Accounting Workbook

2nd Edition

by Tage C. Tracy

A Wiley Brand

Accounting Workbook For Dummies®, 2nd Edition

Published by: **John Wiley & Sons, Inc.,** 111 River Street, Hoboken, NJ 07030-5774, www.wiley.com

Copyright © 2022 by John Wiley & Sons, Inc., Hoboken, New Jersey

Media and software compilation copyright © 2022 by John Wiley & Sons, Inc. All rights reserved.

Published simultaneously in Canada

For general information on our other products and services, please contact our Customer Care Department within the U.S. at 877-762-2974, outside the U.S. at 317-572-3993, or fax 317-572-4002. For technical support, please visit www.wiley.com/techsupport.

Wiley publishes in a variety of print and electronic formats and by print-on-demand. Some material included with standard print versions of this book may not be included in e-books or in print-on-demand. If this book refers to media such as a CD or DVD that is not included in the version you purchased, you may download this material at http://booksupport.wiley.com. For more information about Wiley products, visit www.wiley.com.

Library of Congress Control Number: 2022941422

ISBN 978-1-119-89763-7 (pbk); ISBN 978-1-119-89764-4 (epdf); ISBN 978-1-119-89765-1 (epub)

SKY10055186_091223

Contents at a Glance

Contents at a Glance

Table of Contents

Introduction

First of all, I have to admit that accounting has an image problem. Be honest: What's the first thing that pops into your mind when you see the word "accountant"? You probably think of a nerd wearing a green eyeshade who has the personality of an undertaker (no offense meant to undertakers, of course). Well, I've never worn green eyeshades in my life, and I can assure you that I'm not a nerd (but a bit geeky from time to time). I do own the latest technology gadgets, generally have a good sense of humor (which will be on display throughout this book) and have extensive accounting experience both from the classroom perspective (through my dad, John Tracy, who taught for more than 35 years and was the author of the first edition of this book) as well as from the "street" (I have been operating a financial and accounting consulting business for more than 25 years).

Explaining accounting for nonaccountants is one of mine and my late dad's passions in life, and we've written several books on the topic. In the mid-1990s, our journey started with John Tracy having the opportunity to write *Accounting For Dummies* (Wiley), which is now in its seventh edition. One of our other books is *How To Read A Financial Report* (Wiley), which has been in print for more than 40 years and now is in its ninth edition. This book, *Accounting Workbook For Dummies*, 2nd Edition, fills a gap with our books: That is, they don't incorporate questions and exercises. This book offers plenty of questions to test and improve your understanding of accounting.

Accounting Workbook for Dummies, 2nd Edition, offers a different take on accounting — one that offers new insights and perspectives including covering important recent developments and trends, such as accounting in the digital age. Through my experiences, I have a pretty good idea of how the subject is taught and understood. I don't go out of my way to be contrary or confrontational, but it is important to remember that accounting isn't an exact science and often a bit of an art form. Accounting is full of controversy and differences of opinion. In this book, I state my opinions forcefully and (I hope) clearly.

The spirit of this book is illustrated in two common-told stories. The first concerns the young and eager musician on her first trip to New York City, who gets off the train at Grand Central Terminal and asks the first person she meets on the street: "How do you get to Carnegie Hall?" The answer is: "Practice, practice, practice!" The second story concerns the legendary UCLA basketball coach John Wooden. At the first practice of each year, he taught the players how to tie their shoes so that they wouldn't come loose during a game.

About This Book

Whether it's a small mom-and-pop business or the gargantuan Apple, Inc., every business keeps track of its financial activities and its financial condition. You can't run a business without an accounting system that tells you whether you're making a profit or suffering a loss, whether you have enough cash (or access to capital) to support on-going operations, or your bank account balance is approaching zero, and whether you're in good financial shape or are on the edge of bankruptcy.

Accounting Workbook For Dummies, 2nd Edition, is largely about business accounting. It explains how business transactions are recorded in the accounts of a business and the financial statements that are prepared for a business to report its profit and loss (the income statement), financial condition (the balance sheet), and cash flows (the statement of cash flows). It also explains how business managers, executives, and analysts use accounting information for decision making. (The book doesn't delve into business income taxation, which is the province of professional accountants.)

Most business managers have limited accounting backgrounds, and most have their enthusiasm for learning more about accounting well under control. But, down deep, they're likely to think that they should know more about accounting. Business managers should find this book quite helpful even if they just dip their toes in.

If you're a business bookkeeper or accountant, you can use this book to review the topics you need to know well. It can help you upgrade your accounting skills and savvy and lay the foundation for further advancement. One great thing about *Accounting Workbook For Dummies,* 2nd Edition, is that it offers alternative explanations of accounting topics that are different from the explanations in standard accounting textbooks. The many questions and problems (with clearly explained answers) offer an excellent way to test your knowledge, and nobody knows your exam scores but you.

If you're a student presently enrolled in a beginning accounting course, you can use this book as a supplementary study guide to your textbook, one that offers many supplementary questions and exercises. Perhaps you took an accounting course a few years ago and need to brush up on the subject. This book can help you refresh your understanding of accounting and help you recall things forgotten.

Note: In Part 2, a fictious business is used as the base for the financial examples provided in Chapters 7 through 10 (for consistency purposes). To start Part 3 of the book, Chapters 11 and 12 do not use the same fictious business but rather simpler and more compact fictious business examples are provided to assist you with understanding the concepts more efficiently. I wanted to call this out to avoid any confusion as it relates to carrying forward the financial information presented in Part 2 of the book.

Foolish Assumptions

Mastering accounting is like mastering many other subjects: First, you must understand the basic terminology (the lingo) and the fundamentals. In accounting, you have to work problems to really get a grasp of the topic and technique. Passive reading just isn't enough. In writing this book, I assume that you aren't a complete accounting neophyte. I designed the book as a second step that builds on your basic accounting knowledge and experience. If you have no previous exposure to accounting, you may want to consider first reading *Accounting For Dummies,* 7th Edition (Wiley).

You don't have to be a math wizard to understand accounting; basic high school algebra is more than enough. However, you do have to pay attention to details, just as you have to pay close attention to the words when you study Shakespeare. Accounting involves calculations and using a business/financial calculator is very helpful. In my experience, many people don't take the time to learn how to use their calculators. But that's time well spent. In many of the questions and problems posed throughout the book, I explain how to use a business calculator for the solution.

Icons Used in This Book

Throughout this book, you can find useful "pointers" that save you the trouble of buying a yellow highlighter pen and using sticky notes. These icons draw your attention to certain parts of the text. Think of them as road signs on your journey through accounting.

EXAMPLE

This icon marks the spot of an example question that explains and illustrates an important point. The answer follows the question. It's a good idea to make sure that you understand the answer before attempting the additional questions on the topic on your own. To get the most out of the example questions, don't read the answer right away. First, try to answer the question and then compare my answer with yours and how you got it.

TIP

This icon points out information that you probably would have underlined or highlighted while reading. These points are worth remembering. When reviewing each chapter, read everything with this icon attached in order to get the essentials.

REMEMBER

I use this icon to indicate that I'm building on your background in accounting. Instead of starting at ground zero, I assume that you already know basic points about the topic. If this book were an elevator, this marker would mean that you're ascending from the first floor to the second floor.

WARNING

Simply put, this icon is a red flag that means "watch out." This warning sign means that the topic being explained is a serious and troublesome issue in accounting, so you should pay close attention and handle it with care.

Beyond the Book

In addition to the content in this book, an online Cheat Sheet is provided for quick access to important information on topics from formulas and functions for financial statements to knowing your debits from your credits to choosing the right accounting method for your business. The Cheat Sheet can be found at www.dummies.com — type *Accounting Workbook For Dummies Cheat Sheet* in the search bar.

But, wait, there's more! For those readers who are interested, I have created an online Excel workbook file containing all the figures given in this book plus some extras that you are able to work through. Go to: www.dummies.com/go/accountingwbfd2e to connect with them.

Where to Go from Here

Accounting Workbook For Dummies, 2nd Edition, is designed to maximize modularity. Each chapter stands on its own feet to the fullest extent possible. Of course, it makes sense to read the chapters in order, but you can jump around as the spirit moves you.

You may be a business investor who's interested in how a business is capitalized (Chapter 13), or you may want to review manufacturing cost accounting (Chapter 12). You may be a business manager who needs to know about analyzing profit behavior (Chapter 11), or you may be confused about cash flow (Chapter 10). If you're a student studying for your first accounting exam, I suggest that you start with Part 1 and read the chapters in order.

Finally, in today's economy, accounting is heavily linked to technology so in order to improve your understanding, either go old school and invest in a top-of-the-line business/financial calculator or do what most people do and become a whiz with using Excel, an extremely powerful and user-friendly software that works very well with almost any personal computer and operating system.

1

Business Accounting Basics

Get started with accounting fundamentals.

Understand the financial effects of transactions, specifically sales and expenses.

Discover the basics of the bookkeeping cycle.

Find out about adjusting and closing entries.

Grasp critical topics related to accounting in the digital age.

Chapter **1**

Business Accounting Fundamentals

The purpose of Chapter 1 is relatively simple as the goal is to provide an introduction to the fundamentals of accounting and its importance to businesses. In this chapter, I cover some extremely basic accounting concepts, ideas, and theories that rain or shine, in good times or bad, act as the bedrock of business accounting. Or looking at accounting from a different perspective, I'm drawn to a question my nephew posed to me that caught me somewhat off guard. Simply put, he asked "What is the purpose of accounting?" To this, I responded with two thoughts:

» First, accounting represents the foundation of fairly reporting the financial performance of a business over a period of time (for example, the income statement and statement of cash flows) or a business's financial strength at a point in time (as in the balance sheet). Accounting, when properly functioning, should clearly and fairly measure the economic performance of a legal entity.

» Second, accounting takes on the added responsibility of safeguarding a legal entity's assets and protecting the economic value of a business.

But, before the accounting process can even begin, a starting point must be established, which is identifying the entity being accounted for. A business entity can be legally organized as a partnership, corporation, limited liability company, or other structure permitted by law. Alternatively, a business entity simply may consist of the business activities of an individual, in which case it's called a sole proprietorship. Regardless of how the business entity is legally established, it's treated as a separate entity or distinct person for accounting purposes. And once a legal entity is established, the accounting process can proceed.

Keeping the Accounting Equation in Balance

If you've ever studied accounting, you probably recall the most fundamental accounting equation there is:

Total Assets = Total Liabilities + Owners' Equity

The accounting equation says a lot in very few words. It's like the visible part of an iceberg — a lot of important points are hidden under the water. Notice the two sides to the equation: assets on one side and the claims against the assets on the other side. These claims arise from credit extended to the business (liabilities) and capital invested or retained by owners in the business (owners' equity). (The claims of liabilities are significantly different than the claims of owners; liabilities have seniority and priority for payment over the claims of owners.)

Capital invested means actual investments made in the company by the owners. *Retained by owners* refers to net profits earned by the company that are retained internally, less any distributions or dividends paid to the owners and less any net losses the company may have incurred over the year. In the next paragraph, a total of $6 million of owners' equity is referenced, which could come from $6 million of cash being invested in the company by the owners or it could be the result of $4 million of invested cash, plus $3 million of retained net profits, less $1 million of previous owner dividends. Under either scenario, total owners' equity amounts to $6 million; it just so happens that it comes from different sources.

Suppose a business has $10 million total assets. These assets didn't fall down like manna from heaven (as our old accounting professors were fond of saying). The money for the assets came from somewhere. The business's creditors (to whom it owes its liabilities) may have supplied, say, $4 million of its total assets. Therefore, the owners' equity sources provided the other $6 million.

REMEMBER

Business accounting is based on the two-sided nature of the accounting equation. Both assets and sources of assets are accounted for, which leads, quite naturally, to double-entry accounting. Double entry, in essence, means two-sided. It's based on the general economic exchange model. In economic transactions, something is given, and something is received in exchange. For example, I recently bought an iPod from Apple Computer. Apple gave me the iPod and received my money. Another example involves a business that borrows money from its bank. The business gives the bank a legal instrument called a note promising to return the money at a future date and to pay interest over the time the money is borrowed. In exchange for the note, the business receives the money. (Chapter 3 explains how to implement double-entry accounting.)

Q. Is each of the following equations correct? What key point does each equation raise?

    a. $250,000 Assets = $100,000 Liabilities + $100,000 Owners' Equity

    b. $2,345,000 Assets = $46,900 Liabilities + $2,298,100 Owners' Equity

    c. $26,450 Assets = $675,000 Liabilities − $648,550 Owners' Equity

    d. $4,650,000 Assets = $4,250,000 Liabilities + $400,000 Owners' Equity

A. Each accounting equation offers an important lesson.

    a. Whoops! This accounting equation doesn't balance, so clearly something's wrong. Either liabilities, owner's equity, or some combination of both is $50,000 too low, or the two items on the right-hand side could be correct, in which case total assets are overstated $50,000. With an unbalanced equation such as this, the accountant definitely should find the error or errors and make appropriate correcting entries.

    b. This accounting equation balances, but, wow! Look at the very small size of liabilities relative to assets. This kind of contrast isn't typical. The liabilities of a typical business usually account for a much larger percentage of its total assets.

    c. This accounting equation balances, but the business has a large negative owners' equity. Such a large negative amount of owners' equity means the business has suffered major losses that have wiped out almost all its assets. You wouldn't want to be one of this business's creditors (or one of its owners either).

    d. This accounting equation balances and is correct, but you should notice that the business is highly leveraged, which means the ratio of debt to equity (liabilities divided by owners' equity) is very high, more than 10 to 1. This ratio is quite unusual.

---

1 Which of the following is the normal way to present the accounting equation?

    a. Liabilities = Assets − Owners' Equity

    b. Assets − Liabilities = Owners' Equity

    c. Assets = Liabilities + Owners' Equity

    d. Assets − Liabilities − Owners' Equity = 0

2 A business has $485,000 total liabilities and $1,200,000 total owners' equity. What is the amount of its total assets?

A business has $250,000 total liabilities. At start-up, the owners invested $500,000 in the business. Unfortunately, the business has suffered a cumulative loss of $200,000 up to the present time. What is the amount of its total assets at the present time?

 A business has $175,000 total liabilities. At start-up, the owners invested $250,000 capital. The business has earned $190,000 cumulative profit since its creation, all of which has been retained in the business. What is the total amount of its assets?

Distinguishing Between Cash- and Accrual-Basis Accounting

Cash-basis accounting refers to keeping a record of cash inflows and cash outflows. An individual uses cash-basis accounting in keeping his checkbook because he needs to know his day-to-day cash balance and he needs a journal of his cash receipts and cash expenditures during the year for filing his annual income tax return. Individuals have assets other than cash (such as cars, computers, and homes), and they have liabilities (such as credit card balances and home mortgages). Hardly anyone I know keeps accounting records of their personal noncash assets and their liabilities (aside from putting bills to pay and receipts for major purchases in folders). Most people either maintain a checkbook (for all the old-timers out there) or in today's digital world, manage their banking online and maintain a virtual, real-time summary of inflows and outflows to their bank account. That's about it when it comes to their personal accounting.

Although it's perfect for individuals, cash-basis accounting just doesn't cut it for the large majority of businesses. Cash-basis accounting doesn't provide the information that managers need to run a business, or the information needed to prepare company tax returns and financial reports. Some small personal service businesses (such as barber shops, lawyers, and real estate brokers) can get by using cash-basis accounting because they have virtually no assets other than cash, and they pay their bills right away.

The large majority of businesses use accrual-basis accounting. They keep track of their cash inflows and outflows, of course, but accrual-basis accounting allows them to record all the assets and liabilities of the business. Also, accrual-basis accounting keeps track of the money invested in the business by its owners and the accumulated profit retained in the business. In short, accrual-basis accounting has a much broader scope than cash-basis accounting.

A big difference between cash- and accrual-basis accounting concerns how they measure annual profit of a business. With cash-basis accounting, profit simply equals the total of cash inflows from sales minus the total of cash outflows for expenses of making sales and running the business, or, in other words, the net increase in cash from sales and expenses. With the accrual-basis accounting method, profit is measured differently because the two components of profit — sales revenue and expenses — are recorded differently.

REMEMBER

When using accrual-basis accounting, a business records sales revenue when a sale is made and the products and/or services are delivered to the customer, whether the customer pays cash on the spot or receives credit and doesn't pay the business until sometime later. Sales revenue is recorded before cash is actually received. The business doesn't record the cost of the products sold as an expense until sales revenue is recorded, even though the business paid out cash for the products weeks or months earlier. Furthermore, with accrual-basis accounting, a business records operating expenses as soon as they're incurred (as soon as the business has a liability for the expense), even though the expenses aren't paid until sometime later.

Cash-basis accounting doesn't reflect economic reality for businesses that sell and buy on credit (which is how the vast majority of companies operate in today's economy), carry inventories of products for sale, invest in long-lived operating assets, and make long-term commitments for such things as employee pensions and retirement benefits. When you look beyond small cash-based business, you quickly realize that businesses need the comprehensive recordkeeping system called accrual-basis accounting. I like to call it "economic reality accounting."

The following example question focuses on certain fundamental differences between cash-basis and accrual-basis accounting regarding the recording of sales revenue and expenses for the purpose of measuring profit.

Q. You started a new business one year ago. You've been very busy dealing with so many problems that you haven't had time to sit down and look at whether you made a profit or not. You haven't run out of cash (which for a start-up venture is quite an accomplishment), but you understand that the sustainability of the business depends on making a profit. The following two summaries present cash-flow information for the year and information about two assets and a liability at year-end:

Revenue and Expense Cash Flows for First Year

$558,000 cash receipts from sales

$375,000 cash payments for purchases of products

$340,000 cash payments for other expenses

Two Assets and a Liability at Year-End

$52,000 receivables from customers for sales made to them during the year

$85,000 cost of products in ending inventory that haven't yet been sold

$25,000 liability for unpaid expenses

Compare the profit or loss of your business for its first year according to the cash- and accrual-basis accounting methods.

A. Profit according to cash-basis accounting equals the cash inflow from sales minus the total of cash outflows for expenses (and the total of cash outflows for expenses equals the purchases of products plus other expenses). Thus, under cash-basis accounting, your business has a $157,000 loss for the year ($558,000 sales revenue - $715,000 expenses = $157,000 loss).

Under accrual-basis accounting, you record different amounts for sales revenue and the two expenses, which are calculated as follows:

$558,000 cash receipts from sales + $52,000 year-end receivables from customers = $610,000 sales revenue

$375,000 cash payments for purchases of products − $85,000 year-end inventory of unsold products = $290,000 cost of products sold expense

$340,000 cash payments for other expenses + $25,000 year-end liability for unpaid expenses = $365,000 other expenses

Deducting cost of products sold and other expenses from sales revenue gives a net loss of $45,000 ($610,000 sales revenue − $290,000 cost of products sold − $365,000 other expenses = $45,000 net loss for year).

To answer Questions 5 through 8, please refer to the summary of revenue and expense cash flows and the summary of two assets and a liability at year-end presented in the preceding example question.

---

5 What would be the amount of accrual-basis sales revenue for the year if the business's year-end receivables had been $92,000?

6 What would be the amount of accrual-basis cost of products sold expense for the year if the business's cost of products held in inventory at year-end had been $95,000?

7 What would be the amount of accrual-basis other expenses for the year if the business's liability for unpaid expenses at year-end had been $30,000?

8 Based on the changes for the example given in Questions 5, 6, and 7, determine the profit or loss of the business for its first year.

Summarizing Profit Activities in the Income (Profit & Loss) Statement

As crass as it sounds, business managers get paid to make profit happen. Management literature usually stresses the visionary, leadership, and innovative characteristics of business managers, but these traits aren't worth much if the business suffers losses year after year or fails to establish sustainable profit performance. After all, businesses are profit-motivated, aren't they?

It's not surprising that the income statement takes center stage in business financial reports. The income statement summarizes a company's revenue and other income, expenses, losses, and bottom-line profit or loss for a period of time. It is important to indicate with the income statement what period of time it covers. To say a business generated net income of $10,000 is meaningless if the period for which this profit was generated is not also presented.

The income statement tends to get top billing over the other two primary financial statements (the balance sheet and the statement of cash flows), which I discuss later in this chapter. The income statement is referred to informally as the Profit & Loss or P&L statement, although these titles are seldom used in external financial reports. (Alternatively, it may be titled Earnings Statement or Statement of Operations.)

Financial reporting standards demand that an income statement be presented in quarterly and annual financial reports to owners. But financial reporting rules are fairly permissive regarding exactly what information should be reported and how it's presented (see Chapter 7 for the full scoop on income statement disclosure).

Q. Take a look at this extremely abbreviated and condensed income statement for a business's most recent year. (*Note:* A formal income statement in a financial report must disclose more information than this.)

Income Statement for Year

Sales revenue	$26,000,000
Expenses	24,310,000
Net income	$1,690,000

This business sells products, which are also called goods or merchandise. The cost of products sold to customers during the year was $14,300,000. Expand the condensed income statement to reflect this additional information.

A. Income statement reporting requires a company to show the cost of goods (products) sold as a separate expense and deduct it immediately below sales revenue. The difference must be reported as gross profit (or gross margin). Therefore, the condensed income statement should be expanded as follows:

Income Statement for Year

Sales revenue	$26,000,000
Cost of goods sold	14,300,000
Gross profit	$11,700,000
Other expenses	10,010,000
Net income	$1,690,000

---

9 One rule of income statement reporting is that interest expense and income tax expense be reported separately. The $10,010,000 "Other expenses" in the income statement for the answer to the example question includes $350,000 interest expense and $910,000 income tax. Rebuild the income statement given the information for these additional two expenses. Hint: Profit before interest expense is usually labeled "operating earnings," and profit after interest and before income tax expense is usually labeled "earnings before income tax."

10 No specific rule governs income statement disclosure of advertising expense. Suppose the $10,010,000 "Other expenses" in the income statement for the answer to the example question includes $5,000,000 of advertising expense. Would you favor reporting this as a separate expense in the income statement? Hint: This question calls for your opinion only.

---

11 No specific rule governs income statement disclosure of executive-level compensation. Suppose the $10,010,000 "Other expenses" in the income statement for the answer to the example question includes $3,000,000 of executive-level compensation that includes both base salaries and generous bonuses. Would you favor reporting this as a separate expense in the income statement? Hint: This question calls for your opinion only.

12 Suppose the business distributed $650,000 cash to its shareowners from its profit (net income) for the year in the form of a dividend. Is this cash disbursement treated as an expense?

Assembling a Balance Sheet

The balance sheet is one of the three primary financial statements that businesses report (the other two being the income statement and the cash flow statement or statement of cash flows). The balance sheet summarizes the assets, liabilities, and owners' equity accounts of a business at an instant in time. Prepared at the close of business on the last day of the profit period, the balance sheet presents a "freeze frame" look at the business's financial condition.

REMEMBER

Preparing and reporting a balance sheet takes time, so by the time you read a balance sheet, it's already out-of-date. The business's stream of activities and operations doesn't stop, which means that from the date at which the balance sheet was prepared to when you read it, the business will have engaged in many transactions. These subsequent transactions may have significantly changed its financial condition. For more on the balance sheet, turn to Chapter 8.

TIP

In accounting, the term *balance* refers to the dollar amount of an account, after recording all increases and decreases in the account caused by business activities over a defined period of time. The balance sheet reports the balances of asset, liability, and owners' equity accounts, but it also refers to the equality, or balance, of the accounting equation (see the section "Keeping the Accounting Equation in Balance" earlier in this chapter).

Balance sheets normally list assets and liabilities in order of liquidity. Liquidity means how easy it is to change an asset or a liability into cash. For example: Cash is first in the list of assets, followed by accounts receivable, which are usually turned into cash in 30 days or less. Inventory is next because it usually will be sold and turned into cash within the next 90 days. And equipment, land, and buildings come last because they usually will be held for many years.

On the liability side of the balance sheet, accounts payable, accrued liabilities, and other current liabilities (such as sales tax payable) come first because they are usually paid within 30 to 90 days. Notes payable and payments on long-term loans come next; they're usually paid within a year. And long-term loans that will not be paid within the next year come last. Liabilities come before owners' equity, both due to timing and to agreeing with the order in the accounting equation.

EXAMPLE

Q. The following list summarizes the assets and liabilities of a business at the close of business on the last day of its most recent profit period:

Amounts owed by customers to the business (such as trade accounts receivable): $485,000

Cost of unsold products that will be sold in future periods (such as inventory): $678,000

Cash balance on deposit in checking account with bank: $396,000

Amounts owed by business for unpaid purchases and expenses (such as trade accounts payable): $438,000

Notes payable to bank (on which interest is paid): $500,000

Original cost of long-term operating assets (such as machinery and equipment) that are being depreciated over their useful lives to the business: $950,000

Accumulated depreciation of long-term operating assets: $305,000

Using this information, prepare the business's balance sheet.

A.

Cash	$396,000	Accounts Payable	$438,000
Accounts Receivable	$485,000	Notes Payable	$500,000
Inventory	$678,000	Owners' Equity*	$1,266,000
Fixed Assets (Net of Accumulated Depreciation)	$645,000		
Total Assets	$2,204,000	Total Liabilities and Owners' Equity	$2,204,000

*Owners' equity is determined by deducting the sum of liabilities from total assets.

Note: This balance sheet isn't classified into current assets and current liabilities. Also, owners' equity isn't classified. (Chapter 8 explains the balance sheet in greater detail.)

Use the balance sheet shown in the preceding example to answer Questions 13 through 16.

---

13 Suppose $950,000 of owners' equity consists of profit earned and not distributed by the business. What is this amount usually called in the balance sheet? And, what is the other amount of owners' equity called in the balance sheet?

14 It appears that the business can't pay its liabilities. The two liabilities total $938,000, but the business has a cash balance of only $396,000. Do you agree?

15 Can you tell the amount of profit the business earned in the period just ended?

16 In a balance sheet, assets usually are listed in the order of their "nearness" to cash. Cash is listed first, followed by the asset closest to being converted into cash, and so on. Is the sequence of assets according to normal rules for presenting assets in balance sheets?

Partitioning the Statement of Cash Flows

You could argue that the statement of cash flows is the most important of the three primary financial statements. Why? Because in the long run everything comes down to cash flows. Profit recorded on the accrual basis of accounting has to be turned into cash — and the sooner the better. Otherwise, profit doesn't provide money for growing the business and paying distributions to owners. I have never known a business to fail and go bankrupt because it ran out of assets. Businesses fail because they run out of cash; either from operations not generating cash, lenders unwilling to loan the business cash, or investors not willing to invest more cash. These three elements are disclosed in the statement of cash flows.

By themselves, the income statement and balance sheet don't provide information about the cash flow generated by the business's profit-making, or operating, activities. But people who use financial reports (business managers, lenders, and investors) want to see cash flow information. In short, financial reporting standards require a statement of cash flows. The statement of cash flows begins where the income statement finished off, by presenting the net income or loss for the like reporting period. After this, the statement of cash flows reports cash increases and decreases in three main buckets or groups of information as follows:

>> **Operating activities:** This section of the statement of cash flows starts with the net profit or loss generated by the company over the period and then captures changes in cash occurring from normal operating activity such as increases or decreases in trade accounts receivable, inventory, trade accounts payable, accrued liabilities, and other current assets and liabilities. In addition, you will also note that operating activities include adding back the amount recorded for depreciation and amortization expense. The reason for this is that these expenses represent "non cash" charges to the income statement to account for the periodic estimated use of assets over a period of time. I discuss depreciation and amortization expense in more detail in Chapter 6.

>> **Investing activities:** Include the purchase and construction of long-term operating assets such as land, buildings, equipment, machinery, vehicles, and tools. If a business realizes cash from the disposal of such assets, the proceeds are included in this category of cash flows.

>> **Financing activities:** Include borrowing money from debt sources and paying loans at maturity as well as raising capital from shareowners and returning capital to them. Cash distributions from profit are included in this category of cash flows.

Q. The statement of cash flows for a business's most recent year is presented as follows. Based on the information provided, is it possible to determine the amount of cash flow from operating activities?

Cash flow from operating activities:		?????
Cash flow from investing activities:		
Capital expenditures	($2,345,000)	
Proceeds from disposal of real estate	$225,000	($2,120,000)
Cash flow from financing activities:		
Increase in debt	$1,625,000	
Issue of capital stock shares	$550,000	
Cash dividends to shareholders	($400,000)	$1,775,000
Net cash increase during year		$355,000

A. You can determine the amount of cash flow from operating activities by the following calculations:

$2,120,000 net cash needed for capital expenditures + $355,000 cash balance increase = $2,475,000 total cash needed

$2,475,000 total cash needed − $1,775,000 net cash provided from financing activities = $700,000 cash flow from operating activities

Cash flow from operating activities is explained in more detail in Chapter 8.

You can condense a statement of cash flows, such as the one for the example, into its four basic components as follows (negative numbers appear in parentheses):

Cash flow from operating activities	$700,000
Cash flow from investing activities	($2,120,000)
Cash flow from financing activities	$1,775,000
Net increase in cash during the year	$355,000

TIP

If you know three of the four components in a condensed statement of cash flows, you can determine the fourth factor. Suppose you know the increase or decrease in cash during the year (which is easy enough to determine by comparing the ending cash balance with the beginning cash balance). And suppose you can quickly determine the cash flow from investing activities and the cash flow from financing activities (because there aren't many transactions of these two types during the year). Knowing these three factors, you can quickly determine the cash flow from operating activities. The remainder of the increase or decrease in cash during the year is attributable to operating activities.

Questions 17 through 20 give you three of the four components in a condensed statement of cash flows and ask you to solve for the unknown factor.

Three of the four components of cash flow for the year of a business are as follows:

Cash flow from operating activities	$450,000
Cash flow from investing activities	($725,000)
Cash flow from financing activities	$50,000
Net increase (decrease) in cash during the year	????

Determine the increase or decrease in cash during the year.

 Three of the four components of cash flow for the year of a business are as follows:

Cash flow from operating activities	$2,680,000
Cash flow from investing activities	????
Cash flow from financing activities	$1,250,000
Net increase (decrease) in cash during the year	$400,000

Determine cash flow from investing activities for the year.

 Three of the four components of cash flow for the year of a business are as follows:

Cash flow from operating activities	$650,000
Cash flow from investing activities	($925,000)
Cash flow from financing activities	????
Net increase (decrease) in cash during the year	($65,000)

Determine cash flow from financing activities for the year.

 Three of the four components of cash flow for the year of a business are as follows:

Cash flow from operating activities	????
Cash flow from investing activities	($480,000)
Cash flow from financing activities	($150,000)
Net increase (decrease) in cash during the year	$150,000

Determine cash flow from operating activities for the year.

Tracing How Dishonest Accounting Distorts Financial Statements

It goes without saying that a business should keep its accounting system as honest as the day is long. In preparing its financial statements, a business should be forthright and not misleading. As the late sportscaster Howard Cosell would say, "Tell it like it is." I regret to inform you that some businesses might "tweak" their financial results, others may have errors present in their financial statements, and in a few cases, outright misrepresent their accounting and financial reporting. So, what's the difference?

First, many businesses perform a light amount of cosmetic surgery (also known as tweaking) on their accounting records, touching up their financial condition and profit performance to achieve a specific objective. This practice is popularly called "massaging the numbers" or "financial statement dressing." Professional investors (as in mutual fund managers) and lenders (as in banks) know that a certain amount of accounting manipulation goes on by many businesses, and as a practical matter not much can be done about it (so it is generally tolerated to a large extent).

Second, companies that have relatively poor accounting systems, inexperienced staff, limited financial management infrastructure, and/or that lack proper policies, procedures, and internal controls, may in fact present financial statements that contain errors. It is important to note that presenting financial statements with an error (which may not even be known to the management team) does not mean that the company is intentionally undertaking fraudulent activity. Rather, when errors are present, it's usually due to a lack of accounting knowledge. I'm not attempting to defend companies that have accounting errors present, but there is a significant difference in the intent of management in financial information that has been reported with an error (unintentional) versus a direct misrepresentation (an intentional effort to mislead), which is often referred to as an accounting "irregularity."

WARNING

Third, some businesses (but thankfully a small minority) resort to outright accounting fraud to put a better sheen on profit performance and conceal financial problems. Accounting fraud is popularly called "cooking the books." On one end, think of massaging the numbers as fibbing or putting a spin on the truth and on the other end, accounting fraud as out-and-out lying with the intent to deceive and mislead. Over the past 20 years, legislation has been enacted to help combat accounting fraud, especially after the Enron debacle and bankruptcy in 2001 (the largest at its time). Although progress has been made, accounting fraud still occurs as evidenced by the Wirecard fraud, which reached its peak in 2020. It seems no matter how hard the authorities try, a small number of criminals continue to front run legislation, controls, and regulations to commit accounting fraud. Accounting fraud is illegal, and perpetrators are subject to prosecution under criminal law. Plus, victims can sue the persons responsible for the fraud.

EXAMPLE

Q. Suppose a business has engaged in some accounting fraud to boost its profit for the year just ended. Assume that the business didn't commit any accounting fraud before this year (which may not be true, of course). As the result of fraudulent entries in its accounts, the $2,340,000 bottom-line profit reported in its income statement was overstated by $385,000. How does this dishonest accounting distort the business's balance sheet?

A. Owners' equity is overstated by $385,000 because profit increases owners' equity. And the overstatement of profit may have involved the overstatement of assets, the understatement of liabilities, or a combination of both. To correct this error, owners' equity should be decreased $385,000. As well, assets should be decreased $385,000, or liabilities should be increased $385,000 (or some combination of both).

---

21 Suppose a business commits accounting fraud by deliberately not writing down its inventory of $268,000, which is the cost of certain products that it can no longer sell and will be thrown in the junk heap. How should its balance sheet be adjusted to correct for this accounting fraud, ignoring income tax effects? (Use the answer template provided.)

Cash	Accounts Payable
Accounts Receivable	Notes Payable
Inventory	Owners' Equity
Fixed Assets (Net of Accumulated Depreciation) ____	____
Total Assets	Total Liabilities and Owners' Equity

---

22 Suppose a business commits accounting fraud by deliberately not recording $465,000 liabilities for unpaid expenses at the end of the year. How should its balance sheet be adjusted to correct for this accounting fraud, ignoring income tax effects? (Use the answer template provided.)

Cash	Accounts Payable
Accounts Receivable	Notes Payable
Inventory	Owners' Equity
Fixed Assets (Net of Accumulated Depreciation) ____	____
Total Assets	Total Liabilities and Owners' Equity

Answers to Problems on Elements of Business Accounting

The following are the answers to the practice questions presented earlier in this chapter.

1 Which of the following is the normal way to present the accounting equation?

c. Assets = Liabilities + Owners' Equity

The other three accounting equations are correct from the algebraic equation point of view. However, the accounting equation is usually shown with assets on one side and the two broad classes of claims against the assets on the other side. *Note:* You see answer (b) (Assets – Liabilities = Owners' equity) when the purpose is to emphasize the net worth of a business, or its assets less its liabilities.

2 A business has $485,000 total liabilities and $1,200,000 total owners' equity. What is the amount of its total assets?

Total assets = $1,685,000, which is the total of $485,000 liabilities plus $1,200,000 owners' equity.

3 A business has $250,000 total liabilities. When it was started the owners invested $500,000 in the business. Unfortunately, the business has suffered a cumulative loss of $200,000 up to the present time. What is the amount of its total assets at the present time?

Total assets = $550,000, which is the total of $250,000 liabilities plus $300,000 owners' equity.

Notice that the original $500,000 that the owners invested in the business is reduced by the $200,000 cumulative loss of the business, and owners' equity is now only $300,000.

4 A business has $175,000 total liabilities. Originally, at the time of starting the business, the owners invested $250,000 capital. The business has earned $190,000 cumulative profit since it started (all of which has been retained in the business). What is the total amount of its assets?

Total assets = $615,000, which is the total of $175,000 liabilities and $440,000 owners' equity.

Notice that in addition to the original $250,000 capital invested by owners, the business has earned $190,000 profit, so its total owners' equity is $440,000.

5 What would be the amount of accrual-basis sales revenue for the year if the business's year-end receivables had been $92,000? (For the original numbers, see the section "Distinguishing Between Cash- and Accrual-Basis Accounting.")

Sales revenue ($558,000 cash receipts + $92,000 year-end receivables) = $650,000

6 What would be the amount of accrual-basis cost of products sold expense for the year if the business's cost of products held in inventory at year-end had been $95,000? (For the original numbers, see the section "Distinguishing Between Cash- and Accrual-Basis Accounting.")

Cost of products sold ($375,000 cash payments – $95,000 year-end inventory) = $280,000

(7) What would be the amount of accrual-basis other expenses for the year if the business's liability for unpaid expenses at year-end had been $30,000? (For the original numbers, see the section "Distinguishing Between Cash- and Accrual-Basis Accounting.")

Other expenses ($340,000 cash payments + $30,000 year-end liability) = $370,000

(8) Based on the changes to the example given in Questions 5, 6, and 7, determine the profit or loss of the business for its first year.

In this case, the total of the two expenses (cost of products sold and other expenses) happens to be $650,000, which is exactly equal to sales revenue. So, the business breaks even for the year. This outcome is unusual, of course; the total of expenses for the year is almost always different than total sales revenue for the year.

(9) One rule of income statement reporting is that interest expense and income tax expense be reported separately. The $10,010,000 "Other expenses" in the income statement for the answer to the example question includes $350,000 interest expense and $910,000 income tax. Rebuild the income statement given the information for these additional two expenses. Hint: Profit before interest expense is usually labeled "operating earnings," and profit after interest and before income tax expense is usually labeled "earnings before income tax."

Income Statement for Year

Sales revenue	$26,000,000
Cost of goods sold	14,300,000
Gross margin	$11,700,000
Other expenses	8,750,000
Operating earnings	$2,950,000
Interest expense	350,000
Earnings before income tax	$2,600,000
Income tax expense	910,000
Net income	$1,690,000

REMEMBER

Burying interest expense or income tax expense in a broader expense category such as "other expenses" or "general expenses" is unacceptable. Interest and income tax expenses are reported toward the bottom of the income statement. They're viewed as nonoperating expenses, which means that they depend on how the business is financed and its income tax situation.

(10) No specific rule governs income statement disclosure of advertising expense. Suppose the $10,010,000 "Other expenses" in the income statement for the answer to the example question includes $5,000,000 of advertising expense. Would you favor reporting this as a separate expense in the income statement? Hint: This question calls for your opinion only.

Well, there's no rule against disclosure of advertising expense — that's for sure. Because it's such a large expense, I favor disclosing it in the income statement. But most businesses are very sensitive about disclosing their advertising expense and, in fact, don't disclose this expense in their income statements.

(11) No specific rule governs income statement disclosure of executive-level compensation for privately held businesses. For public companies, this is not the case as U.S. Securities and Exchange Commission (SEC) reporting generally requires the disclosure of executive salaries and other important and sensitive data (in Proxy statements and Form 10-K reporting).

Suppose the $10,010,000 "Other expenses" in the income statement for the answer to the example question includes $3,000,000 of executive-level compensation that includes both base salaries and generous bonuses. Would you favor reporting this as a separate expense in the income statement? Hint: This question calls for your opinion only.

Oh boy! This is a hot potato question. I'm all for open, frank, and transparent disclosure in financial reports, but this is like believing in Santa Claus. Most private businesses are very reluctant to disclose executive-level compensation in their income statements or elsewhere in their financial reports. With no rule forcing such disclosure in their income statements, most businesses don't reveal this piece of information. You can ask for executive-level compensation information if you're on the board of directors of the business, but as an outside shareowner, don't expect to get this information.

12 Suppose the business distributed $650,000 cash to its shareowners from its profit (net income) for the year. Is this cash disbursement treated as an expense?

No, cash distributions from profit to the shareowners of a business aren't an expense. In other words, net income is before any distributions to shareowners.

TIP

Income statements generally don't disclose information regarding distributions from profit (net income) during the year. To be more accurate, I should say that an income statement doesn't have to disclose this information. However, some businesses don't end their income statements at bottom-line net income: They add net income to the retained earnings balance at the start of the year and deduct distributions from net income during the year to arrive at the year-end balance of retained earnings. But such disclosure isn't common practice. Distributions from net income usually are reported in a separate financial statement called the statement of changes in owners' equity, which I discuss in Chapter 8.

13 Suppose $950,000 of owners' equity consists of profit earned and not distributed by the business. What is this amount usually called in the balance sheet? And, what is the other amount of owners' equity called in the balance sheet?

The $950,000 of owners' equity over and above the amount of capital invested by the owners typically is called retained earnings. To be more precise, business corporations and limited liability companies use this term. (If a business is organized legally as a partnership or as a proprietorship, it follows different practices for reporting the owners' equity.)

14 It appears that the business can't pay its liabilities. The two liabilities total $938,000, but the business has a cash balance of only $396,000. Do you agree?

A business isn't expected to hold cash equal to the total of its liabilities. In my opinion, this business wouldn't be judged insolvent, although this judgment depends on how conservative or strict you are in evaluating solvency. The business's cash flow prospects are the key factor. The accounts receivable will be collected in the short-run, and this incoming cash will be available for paying the business's liabilities. The inventory held by the business will be sold during the short-run and will generate cash flow. Further, I don't know when the Notes Payable becomes due; it may not be due for several months, by which time more sales and collections of receivables that are not yet on the balance sheet may be available to pay the Notes Payable.

15 Can you tell the amount of profit the business earned in the period just ended?

No, a balance sheet doesn't report profit (net income) for the most recent period. You look to the income statement for this key figure.

(16) In a balance sheet, assets usually are listed in the order of their "nearness" to cash. Cash is listed first, followed by the asset closest to being converted into cash, and so on. Is the sequence of assets according to normal rules for presenting assets in balance sheets?

Yes, the sequence is correct according to conventional rules for reporting assets in a balance sheet. Cash is listed first, followed by assets according to their "nearness" to cash. In the example, the business doesn't have short-term investments in marketable securities. So, its accounts receivable asset is listed second, after cash, because these receivables will be collected in the short-term. Inventory is listed after accounts receivable because this asset consists of products that have to be sold before they can be converted into cash.

(17) Based on the three of four components of cash flow for the year of a business that follow, determine the increase or decrease in cash during the year.

Cash flow from operating activities	$450,000
Cash flow from investing activities	($725,000)
Cash flow from financing activities	$50,000
Net increase (decrease) in cash during the year	????

Cash decreased $225,000 during the year.

(18) Based on the three of four components of cash flow for the year of a business that follow, determine cash flow from investing activities for the year.

Cash flow from operating activities	$2,680,000
Cash flow from investing activities	????
Cash flow from financing activities	$1,250,000
Net increase (decrease) in cash during the year	$400,000

Cash flow from investing activities for the year is a negative $3,530,000. In other words, the net cash decrease from investing activities was $3,530,000 during the year.

(19) Based on the three of four components of cash flow for the year of a business that follow, determine cash flow from financing activities for the year.

Cash flow from operating activities	$650,000
Cash flow from investing activities	($925,000)
Cash flow from financing activities	????
Net increase (decrease) in cash during the year	($65,000)

Cash flow from financing activities for the year is $210,000. In other words, the net cash increase from financing activities was $210,000 during the year.

(20) Based on the three of four components of cash flow for the year of a business that follow, determine cash flow from operating activities for the year.

Cash flow from operating activities	????
Cash flow from investing activities	($480,000)
Cash flow from financing activities	($150,000)
Net increase (decrease) in cash during the year	$150,000

Cash flow from operating activities for the year is $780,000. In other words, the net cash increase from sales and expense (operating) activities was $780,000 during the year.

(21) Suppose a business commits accounting fraud by deliberately not reducing the cost of its inventory by $268,000, which is the cost of certain products that are obsolete, can no longer be sold, and will be thrown in the junk heap. How should its balance sheet be adjusted to correct for this accounting fraud, ignoring income tax effects?

The changes in the balance sheet to correct the fraudulent error are:

Cash		Accounts Payable	
Accounts Receivable		Notes Payable	
Inventory	($268,000)	Owners' Equity	($268,000)
Fixed Assets (Net of Accumulated Depreciation)	_____		_____
Total Assets	($268,000)	Total Liabilities and Owners' Equity	($268,000)

(22) Suppose a business commits accounting fraud by deliberately not recording $465,000 of liabilities for unpaid expenses at the end of the year. How should its balance sheet be adjusted to correct for this accounting fraud, ignoring income tax effects?

The changes in the balance sheet to correct the fraudulent error are:

Cash		Accounts Payable	$465,000
Accounts Receivable		Notes Payable	
Inventory		Owners' Equity	($465,000)
Fixed Assets (Net of Accumulated Depreciation)	_____		_____
Total Assets		Total Liabilities and Owners' Equity	

Chapter **2**

Financial Effects of Transactions

The following three financial statements are the financial anchors and reference points of every business:

» Balance sheet: Summarizes the business's assets, liabilities, and owners' equity at the end of a period

» Income statement: Summarizes the profit-making transactions of the business for a period of time (usually monthly, quarterly, or annually); also known as the profit and loss (P&L) statement

» Statement of cash flows: Summarizes the business's cash transactions for the same period of time.

The first job of accounting is to faithfully record all the business financial transactions (referred to as simply transactions through the balance of this chapter) in a complete, accurate, reliable, and timely manner (referred to as CART) so that the financial statements listed can be prepared from the financial transaction records. If you're more the visual type, try this on for size:

Transactions → Accounting Process → Financial Statements

Transactions are the heartbeat of every business, which is why accountants, above all else, must know how to record them. This chapter separates business transactions into their main types and pays particular attention to how profit-making transactions — specifically, sales and expenses — impact the financial condition of a business.

Note: I do not use debits and credits (reserved for Chapter 3) in this chapter. Instead, this chapter keeps the focus on the balance sheet, which is the summary of the financial condition of a business.

Classifying Business Transactions

Businesses are profit-motivated, so one basic type of transactions is obvious: profit-making transactions. In a nutshell, profit-making transactions consist of making sales and incurring expenses. Well, if you want to be picky, a business may have other income in addition to sales revenue, and it may record losses in addition to expenses. But the bread-and-butter profit-making activities of a business are making sales and keeping expenses under control. The profit-making transactions of a business over a period of time are reported in its income statement (which I cover in more detail in Chapter 7).

A business's other transactions fall into three basic categories:

>> Set-up and follow-up transactions for sales and expenses: Includes collecting cash from customers after sales made on credit are recorded; the purchase of products (goods) that are held for some time before being sold, at which time the expense is recorded; and making cash payments for expenses after the expenses are recorded

>> Investing activities (transactions): Includes the purchase, construction, and disposals of long-term operating assets such as buildings, machinery, equipment, and tools

>> Financing activities (transactions): Includes borrowing money and repaying amounts borrowed; owners investing capital in the business and the business returning capital to them; and making cash distributions to owners based on the profit earned by the business

REMEMBER

Investing and financing activities of a particular period are reported in that period's statement of cash flows (refer to Chapter 10 for a more complete overview). In contrast, set-up and follow-up transactions for sales and expenses stay in the background, meaning that they are not separately reported in a financial statement. Nevertheless, these transactions are essential to the profit-making process.

Consider, for instance, the purchase of products for inventory. As far as profit is concerned, nothing happens until the business makes a sale of that inventory and records the cost of goods sold expense against the revenue from the sale. Because the business needs to have the products available for sale, the purchase of inventory is the important first step, or set-up transaction.

In understanding accounting, you first need to be very clear about which type of transaction you're looking at.

EXAMPLE

Q. During the year, a business engaged in the following transactions:

a. Borrowed money from a lender (for example, a bank)

b. Purchased products that it put in inventory to be sold to customers at a later date

c. Bought new delivery trucks that will be used for several years

d. Sold to customers products that had been held in inventory

For each transaction, identify which type of transaction it is according to the four basic types:

- Profit-making activities (sales and expenses)
- Set-up and follow-up transactions for sales and expenses
- Investing activities
- Financing activities

A. The transactions and types match up as follows:

a. Financing activities

b. Set-up and follow-up transactions for sales and expenses

c. Investing activities

d. Profit-making activities

TIP

Purchasing and constructing assets that have multi-year lives are long-term investments, which are classified as investing activities.

 A business's shareowners invest additional capital in the business. Which type of transaction is this?

 A business records employees' wages and salaries for the period. Which type of transaction is this?

3 A business records the cost of electricity and gas used during the period. Which type of transaction is this?

4 A business pays a vendor for a previous purchase of products bought on credit. Which type of transaction is this?

Seeing Both Sides of Business Transactions

The accountant's job is to capture all the transactions of the business, determine the financial effects of every transaction, record every transaction in the business's accounts, and from the accounts, prepare the financial statements.

To carry out their mission, accountants must understand how transactions (and certain other events) affect the financial condition of the business. To illustrate the impact of transactions, consider the case of a business that has been in operation for many years. Its condensed balance sheet at the start of the year appears in Figure 2-1.

Most businesses report more than just the four kinds of assets shown in Figure 2-1, but these four are the hard-core assets of a business that sells both products and services. ("PP&E" stands for property, plant, and equipment, which is the generic name for the long-term operating assets of a business. The term "net" means that the amount of accumulated depreciation that has been recorded up to this time is deducted from the cost of the assets.)

Liabilities are divided into two types based on their sources:

>> Those that arise out of operating activities

>> Those that result from borrowing money on interest-bearing debt

Operating liabilities are short-term and do not bear interest. Owners' equity is shown in two different accounts in Figure 2-1. The first is for capital invested in the business by its owners. This source of owners' equity is segregated from the other owners' account, which expresses profit that has been earned and retained by the business.

In Figure 2-1, you can see that the total assets and the total liabilities plus owners' equity appear below the line. This information is the accounting equation of the business. The accounting equation is in balance, as it should be, of course.

Condensed Balance Sheet

Cash	$250,000	Operating liabilities		$350,000
Receivables	$300,000	Interest-bearing liabilities		$500,000
Inventory	$400,000	Owner's invested capital		$250,000
PP&E, net	$550,000	Owner's retained earnings		$400,000
Assets	$1,500,000 =	Liabilities and Owner's Equity		$1,500,000

FIGURE 2-1: Condensed balance sheet of a business.

EXAMPLE

Q. Refer to the eight basic accounts presented in the condensed balance sheet shown in Figure 2-1 — the four assets, the two liabilities, and the two owners' equities. How does each of the following transactions change the company's financial condition?

a. The business borrows $500,000 and signs a legal instrument called a note payable to the lender, promising to pay interest over the life of the loan and to return $500,000 at a future date.

b. The business invests $250,000 in a new machine that it will use for several years and pays for the purchase with a check.

c. The business owners invest an additional $750,000 in the business to aid in its growth and expansion.

d. The business distributes $100,000 of the profit it earned during the year to its shareowners.

A. **a.** Condensed Balance Sheet

Cash	+$500,000	Operating liabilities	
Receivables		Interest-bearing liabilities	+$500,000
Inventory		Owners' invested capital	
PP&E, net		Owners' retained earnings	
Assets	+$500,000 =	Liabilities and Owners' Equity	+$500,000

No interest expense is recorded when the money is borrowed because interest is a time charge for using borrowed money. Interest expenses will be recorded in each future period the money is borrowed, starting at the time the money is borrowed.

b. Condensed Balance Sheet

Cash	–$250,000	Operating Liabilities	
Receivables		Interest-bearing Liabilities	
Inventory		Owners' Invested Capital	
PP&E, net	+$250,000	Owners' Retained Earnings	
Assets	=	Liabilities and Owners' Equity	

There is no change in total assets but rather an exchange among assets: Cash decreases $250,000 with the cost of the new machine. Keep in mind that the cost of the machine will be charged as a depreciation expense over future periods in which the machine is used.

c. Condensed Balance Sheet

Cash	+$750,000	Operating Liabilities	
Receivables		Interest-bearing Liabilities	
Inventory		Owners' Invested Capital	+$750,000
PP&E, net		Owners' Retained Earnings	
Assets	+$750,000 =	Liabilities and owners' equity	+$750,000

In this situation, total assets (that is, cash) increases $750,000 as a result of the owner investing this amount into the business. To balance the equation, owner's invested capital increases by $750,000 to reflect the additional investment.

d. Condensed Balance Sheet

Cash	–$100,000	Operating Liabilities	
Receivables		Interest-bearing Liabilities	
Inventory		Owners' Invested Capital	
PP&E, net		Owners' Retained Earnings	–$100,000
Assets	–$100,000 =	Liabilities and Owners' Equity	–$100,000

Profit is recorded in owners' retained earnings. Profit increases this account, and distributions from profit decrease the account. In this situation, a distribution of profit was made to the owner which reduced cash by $100,000 and owners' retained earnings by the same amount.

---

5 Suppose that all revenue transactions during the year increase cash and that all expense transactions during the year decrease cash. In other words, suppose no other assets and no operating liabilities are affected by the profit–making activities of the business during the year (this scenario isn't realistic and is assumed only for this problem). The net income (bottom–line profit) of this atypical business for the year is $950,000. How does profit change its financial condition?

Condensed Balance Sheet

Cash		Operating Liabilities
Receivables		Interest-bearing Liabilities
Inventory		Owners' Invested Capital
PP&E, net		Owners' Retained Earnings
Assets	=	Liabilities and Owners' Equity

---

6 During the year, a business borrowed $850,000 and used $750,000 of those funds to invest in new long–term operating assets. How do these actions change its financial condition?

Condensed Balance Sheet

Cash		Operating Liabilities
Receivables		Interest-bearing Liabilities
Inventory		Owners' Invested Capital
PP&E, net		Owners' Retained Earnings
Assets	=	Liabilities and Owners' Equity

A freak flood caused extensive damage to inventory. Unfortunately, these losses weren't insured, and the business had to write off $175,000 of its inventory. Ignoring the income tax effects of this write-off, how does this event change the business's financial condition?

Condensed Balance Sheet

Cash	Operating Liabilities
Receivables	Interest-bearing Liabilities
Inventory	Owners' Invested Capital
PP&E, net	Owners' Retained Earnings
Assets	= Liabilities and owners' equity

 A note payable liability came due (meaning it reached its maturity date) during the year, and the business decided not to renew (or rollover) this loan. Accordingly, the business paid $500,000 to the lender, and the note payable was cancelled. (All interest expense on this debt was recorded correctly during the year.) How did paying off the note payable change the business's financial condition?

Condensed Balance Sheet

Cash	Operating Liabilities
Receivables	Interest-bearing Liabilities
Inventory	Owners' Invested Capital
PP&E, net	Owners' Retained Earnings
Assets	= Liabilities and Owners' Equity

Concentrating on Sales

One of the most quoted sayings in business is, "Nothing happens until you sell it." (Another is, "There's no such thing as a free lunch," but I digress.) Well, there's no doubt that a business has to make sales that generate enough sales revenue to overcome its expenses, leaving a residual of profit. As I'm sure you know, this is a tall task and much easier said than done.

The effect that making a sale has on a business's financial condition depends on when cash is collected from the sale. By the way, when I refer to "cash," this includes both the physical receipt of cash (which is relatively uncommon in today's economy) or more importantly, the electronic receipt of cash via credit cards, debit cards, electronic payment services, bank processed ACHs or wires, and so on. Over the past 20 years, the transition away from using cash and checks to leveraging electronic forms of payments has been extraordinary and is a subject I cover in more depth in Chapter 5.

Regarding cash collection, sales come in three flavors:

» **Cash sales:** Cash is collected when the business makes the sale and delivers the product and/or service to the customer. A classic example of this is a customer purchase of food at a fast-food restaurant where cash is exchanged for the food received.

» **Credit sales:** Cash isn't collected until sometime after the sale is made; the customer is given a period of time before they have to pay the business. Here, a perfect example is centered in a law firm providing services to a customer and granting 30 days to the customer to remit payment.

» **Advance payment sales:** The customer pays the business before the sale is consummated, that is, before the business delivers the product and/or service to the customer. For example, Tesla requires customers to provide a deposit at the point a car is ordered, and then the customer pays the balance upon delivery of the vehicle.

In short, cash may be collected at the time of the sale, after this time, or before this time.

REMEMBER No doubt you're familiar with cash and credit sales. However, you may be a little rusty, from an accounting point of view, on advance payment sales. For this type of sale, at the time of receiving an advance payment, like with the Tesla the customer is buying, the business does not record a sale; instead, it records a liability that stays on the books until the product or service is actually delivered to the customer. This specific liability is one of the business's operating liabilities.

For example, in today's economy, paying in advance for a software subscription is quite common as the company providing access to the software will often bill the customer in advance for the entire year. The company selling the software subscription cannot record the amount billed to the customer as sales revenue as the services rendered are provided over a year. (Until the services are used, the company should maintain a liability which is often referred to as unearned revenue.) In effect, the selling company must defer the revenue and recognize it over the contract period to properly match earned revenue with operating expenses incurred.

Another example might hit closer to home: If you give gift certificates to others as birthday or holiday presents, this would be another example of an advance payment sale. The liability of the advance payment sale is extinguished as gift certificates are redeemed for goods or services.

Suppose I tell you that a business recorded $3,200,000 sales revenue for the year just ended. Can you tell me how its balance sheet changed as the result of that sales revenue? No, you can't — unless the business makes only cash sales. If the business makes credit sales or collects advance payments from customers for future sales, then the changes in its balance sheet caused by sales are a little more involved. Sorry, but this is a business fact of life.

Q. A business makes all three kinds of sales — cash, credit, and advance payment. For the latest year, it recorded $3,200,000 total sales revenue. Its sales caused its receivable balance to increase $75,000 during the year, and its operating liabilities balance to increase $50,000 during the year. How did sales for the year change its financial condition?

EXAMPLE

A. Its sales cause the following changes in the financial condition of the business:

Condensed Balance Sheet

Cash	+$3,175,000	Operating Liabilities		+$50,000
Receivables	+$75,000	Interest-bearing Liabilities		
Inventory		Owners' Invested Capital		
PP&E, net		Owners' Retained Earnings		+$3,200,000
Assets	+$3,250,000 =	Liabilities and Owners' Equity		+$3,250,000

Some important points to note in this scenario are:

- Credit sales cause receivables to increase $75,000 during the year, so the year-end balance of receivables is $75,000 higher than the start-of-year balance. Generally speaking, receivables increase when sales increase year-to-year.

- Advance payment sales cause operating liabilities to increase $50,000 during the year, so the year-end balance of the liability for advance payments from customers is $50,000 higher than the start-of-year balance. Generally speaking, this liability increases when sales increase year-to-year.

- Accounting can sometimes look like a puzzle with missing pieces, but it really isn't that difficult. From the accounting equation (which is nothing more than basic math), you know the liabilities plus the owners' equity have increased a total of $3,250,000. To stay in balance, the asset side has to increase the same amount. On the asset side of the puzzle, you know receivables has increased $75,000. One missing piece of the puzzle is the amount that cash increased. To keep the accounting equation in balance, cash has to have increased $3,175,000.

---

9 A business sells only to other businesses and makes all sales on credit; it doesn't have any cash sales or advance payment sales. During the year, the business made $35,000,000 sales. From these sales, the business collected $31,500,000 during the year, and it also collected the $3,250,000 receivables balance at the start of the year. What are the effects of these collections on the business's financial condition?

Condensed Balance Sheet

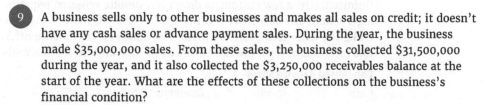

Cash	Operating Liabilities	
Receivables	Interest-bearing Liabilities	
Inventory	Owners' Invested Capital	
PP&E, net	Owners' Retained Earnings	
Assets	= Liabilities and Owners' Equity	

A business requires advance payments on all sales. In other words, it collects cash from customers before products are delivered to them later. During the year, the business received $12,500,000 in advance payments from customers. By the end of the year, the business had delivered 85 percent of products to customers for advance payments received during the year. Also, the business delivered products to customers during the year that fully discharged the $1,500,000 balance in liability for advance payments at the start of the year. What are the effects of these exchanges on the business's financial condition?

Condensed Balance Sheet

Cash		Operating Liabilities
Receivables		Interest-bearing Liabilities
Inventory		Owners' Invested Capital
PP&E, net		Owners' Retained Earnings
Assets	=	Liabilities and Owners' Equity

 During the year, a business made $3,650,000 cash sales. The business has a very liberal product return policy and, therefore, accepted product returns from customers and refunded $450,000 cash. What are the effects of these returns on the business's financial condition?

Condensed Balance Sheet

Cash		Operating Liabilities
Receivables		Interest-bearing Liabilities
Inventory		Owners' Invested Capital
PP&E, net		Owners' Retained Earnings
Assets	=	Liabilities and Owners' Equity

12 During its first year of business, a company made $6,250,000 credit sales. The business collected $5,600,000 cash from customers during the year from these sales. Unfortunately, a few customers didn't pay despite repeated requests and threats of legal action. The business cut off credit to these "deadbeat" customers and refused to make any more credit sales to them. The business had to write off $150,000 uncollectible receivables. What are the effects of these events on its financial condition?

Condensed Balance Sheet

Cash		Operating Liabilities
Receivables		Interest-bearing Liabilities
Inventory		Owners' Invested Capital
PP&E, net		Owners' Retained Earnings
Assets	=	Liabilities and Owners' Equity

Concentrating on Expenses

Just as cash is collected before, after, or at the time of sale, cash is paid before, after, or at the time that an expense is recorded. The following are some examples of cash payment for expenses:

>> Paying cash before an expense is recorded: The expense of cost of goods (products) sold is not recorded until the sale is made. (Products are bought and paid for before they're sold to customers.) Another example is that businesses pay for an annual insurance policy in advance that provides coverage for the next twelve months. The insurance expense is recorded monthly as the services are consumed.

>> Paying cash after an expense is recorded: A business records utility expenses as the service is delivered but does not pay for the utility expense until the following month.

>> Paying cash when an expense is recorded: Wages and salaries expenses are generally recorded at the time employees are paid.

REMEMBER

Most businesses invest in long-term operating assets, the cost of which (that is, the estimated annual usage of the asset) is charged to depreciation expense over many years. Essentially, a business pays for the asset today, but the cost of the asset is recorded as expense over several future years as the business receives the benefits from the asset. Depreciation expense is an estimate of the amount of the cost of the asset consumed or used in earning revenue over future periods. Depreciation is a way to match revenue and expense. For example, as a CPA, I do tax returns for clients. In today's world, I have to have a computer that will run the latest tax software. I buy a $2,000 computer today that I will use to do tax returns for the next five years. I will record that computer as a long-term asset today and depreciate it over five years to match the cost of the computer with the revenue I earn from doing tax returns with that computer over the next five years.

Suppose I tell you that a business recorded $3,000,000 total expenses for the year just ended. Does this simply mean that cash decreased this amount? Hardly! Recording expenses involves other assets than just cash — it involves operating liabilities and depreciating long-term assets as well.

EXAMPLE

Q. Refer back to the business examined in the "Concentrating on Sales" section to complete that business's profit accounting for the year. Expenses are now dealt with to close the profit circle. During the year just ended, the business recorded all three types of expenses — expenses recorded before, after, and at the time of paying the expense. For the year, the business recorded $3,000,000 total expenses. These expenses caused inventory to increase $50,000 during the year, PP&E, net to decrease $75,000 (because depreciation on the assets was recorded), and operating liabilities to increase $45,000. How did the company's expenses change its financial condition?

A. Here's a realistic scenario for how expenses change the financial condition of the business:

Condensed Balance Sheet

Cash	–$2,930,000	Operating Liabilities	+$45,000
Receivables		Interest-bearing Liabilities	
Inventory	+$50,000	Owners' Invested Capital	
PP&E, net	–$75,000	Owners' Retained Earnings	–$3,000,000
Assets	–$2,955,000 =	Liabilities and Owners' Equity	–$2,955,000

Some important points to note in this scenario follow:

- The business recorded $75,000 depreciation expense for the year, so its long-term operating assets (PP&E, net) decrease this amount.

- The $50,000 increase in inventory may strike you as an odd effect of expenses. Keep in mind, however, that a business can purchase or manufacture more inventory than it sells during the year, in which case its inventory balance increases. That's exactly what happened in this example.

- The business has $45,000 more operating liabilities at year-end than it did at the start of the year. In other words, its unpaid expenses at the end of the year are $45,000 more than at the beginning of the year.

- Using the missing piece of the puzzle approach, we have now filled in the pieces for liabilities and owners' equity side if the accounting equation. Liabilities increased $45,000. Owners' equity decreased $3,000,000 for a net decrease of $2,955,000 of total liabilities and owners' equity. Total assets have to decrease by that same amount to keep the accounting equation in balance. We know inventory increased $50,000 and PP&E net decreased $75,000 for a net decrease in assets of $25,000. That leaves only cash to decrease $2,930,000 to keep the accounting equation in balance.

---

13 A business recorded $4,500,000 total expenses for the year. The expenses caused $100,000 increase in its operating liabilities, and a $200,000 depreciation expense was recorded in the year. There was no change in inventory during the year (which is unusual). How did expenses change the financial condition of the business?

Condensed Balance Sheet

Cash		Operating Liabilities
Receivables		Interest-bearing Liabilities
Inventory		Owners' Invested Capital
PP&E, net		Owners' Retained Earnings
Assets	=	Liabilities and Owners' Equity

A business leases (rents these assets instead of owning them) all its long-term operating assets (buildings, machines, vehicles, and so on). Thus, it has no depreciation expense. For the year just ended, the business recorded $2,450,000 total expenses. Expenses caused $75,000 increase in operating liabilities. Inventory increased $45,000 during the year. How did expenses change the financial condition of the business?

Condensed Balance Sheet

Cash		Operating Liabilities
Receivables		Interest-bearing Liabilities
Inventory		Owners' Invested Capital
PP&E, net		Owners' Retained Earnings
Assets	=	Liabilities and Owners' Equity

 A business was just about ready to prepare its financial statements for the year when a sharp-eyed bookkeeper noticed that the business had failed to accrue (record) certain liabilities for unpaid expenses at the end of the year. So, a correcting entry has to be made. The amount of these liabilities for unpaid expenses at year-end is $38,000. What changes in financial condition does recording this additional amount of expense for the year cause? (Ignore income tax effects.)

Condensed Balance Sheet

Cash		Operating Liabilities
Receivables		Interest-bearing Liabilities
Inventory		Owners' Invested Capital
PP&E, net		Owners' Retained Earnings
Assets	=	Liabilities and Owners' Equity

---

16 A business decides to engage in accounting fraud to improve its profit performance for the year. Of course, as explained in Chapter 1, this is unethical and illegal, but the chief executive of the business is desperate, and the chief accountant agrees to conspire with the chief executive to carry out this accounting fraud. They decide that they can't manipulate sales revenue for the year, so the accounting fraud has to be done on the expense side of the ledger. The changes in financial condition caused by the actual expenses of the business for the year are given. How might management go about misstating the expenses in order to boost profit $125,000? (Note: You have to think like a crook to work this problem.)

Condensed Balance Sheet

Cash	-$4,800,000		Operating Liabilities	+$275,000
Receivables			Interest-bearing Liabilities	
Inventory	+$50,000		Owners' Invested Capital	
PP&E, net	-$400,000		Owners' Retained Earnings	-$5,425,000
Assets	-$5,150,000	=	Liabilities and Owners' Equity	-$5,150,000

Determining the Composite Effect of Profit

To determine the profit or loss of a business for the year, it's necessary to blend sales revenue and expenses together. The equation for profit is as follows:

Profit = Sales Revenue – Expenses

For example,

Sales Revenue	$3,200,000
Less: Expenses	–3,000,000
Equals: Profit	$200,000

Determining the effects of profit on the year-end financial condition of a business is a little more involved than the profit computation. You merge the two summaries of changes in financial condition presented earlier in this chapter — one from revenue (see the section "Concentrating on Sales") and the second from expenses (see the section "Concentrating on Expenses") — to determine the composite effect on assets, liabilities, and owners' retained earnings.

REMEMBER

Two kinds of balance sheet accounts generally aren't affected by sales and expense transactions: interest-bearing liabilities (although interest expense is usually recorded at some point and may impact current liabilities) and owners' invested capital.

EXAMPLE

Q. What is the composite change in the year-end financial condition of the business caused by its profit-making activities over the year? Refer back to the financial condition changes caused by sales and expenses, which are presented earlier in the chapter (see the example questions in the sections "Concentrating on Sales" and "Concentrating on Expenses"), to answer this question.

A. Combining the changes caused from sales with the changes caused from expenses gives the following:

Condensed Balance Sheet – Composite Net Changes From Sales and Expenses

Cash	+$245,000	Operating Liabilities		+$95,000
Receivables	+$75,000	Interest-bearing Liabilities		
Inventory	+$50,000	Owners' Invested Capital		
PP&E, net	–$75,000	Owners' Retained Earnings		+$200,000
Assets	+$295,000	= Liabilities and Owners' Equity		+$295,000

TIP

To determine each amount of change, combine the change caused by sales and the change caused by expenses. For instance, sales increase cash $3,175,000 and expenses decrease cash $2,930,000, so the net change is $245,000 increase.

Suppose that expenses for the year caused the following changes in the company's financial condition:

Condensed Balance Sheet

Cash	-$2,880,000		Operating Liabilities	+$150,000
Receivables			Interest-bearing Liabilities	
Inventory	+$25,000		Owners' Invested Capital	
PP&E, net	-$95,000		Owners' Retained Earnings	-$3,100,000
Assets	-$2,950,000	=	Liabilities and Owners' Equity	-$2,950,000

What is the composite effect on financial condition from the company's profit–making activities for the year? (Assume that changes in financial condition from its sales are the same.)

Condensed Balance Sheet

Cash			Operating Liabilities	
Receivables			Interest-bearing Liabilities	
Inventory			Owners' Invested Capital	
PP&E, net			Owners' Retained Earnings	
Assets		=	Liabilities and Owners' Equity	

 Suppose that sales for the year caused the following changes in the company's financial condition:

Condensed Balance Sheet

Cash	+$3,000,000		Operating Liabilities	- $50,000
Receivables	+$250,000		Interest-bearing Liabilities	
Inventory			Owners' Invested Capital	
PP&E, net			Owners' Retained Earnings	+$3,300,000
Assets	+$3,250,000	=	Liabilities and Owners' Equity	+$3,250,000

What is the composite effect on financial condition from the company's profit–making activities for the year? (Assume that changes in financial condition from expenses are the same.)

Condensed Balance Sheet

Cash			Operating Liabilities	
Receivables			Interest-bearing Liabilities	
Inventory			Owners' Invested Capital	
PP&E, net			Owners' Retained Earnings	
Assets		=	Liabilities and Owners' Equity	

Starting with the financial condition of the business at the beginning of the year (see "Seeing Both Sides of Business Transactions" earlier in this chapter) and the changes caused by its profit-making activities during the year (see "Determining the Composite Effect of Profit" earlier in this chapter), what is its financial condition at the end of the year, ignoring other transactions that occurred during the year?

To help you work this problem, the company's financial condition at the start of the year is repeated here (from Figure 2-1):

Condensed Balance Sheet

Cash	$250,000		Operating Liabilities	$350,000
Receivables	$300,000		Interest-bearing Liabilities	$500,000
Inventory	$400,000		Owners' Invested Capital	$250,000
PP&E, net	$550,000		Owners' Retained Earnings	$400,000
Assets	$1,500,000	=	Liabilities and Owners' Equity	$1,500,000

Condensed Balance Sheet

Cash		Operating Liabilities
Receivables		Interest-bearing Liabilities
Inventory		Owners' Invested Capital
PP&E, net		Owners' Retained Earnings
Assets	=	Liabilities and Owners' Equity

---

20 Building on your answer to Question 19, assume that the business had other non-profit transactions during the year, as follows:

- Increased its interest-bearing liabilities $100,000.

- Paid $80,000 distribution from profit to its shareowners

Taking into account these additional transactions, what is the financial condition of the business at the end of the year?

Condensed Balance Sheet

Cash		Operating Liabilities
Receivables		Interest-bearing Liabilities
Inventory		Owners' Invested Capital
PP&E, net		Owners' Retained Earnings
Assets	=	Liabilities and Owners' Equity

Answers to Problems on Financial Effects of Transactions

The following are the answers to the practice questions presented earlier in this chapter.

(1) A business's shareowners invest additional capital in the business. Which type of transaction is this?

Financing activity. To start a business, its owners invest an initial amount of capital (usually money) and from time to time after start-up, they may invest more capital in the business.

(2) A business records employees' wages and salaries for the period. Which type of transaction is this?

Profit-making activity. Wages and salaries is a basic type of expense of all businesses.

(3) A business records the cost of electricity and gas used during the period. Which type of transaction is this?

Profit-making activity. The cost of utilities is a basic expense of all businesses.

(4) A business pays a vendor for a previous purchase of products bought on credit. Which type of transaction is this?

Set-up and follow-up transactions for sales and expenses. This payment is the follow-up transaction that completes the previous purchase on credit.

(5) Suppose that all revenue transactions during the year increase cash and that all expense transactions during the year decrease cash. In other words, suppose no other assets and no operating liabilities are affected by the profit-making activities of the business during the year (this scenario isn't realistic and is assumed only for this problem). The net income (bottom-line profit) of this atypical business for the year is $950,000. How does profit change its financial condition?

Condensed Balance Sheet

Cash	+$950,000	Operating Liabilities	
Receivables		Interest-bearing Liabilities	
Inventory		Owners' Invested Capital	
PP&E, net		Owners' Retained Earnings	+$950,000
Assets	+$950,000 =	Liabilities and Owners' Equity	+$950,000

(6) During the year, a business borrowed $850,000 and used $750,000 of those funds to invest in new long-term operating assets. How do these actions change its financial condition?

Condensed Balance Sheet

Cash	+$100,000	Operating Liabilities	
Receivables		Interest-bearing Liabilities	+$850,000
Inventory		Owners' Invested Capital	
PP&E, net	+$750,000	Owners' Retained Earnings	
Assets	+$850,000 =	Liabilities and Owners' Equity	+$850,000

(7) A freak flood caused extensive damage to inventory. Unfortunately, these losses weren't insured, and the business had to write off $175,000 of its inventory. Ignoring the income tax effects of this write-off, how does this event change the business's financial condition?

Condensed Balance Sheet

Cash		Operating Liabilities		
Receivables		Interest-bearing Liabilities		
Inventory	–$175,000	Owners' Invested Capital		
PP&E, net		Owners' Retained Earnings	–$175,000	
Assets	–$175,000 =	Liabilities and Owners' Equity	–$175,000	

(8) A note payable liability came due (meaning it reached its maturity date) during the year, and the business decided not to renew (or rollover) this loan. Accordingly, the business paid $500,000 to the lender, and the note payable was cancelled. (All interest expense on this debt was recorded correctly during the year.) How did paying off the note payable change the business's financial condition?

Condensed Balance Sheet

Cash	–$500,000	Operating Liabilities		
Receivables		Interest-bearing Liabilities	–$500,000	
Inventory		Owners' Invested Capital		
PP&E, net		Owners' Retained Earnings		
Assets	–$500,000 =	Liabilities and Owners' Equity	–$500,000	

(9) A business sells only to other businesses and makes all sales on credit; it doesn't have any cash sales or advance payment sales. During the year, the business made $35,000,000 sales. From these sales, the business collected $31,500,000 during the year, and it also collected the $3,250,000 receivables balance at the start of the year. What are the effects of these collections on the business's financial condition?

Condensed Balance Sheet

Cash	+$34,750,000	Operating Liabilities		
Receivables	+$250,000	Interest-bearing Liabilities		
Inventory		Owners' Invested Capital		
PP&E, net		Owners' Retained Earnings	+$35,000,000	
Assets	+$35,000,000 =	Liabilities and Owners' Equity	+$35,000,000	

The business added $35,000,000 to receivables from its credit sales during the year. It collected $34,750,000 on receivables during the year ($31,500,000 + $3,250,000). Therefore, receivables increased $250,000, as you see in the preceding balance sheet.

(10) A business requires advance payments on all sales. In other words, it collects cash from customers before products are delivered to them later. During the year, the business received $12,500,000 in advance payments from customers. By the end of the year, the business had delivered 85 percent of products to customers for advance payments received during the year. Also, the business delivered products to customers during the year that fully discharged the $1,500,000 balance in liability for advance payments at the start of the year. What are the effects of these exchanges on the business's financial condition?

Condensed Balance Sheet

Cash	+$12,500,000		Operating Liabilities		+$375,000
Receivables			Interest-bearing Liabilities		
Inventory			Owners' Invested Capital		
PP&E, net			Owners' Retained Earnings		+$12,125,000
Assets	+$12,500,000	=	Liabilities and Owners' Equity		+$12,500,000

The business fulfilled 85 percent of its advanced payment for sales during the year, which means it recorded $10,625,000 sales revenue from the current year's advanced sales. Also, the company earned $1,500,000 by delivering products to "pay off" the balance in the liability account for advance payments at the start of the year. Sales revenue is the sum of the two, or $12,125,000. The business has not delivered on 15 percent of its $12,500,000 advance payment sales during the year, which gives it a $1,875,000 increase in the liability for the current year's advance sales offset by the $1,500,000 decrease in the liability for the prior year's advance sales that were recognized in the current year, leaving a net current year-end balance in this liability of $375,000. By the way, if you got this answer right the first time around, congratulations! This is a tough problem.

(11) During the year, a business made $3,650,000 cash sales. The business has a very liberal product return policy and, therefore, accepted product returns from customers and refunded $450,000 cash. What are the effects of these returns on the business's financial condition?

Condensed Balance Sheet

Cash	+$3,200,000		Operating Liabilities		
Receivables			Interest-bearing Liabilities		
Inventory			Owners' Invested Capital		
PP&E, net			Owners' Retained Earnings		+$3,200,000
Assets	+$3,200,000	=	Liabilities and Owners' Equity		+$3,200,000

The cash refunded of $450,000 decreased both the cash received during the year and the net sales recorded during the year.

(12) During its first year of business, a company made $6,250,000 credit sales. The business collected $5,600,000 cash from customers during the year from these sales. Unfortunately, a few customers didn't pay despite repeated requests and threats of legal action. The business cut off credit to these "deadbeat" customers and refused to make any more credit sales to them. The business had to write off $150,000 uncollectible receivables. What are the effects of these events on its financial condition?

Condensed Balance Sheet

Cash	+$5,600,000		Operating Liabilities		
Receivables	+$500,000		Interest-bearing Liabilities		
Inventory			Owners' Invested Capital		
PP&E, net			Owners' Retained Earnings		+$6,100,000
Assets	+$6,100,000	=	Liabilities and Owners' Equity		+$6,100,000

In its income statement for the year, the business reports $6,250,000 sales revenue and $150,000 bad debts expense for the receivables written-off during the year. So, the net effect on owners' retained earnings is an increase of $6,100,000. The business increased cash by $5,600,000 leaving an increase in receivables of $500,000 to keep the accounting equation in balance.

(13) A business recorded $4,500,000 total expenses for the year. The expenses caused $100,000 increase in its operating liabilities, and a $200,000 depreciation expense was recorded in the year. There was no change in inventory during the year (which is unusual). How did expenses change the financial condition of the business?

Condensed Balance Sheet

Cash	−$4,200,000	Operating Liabilities	+$100,000
Receivables		Interest-bearing Liabilities	
Inventory		Owners' Invested Capital	
PP&E, net	−$200,000	Owners' Retained Earnings	−$4,500,000
Assets	−$4,400,000 =	Liabilities and Owners' Equity	−$4,400,000

Owners' equity decreased $4,500,000 and operating liabilities increased $100,000 leaving a net decrease of $4,400,000 in liabilities and owners' equity. Depreciation expense of $200,000 caused a decrease of that amount in PP&E, net. With no change in Inventory, that leaves a decrease in cash of $4,200,000 to keep the accounting equation in balance.

(14) A business leases (rents these assets instead of owning them) all its long-term operating assets (buildings, machines, vehicles, and so on). Thus, it has no depreciation expense. For the year just ended, the business recorded $2,450,000 total expenses. Expenses caused $75,000 increase in operating liabilities. Inventory increased $45,000 during the year. How did expenses change the financial condition of the business?

Condensed Balance Sheet

Cash	−$2,420,000	Operating Liabilities	+$75,000
Receivables		Interest-bearing Liabilities	
Inventory	+$45,000	Owners' Invested Capital	
PP&E, net		Owners' Retained Earnings	−$2,450,000
Assets	−$2,375,000 =	Liabilities and Owners' Equity	−$2,375,000

Owners' equity decreased $2,450,000, and operating liabilities increased $75,000 leaving a net decrease of $2,375,000 in liabilities and owners' equity. There was no depreciation expense for the year. Inventory increased $45,000, leaving a decrease in cash of $2,420,000 to keep the accounting equation in balance.

(15) A business was just about ready to prepare its financial statements for the year when a sharp-eyed bookkeeper noticed that the business had failed to accrue (record) certain liabilities for unpaid expenses at the end of the year. So, a correcting entry has to be made. The amount of these liabilities for unpaid expenses at year-end is $38,000. What changes in financial condition does recording this additional amount of expense for the year cause? (Ignore income tax effects.)

Condensed Balance Sheet

Cash		Operating Liabilities	+$38,000
Receivables		Interest-bearing Liabilities	
Inventory		Owners' Invested Capital	
PP&E, net		Owners' Retained Earnings	−$38,000
Assets	=	Liabilities and Owners' Equity	

REMEMBER

The income tax effect of recording the additional $38,000 expenses is not reflected in this answer. The additional $38,000 is deductible to figure taxable income, so the income tax expense for the year would decrease and since nothing on the Asset side changed, the off-setting change has to be an increase in operating liabilities.

16 A business decides to engage in accounting fraud to improve its profit performance for the year. Of course, as explained in Chapter 1, this is unethical and illegal, but the chief executive of the business is desperate, and the chief accountant agrees to conspire with the chief executive to carry out this accounting fraud. They decide that they can't manipulate sales revenue for the year, so the accounting fraud has to be done on the expense side of the ledger. The changes in financial condition caused by the actual expenses of the business for the year are given. How might management go about misstating the expenses in order to boost profit $125,000? (Note: You have to think like a crook to work this problem.)

Condensed Balance Sheet

Cash	Operating Liabilities	–$125,000
Receivables	Interest-bearing Liabilities	
Inventory	Owners' Invested Capital	
PP&E, net	Owners' Retained Earnings	+$125,000

Thinking like a crook, we probably would manipulate liabilities for unpaid expenses; we would deliberately not record $125,000 of these liabilities. The effects of this manipulation are shown in the condensed balance sheet. As you see, operating liabilities are understated $125,000. Therefore, total expenses for the year are $125,000 lower, and net income is $125,000 higher (before income tax is taken into account). Doing accounting fraud this way may deceive auditors because there's no record of these unrecorded liabilities in the accounts. Increasing cash or receivables or inventory or decreasing depreciation expense would all achieve the same result but would be easier for an auditor to detect. However, a sharp auditor may notice something missing if he or she looks carefully for unrecorded liabilities.

17 Suppose that expenses for the year caused the following changes in the company's financial condition:

Condensed Balance Sheet

Cash	–$2,880,000	Operating Liabilities		+$150,000
Receivables		Interest-bearing Liabilities		
Inventory	+$25,000	Owners' Invested Capital		
PP&E, net	–$95,000	Owners' Retained Earnings		–$3,100,000
Assets	–$2,950,000	=	Liabilities and Owners' Equity	–$2,950,000

What is the composite effect on financial condition from the company's profit-making activities for the year? (Assume that changes in financial condition from its sales are the same.)

Condensed Balance Sheet

Cash	+$295,000	Operating Liabilities		+$200,000
Receivables	+$75,000	Interest-bearing Liabilities		
Inventory	+$25,000	Owners' Invested Capital		
PP&E, net	–$95,000	Owners' Retained Earnings		+$100,000
Assets	+$300,000	=	Liabilities and Owners' Equity	+$300,000

Each of the answers to Questions 17 through 20 are looking for the composite effect of profit on the condensed balance sheet accounts as described in the example in the section "Determining the Composite Effect of Profit."

For Question 17 you must combine the impact on each account for sales from the condensed balance sheet for sales in the section "Concentrating on Sales" with the condensed balance sheet for expenses shown.

18. Suppose that sales for the year caused the following changes in the company's financial condition:

Condensed Balance Sheet

Cash	+$3,000,000	Operating Liabilities		– $50,000
Receivables	+$250,000	Interest-bearing Liabilities		
Inventory		Owners' Invested Capital		
PP&E, net		Owners' Retained Earnings		+$3,300,000
Assets	+$3,250,000 =	Liabilities and Owners' Equity		+$3,250,000

What is the composite effect on financial condition from the company's profit–making activities for the year? (Assume that changes in financial condition from expenses are the same.)

Condensed Balance Sheet

Cash	+$70,000	Operating Liabilities		–$5,000
Receivables	+$250,000	Interest-bearing Liabilities		
Inventory	+$50,000	Owners' Invested Capital		
PP&E, net	–$75,000	Owners' Retained Earnings		+$300,000
Assets	+$295,000 =	Liabilities and Owners' Equity		+$295,000

For Question 18 you must combine the impact on each account for sales from the condensed balance sheet for sales shown in Question 18 with the condensed balance sheet for expenses in the section "Concentrating on Expenses."

19. Starting with the financial condition of the business at the beginning of the year (see "Seeing Both Sides of Business Transactions" earlier in this chapter) and the changes caused by its profit–making activities during the year (see "Determining the Composite Effect of Profit" earlier in this chapter), what is its financial condition at the end of the year, ignoring other transactions that occurred during the year?

To help you work this problem, the company's financial condition at the start of the year is repeated here (from Figure 2–1):

Condensed Balance Sheet

Cash	$250,000	Operating Liabilities	$350,000
Receivables	$300,000	Interest-bearing Liabilities	$500,000
Inventory	$400,000	Owners' Invested Capital	$250,000
PP&E, net	$550,000	Owners' Retained Earnings	$400,000
Assets	$1,500,000 =	Liabilities and Owners' Equity	$1,500,000

Condensed Balance Sheet

Cash	$495,000		Operating Liabilities	$445,000
Receivables	$375,000		Interest-bearing Liabilities	$500,000
Inventory	$450,000		Owners' Invested Capital	$250,000
PP&E, net	$475,000		Owners' Retained Earnings	$600,000
Assets	$1,795,000	=	Liabilities and Owners' Equity	$1,795,000

For Question 19 you must combine the impact on each account for sales from the condensed balance sheet for sales shown in Question 19 and in Figure 2-1 with the condensed balance sheet for expenses in the section "Determining the Composite Effect of Profit."

(20) Building on your answer to Question 19, assume that the business had other non-profit transactions during the year, as follows:

- Increased its interest-bearing liabilities $100,000.

- Paid $80,000 distribution from profit to its shareowners

Taking into account these additional transactions, what is the financial condition of the business at the end of the year?

Condensed Balance Sheet

Cash	$515,000		Operating Liabilities	$445,000
Receivables	$375,000		Interest-bearing Liabilities	$600,000
Inventory	$450,000		Owners' Invested Capital	$250,000
PP&E, net	$475,000		Owners' Retained Earnings	$520,000
Assets	$1,815,000	=	Liabilities and Owners' Equity	$1,815,000

For Question 20 you must combine the impact on each account for sales from the condensed balance sheet for sales shown in Question 19 and Figure 2-1 with the condensed balance sheet for expenses in the section "Determining the Composite Effect of Profit" adding to this last Balance Sheet the additional transactions given in Question 20. After you have added the transactions, you will need to re-calculate the amount for cash in this last balance sheet.

Chapter **3**

Getting Started in the Bookkeeping Cycle

The bookkeeping and recordkeeping system of a business requires an accountant to do the following:

» Establish the chart of accounts in which the financial transactions of the business are recorded.

» Record original entries for financial transactions of the business as they occur day by day or in this hyper technically enabled world, in a real-time basis when the financial transaction actually occurs.

» Use the debits and credits system for recording financial transactions in order to keep the books (accounts) of the business in balance.

» Record additional adjusting entries at the end of the period to adjust revenue and expense accounts in order to ensure the net profit or loss is correctly reported, assets are properly accounted for, and the statement of cash flows is accurate.

» Record certain "housekeeping" entries, called closing or period end entries, to bring the accounting process for the year to a close including both the income statement and balance sheet.

This chapter explains the first three elements: the chart of accounts, original entries, and debits and credits. Chapter 4 completes the recordkeeping cycle by explaining the last two elements: adjusting entries and closing entries. I should also note that the chart of accounts, original entries, and debits and credits usually only impact two of the three financial statements previously discussed in Chapter 2, the income statement and the balance sheet. The reason for this is that the statement of cash flows is derived from the final financial information presented in the balance sheet and income statement as this is where source financial transactions are captured and recorded. By *source financial transactions,* I mean the meat and potatoes of financial and accounting transactions, such as recording customer sales, applying customer payments, capturing vendor expenses, processing payments to vendors, purchasing inventory, and so on. This will become clearer as you work through the rest of this chapter.

TIP

It makes no difference whether the bookkeeping process is handled by a person recording entries by hand (popularly envisioned wearing a green eyeshade and arm garters and making entries with a quill pen, which, of course, is very outdated these days), a 21st-century book-keeper working at a computer keyboard, or a modern accountant capturing financial transactions in real-time fashion using integrated software to perform this task. The recordkeeping process is fundamentally the same: Adopt a chart of accounts, make original entries using debits and credits to keep the books in balance, make adjusting entries to get profit for the period right, and close the books at the end of the year. Apple does it this way, and so should your local convenience store (hopefully). The process reminds me of the saying: "The more things change, the more things stay the same."

Constructing the Chart of Accounts

Accounts are the basic building blocks of an accounting system. An account is a category of information, like a file in which a certain type of information is stored. The reason for establishing an account is that the business needs specific information pulled together in order to prepare a financial statement or some other accounting report.

The first step in setting up an accounting system is to identify the particular accounts that are needed. The financial effects of transactions are recorded as increases or decreases in accounts, and you can't make an accounting entry for a transaction without having accounts to increase or decrease. In short, no accounts mean no accounting!

Suppose you're the chief accountant of a new business. It's your very first day on the job. Where do you start (after finding the restroom)? Your first order of business is to establish the chart of accounts that will be used to record the transactions of the business. The chart of accounts becomes the official set of accounts that you use to record the effects of transactions. Unless you authorize the creation of a new account, the accounts in the chart are the only ones you use.

TIP

The need for one account in the chart of accounts, the cash account, is pretty obvious. A business needs to know how much money it has in its checking account with its bank, so it must establish a cash account and record cash receipts and disbursements in the account. Which other accounts are needed? This is the $64,000 question. To answer this question, the chief accountant looks to the information the business needs to report in its financial statements (provided to both internal and external parties) and income tax and other governmental based returns (the two major information demands on the accounting system of a business).

For most businesses, the chart of accounts is typically structured using one of two formats – alpha or numeric:

>> **Alpha Chart of Accounts:** Smaller businesses that aren't overly sophisticated will often use a simple alpha based chart of accounts. That is, the accounts used are referenced by an alphabetical name such as cash, operating bank account (and the name of the bank), trade accounts receivables, prepaid expenses, and so on. The reason an alpha based chart of accounts is used is for simplicity.

>> **Numeric Chart of Accounts:** For larger and more sophisticated businesses, the chart of accounts is usually structured using a numeric format, which also includes a name. For example, 1001 – Cash would represent the account used to capture cash transactions, 1201 – Trade Accounts Receivables would represent the account used to capture customer sales made on credit, and so on. The reason a numeric based chart of accounts is used is to support more complex business models and provide more accurate financial reporting and analysis.

In either case, it is important to remember that almost all businesses structure their chart of accounts starting with current assets, then long-term assets, moving to current liabilities, long-term liabilities, owners' equity, and then closing out the chart of accounts with sales revenue, costs of sales, operating expenses, and other expenses and income. In fact, a very common chart of account numeric structure is to reserve all 1,000 accounts for assets, 2,000 accounts for liabilities, 3,000 accounts for owners' equity, 4,000 accounts for sales revenue, 5,000 accounts for costs of sales, 6,000 accounts for operating expenses, and 7,000 accounts for other expenses, income, and taxes. This provides for a very logical reporting structure, something accountants love. I highly recommend a numeric chart of accounts as it provides more logic and flexibility as it relates to financial reporting.

As previously noted, business corporations are required to file numerous governmental required reports and returns including the dreaded annual form 1120 (for regular C corporations) or 1120-S (for S corporations) with the Internal Revenue Service (IRS). On the first page of the Form 1120 (which I encourage you to review online at https://www.irs.gov/pub/firs-pdf/f1120.pdf), the following revenue and income information is required to be reported:

>> Line 1a Gross receipts or sales

>> Line 1b Returns and allowances

>> Line 1c Balance. Subtract Line 1b from Line 1a.

>> Line 2 Cost of goods sold

>> Line 3 Gross profit. Subtract Line 2 from Line 1c.

>> Line 4 Dividends

>> Line 5 Interest

>> Line 6 Gross rents

>> Line 7 Gross royalties

Q. Which accounts should the business establish to provide the information required in the first part of its annual income tax return?

A. The business should establish the following accounts:

- Sales revenue for gross revenue from sales to customers
- Sales returns and allowances for returns of products and price reductions after making sales
- Cost of goods sold expenses for the cost of products sold to customers
- Dividend income for income from investments in stocks of other companies
- Interest income for interest earned on investments and loans
- Rental income for income from property being rented to others
- Royalty income for income from mineral rights, copyrights, and so on owned by the business

TIP

The exact titles of these accounts vary from business to business. However, the account titles listed here are fairly typical. The sales returns and allowance account is a contra account to the sales revenue account, which means that it offsets the sales revenue account. Generally, the sales returns and allowance account is used to capture customer returns and/or other adjustments provided to satisfy the customer (for example, an allowance of 10 percent is provided to the customer to quell a delayed shipment complaint). The balance in this account is deducted from sales revenue to determine net sales revenue, which is reported on Line 1c on Form 1120. If a business knows that it won't have any income from dividends, interest, rents, and royalties, then it shouldn't bother to establish accounts for these sources of income. No account is needed for Line 1c or Line 3 because they're calculated amounts, not balances of accounts.

 A business rents the building that houses its retail store, its warehouse, and its administrative offices. It pays rent via check, so obviously the business needs a bank account. Should the business include an expense account for rent in its chart of accounts?

 A business borrows money from its bank. Identify the liability account and the expense account that it should include in its chart of accounts for the borrowing of money and associated cost of borrowing the money (hint, interest).

3 A business employs a typical range of employees — janitors, salespeople, bookkeepers, truck drivers, managers, and so on. It provides a basic retirement plan and pays the premiums for employees' medical and hospital insurance. The annual income tax return filed with the IRS requires the following information: compensation of officers; salaries and wages; employee benefit program; and pension and profit-sharing plans. Should the business include a separate expense account for each of these compensation elements in its chart of accounts?

4 The income tax Form 1120 for business corporations requires the reporting of the following assets: trade notes and accounts receivables; buildings and other depreciable assets; and loans to shareholders. Should the business include separate accounts for each of these assets in its chart of accounts? (These are only three of many items of information that the IRS requires to be reported in the balance sheet that must be included in a business's annual income tax returns.)

Distinguishing Real and Nominal Accounts

Businesses keep two types of accounts:

>> Real accounts are those reported in the balance sheet, which is the summary of the assets, liabilities, and owners' equities of a business.

The label *real* refers to the continuous, permanent nature of this type of account. Real accounts are active from the first day of business to the last day. (A real account could have a temporary zero balance, in which case it's not reported in the balance sheet.) Real accounts contain the balances of assets, liabilities, and owners' equities at a specific point in time, such as at the close of business on the last day of the year. A real account is a record of the amount of asset, liability, or owners' equity at a precise moment in time. The balance in a real account is the net amount after subtracting decreases from increases in the account.

>> Nominal accounts are those reported in the income statement, which is the summary of the revenue and expenses of a business for a period of time.

Balances in nominal accounts are cumulative over a period of time. Take the balance in the sales revenue account at the end of the year, for example. This balance is the total amount of sales over the entire year. Likewise, the balance in advertising expense is the total amount of advertising expense over the entire year. At the end of the period, the accountant uses the balances in the nominal accounts of a business to determine its net profit or loss for the period — this is the main reason for keeping the nominal accounts.

Here's a rough analogy to help you understand the difference between real and nominal accounts: Consider the water held behind a dam at a particular point in time. The water is real because you can dip your toe in it. Compare this body of water with the total amount of water that flowed through the dam over the last year. This water isn't there because it has already gone downriver. This amount is the measure of total flow for a period of time. Assets are like the water behind the dam, and sales revenue is like the flow of water over the year.

Nominal (revenue and expense) accounts are closed at the end of the year. After these accounts have done their jobs accumulating amounts of sales and expenses for the year 2022, for example, their balances are closed. Their balances are reset to zero to start the year 2023. Nominal accounts are emptied out to make way for accumulating sales revenue and expenses during the following year. I cover closing entries in nominal accounts in Chapter 4.

EXAMPLE

Q. A business has just released its financial report for the year just ended, which includes its balance sheet at year-end and its income statement for the year. You take the time to count the number of accounts in each statement and find 20 accounts in the balance sheet and 6 accounts in the income statement. These accounts do not include calculated amounts, such as the total of assets in the balance sheet and gross profit in the income statement. How many accounts of each type and in total does the business need?

A. The absolute minimum number of accounts that a business needs is 20 balance sheet (real) accounts and 6 income statement (nominal) accounts. Otherwise, it doesn't have enough separation of information to prepare its two financial statements. In actual practice, businesses keep many more accounts than they report in their balance sheets and income statements.

TIP

If you were to look at the chart of accounts maintained by even a relatively small business, you'd find hundreds of accounts (maybe more). For example, a business may keep a separate account for each checking account it uses but, in its balance sheet, report only one cash account, which is the combined total of all its separate checking and other cash accounts. Similarly, the business may keep different notes payable accounts, one for each note payable obligation, but combine all into one total liability amount in its balance sheet. Another example is a business that keeps different sales revenue accounts, categorized by product lines, sales territories, and so on. It reports only one total sales revenue account in its income statement. (Public businesses are subject to disclosure rules regarding segment reporting of sales, which is too technical to go into here.)

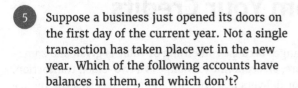

5 Suppose a business just opened its doors on the first day of the current year. Not a single transaction has taken place yet in the new year. Which of the following accounts have balances in them, and which don't?

a. Cash

b. Notes payable

c. Sales revenue

d. Owners' equity — Invested capital

e. Wages and salaries expense

f. Inventory

6 This question focuses on just two accounts taken from the chart of accounts of a business that makes credit sales. The first is a real account, accounts receivable. The second is a nominal account, sales revenue. Are increases and decreases recorded in both accounts during the year, or are only increases recorded during the year?

7 The following condensed balance sheet presents eight core accounts of a business. Which of the eight accounts have a high frequency of transactions recorded in them during the year, and which have a low frequency of transactions? In other words, which of these eight are busy accounts, and which are not?

Condensed Balance Sheet

Cash	$250,000		Operating Liabilities	$350,000
Receivables	$300,000		Interest-bearing Liabilities	$500,000
Inventory	$400,000		Owners' Invested Capital	$250,000
PP&E, net	$550,000		Owners' Retained Earnings	$400,000
Assets	$1,500,000	=	Liabilities and Owners' Equity	$1,500,000

8 A good friend is reading the most recent financial statements prepared for your business. In the balance sheet, they come across the account called "owners' equity — retained earnings." She asks you, "Is this an asset account? If it is, is it money in the bank?" How do you answer?

Knowing Your Debits from Your Credits

Business transactions are economic exchanges because something of value is given and something of value is received. By its very nature, an economic exchange is a two-sided transaction. For example, a business sells a product or delivers a service for $400. It receives the money (either immediately or later) and gives the product to the customer or provides a service. In another example, a business receives $10 million from a lender and gives the lender a legal instrument called a note that promises to return the money at a future date and to pay interest every period starting from the date of the loan forward.

Accountants and bookkeepers use an ingenious scheme to record transactions while keeping the accounting equation constantly in balance — it's called double-entry accounting. This method has been in use a long time. In fact, a book published in 1494 describes the method. What do you think of that?

REMEMBER

Double-entry accounting records both sides of a transaction, and the accounting equation remains in balance as transactions are recorded. For example, if a transaction decreases cash $25,000, then the other side of the transaction is a $25,000 increase in some other asset, or a $25,000 decrease in a liability, or a $25,000 increase in an expense (to cite three possibilities).

To keep the accounting equation in balance as they record transactions, accountants use the system of debits and credits. The famous German philosopher Goethe is reputed to have called double-entry accounting "one of the finest inventions of the human mind." Well, I'm not sure that this bookkeeping technique deserves such high praise, but it's undeniable that the debits and credits method has been in use over six centuries.

Figure 3-1 summarizes the basic rules for debits and credits. By long-standing convention, debits are shown on the left and credits on the right. An increase in a liability, owners' equity, revenue, and income account is recorded as a credit, so the increase side is on the right. The recording of all transactions follows these rules for debits and credits.

Assets		Liabilities and Owner's Equities	
Increases	Decreases	Decreases	Increases
Debits	*Credits*	*Debits*	*Credits*

Expenses and Losses		Revenue and Income	
Increases	Decreases	Decreases	Increases
Debits	*Credits*	*Debits*	*Credits*

FIGURE 3-1: Rules for debits and credits.

WARNING

Practically everyone has trouble with the rules of debits and credit. (I certainly did!) Frankly, the rules aren't very intuitive. Learning the rules for debits and credits is a rite of passage for bookkeepers and accountants. The only way to really understand the rules is to make accounting entries — over and over again. After a while, using the rules becomes like tying your shoes — you do it without even thinking about it.

TIP

Notice the horizontal and vertical lines under the accounts in Figure 3-1. These lines form the letter "T." Accountants refer to these as T accounts. (Very clever of accountants, no?) Although the actual accounts maintained by a business don't necessarily look like T accounts, accounts usually have one column for increases and another column for decreases. In other words, an account has a debit column and a credit column. Also, an account may have a running balance column to continuously keep track of the account's balance.

In the following example question, the number of accounts is limited to simplify the problem; even a small business typically needs more than 100 accounts.

MAKING MORE SENSE OUT OF DEBITS AND CREDITS

Note the accounting equation: Assets = Liabilities + Owners' Equity.

Assets are on the left side of the equation. Assets are increased with debits, which are shown on the left side of a T account and the left side of journal columns. That leaves the right side or the credit side of the T account to be used to decrease assets.

Liabilities and owners' equity are on the right side of the equation. Liabilities and owners' equity are increased with credits, which are shown on the right side of a T account and the right side of journal columns. That leaves the left side or the debit side of the T account to be used to decrease liabilities and owners' equity.

Revenues and expenses are T accounts that are a part of owners' equity — retained earnings. Revenues increase retained earnings, and since they are part of owners' equity, which is on the right side of the accounting equation, revenues are increased with credits, which are on the right side of T accounts.

Expenses are also a part of owners' equity – retained earnings. And since an increase in expenses decreases retained earnings and decreases in retained earnings are shown on the left side or debit side of the T accounts; then increases in expense accounts are shown on the left side or debit side of the T accounts.

After you have learned to use T accounts, they are a great tool in understanding or explaining accounting entries.

Q. Suppose a small business keeps just the following eight accounts.

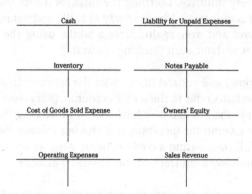

The business's transactions during the year include:

a. Made sales during the year for $2,400 (all were cash sales)

b. The cost of goods sold during the year was $1,600 for product taken out of inventory

c. Incurred $425 in operating expenses, which will be paid sometime later

d. Borrowed $10,000 from bank (ignore the interest expense on this note)

e. Cut a check for $275 in payment of operating expenses; these expenses haven't been recorded previously in a liability account

How should these transactions be recorded in the business's accounts?

A. The following figure shows how the transactions are recorded in the business's accounts. (The letters in the entries correspond to the transactions listed in the question.) In each transaction, the debit amount equals the credit amount.

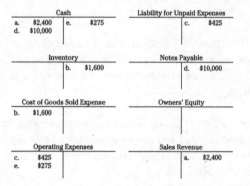

In every account, debits are on the left, and credits are on the right. And don't forget that increases in assets and expenses are recorded as debits, and increases in liabilities and sales revenue are recorded as credits. These few transactions are a very small sample of the large number of transactions the business makes over the course of one year.

Questions 9 through 12 use the same eight accounts given in the preceding example question.

9 The business purchases products for inventory and pays $3,500 cash for the purchase. How should this transaction be recorded in the accounts?

---

10 The business pays the $425 liability for the operating expenses noted in the example question's transaction list. How should this transaction be recorded in the accounts?

---

11 The business pays a note payable that came due in the amount of $5,000. (Ignore interest expense.) How should this transaction be recorded in the accounts?

---

12 The owners invest an additional $25,000 in the business. How should this transaction be recorded in the accounts?

Making Original Journal Entries

To explain and illustrate double-entry recordkeeping in the preceding section, I enter the effects of transactions directly into accounts. By keeping the number of accounts to a minimum, you can see the "big picture" because all assets, liabilities, owners' equity, revenue, and expenses fit on one page. Looking at accounts this way is a useful first step in understanding the rules of debits and credits.

However, with a large number of accounts, recording the effects of transactions directly in the accounts of a business isn't practical. The debits are in one account, and the credits are in another account, and the accounts may be far removed from one another. A much more useful method is to record every transaction such that both sides of the transaction are in one place; keep the debit(s) and credit(s) in the entry for the transaction next to each other.

Therefore, the standard practice is to record transactions first in journal entries so that both sides of a transaction are recorded in one place. A journal is like a diary in that it's a chronological listing of transactions. After journal entries have been recorded, the debits and credits of the transactions are recorded in the accounts of the business. The debits and credits are delivered to their proper addresses, which in accounting parlance is called posting to the accounts.

The journey from transactions to financial statements is as follows:

Transactions → Journal Entries → Posting to Accounts → Financial Statements

TIP

One reason for keeping journals instead of recording the effects of transactions directly in accounts is that a business needs a chronological listing of all its transactions in one place. With journals, each transaction is stored in one place and is available for inspection and review. At a later date, a question or challenge may arise regarding how a transaction was recorded, and the journals allow direct access to original recording of the transaction, which is especially important for audit purposes.

Businesses use several specialized journals, usually one for each basic type of transaction. A typical business has a sales journal, purchases journal, cash receipts journal, cash disbursements (payments) journal, payroll journal, and perhaps other journals as well. In addition, a business needs one general journal in which it records low frequency and non-routine accounting entries. Adjusting and closing entries made at the end of the year (discussed in Chapter 4) are recorded in the general journal.

REMEMBER

Today, businesses use computer-based bookkeeping/accounting systems, which are often now structured to be accessed on-line and in real time (how times have changed). The days of manual journals and accounts are history. Using computerized systems, accountants do the same things that were done in traditional bookkeeping systems, including constructing a chart of accounts, recording journal entries for transactions, posting the debits and credits of journal entries in the accounts, making end-of-period adjusting entries, and using the accounts to prepare financial statements. The reason I mention this is that the use of journals is alive and well but in automated computer systems, the line between the general ledger and journals often blends together.

Q. A business makes $2,350 cash sales for the day, which are paid for by the customer with a debit card. What is the journal entry for these sales?

EXAMPLE

A. I can't show you the process for entering the information for this sales transaction into a computer-based accounting system, so here's the hand-written journal entry:

Bank Account #123	$2,350
Sales Revenue	$2,350

REMEMBER This journal entry follows the conventional format for journal entries in that debits appear first and on the left and credits come second and are indented to the right. (This layout jibes with the rules for debits and credits shown in Figure 3-1.) In this journal entry, the bank account used to capture the customer payment, in this cash Bank Account #123 is debited, or increased $2,350; the sales revenue account is credited, or increased $2,350.

---

 13 What is the explanation for this journal entry?

Inventory	$48,325
Accounts Payable	$48,325

 14 What is the explanation for this journal entry?

Cash	$250,000
Notes Payable	$250,000

 15 What is the explanation for this journal entry?

Rent Expense	$48,325
Cash	$48,325

 16 What is the explanation for this journal entry?

Accounts Payable	$19,250
Cash	$19,250

Please note that when I use the account "cash," we're really not saying that physical cash is changing hands but rather payments to vendors for inventory or rent are being processed via a check or electronic form of payment. Hence, businesses will not generally use the term "cash" in the chart of accounts but rather will use different bank accounts to receive customer payments (in the example bank account #123) or process vendor payments (bank account #456). The reason different bank accounts are used to capture customer payments (an inflow) or process vendor payments (an outflow) is for internal accounting control purposes and help safeguard company assets.

Recording Revenue and Income

In Chapter 2, I explain that when making sales, a business receives cash at the time of making the sale, after the time of sale, or before the time of sale. What about when customers pay with credit cards, debit cards, or other forms of electronic payments? As you know, individuals use credit and debit cards for a large percent of their purchases from businesses. A third form of electronic payment is gaining popularity as well, using third-party apps (such as, PayPal). As far as businesses are concerned, credit card sales are virtually the same as cash sales. The business immediately transmits its credit card receipts to its bank or merchant account for deposit into its checking account. The only real difference is that actual cash payments are received at that point in time whereas credit and debit card sales can sometimes take 24 to 72 hours to actually receive.

A business doesn't get one hundred cents on the dollar when it makes a sale using a credit card or debit card. Banks discount the credit and debit card amounts. For example, assume a bank discounts 3.0 percent from the credit card amount (not an uncommon discount rate). Therefore, for a $100.00 credit card receipt, the bank puts only $97.00 in the business's checking account. The credit card discount rate can be higher or lower depending on several factors, but a 3.0 percent discount rate is in the ballpark for many businesses.

In addition to sales revenue, a business may have other sources of income. A prime example is investment income. Many businesses invest their spare cash in short-term marketable securities that pay interest. Some businesses make loans to officers and employees and charge interest on the loans, which generates interest income, of course. Legally, a business faces few restrictions on the types of investments it can make unless the business adopts formal limits on permissible investments.

EXAMPLE

Q. For a particular business, the day's sales are summarized as follows:

Cash sales	$3,500
Credit card sales	$14,800
Credit sales	$23,400

Its bank discounts 2.75 percent from credit card sales. In journal entry form, record the sales activity of the business for the day.

A. The separate journal entries for the three types of sales for the day are:

Cash	$3,500	
Sales Revenue		$3,500

Cash sales for day.

Credit Card Discount Expense	$407	
Cash	$14,393	
Sales Revenue		$14,800

Credit card sales for day, discounted by bank.

Accounts Receivable	$23,400	
Sales Revenue		$23,400

Credit sales for the day.

Here are a few things to note in these entries:

- These account titles are typical but not universal. Different businesses use slightly different account titles.

- Credit card discount expense is recorded for the credit card sales; in this case, the calculation is $14,800 face value of credit card charges × 2.75 percent discount fee charged by bank = $407. Sales revenue is recorded gross, or before the bank's discount is deducted.

17 For the day, a business makes $38,900 credit sales to other businesses. How should these credit sales be recorded? (Use the journal entry format shown in the preceding example answer.)

18 For the day, a business makes $48,000 of sales which customers pay with a credit card. It immediately sends the credit card information to its bank, which deducts 2.5 percent on credit card charges and puts the remainder in the business's checking account. How should these sales made with credit card payments be recorded? (Use the journal entry format shown in the preceding example answer.)

19 Over the course of a business day, a few customers return products to the business. For the day, the total of customer returns is $2,300, and the business refunds cash to these customers. How should the product returns be recorded? (Use the journal entry format shown in the preceding example answer.)

20 A business invests in short-term government securities to earn income on excess cash that it doesn't need for its day-to-day operations. It just received a $4,500 check from the government for interest earned over the last six months. None of this income has been recorded yet. How should this income be recorded? (Use the journal entry format shown in the preceding example answer.)

Recording Expenses and Losses

How many expense accounts should a business maintain? There's no easy answer to this question. The glib answer is "As many as it needs." To make a profit, business managers have to control expenses, and this task requires a good deal of specific information about expenses.

To get an idea of the broad range of expenses a business may have and, therefore, needs to account for, imagine a business with $10 million annual sales revenue. With that much revenue, you know right off that this company isn't a small, storefront operation. The business probably has more than 50 employees and hundreds or thousands of customers. It may have several locations, and it pays property taxes on its real estate. The business may manufacture the products it sells, or it may be a retailer that buys products in condition for resale. Most likely, it buys insurance coverage to protect against various risks. It also probably advertises the products it sells. For a $10 million business like this one, I would expect to find several hundred different expense accounts — even a thousand or more wouldn't surprise me.

Most businesses with $10 million annual sales revenue have total annual expenses of more than $9 million, or more than 90 percent of their sales revenue. Few businesses earn 10 percent or higher bottom-line profit on their sales revenue. As you may have already figured out, it takes a lot of accounts to keep track of over $9 million expenses.

REMEMBER

Accountants record expenses by decreasing assets or increasing liabilities. Sounds straightforward enough, doesn't it? It ain't! Many different assets and liabilities are credited in making expense entries. The amounts recorded for certain expenses aren't definite or clear-cut. To complicate matters further, the liabilities used to record certain expenses are nebulous and difficult to understand. Frankly, expense accounting is a hodgepodge, so strap on your seat belt.

Figure 3-2 presents a broad overview of expenses. This summary matches expenses with the balance sheet accounts that are credited in recording the expenses. For instance, in recording cost of goods sold expense, the inventory asset account is credited. Many different expenses are recorded when cash disbursements for the expenses are made. Figure 3-2 shows that a specific expense account is recorded when a cash payment is made. The expense could be one of many in the business's chart of accounts.

Expense Account Debited	*Balance Sheet Account Credited*
	Assets
Many specific expenses	Cash
Bad debts expense	Accounts receivable
Cost of goods sold expense	Inventory
Several specific expenses	Prepaid expenses
Depreciation expense	Fixed Assets
	Liabilities
Many specific expenses	Account payable
Several specific expenses	Accrued expense liabilities
Income tax expense	Income tax payable
Labor cost expense	Employee's retirement liability
Income tax expense	Deferred income tax liability
	Owner's Equity
Stock option expense	Invested capital
	Retained earnings

FIGURE 3-2: Balance sheet accounts credited in recording expenses.

Q. A business has three expenses that it must record:

- The business issued a $45,000 check to its advertising agency for spot commercials that appeared on local television during last month; this cost has not been recorded yet.

- The accountant calculated that depreciation for the period is $306,500.

- The accountant calculated that the cost of vacation and sick pay accumulated by employees during the period just ended is $15,400; employees have taken none of this time yet.

What journal entries should be recorded for these expenses?

A. The following journal entries are recorded for the three expenses:

Advertising Expense	$45,000	
Cash		$45,000

Because no expense has been recorded before the time of making cash payment, the advertising expense account is debited (increased) at the time of making payment.

Depreciation Expense	$306,500	
Accumulated Depreciation		$306,500

The cost of a long-term operating asset, also called a fixed asset, is allocated over the estimated useful life of the asset, so a fraction of the cost is charged to the depreciation expense account each period. The fixed asset is credited (decreased) — not by a direct credit in the asset account but by a credit in the contra account, accumulated depreciation. The balance in this contra account is deducted from the original cost of the fixed asset.

Employees' Benefits Expense	$15,400	
Accrued Expense Liability		$15,400

Some expenses accrue, or build up over time, even though the business doesn't receive a bill for the expense. A good example is vacation and sick pay accumulated by employees. Rather than waiting until individual employees actually take time off to record the expense, the creeping liability for this expense is recorded each period. When the employees are paid for vacation and sick time, the liability is debited (decreased).

21 The business's cost of goods sold for its sales during the period is $938,450. The sales revenue for these sales has been recorded. What journal entry should be made for this expense?

22 The business just received a bill for $15,000 from the outside security firm that guards its warehouse and offices. No entry has been made for this expense yet, and the business normally waits several weeks to pay this bill. What journal entry should be made for this expense?

23 Its actuarial firm informs the business that the cost of its employees' retirement pension benefit for the period is $565,000. According to the contract with its employees, the business decides to transfer $300,000 to the trustee of the pension plan and to defer payment of the remainder until a later time (which it has the option to do). No entry has been made for this expense yet. What journal entry should be made for this expense?

24 Unfortunately, one of the major customers of the business declared bankruptcy. This customer owes the business $35,000. The business has already recorded the credit sale to the customer and the cost of goods sold for the sale. After careful analysis, the business comes to the conclusion that it will not collect a dime from this customer. The business doesn't record an expense caused by uncollectible receivables until it actually writes off the receivable. What journal entry should be made for this expense?

Recording Set-Up and Follow-Up Transactions for Revenue and Expenses

Chapter 2 explains the basic types of business transactions, one of which consists of those transactions that take place before or after revenue and expenses are recorded. These set-up and follow-up transactions are supporting transactions for the profit-making activities of a business. These transactions are necessary, as you can see in the following examples:

>> Buying products for inventory (the goods are held in inventory until they're sold and delivered to customers)

>> Collecting receivables from customers

>> Paying liabilities for products, supplies, and services that were bought on credit

>> Paying certain expenses in advance, such as for insurance policies, shipping containers, and office supplies

REMEMBER

Profit-making activities are reported in the income statement, and investing and financing activities are reported in the statement of cash flows. In contrast, set-up and follow-up transactions for revenue and expenses aren't reported in a financial statement. Nevertheless, these housekeeping activities have financial consequences and must be recorded in the accounts of a business. Although no revenue or expense account is involved in recording these activities, these transactions change assets and liabilities.

EXAMPLE

Q. A business purchases fire insurance on its building and contents. The insurance policy covers the next six months. The business writes a check for $25,000 to the insurance company. Also, the business recently purchased $328,000 of products for inventory on credit. The products were delivered to the company's warehouse, and after inspection, the company accepted the products. Record these two transactions in journal entry form.

A. The journal entries for the two transactions are as follows:

Prepaid Expenses	$25,000
Cash	$25,000

The cost of insurance policies is entered in the asset account called prepaid expenses. Over the six months of insurance coverage, the cost is allocated to insurance expense. The payment for the insurance policy decreases one asset (cash) and increases another asset (prepaid expenses).

Inventory	$328,000
Accounts Payable	$328,000

The purchase of products doesn't result in an expense; rather, the transaction is the acquisition of an asset called inventory. The cost of products remains in the asset account until the products are sold to customers, at which time the cost of goods sold expense is recorded, and the asset inventory is decreased. Because the purchase was made on credit, the liability accounts payable is credited (increased). When this liability is paid later, the account is debited (decreased), and cash is decreased.

25 The business buys on credit a large supply of shipping containers that should be enough for the next six months of deliveries. The bill for the purchase is $26,500, and the business will pay it in about 30 days. What journal entry should be made for this transaction?

26 The business receives $49,000 from customers in payment for their previous purchases on credit from the business. To encourage prompt payment, the business offered its customers a 2 percent discount off the sales invoice amount if they paid within ten days of sale, and all the customers took advantage of this incentive. What journal entry should be made for this transaction?

27 The business enters into a contract with a major supplier in which it agrees to buy a minimum amount of products every month over the next five years. Also, set prices are established in the contract. As of yet, the business hasn't made a purchase under this contract, but it expects to do so in the near future. Should a journal entry be made for entering into this contract?

28 A few days after recording the purchase of products on credit, the business discovers that some of the products are defective. The business hasn't paid for the purchase yet, and the vendor agrees to accept return of these defective products for full credit. The products returned to the vendor cost $16,300. What journal entry should be made for this transaction?

Recording Investing and Financing Transactions

Suppose a business recorded 10,000 transactions during the year. The large majority would be sales and expense transactions and the set-up and follow-up transactions for sales and expenses. Perhaps fewer than 100 would be investing and financing transactions. Though few in number, investing and financing transactions are very important and usually involve big chunks of money. In fact, these two types of transactions are reported in the statement of cash flows — that ought to tell you something.

REMEMBER

Investing activities include the purchase and construction of long-term operating assets, such as land, buildings, machines, equipment, vehicles, and so on. In general, these investments are called capital expenditures. (The term *capital* refers to the large amounts of money invested in the assets as well as the long-term nature of these investments.) These economic resources are also called fixed assets. They're not held for sale in the normal course of business; rather, they're held for use in the operations of the business. When grouped together in a balance sheet, fixed assets are typically labeled property, plant, and equipment. Eventually, the business disposes of these assets by trading them in for new assets, selling them off for residual value, or just having the junk collector come and haul them away.

Investing transactions include acquisitions of other long-term assets, such as intangible resources (patents or the creation of video content such as a movie, for example), rental real estate, and research projects in the development stage. For example, a business could invest in a sports franchise, such as the Las Vegas Raiders. (Being a Denver Broncos fan, I doubt if I would buy the stock shares of a business that invested in the Las Vegas Raiders — just kidding!)

REMEMBER

Financing activities basically fall into three categories:

>> A business borrows money on the basis of interest-bearing debt and either pays these loans at their maturity dates or renews them.

>> A business raises capital (usually money) from shareowners and may return some of the invested capital to them.

>> A business distributes cash to its shareowners based on its profit performance.

These are the three basic kinds of financing activities. Large public corporations engage in much more complex and sophisticated financing deals and instruments than these basic types, but those activities are beyond the scope of this book.

EXAMPLE

Q. The investing and financing activities for the year of a new, start-up business corporation are summarized as follows:

- Received $10,000,000 from a venture capital (VC) firm; in exchange, the business signed a $5 million note payable (interest-bearing, of course) to the VC firm and issued shares of stock to the VC firm equal to 10 percent of the total number of shares of stock issued by the business

- Purchased various long-term operating assets for total cash payments of $6,000,000

Make the journal entries for these investing and financing activities.

A. The journal entries for these investing and financing activities are as follows:

Cash	$10,000,000	
Notes Payable		$5,000,000
Owners' Equity — Invested Capital		$5,000,000
Property, Plant, & Equipment	$6,000,000	
Cash		$6,000,000

One-half of the money invested in the start-up business by the VC firm is secured by a note payable on which the business has to pay interest. This transaction is recorded in the notes payable liability account to indicate that the business has the legal obligation to pay interest and to pay the loan at its maturity date. The other half of the money that the VC firm put in the business is attributed to the account for capital stock shares issued by the business. The account title property, plant, and equipment is a generic title for long-term operating assets. The business would maintain more-specific accounts for each major asset purchased, such as buildings, machinery, vehicles, and so on.

---

  29 A business corporation needed more capital to expand and grow, so it issued additional stock shares for a total of $25,000,000. What journal entry should be made for this financing transaction?

  30 A business has had a very good year; its $58,000,000 net income for the year is an all-time high. Being in a generous mood, its board of directors declares a whopping cash distribution of $30,000,000 based on the business's record-setting performance. What journal entry should be made for this financing transaction?

Answers to Problems on the Bookkeeping Cycle

The following are the answers to the practice questions presented earlier in this chapter.

(1) A business rents the building that houses its retail store, its warehouse, and its administrative offices. It pays rent by check, so obviously the business needs a bank account. Should the business include an expense account for rent in its chart of accounts?

Sure; the business definitely needs a rent expense account in which to record the payments to the landlord.

(2) A business borrows money from its bank. Identify the liability account and the expense account that it should include in its chart of accounts for the borrowing of money.

The business needs a notes payable liability account and an interest expense account. In fact, it needs a separate note payable liability account for each loan from the bank, although it probably needs only one interest expense account.

(3) A business employs a typical range of employees — janitors, salespeople, bookkeepers, truck drivers, managers, and so on. It provides a basic retirement plan and pays the premiums for employees' medical and hospital insurance. The annual income tax return filed with the IRS requires the following information: compensation of officers; salaries and wages; employee benefit program; and pension and profit-sharing plans. Should the business include a separate expense account for each of these compensation elements in its chart of accounts?

Because the business needs to separate out information for the various components of its total cost of labor according to the categories required in its income tax return, it should set up a separate expense account for each of the categories listed in the question.

TIP Most businesses don't disclose detailed information about their labor costs in their income statements as required in their federal income tax returns. If total labor cost is disclosed — and not all businesses disclose this expense separately — it's typically reported as one total amount. You seldom see compensation of officers reported as a separate expense in an income statement, although there's no rule against doing so.

(4) The income tax Form 1120 for business corporations requires the reporting of the following assets: trade notes and accounts receivables; buildings and other depreciable assets; and loans to shareholders. Should the business include separate accounts for each of these assets in its chart of accounts? (These are only three of many items of information that the IRS requires to be reported in the balance sheet that must be included in a business's annual income tax returns.)

The fairly obvious answer is that a business should establish separate accounts for these different assets. Typical titles for these accounts are: accounts receivable; notes receivable; buildings; machinery; equipment; vehicles; and loans to offices and shareholders. Exact titles vary from business to business.

(5) Suppose a business just opened its doors on the first day of the current year, and not a single transaction has taken place yet in the new year. Which of the following accounts have balances in them, and which don't?

- Cash
- Notes payable
- Sales revenue
- Owners' equity — Invested capital
- Wages and salaries expense
- Inventory

The real accounts, which are cash, notes payable, owners' equity — invested capital, and inventory, start the year with balances, rolling over from the previous year-end.

The nominal accounts, which are sales revenue and wages and salaries expense, start the year with zero balances.

(6) This question focuses on just two accounts taken from the chart of accounts of a business that makes credit sales. The first is a real account, accounts receivable. The second is a nominal account, sales revenue. Are increases and decreases recorded in both accounts during the year, or are only increases recorded during the year?

Both increases and decreases are recorded in the accounts receivable asset account. Increases are recorded for sales made on credit, and decreases are recorded for collections from customers. In contrast, the sales revenue account records only increases during the year. To be more precise, some decreases may be recorded in this revenue account, but they're the exception rather than the rule. After recording sales revenue, an error may be discovered that requires a decrease in the account to correct the error.

(7) The following condensed balance sheet presents eight core accounts of a business. Which of the eight accounts have a high frequency of transactions recorded in them during the year, and which have a low frequency of transactions? In other words, which of these eight are busy accounts, and which are not?

Condensed Balance Sheet

Cash	$250,000		Operating Liabilities	$350,000
Receivables	$300,000		Interest-bearing Liabilities	$500,000
Inventory	$400,000		Owners' Invested Capital	$250,000
PP&E, net	$550,000		Owners' Retained Earnings	$400,000
Assets	$1,500,000	=	Liabilities and Owners' equity	$1,500,000

The high frequency accounts are cash; receivables; inventory; and operating liabilities. The low frequency accounts are PP&E, net; interest-bearing liabilities; owners' invested capital; and owners' retained earnings.

(8) A good friend is reading the most recent financial statements prepared for your business. In the balance sheet, they come across the account called "owners' equity — retained earnings." She asks you, "Is this an asset account? If it is, is it money in the bank?" How do you answer?

WARNING

No, no, no, no! Many people assume that retained earnings is an asset account and, in particular, that it's money stashed away someplace. (The title of the account may suggest this misleading interpretation.) You should stress that the cash in the bank account is listed under assets in the balance sheet as part of cash. And that cash is a part of the total assets of the business, which includes accounts receivable, inventory, buildings, and so on.

Owners' equity – retained earnings is on the other side of the balance sheet and is part of total owners' equity. Retained earnings is a sum of all the earnings the business has ever had since it began, less any losses the business has ever had, less the amount of any dividends that the business ever paid out to owners. Total owners' equity includes retained earnings plus investments made by owners. Total owners' equity plus total liabilities show the source of all of the business's assets.

Basically, the financial report says that $400,000 of the $1,500,000 total assets of the business is from the earning of profit over the years that has been retained and not distributed to its owners. The total assets of $1,500,000 are supplied by the operating liabilities of $350,000 plus the interest-bearing liabilities of $500,000 and the total owners' equity of $650,000 ($250,000 invested plus $400,000 retained earnings).

9 The business purchases products for inventory and pays $3,500 cash for the purchase. How should this transaction be recorded in the accounts?

Inventory	Cash
$3,500	$3,500

10 The business pays the $425 liability for the operating expenses noted in the example question's transaction list. How should this transaction be recorded in the accounts?

Liability for Unpaid Expenses	Cash
$425	$425

11 The business pays a note payable that came due in the amount of $5,000. (Ignore interest expense.) How should this transaction be recorded in the accounts?

Notes payable	Cash
$5,000	$5,000

12 The owners invest an additional $25,000 in the business. How should this transaction be recorded in the accounts?

Cash	Owners' Equity
$25,000	$25,000

(13) What is the explanation for this journal entry?

Inventory $48,325
    Accounts Payable $48,325

This entry records purchase of products on credit.

(14) What is the explanation for this journal entry?

Cash $250,000
    Notes Payable $250,000

This entry records the borrowing of money on the basis of an interest-bearing note.

(15) What is the explanation for this journal entry?

Rent Expense $48,325
    Cash $48,325

This entry records rent payments to the landlord.

(16) What is the explanation for this journal entry?

Accounts Payable $19,250
    Cash $19,250

This entry records the payment of amounts owed for previous purchases on credit.

(17) For the day, a business makes $38,900 credit sales to other businesses. How should these credit sales be recorded?

Accounts Receivable $38,900
    Sales Revenue $38,900

(18) For the day, a business makes $48,000 credit card sales to individuals. It immediately sends the credit card information to its bank, which deducts 2.5 percent on credit card charges and puts the remainder in the business's checking account. How should these credit card sales be recorded?

Cash $46,800
Credit Card Discount Expense $1,200
    Sales Revenue $48,000

(19) Over the course of a business day, a few customers return products to the business. For the day, the total of customer returns is $2,300, and the business refunds cash to these customers. How should the product returns be recorded?

Sales Returns & Allowances $2,300
    Cash $2,300

TIP

In this scenario, the debit isn't in the sales revenue account but rather in sales returns and allowances account, which is the contra account to sales revenue. The balance in this account is deducted from sales revenue to determine net sales revenue, and the balance in sales returns and allowances is compared with the balance in sales revenue to gauge the returns against sales. (Also, I should mention that a second entry should be made to record the return of products to inventory. The question doesn't give the cost of the goods returned by customers, so you're not asked to include this entry.)

(20) A business invests in short-term government securities to earn income on excess cash that it doesn't need for its day-to-day operations. It just received a $4,500 check from the government for interest earned over the last six months. None of this income has been recorded yet. How should this income be recorded?

Cash	$4,500	
Investment Income		$4,500

(21) The business's cost of goods sold for its sales during the period is $938,450. The sales revenue for these sales has been recorded. What journal entry should be made for this expense?

Cost of Goods Sold Expense	$938,450	
Inventory		$938,450

(22) The business just received a bill for $15,000 from the outside security firm that guards its warehouse and offices. No entry has been made for this expense yet, and the business normally waits several weeks to pay this bill. What journal entry should be made for this expense?

Security Guard Expense	$15,000	
Accounts Payable		$15,000

(23) Its actuarial firm informs the business that the cost of its employees' retirement pension benefit for the period is $565,000. According to the contract with its employees, the business decides to transfer $300,000 to the trustee of the pension plan and to defer payment of the remainder until a later time (which it has the option to do). No entry has been made for this expense yet. What journal entry should be made for this expense?

Employees' Benefit Expense	$565,000	
Cash		$300,000
Employees' Retirement Liability		$265,000

WARNING

Determining the annual cost of a defined benefits pension plan is an exceedingly complex computation. The Financial Accounting Standards Board (FASB) lays down the general rules for United States businesses. You have to be a CPA to wade through all these rules, and even some CPAs find it tough going. I should mention that many business corporations defer funding of their employee pension plans. Some of these companies have gone into bankruptcy, making their ability to fully fund their pension plans doubtful.

24 Unfortunately, one of the major customers of the business declared bankruptcy. This customer owes the business $35,000. The business has already recorded the credit sale to the customer and the cost of goods sold for the sale. After careful analysis, the business comes to the conclusion that it will not collect a dime from this customer. The business doesn't record an expense caused by uncollectible receivables until it actually writes off the receivable. What journal entry should be made for this expense?

Bad Debts Expense	$35,000
Accounts Receivable	$35,000

TIP

I deliberately made this bad debt that has to be written off as uncollectible a relatively large amount in order to call your attention to this problem. Basically, the business gave away its products for nothing. That really smarts! Of course, the business should shut off credit privileges to this customer and also consider reporting this incident to credit-rating agencies.

25 The business buys on credit a large supply of shipping containers that should be enough for the next six months of deliveries. The bill for the purchase is $26,500, and the business will pay it in about 30 days. What journal entry should be made for this transaction?

Prepaid Expenses	$26,500
Accounts Payable	$26,500

When some of the containers are used to ship the products sold to customers, an entry is made to remove the appropriate amount from the prepaid expenses asset account and to charge this amount to an expense, such as transportation or shipping expense. The prepaid expense account may be called something more specific, such as shipping containers.

26 The business receives $49,000 from customers in payment for their previous purchases on credit from the business. To encourage prompt payment, the business offered its customers a 2 percent discount off the sales invoice amount if they paid within ten days of sale, and all the customers took advantage of this incentive. What journal entry should be made for this transaction?

Cash	$49,000
Sales Discounts	$1,000
Accounts Receivable	$50,000

In recording sales, you record the full amount (before any prompt payment discount) in the sales revenue account and in the accounts receivable account. Therefore, the accounts receivable account for these sales has a balance of $50,000. This amount is fully discharged when the customers take the 2 percent prompt payment discount ($50,000 × 2 percent = $1,000). The business records $1,000 in the sales discounts account, which is usually viewed as a sales revenue contra account (not an expense account).

27 The business enters into a contract with a major supplier in which it agrees to buy a minimum amount of products every month over the next five years. Also, set prices are established in the contract. As of yet, the business hasn't made a purchase under this contract, but it expects to do so in the near future. Should a journal entry be made for entering into this contract?

Even though it's an important event, no entry is made for entering into this purchase contract. However, financial reporting disclosure standards require that salient details of this contract be presented in a footnote to the financial statements. The one escape clause, or loophole, in this disclosure standard is that the business doesn't have to disclose the details of the contract if it judges that the contract isn't material, or significant in the affairs of its operations.

28 A few days after recording the purchase of products on credit, the business discovers that some of the products are defective. The business hasn't paid for the purchase yet, and the vendor agrees to accept return of these defective products for full credit. The products returned to the vendor cost $16,300. What journal entry should be made for this transaction?

Accounts Payable	$16,300
Inventory	$16,300

TIP Some accountants argue that instead of crediting the asset inventory in a scenario such as this, a contra account called purchase returns and allowances should be credited. The balance in this contra account is deducted from total purchases for the year to determine net purchases. Unless purchase returns are a serious problem, I favor the entry shown.

29 A business corporation needed more capital to expand and grow, so it issued additional stock shares for a total of $25,000,000. What journal entry should be made for this financing transaction?

Cash	$25,000,000
Owners' Equity — Invested Capital	$25,000,000

30 A business has had a very good year; its $58,000,000 net income for the year is an all-time high. Being in a generous mood, its board of directors declares a whopping cash distribution of $30,000,000 based on the business's record-setting performance. What journal entry should be made for this financing transaction?

Owners' Equity — Retained Earnings	$30,000,000
Cash	$30,000,000

TIP Instead of directly debiting (decreasing) the retained earnings account, as shown in the entry above, some accountants favor making two entries for dividends, as follows:

Dividends	$30,000,000
Cash	$30,000,000

Owners' Equity — Retained Earnings	$30,000,000
Dividends	$30,000,000

As you can see, the end result is the same: The retained earnings account is decreased by the amount of the dividends.

Chapter **4**

The Bookkeeping Cycle: Adjusting and Closing Entries

The end of its fiscal year is a very important time for a business. Accountants prepare the business's income statement and statement of cash flows for the year as well as its balance sheet. The board of directors critically reviews these financial statements to assess the business's financial performance and position and to plan the future course of the business. The financial statements are sent to lenders and shareowners who make their lending and investment decisions based on these accounting reports.

In short, the annual financial statements of a business are extraordinarily important. Accordingly, the financial statements require extraordinarily good accounting; financial statements are no better than the quality of accounting behind them. As I explain in Chapter 3, good accounting demands a well-designed and reliable recordkeeping system, one that records the business's transactions during the period in a complete, accurate, reliable, and timely manner.

This chapter moves on to the additional accounting procedures done at the end of the period. An accountant can't use a business's various accounts to prepare financial statements until these end-of-period accounting steps are completed. As the saying goes, "It ain't over until the fat lady sings."

Getting Accurate with Adjusting Entries

During an accounting period, certain expenses either aren't recorded or aren't fully recorded. The accountant waits until the end of the period and records adjusting entries for these expenses. In addition to expenses, revenue and income accounts may also need adjusting entries at the end of the period. Adjusting entries complete the profit accounting process for the period.

REMEMBER

The term "adjusting" doesn't mean "fiddling with." Adjusting entries aren't made to manipulate profit, such as to move profit closer to the forecast target for the period. Rather, an accountant makes adjusting entries to make profit for the period as accurate as possible. In other words, adjusting entries make revenue and expenses correct for the period, and without them, the bottom-line net income for the period would be wrong. Keep in mind that the managers, directors, lenders, and shareowners of a business rely on the profit number more than any other figure in the business's financial statements.

As you may know, businesses prepare quarterly (three-month) financial statements. In this chapter, I focus on the annual (twelve-month) accounting period. In the business world (and for economic analysis in general), one year is the standard time unit. One year includes the complete cycle of seasonal variations that many businesses experience. The annual income statement draws the most attention in business financial reporting, and everyone holds the annual income statement to high standards of accounting.

In broad overview, year-end adjusting entries are needed for two reasons:

>> To correct errors, miscalculations, revisions to estimates, and so on, that may have crept into the recordkeeping process over a period of time.

>> To make final entries for the year in revenue, income, expense, and loss accounts so that the profit or loss for the year is reasonably accurate and fairly measures the economic performance of a company. This is also the purpose of GAAP (generally accepted accounting principles) as the goal is to ensure a company's income statement presents fairly the results of operations for the year. Both of these statements are correct and draw the same conclusion, the fair representation of a company's economic performance over a period of time.

WARNING

An accounting system involves an enormous amount of data and detail, so safeguards and procedures should be put in place to prevent bookkeeping errors. A business is well-advised to conduct a thorough search at the end of the year for bookkeeping errors that have gone undetected. In the section "Instituting Internal Controls" later in the chapter, I discuss internal accounting controls that should be put into place to minimize bookkeeping errors. Despite their best efforts, most businesses find that errors sneak into their bookkeeping systems.

Q. At year-end, the business searches for bookkeeping errors that may have gone undetected. Based on its year-end review, the business discovers that some office and computer supplies were thrown away and no entry was made. (The supplies were thrown out because they were no longer of any use, but the bookkeeping department wasn't informed that the supplies had been put in the dumpster.) Generally, at the time of purchase, the costs of office and computer supplies are entered (debited) in an asset account called prepaid expenses. As these supplies are used, the appropriate amount of cost is removed from the asset account and recorded to expense. The cost of the discarded supplies was $4,800. What adjusting entry should be made to correct this error?

A. The entry to correct the error of not recording the cost of supplies thrown away is:

Office and Computer Supplies Expense	$4,800
Prepaid Expenses	$4,800

You could argue that throwing away office and computer supplies causes a special type of loss that should be recorded in a separate loss account, but I think that most accountants would put the cost of discarded office and computer supplies in the regular expense account.

---

1 In its year-end review for errors, a business discovers that the recent bill from its law firm was entered as $6,500 instead of $5,600, which is the correct amount. The bill has not been paid yet. What adjusting entry should be made to correct this error?

2 In its year-end review for errors, a business discovers that an order of products was shipped to a customer, and the cost of the products was correctly charged to cost of goods sold expense. However, the paperwork for this particular sales order wasn't sent to the bookkeeping department on time. Therefore, the sale hasn't been recorded. The total price for this credit sale is $36,260. What adjusting entry should be made to correct this error?

3 The $1,500 trash collection bill for the last month of the fiscal year normally arrives before the end of the month. However, the waste management company didn't get its bills out on time, so the expense hasn't been recorded. What adjusting entry should be made to correct this error?

4 In the hustle and bustle of the end-of-year accounting activities, the bookkeeper simply forgot to record the business's social security taxes on its last payroll in the year. As you may know, a business employer pays social security taxes equal to the amount withheld from employees' paychecks. The amount of employer's social security tax for the last pay period is $29,600. What adjusting entry should be made to correct this error?

Breaking Down the End-of-Year Adjusting Entries

The chief accountant of a business, usually known as the controller, must know which end-of-year adjusting entries should be made and should follow through to make sure that these critical entries are recorded correctly. In most businesses, the controller takes a hands-on approach in recording adjusting entries at the end of the year. Recording year-end adjusting entries marks a dividing line between bookkeeping and accounting. Bookkeeping consists of following established rules for accounting and recordkeeping with a heavy focus on managing and accounting for high volumes of financial transactions, whereas the chief accountant makes and enforces the accounting policies, procedures, and controls (the "rules") and takes charge of the year-end adjusting entries with the goal of preparing financial statements and reports in accordance with GAAP.

Recording depreciation expense

The theory of depreciation isn't complicated. Businesses invest in long-term operating assets such as land, buildings, machines, equipment, delivery trucks and cars, forklifts, office furniture, computers, and so on. These are called fixed assets because they are tangible assets that have long-term useful lives. Further, the term "fixed" also implies that the assets aren't held for sale in the normal course of business such as inventory. In a balance sheet, these assets typically are reported in a category called *property, plant, and equipment* (although reporting practices vary on this point).

WARNING

A basic principle of accounting is to match revenue and expenses. For financial statement purposes, charging the entire cost of fixed assets to expense at the time they're bought or constructed wouldn't be very smart. The obvious thing to do is to allocate the cost of a fixed asset over the years of its useful life; this practice is called depreciation. Ah, but here's the rub. Can you predict the future useful life of a fixed asset? A building may stand 40 or 50 years — or more. Some machines don't really wear out; with proper maintenance and repair, they could last indefinitely. Another complicating factor is that businesses replace many fixed assets before the end of their useful lives — not because they wear out physically, but because they become obsolete and inefficient.

TIP

Congress charges the Internal Revenue Service (IRS), everyone's favorite government agency, with the responsibility of implementing income tax legislation. The income tax law and IRS rulings deal with depreciation in a practical, if not entirely correct theoretical, manner. Useful life guidelines have been established for several categories of fixed assets. Generally speaking, these estimates are shorter than the actual useful lives of fixed assets.

For example, a business building is depreciated over 39 years, even though many buildings are used longer, and trucks are depreciated over five years, even though they may be driven for more years. As a practical matter, many businesses (probably the majority) simply adopt the depreciation useful life estimates permitted under the federal income tax law, although the estimates conflict with economic reality to a certain extent.

Even worse (from a viewpoint of what to record as depreciation, much better for reducing business tax liability) to encourage businesses to invest in equipment, the Tax Cut and Jobs Act of 2017 allowed for up to $1 million (adjusted for inflation) of purchase cost per year of equipment with useful lives of 20 years or less, to be written off for tax purposes in the year purchased. So, while charging the entire cost of fixed assets to expense at the time they're bought or constructed wouldn't be very smart for financial statement purposes, it is now allowed for tax purposes. This is only one of the areas where businesses will legally have two sets of books: one for financial statements and one for tax returns.

Depreciation also raises the question of whether each year of using a fixed asset should be charged with the same amount of depreciation. Or should some years be hit with more depreciation expense than others? Generally, the answer to this question boils down to a choice between the straight-line depreciation method (an equal amount is charged to expense each year) and an accelerated depreciation method (earlier years are hit with more expense than later years). I explain depreciation in-depth in Chapter 6. My purpose here is simply to illustrate the year-end adjusting entry for depreciation.

Q. A business bought new computer software for $57,750 at the start of the year. It estimates the useful life of the computer software to be three years and, thus, will depreciate the software cost over three years. The straight-line method (equal amounts per year) is used. The business has not recorded any depreciation on this software during the year. What year-end adjusting entry is recorded for depreciation of the computer software?

EXAMPLE

A. Computer software isn't your typical depreciable fixed asset. Because it's hard to see or touch computer software, you may consider it to be an intangible asset. (I discuss intangible assets in the next section.) However, computer software is part and parcel of using computer hardware, and computer hardware isn't good for anything without software to tell it what to do.

The entry to record the annual depreciation on the computer software is

Depreciation Expense — Computer Software	$19,250
Accumulated Depreciation — Computer Software	$19,250

TIP

In the entry, I debit a specific depreciation expense account, but this doesn't mean that this depreciation account is disclosed separately in the business's income statement. Probably it's grouped with other depreciation expense accounts, and only one total depreciation expense is reported in the income statement. A full-year depreciation amount is recorded because the business has used the asset the entire year. The calculation is $57,750 ÷ 3 years = $19,250 per year.

Instead of crediting (decreasing) the fixed asset account, the standard accounting practice is to credit accumulated depreciation, which is the contra account to the fixed asset account. In essence, the contra account is the credit side of the fixed asset account. It's maintained so that both the original cost of fixed assets and the cumulative depreciation amount on the fixed assets are available for reporting in the balance sheet.

---

5 Based on its depreciation schedules, the annual depreciation on the business's machinery is $420,000. The business uses the straight-line depreciation method. The business recorded a machinery depreciation expense at the end of each quarter during the year, but no entry has been made for the fourth and final quarter. What adjusting entry for machinery depreciation should be recorded at year-end?

6 Rather than own the real estate, a business leases its land and buildings. The lease agreement calls for monthly rents. Does the business record depreciation on this real estate?

7 A bookkeeper who was recently hired by a business recorded the depreciation expense on delivery trucks for the year as follows:

Depreciation Expense — Delivery Trucks	$215,000
Delivery Trucks	$215,000

Is this entry wrong?

8 On the last day of the year, a particular piece of equipment that originally cost $87,500 many years ago was removed from the production line and put on the shipping dock. The equipment is of no further use to the business and will be hauled away to the junk heap in a few days. The asset is fully depreciated. What entry should be made for the retirement of the fixed asset?

Recording amortization expense

In addition to tangible fixed assets, a business may invest in intangible assets, which can't be seen or touched. The value of an intangible asset is rooted in law. For example, a patent gives the owner the exclusive legal right to use the patent in the pursuit of profit. No one else can legally use the patent without being held liable for infringement. There are all sorts of intangible assets. For instance, a business may purchase a list consisting of thousands of names of potential customers or acquire the right to use an established trade name and logo.

REMEMBER The acquisition of an intangible asset is recorded as a debit (increase) in an asset account. The cost of an intangible asset usually is allocated over its predicted useful life to the business, much like depreciation (see the preceding section). Allocating the cost of an intangible asset to expense over the years of its useful life is called amortization.

Q. A business invests in a franchise, which gives it the right to operate under a well-known trade name and logo. The franchise contract is for ten years, and the business pays $250,000 to the franchisor. What adjusting entry should be made at the end of the first year concerning the cost of the franchise?

A. At the end of the first year, the business has used up one year of the ten-year franchise investment. Therefore, the following year-end adjusting entry is made:

Franchise Amortization Expense	$25,000
Franchise	$25,000

Generally, the straight-line amortization method is used, which means that an equal amount is charged to expense each year. The asset account is credited (decreased) in recording amortization expense. A contra account is not used to accumulate amortization.

---

 9 A business pays the owner of a patent $500,000 for the right to use the patent for a period of five years.

   a. What entry should be made for the purchase of the patent right?

   b. What adjusting entry should be made one year later?

 10 The business signs a ten-year contract with the inventor of a secret process that it will use in its manufacturing operations. As an incentive to agree to the contract, the business immediately pays the inventor $1,000,000. In addition, the business agrees to pay the inventor a royalty equal to five percent of its sales revenue from these products over the next ten years.

   a. What entry should be made for the initial payment to the inventor?

   b. What adjusting entry should be made one year later?

Recording other adjusting entries

Depending on the business, year-end adjusting entries are made for:

» Investment income that has been earned but not recorded

» Bad debts expense (caused by uncollectible accounts receivable)

» Inventory losses due to shrinkage and write-downs required by the lower of cost or market (LCM) accounting rule

>> Estimated reserve for sales returns that naturally occur after a heavy selling period (for example, sales returns to retailers in January are generally very high after the holiday selling season)

>> Losses due to asset impairments

>> Buildup of liabilities for operating expenses that haven't been recorded such as period end bonuses due but not paid to employees, commissions earned but not paid to sales reps, and other similar items

>> Income tax liability based on the final determination of income tax for the year

>> Liability for product warranty and guarantee costs

>> Proper recording of unearned or deferred revenue that customers have paid for but are earned over a period of time

>> Increases in liability for unfunded employees' retirement benefits and for post-retirement medical and healthcare benefits

>> Potential losses and liabilities that may arise from unfavorable legal actions

This list is quite a dog's breakfast, isn't it? And I don't even list all possible adjusting entries made by businesses as in some cases, it can number well into the hundreds for larger businesses! This list should give you some idea of the burden on the chief accountant of a business to make sure that all its revenue and expenses are correctly recorded for the year.

EXAMPLE

Q. A business makes mostly credit sales. At the end of the year, its accountant does an aging analysis of its accounts receivables, analyzing the receivables according to how old they are. Generally, the older a receivable is, the greater the risk of not collecting it or not collecting the entire amount owed by the customer. At the end of the year, the business has $4,538,600 total accounts receivable. This ending balance doesn't include specific accounts receivable that were written off during the period. Based on its aging analysis, the business estimates that sooner or later about $95,000 of the ending balance of its accounts receivable will not be paid by customers. What year-end adjusting entry is made?

A. There are two methods of accounting for bad debts expense. In the direct write-off method, no expense is recorded until specific accounts receivable are actually written off. Under this method, no adjusting entry is made at year-end because the business hasn't identified specific customers' accounts from its accounts receivable at year-end that should be written off. During the year, the business did write off specific receivables, and bad debts expense was debited (increased) in these entries. Only these write-offs are recorded in the bad debts expense account.

In the allowance method, based on the estimated amount of accounts receivable that will have to be written off in the future, the following entry is made:

Bad Debts Expense	$95,000	
Allowance for Doubtful Accounts		$95,000

Allowance for doubtful accounts is the contra account to the accounts receivable asset account.

I don't discuss several bookkeeping procedures connected with the allowance method for recording bad debts expense because the goal simply is to illustrate that bad debt expense can be recorded before specific accounts receivable are actually identified and written off as uncollectible. The compelling theory of the allowance method is that the expense is recorded in the same period as the credit sales that generated the bad debts. For large companies, it's inevitable that some amount of sales will not be collected. On the other hand, estimating the amount of future write-offs of accounts receivable is very tricky and is open to manipulation. As a matter of fact, the IRS doesn't permit businesses other than financial institutions to use the allowance method.

The following questions offer examples of common year-end adjusting entries made by businesses, but a particular business doesn't necessarily make every one of the following adjusting entries. For instance, consider a business that makes only cash sales and no credit sales. This business doesn't have bad debts expense from uncollectible accounts receivable, but it does have expenses from taking counterfeit currency, accepting bad checks, making mistakes in giving change to customers, and thefts from cash registers.

 11 A business makes almost all credit sales. At the end of the year, the business has $485,000 total accounts receivable. This ending balance doesn't include $28,500 specific accounts receivable that were written off during the period. The business estimates that customers will not pay $6,500 of the ending balance of its accounts receivable. What year-end adjusting entry is made?

 12 The business has more cash than it needs for day-to-day operations, so the excess cash is invested in short-term marketable securities that pay interest. During the year, the business receives interest checks, which it records in the interest income account. At the end of the year, $48,500 interest has been earned but not yet received. This interest will be included in the interest checks the business receives next year. The business hasn't recorded this earned interest. What adjusting entry is made at the end of the year?

13 At the end of the year, the business owes its employees $58,300 for accumulated vacation and sick pay. This amount will be paid when employees actually take their vacations and time off for sick leave. No entry has been made for this accrued liability. What adjusting entry is made at the end of the year?

14 Based on the final determination of its federal income tax for the year, the business owes $431,500. During the year, it made $3,978,500 total installment payments towards its income tax, which were charged (debited) to its income tax expense account. The $431,500 balance still owed to the government will be paid when the business's income tax return is filed later.

a. What adjusting entry is made at the end of the year?

b. What is the amount of income tax expense reported in its income statement for the year?

15 At the end of the year, the business owes $10,000,000 on interest-bearing notes payable. During the year, it records interest expense as it's paid to lenders. Accordingly, the business recorded $515,400 interest expense during the year. At the close of the year, it owes $97,500 interest that hasn't yet come due for payment and that hasn't been recorded.

a. What adjusting entry is made at the end of the year?

b. What is the amount of interest expense reported in its annual income statement?

16 At the end of the year, the business counts and inspects its ending inventory of products on hand, which is stored in its warehouse and retail sales areas. Usually, employees discover some damaged and spoiled products that can't be sold. This year is no exception. The cost of spoiled and damaged products that will have to be thrown away is $26,300. What adjusting entry is made?

Closing the Books on the Year

The annual income statement of a business is prepared from its revenue, other income, expense, and loss accounts for the year. Indeed, where else could information for preparing the income statement come from? Accountants use these accounts to determine the amount of profit or loss for the year. I needn't remind you how important the annual profit number is to the managers and directors of the business as well as its lenders and shareowners.

Even a modest-size business may have 100 or so revenue accounts and 1,000 or so expense accounts. Managers need a lot of detailed information to run their businesses, so they depend on their accountants to generate regular reports that provide the detailed account information they need for decision-making and management control. In sharp contrast, relatively few lines of information are included in the external income statement distributed to a business's lenders and shareowners. In its external income statement, the business compresses its many revenue accounts into only one or two sales revenue lines and its many expense accounts into relatively few expense lines. (I cover this funneling of information in Chapter 7.)

After the business has prepared its annual financial statements, the revenue and expense accounts have served their dual purpose — to provide information for preparing the income statement and to aid in determining profit or loss for the year. What happens to these revenue and expense accounts after the year is concluded? The traditional bookkeeping procedure is to make closing entries in the accounts. These special entries close, or shut down, the revenue and expense accounts for the year just ended. Also, the amount of profit or loss for the year is recorded in the retained earnings account.

In the few pages I have here to illustrate closing entries, I can't show you a hundred revenue accounts and a thousand expense accounts. So, in the following example, I use just one sales revenue account and only four expense accounts. This scenario isn't realistic, but it gets the point across.

Q. At the end of the year, after all year-end adjusting entries have been made and posted, the balances in the revenue and expense accounts of the business are as follows:

Cost of Goods Sold Expense		Sales Revenue	
$2,725,000			$4,526,500

Selling & Administrative Expenses	
$1,228,500	

Interest Expense	
$175,000	

Income Tax Expense	
$138,000	

What entry is made to close the nominal accounts and enter the profit or loss for the year?

A. The journal entry to close the books is as follows:

Sales Revenue	$4,526,500	
Cost of Goods Sold Expense		$2,725,000
Selling & Administrative Expenses		$1,228,500
Interest Expense		$175,000
Income Tax Expense		$138,000
Owners' Equity — Retained Earnings		$260,000

TIP

The debit to sales revenue and the credits to expenses close out these accounts. The $260,000 profit for the year (sales revenue less all expenses) is recorded in the retained earnings account, where it belongs. Are the books still in balance? In other words, is the accounting equation still in balance after making this entry? Sure. The total credit in this closing entry equals the total debit. So, this entry doesn't throw the accounting equation out of balance.

---

17 Refer to the closing entry in the answer to the example in this section. The T accounts before the closing entry is recorded are provided here. What are the balances in the revenue and expense accounts after the closing entry is posted?

Cost of Goods Sold Expense		Sales Revenue	
$2,725,000			$4,526,500

Selling & Administrative Expenses	
$1,228,500	

Interest Expense	
$175,000	

Income Tax Expense	
$138,000	

---

18 The business is organized legally as a partnership and therefore doesn't pay income tax. (A partnership's annual taxable income or loss is passed through to its partners who pick up their share of profit or loss in their individual income tax returns.) Year-end adjusting entries have been recorded and posted, and the business's revenue and expense accounts are provided here. What closing entry is recorded?

Cost of Goods Sold Expense		Sales Revenue	
$687,500			$1,764,500

Selling & Administrative Expenses	
$674,300	

Interest Expense	
$76,500	

Instituting Internal Controls

Have you ever made an error in your checkbook or forgot to pay a bill on time? Have you ever misplaced an important document that you desperately needed but couldn't find? Have you started to fill out a loan application and realized that you don't keep records for the types of information the lender wants to know? (Trust me; you don't want to know my answers to these questions.) Your individual bookkeeping system may have holes in it, but you can probably get by. In contrast, a business can't get by if its bookkeeping system is full of errors and doesn't provide the information accountants need. A good accounting system is a matter of life and death for a business.

A business accounting system has many components:

» The forms, procedures, policies, and on-line security protocols used to facilitate business transactions and activities, such as making purchases, paying bills, depositing cash receipts in the bank, preparing payroll checks, and so on

» The chart of accounts, which I discuss in Chapter 3

» The bookkeeping procedures used to record its transactions, which should work perfectly if no errors are made

» The computer system and accounting software utilized as an invaluable tool to assist with managing the accounting function (Note that a company may not use technology to support the accounting function, but these instances are extremely rare in today's world.)

Bookkeeping errors can happen, of course. (I presume you've heard of Murphy's Law: "If something can go wrong, it will.") To counteract bookkeeping errors, a layer of internal accounting controls is superimposed on the recordkeeping procedures of the business. This layer of controls builds redundancy into the accounting system in that accountants take extra steps to double-check the data and information recorded in the original entries and accounts. It's like looking at your speedometer not once but twice to make sure your speed is acceptable. Businesses know that effective internal accounting controls reduce the incidence of recordkeeping errors to a minimum, and that's extremely important.

The accountant's function extends beyond establishing and policing internal accounting controls. The accounting department is assigned responsibility for designing and enforcing controls to guard against a broad range of threats facing the business. Businesses are at risk from all sorts of dishonesty, theft, and fraud. They handle a lot of cash and have valuable assets and have direct control over large amounts of invaluable data (a very important concept in today's technology-based world), so businesses are natural targets for people who steal and cheat. Everyone that a business deals with poses a potential risk.

Another serious problem to consider is that instead of being the victim, a business may be the perpetrator of wrongdoing. A business may cheat its employees and customers, knowingly violate laws, or resort to accounting fraud to make its financial statements look better than the facts support. In other words, a business may cook its books. You may have heard about Enron and other high profile accounting fraud scandals that led to the passage of the federal Sarbanes-Oxley Act of 2002. This legislation puts a heavy burden on the top-level executives of public companies to certify that their businesses have effective controls to prevent fraudulent financial reporting. (For more on the Sarbanes-Oxley Act, see *Sarbanes-Oxley For Dummies* by Jill Gilbert Welytok [Wiley].)

The chief accountant of a business has to make sure basic internal accounting controls are in place and working effectively to minimize bookkeeping errors. In addition, they are responsible for establishing effective controls that prevent employee theft and embezzlement as well as fraud against the business by its customers, vendors, and the other outside parties it deals with. Furthermore, a business needs to adopt controls to prevent it from issuing fraudulent financial statements. All this is a tall order, to say the least!

EXAMPLE

Q. The business has established an internal control procedure that, for every cash disbursement $2,500 or more, a second manager must countersign the check. The manager who has authority to initiate the disbursement signs the check and then sends the check with supporting documentation to the second manager for his or her signature. What is the logic of this control?

A. The theory behind this internal control procedure is that the second manager will make a careful review and judge whether the payment is for a legitimate purpose and is reasonable in amount. If two persons have to sign off on expenditures over a certain amount, then they would have to collude to pull off a scam against the business. Even if someone were inclined to make a quick buck and didn't care how you did it, they probably wouldn't be in cahoots with another untrustworthy crook.

19 The purchasing manager of the business has authority to issue purchase orders. He also inspects shipments as they arrive, approves vendors' invoices for payment, and mails checks to the vendors. Do you see any potential problems here?

20 A business doesn't bother to reconcile its monthly bank statement balance and its cash account balance, claiming that its bookkeepers have more important things to do and, besides, the bank never makes a mistake. What do you think?

Answers to Problems on the Bookkeeping Cycle

The following are the answers to the practice questions presented earlier in this chapter.

(1) In its year-end review for errors, a business discovers that the recent bill from its law firm was entered as $6,500 instead of $5,600, which is the correct amount. The bill has not been paid yet. What adjusting entry should be made to correct this error?

Accounts Payable	$900
Legal Expense	$900

TIP

This type of error is called a transposition error because two digits in the number are transposed, or switched. It's a common error. Experienced bookkeepers and accountants know that this type of error is divisible by nine. (The difference caused by any two digits you transpose is always divisible by nine.)

(2) In its year-end review, for errors a business discovers that an order of products was shipped to a customer, and cost of the products was correctly charged to cost of goods sold expense. However, the paperwork for this particular sales order wasn't sent to the bookkeeping department on time. Therefore, the sale hasn't been recorded. The total price for this credit sale is $36,260. What adjusting entry should be made to correct this error?

Accounts Receivable	$36,260
Sales Revenue	$36,260

The sales revenue for this sale should be recorded because the sale was completed, and the products were delivered to the customer. The sale should be recorded to match revenue and expense. If this error isn't corrected, a mismatch will occur because the expense is in this year but the revenue will be in next year.

(3) The $1,500 trash collection bill for the last month of the fiscal year normally arrives before the end of the month. However, the waste management company didn't get its bills out on time, so the expense hasn't been recorded. What adjusting entry should be made to correct this error?

Trash Collection Expense	$1,500
Accounts Payable	$1,500

This entry records the 12th month of expense for the year. If this entry were not recorded, only 11 months of trash collection expense would be recorded for the year. Also, the amount owed to the trash collection company is clearly a liability of the business and should be included in its accounts payable balance at the end of the year.

(4) In the hustle and bustle of the end-of-year accounting activities, the bookkeeper simply forgot to record the business's social security taxes on its last payroll in the year. As you may know, a business employer pays social security taxes equal to the amount withheld from

employees' paychecks. The amount of employer's social security tax for the last pay period is $29,600. What adjusting entry should be made to correct this error?

Social Security Tax Expense	$29,600
Social Security Taxes Payable	$29,600

TIP

Most businesses put both the social security taxes withheld from employees' wages and the equal amount paid by the business in one liability account for social security taxes payable.

(5) Based on its depreciation schedules, the annual depreciation on the business's machinery is $420,000. The business uses the straight-line depreciation method. The business recorded a machinery depreciation expense at the end of each quarter during the year, but no entry has been made for the fourth and final quarter. What adjusting entry for machinery depreciation should be recorded at year-end?

Machinery Depreciation	$105,000
Accumulated Depreciation — Machinery	$105,000

Note: By the end of the year, the business had already recorded three quarters of depreciation on its machinery. In the year-end adjusting entry, only the last quarter of the total annual depreciation expense is recorded.

(6) Rather than own the real estate, a business leases its land and buildings. The lease agreement calls for monthly rents. Does the business record depreciation on this real estate?

No, because there's no depreciation expense to record. As each lease payment is made, the business records rent expense, which takes the place of depreciation expense (which would be recorded if the business owned the building).

(7) A bookkeeper who was recently hired by a business recorded the depreciation expense on delivery trucks for the year as follows:

Depreciation Expense — Delivery Trucks	$215,000
Delivery Trucks	$215,000

Is this entry wrong?

The debit to depreciation expense is correct, but the wrong account is credited. The credit should be made in the Accumulated Depreciation — Delivery Trucks account, which is the contra account to the Delivery Trucks asset account.

TIP

Standard practice is to report the original cost of fixed assets in the balance sheet and to deduct the cumulative amount of depreciation from original cost. To have this information available for preparing the balance sheet, the accumulated depreciation account is credited when recording depreciation expense.

(8) On the last day of the year, a particular piece of equipment that originally cost $87,500 many years ago was removed from the production line and put on the shipping dock. The equipment is of no further use to the business and will be hauled away to the junk heap in a few days. The asset is fully depreciated. What entry should be made for the retirement of the fixed asset?

Accumulated Depreciation — Equipment	$87,500
Equipment	$87,500

WARNING

When a fixed asset is retired and removed from service, its cost and accumulated depreciation should be removed from the accounts. The fixed asset is fully depreciated, so the balance in the accumulated depreciation account is equal to the original cost of the fixed asset. Not making this entry would inflate the balances of the fixed asset account and of its contra account. If the equipment had not been fully depreciated, the accumulated adjustment account would have been less than the cost of the equipment. You would still make the above entry to write off the original cost of the equipment and the current balance in the Accumulated Depreciation – Equipment account. To keep the accounting equation in balance, you would need an additional debit to make your total debits equal your total credits. This additional debit would be to an account Loss on Disposal of Equipment or something with a similar name.

9 A business pays the owner of a patent $500,000 for the right to use the patent for a period of five years.

a. What entry should be made for the purchase of the patent right?

The entry to record the purchase of the patent is:

Patent	$500,000	
Cash		$500,000

b. What adjusting entry should be made one year later?

The entry to record the first-year amortization expense on the patent is:

Patent Amortization Expense	$100,000	
Patent		$100,000

The business has the right to use the patent for only five years. Therefore, it should amortize the cost of the patent right over the five-year period. Generally, the straight-line method of allocation is used for amortizing the cost of an intangible asset. So, $100,000 expense (1/5 of $500,000) is recorded each year. The amortization is recorded as a direct reduction (credit) in the intangible asset account.

10 The business signs a ten-year contract with the inventor of a secret process that it will use in its manufacturing operations. As an incentive to agree to the contract, the business immediately pays the inventor $1,000,000. In addition, the business agrees to pay the inventor a royalty equal to five percent of its sales revenue from these products over the next ten years.

a. What entry should be made for the initial payment to the inventor?

The entry to record the purchase of the rights to the secret process is:

Secret Process	$1,000,000	
Cash		$1,000,000

b. What adjusting entry should be made one year later?

The entry to record the first-year amortization expense on the cost of the secret process is:

Secret Process Amortization Expense	$100,000	
Secret Process		$100,000

TIP

The purpose of this question is to illustrate that the cost of the intangible asset should be amortized over the life of the contract to use the secret process. To be more accurate, however, this is a cost of production. The amortization amount should be charged to the cost of the products that are manufactured using the secret process. When these products are sold, their costs are charged to the cost of goods sold expense account. So, the amortization ends up in the cost of goods sold expense account. Likewise, depreciation on fixed assets that are used in a company's manufacturing process is charged to the cost of products manufactured.

11 A business makes almost all credit sales. At the end of the year, the business has $485,000 total accounts receivable. This ending balance doesn't include $28,500 specific accounts receivable that were written off during the period. The business estimates that customers will not pay $6,500 of the ending balance of its accounts receivable. What year-end adjusting entry is made?

If the business uses the direct write-off method, no adjusting entry is made at the end of the year. Only the receivables actually written off during the year are included in bad debts expense. So, its bad debts expense for the year is $28,500.

If the business uses the allowance method, the following adjusting entry is made at the end of the year:

Bad Debts Expense	$6,500
Allowance for Doubtful Accounts	$6,500

Its bad debts expense for the year is $35,000 ($28,500 specific accounts written off during the year + $6,500 recorded in this adjusting entry).

12 The business has more cash than it needs for day-to-day operations, so the excess cash is invested in short-term marketable securities that pay interest. During the year, the business receives interest checks, which it records in the interest income account. At the end of the year, $48,500 interest has been earned but not yet received. This interest will be included in the interest checks the business receives next year. The business hasn't recorded this earned interest. What adjusting entry is made at the end of the year?

The following year-end adjusting entry is made to pick up the additional amount of interest income that has been earned but not received:

Accrued Interest Receivable	$48,500
Interest Income	$48,500

When the interest income checks are received next year, the bookkeeper has to remember that $48,500 interest income has already been recorded. Accordingly, when the interest income checks are received, $48,500 is entered as a credit in the accrued interest receivable asset account.

13 At the end of the year, the business owes its employees $58,300 for accumulated vacation and sick pay. This amount will be paid when employees actually take their vacations and time off for sick leave. No entry has been made for this accrued liability. What adjusting entry is made at the end of the year?

The year-end adjusting entry for the accumulation of vacation and sick pay is as follows.

Wages and Salaries Expense	$58,300	
Accrued Operating Liabilities Payable		$58,300

TIP

The titles of the accounts debited and credited in this year-end entry vary from business to business. For example, a separate expense account for employees' benefits can be used instead of debiting all labor costs in one general wages and salaries expense account. And the exact title of the liability account credited may vary; separate accounts may be used for each specific liability.

(14) Based on the final determination of its federal income tax for the year, the business owes $431,500. During the year, it made $3,978,500 total installment payments towards its income tax, which were charged (debited) to its income tax expense account. The $431,500 balance still owed to the government will be paid when the business's income tax return is filed later.

a. What adjusting entry is made at the end of the year?

The year-end adjusting entry to record the full amount of income tax expense for the year is as follows:

Income Tax Expense	$431,500	
Income Tax Payable		$431,500

b. What is the amount of income tax expense reported in its income statement for the year?

The amount of income tax expense reported in its income statement is $4,410,000, which is the total of the installment payments made during the year plus the amount recorded in the year-end adjusting entry.

(15) At the end of the year, the business owes $10,000,000 on interest-bearing notes payable. During the year, it records interest expense as it's paid to lenders. Accordingly, the business recorded $515,400 interest expense during the year. At the close of the year, it owes $97,500 interest that hasn't yet come due for payment and that hasn't been recorded.

a. What adjusting entry is made at the end of the year?

The year-end adjusting entry for unpaid interest expense is:

Interest Expense	$97,500	
Accrued Interest Payable		$97,500

b. What is the amount of interest expense reported in its annual income statement?

The interest expense reported in its annual income statement for the year is $612,900, which is the total of the interest payments during the year plus the amount recorded in the year-end adjusting entry.

(16) At the end of the year, the business counts and inspects its ending inventory of products on hand, which is stored in its warehouse and retail sales areas. Usually, employees discover some damaged and spoiled products that can't be sold. This year is no exception. The cost of spoiled and damaged products that will have to be thrown away is $26,300. What adjusting entry is made?

The business should make the following year–end adjusting entry:

Cost of Goods Sold Expense	$26,300	
Inventory		$26,300

TIP

Some accountants may disagree about the account I debit in this adjusting entry. Some amount of spoilage and damage from handling products is unavoidable and a normal cost of receiving, moving, storing, and handling products. Therefore, I include this amount in the cost of goods sold expense. On the other hand, an unusually high percent of products could be thrown away — beyond what's normal for the business. In such a situation, I would record the excess cost as a special expense, such as loss from damaged products. Regardless of which expense account is debited, accountants definitely agree that the cost of products thrown out should be recorded to expense in the year.

(17) Refer to the closing entry in the answer to the example in this section. The T accounts after the closing entry is posted are provided here. What are the balances in the revenue and expense accounts after the closing entry is posted?

Cost of Goods Sold Expense			Sales Revenue	
$2,725,000	$2,725,000		$4,526,500	$4,526,500

Selling & Administrative Expenses	
$1,228,500	$1,228,500

Interest Expense	
$175,000	$175,000

Income Tax Expense	
$138,000	$138,000

As you can see, the accounts have zero balances. They have served their purposes for the year and are shut down and made ready for next year.

(18) The business is organized legally as a partnership and therefore doesn't pay income tax. (A partnership's annual taxable income or loss is passed through to its partners who pick up their share of profit or loss in their individual income tax returns.) Year-end adjusting entries have been recorded and posted, and the business's revenue and expense accounts are provided here. What closing entry is recorded?

Cost of Goods Sold Expense			Sales Revenue	
$687,500				$1,764,500

Selling & Administrative Expenses	
$674,300	

Interest Expense	
$76,500	

The following closing entry is recorded.

Sales Revenue	$1,764,500	
Cost of Goods Sold Expense		$687,500
Selling & Administrative Expenses		$674,300
Interest Expense		$76,500
Partners' Equity		$326,200

The annual profit of a partnership is allocated among the individual partners' equity (also called capital) accounts. In this entry, only one general partners' equity account is shown. Generally, partnerships don't separate between invested capital and retained earnings, as do corporations.

(19) The purchasing manager of the business has authority to issue purchase orders. He also inspects shipments as they arrive, approves vendors' invoices for payment, and mails checks to the vendors. Do you see any potential problems here?

This business is asking for trouble. Assigning all these different functions to the same person violates a fundamental tenet of internal control: the separation of duties. Giving the purchasing manager control over the procurement process from start to finish is dangerous; ideally, a different person should be in charge of each of the steps listed in the question. For example, someone other than the purchasing manager should inspect shipments as they arrive on the receiving dock to make sure the items received match up with the items listed on the invoice from the vendor, and a different person should mail checks to vendors. If I were the boss, I'd tell the purchasing manager that their time is too valuable to do all these things and that they should focus on getting better prices.

(20) A business doesn't bother to reconcile its monthly bank statement balance and its cash account balance, claiming that its bookkeepers have more important things to do and, besides, the bank never makes a mistake. What do you think?

A business should routinely reconcile its monthly bank statement balance and its cash account balance. Even if the bank "never" makes an error (yeah, right!), the bookkeeper may make errors in recording cash receipts and payments. Also, keep in mind that the monthly bank statement reports checks from customers that have bounced (for insufficient funds) and unusual charges by the bank that the business may not have recorded as well as regular charges that the business may wait to record until it gets its monthly bank statement.

I should also note that in this day where electronic data and payment processing are now the rule, the risk of an outside party "hacking" a company and siphoning off funds is a very real risk. In short, the bookkeeper should make time at a minimum to complete a monthly reconciliation and establish procedures to monitor bank account activity on a weekly or even daily basis (with the assistance of a bank that can layer in fraudulent activity monitoring software).

IN THIS CHAPTER

» Using technology in accounting:
The more things change; the more
things stay the same

» Understanding accounting
systems and the cloud

» Processing payments and
protecting cash while leveraging
technology

» Applying technology to assist with
managing the accounting function

Chapter **5**

Accounting in the Digital Age

Throughout the past ten years, the rate of change in technological advancements clearly has been nothing short of mind-numbing. The computing power now possessed in a mobile format (cellphones, tablets, laptops, and yes, even watches and glasses) that allows for real-time access to data, information, articles, content, videos, and just about everything else has transformed how businesses operate, assess financial performances, manage employees, and interact with customers. These technological trends have been further amplified and accelerated by the COVID pandemic that hit the world in early 2020 (and is still present as I write this book), as the move toward remote working and learning has pushed what was once a luxury or nice to have (that is, I can work from home once a week) to a must-have (employees demanding that employers provide work-from-home or remote-working solutions).

This trend is highly prevalent in the heavy data processing and financial transaction side of businesses, including the information technology operations (such as IT or MIS), financial analysis and planning, and accounting. This chapter is dedicated to covering critical topics related to performing and managing the accounting function in the digital age by evaluating the topics from two perspectives:

>> First, what is the latest technological trend or tool that is available to businesses to assist with managing the accounting functions more efficiently?

>> Second, what risks are present with these technological trends or tools, and how does the accounting function need to adapt or evolve to manage these risks?

Keeping a Few Foundational Accounting Concepts in Mind

REMEMBER

Before I dive into the latest and greatest technological trends and tools, I draw your attention to these base accounting concepts that never go out of style and always remain the foundation of accounting:

>> **CART:** Every accounting system, whether 100-percent automated or still being maintained in the dark ages on green ledger sheets, should always strive to produce *complete, accurate, reliable,* and *timely* financial information on which to base sound business decisions. This has been, is, and will always be the primary goal and objective of accounting systems.

>> **SGA:** Accounting systems, whether maintained in the cloud or on the ground, must be designed, controlled, and managed to ensure that company assets are always safeguarded. Never has this been more important. SGA, which stands for safeguarding assets, ensures that physical assets are properly insured and access is restricted to avoid theft. And, more importantly, invaluable company digital data (such as vital customer sales and operating information) is protected from both criminals and competitors.

>> **GIGO or DIGO:** The old saying of *garbage in, garbage out* is more important now than ever before. DIGO stands for *data in, garbage out.* The tendency in the modern accounting era is to assume that if the data flowing into the accounting system has been digitized and/or is supported by blockchain-enabled digital ledgers, then the data is more apt to be correct and free of errors. Don't make this rookie mistake; errors are just as likely to occur with digitized business transactions and records, but if the flow of these records (through the accounting and financial information reporting system) is left unchecked, it can pollute a financial reporting system very quickly and create even more damage if the output reaches decision-makers who ultimately base decisions on erroneous information.

>> **Art versus science:** The profession of accounting is governed by numerous organizations (for example, the Financial Accounting Standards Board, or FASB) that have for decades assisted with documenting guidelines, policies, and procedures for accountants to utilize when preparing company financial information (that is, GAAP — generally accepted accounting principles). Further, colleges, universities, trade schools, and other institutions attempt to educate future accountants to apply GAAP in a consistent manner. But don't forget that accounting still remains a profession that incorporates a significant number of opinions, subjectivity, and for lack of a better term, creativity (the art side of the equation) that technology most likely will never be able to replace.

REMEMBER

The advances made in technology and the digital economy have had a profound and positive impact on the accounting function. These advances have made life so much easier on so many fronts for accountants; one of the single biggest benefits has been allowing accountants to shift their focus and efforts from wasting time on processing data, paperwork, and financial transactions to being able to analyze and interpret accounting and financial reports and data. This is undoubtedly a huge benefit, but one that can be achieved only by keeping in mind two critical concepts:

>> Data integrity has been, is, and will always be of utmost importance; in today's rapid-paced global economic environment, DIGO (data in, garbage out) is not acceptable, and it can be fatal to a business.

>> Developing and implementing proper accounting controls, policies, and procedures to protect the security of all financial data and information has reached an entirely new level given the risks associated with digitizing source documents. As I note in the next section, security, security, and security are the critical buzzwords with accounting systems and software.

REMEMBER

As you work your way through the remainder of this chapter, I want to reinforce that the current technology-based tools available to accountants are absolutely wonderful to have and use, and they have, without question, made accounting systems more efficient. But these technology-based tools have added an entirely new layer of financial and operational management risks that must be proactively managed to achieve the two primary goals of CART and SGA. Remember the old saying "The more things change; the more things stay the same"? This certainly applies to the business accounting function today, tomorrow, or 20 years from now.

EXAMPLE

Q. If you can't tell, I'm big on using acronyms in this book and for good reason; the world of accounting uses acronyms extensively, so the sooner you get accustomed to learning the accounting lingo and using acronyms, the better. To start this chapter off with a bit of humor (always a refreshing break when dealing with such a vibrant topic as accounting, yes, this is sarcasm), let me offer up three acronyms that are often used by accountants and finance types, especially when it comes to making estimates and preparing budgets or financial forecast — BOTE, WAG, and SWAG. What do they stand for?

A. And the answers to these rather "colorful" acronyms is Back of the Envelop, Wild Ass Guess, and Scientific Wild Ass Guess. Although you may get a chuckle from these definitions, I'd like to emphasize just how real these acronyms are and how often they're used in the business and accounting world.

As previously noted, accounting is just as much of an art form as it is a science, and sometimes, estimates or best guesses need to be applied on the accounting front. For example, during the first couple of years a business is in operations and sells products to customers via ecommerce channels, it may have success selling certain products that quickly sell out and not as much success with other products that are "slow moving" (that end up sitting in the warehouse). The question that needs to be asked is simple — Are the slow-moving products worth anything at the end of the first or second year of operations, or do they need to be written off as worthless inventory? Even though the company may have some data to help evaluate the likelihood of the products selling moving forward, consumer buying habits can be very fickle and quickly change, which could render the products held in inventory worthless very quickly. Enter in the concept of SWAG as the accounting department is assigned the task of estimating just how much of the inventory may be worthless or whether its value is impaired. Unfortunately, the company does not have a decade of operating experience and data trends to calculate this figure, so it falls back on preparing a SWAG to help determine what inventory may be at risk. This is a very real and frequently occurring situation and has been amplified even more by the rapid paced, technology dependent world we now live in.

 True or false? Advancements in technology have guaranteed that the accuracy and reliability of accounting information is greater today than it's ever been in the past.

What statement makes the most sense here? Safeguarding physical or tangible assets such as equipment, inventory, and buildings is more important, of equal importance, or less important than safeguarding intangible assets such as customer data, trade secrets, and critical algorithms?

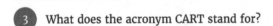 What does the acronym CART stand for?

Using Accounting Software and the Services of an Expert

It's possible, though not likely, that a very small business would keep its books the old-fashioned way: Record all transactions and do all the other steps of the bookkeeping cycle with pen and paper and by making handwritten entries using the old green ledger sheets. However, even a small business has a relatively large number of transactions that have to be recorded in journals and accounts, to say nothing about the end-of-period steps in the bookkeeping cycle (covered in Chapter 4). Therefore, almost all companies today manage accounting processes and financial transactions using fairly sophisticated accounting software designed to handle large volumes of digital data. In fact, you would be absolutely amazed at how far accounting software has come over the past 10 years as the software solutions available today are light years ahead of the dark ages from just 20 years ago.

When mainframe computers were introduced in the 1950s and 1960s, one of their very first uses were for accounting chores. However, only large businesses could afford these electronic behemoths. Smaller businesses didn't use computers for accounting until some years after personal computers came along in the 1980s. A bewildering array of computer software packages is available today for small, medium, and large businesses. Some larger corporations develop and utilize their own computer-based accounting systems (that is, they write their own code), but more and more large companies are utilizing ERP (enterprise resource planning) systems to support their accounting requirements. Indeed, more than 1,000 accounting software systems are listed on the Software Advice website; check out the current numbers at www.softwareadvice.com/accounting.

Many businesses do their accounting work in-house, on the ground at their own locations. They use on-the-premises computers, develop or buy accounting software, and control their own backup files. They may use an outside firm to handle certain accounting chores, particularly payroll. Alternatively, a business can do some or most of its accounting in the cloud. The term *cloud* refers to large-scale offsite computer servers that a business connects with over the internet. The cloud can be used simply as the backup storage location for the company's accounting records. Cloud servers have the reputation of being very difficult to break into by hackers. Cloud providers offer a variety of accounting and business software and services that are too varied to discuss here. In short, a business can do almost all its accounting in the cloud. Of course, the business still needs very strong controls over the transmission of accounting information to and from the cloud. More and more businesses are switching to the cloud for doing more and more of their accounting tasks.

Except for larger entities that employ their own accounting software and information technology experts, other businesses find that they need the consultation of outside IT (information technology) experts in choosing, implementing, upgrading, and replacing accounting software.

If I was giving a talk to owners/managers of small to medium-sized businesses, I would offer the following words of advice about accounting software:

>> Choose your accounting software carefully. It's hard to pull up stakes and switch to another software package. Changing even just one module, such as payroll or inventory, in your accounting software can be quite difficult.

>> In evaluating accounting software, you and your accountant should consider four main factors: ease of use, whether it has the particular features and functionalities you need, the likelihood that the vendor will continue in business and be around to update and make improvements in the software, and, of course, the cost of the software.

>> In real estate, the prime concern is "location, location, location." The watchwords in accounting software are "security, security, security." You need very tight controls over all aspects of using the accounting software and over who is authorized to make changes in any of the modules of the accounting software.

>> Even when using advanced, sophisticated accounting software, a business must design the specialized reports it needs for its various managers and make sure that these reports are generated correctly from the accounting database.

>> Never forget "garbage in, garbage out" (see the previous section and the reference to DIGO). Data entry errors can be a serious problem in computer-based accounting systems. Here's a personal example: My dad's retirement fund manager entered the birthdate of my mom incorrectly. Because of a common transposition error, my mom was recorded as 27 years younger than my dad. This mistake would have caused them grief with the IRS and resulted in their receiving much less monthly retirement income than they were entitled to. Fortunately, they had already calculated the correct amount, and after many telephone calls, they got this straightened out.

  It's next to impossible to eliminate data entry errors altogether. Even barcode readers make mistakes, and barcode tags themselves may have been tampered with. A business should adopt strong controls to minimize these input errors as well as strong internal controls for the verification of data entry.

>> Make sure your accounting software leaves good audit trails (which you need for management control) for your CPA when they audit your financial statements and for the IRS when it decides to audit your income tax returns. The lack of good audit trails looks very suspicious to the IRS.

>> Online accounting systems that permit remote input and access over the internet or a local area network with multiple users present special security problems. Think twice before putting any part of your accounting system online (and if you do, institute airtight controls).

Smaller businesses and even many medium-sized businesses don't have the budget to hire full-time information system and information technology (IT) specialists. They use consultants to help them select accounting software packages, install software, and get it up and running. Like other computer software, accounting programs are frequently revised and updated. A consultant can help keep a business's accounting software up to date, correct flaws and security weaknesses in the program, and take advantage of its latest features.

Controlling and Protecting Money Flows in the Electronic Age

For most businesses, the most targeted asset for theft is good old-fashioned cash. The reason is simple: It is the most liquid asset for criminals to steal and dispose of. Types of cash can range significantly:

>> A small amount of currency that resides in a cash register at a retailer

>> Currency that a bank keeps on hand in a bank teller's drawer

>> Currency that is deposited into and held in a business's checking, savings, trust, or investment accounts at a bank

Needless to say, the use of physical cash has been significantly reduced over the years as other forms of electronic payments replace the need to exchange physical cash. Per a report issued by the Federal Reserve Bank of San Francisco in 2020, consumers used cash in 26 percent of all transactions in 2019, down from 30 percent in 2017. Looking out further (although the exact numbers are not available yet), it is anticipated that the use of cash will see another major decrease because of COVID, given the explosion in direct-to-consumer business models and direct delivery companies such as Amazon, Grubhub, and others.

The reason I highlight these trends is not to state the obvious but rather to emphasize that while the form in which payments are made is changing (from cash to electronic), the sheer volume of electronic payments has exploded over the past ten years. Per a study offered by the CPA Practice Advisor, global digital payments are anticipated to reach $6.6 trillion by 2021, a 40 percent increase in just two years. So basically, every operating business has had to adapt and evolve to the changing landscape to process and receive electronic payments. This, in turn, has driven the requirement of companies to ensure they develop and implement proper policies and procedures to safeguard company assets because criminals are going to follow the cash; if they can't steal it from a retail store, they'll devise systems to steal money electronically.

All companies need to process payments on two fronts:

>> For cash inflows, companies must ensure that customers can remit payments for the goods or services purchased in the most efficient and friendly manner possible.

>> For cash outflows, companies must devise systems to ensure their vendors, suppliers, and employees are paid in an accurate and timely fashion.

For large businesses (think of Walmart and Amazon), the ebb and flow of payment processing (both inflows and outflows) can range in the tens of thousands of transactions daily, so these organizations have developed extremely sophisticated systems to track these payment flows. For small to medium-sized businesses, processing electronic payments is just as important and valuable to the organization to which they devised specific strategies and third-party relationships to assist with managing payment flows (and controlling risks). Find out more about digitally protecting money flows in the following sections.

Processing payroll

Most businesses rely on third-party payroll processing organizations (for example, ADP or Paychex) to manage the task of paying employees. There are so many advantages to using third-party payroll processing organizations that the reasons are almost too many to list, but the primary pluses are centered in the following:

>> Ease in complying with federal and state payroll tax regulations by expert third parties

>> Processing direct deposit of payroll to the employees' bank account (to avoid issuing actual checks)

>> External control of sensitive employee compensation and personal information by a third party

>> Direct online access to payroll records when pay rates, withholdings, and so on need to be changed

Long gone are the days of calling in payroll to your account rep on a semi-monthly basis; these days, you simply log on and update employee pay information in real time. But a word of caution, as access to on-line employee data and pay information can cut both ways. On one front, the employee's personal data is protected along with pay rates, deductions, and so on, by an expert and independent third party. However, if a security breach occurs and access to the pay records is compromised, then an enormous amount of highly confidential employee data could occur (think social security numbers). Ensuring the tightest security systems and controls are established is absolutely essential when dealing with payroll.

Monitoring bank accounts

Bank account information needs to be provided to your customers (so they can process electronic payments to your business) and to vendors and suppliers (so they can receive payments from your business). With so much bank account information floating around in the cyberworld, it can be very helpful to set up unique bank accounts used for specific fund control purposes.

TIP

For example, a company may have a unique bank account set up for the sole purpose of receiving customer payments. This account is monitored every day, and the excess funds are "swept" or consolidated into the company's primary operating account. The same concept holds for payroll accounts as well as vendor payment accounts because these may be funded with just enough money to cover the payments being made. The idea is to avoid concentrating funds in an account that may have more risk of being accessed from unwanted third parties or criminals. If a loss is realized, the loss can be minimized with only a limited amount of funds exposed at any time. The idea is to receive and sweep (customer payments) and remit and fund (vendor/supplier payments).

Surveying bank forms of electronic payments

Check out how banks process payments via the traditional banking route, which includes using a wide range of options:

>> Completing transfers via bank wires (domestic or international)

>> Processing ACH (automated clearing house) transfers

>> Processing bank transfers (you and your vendor both use the same bank so you can transfer funds internally, within the bank)

>> Using bank-provided vendor pay-bill systems (a vendor wants to be paid with a check, which you process electronically online through the bank, so it generates and distributes the physical check, alleviating the need for checks to be generated in-house)

REMEMBER

Other forms of bank payments are available as well, but the general idea here is to leverage the extensive knowledge and security the bank has set up and implemented to process electronic payments in a tightly controlled and secure environment. Banks are highly regulated and operate in an industry that demands the highest level of trust from the public. Banks have, over the decades, devised payment processing systems that are some of the securest in the world, so why not utilize this expertise to protect your hard-earned cash?

Checking out non-bank forms of electronic payments

It seems that every day a new form of electronic payment is being devised. These include using credit cards, debit cards, PayPal, Apple Pay, Amazon Pay, Venmo, and similar types of electronic payment services. Please note that when I use the term "non-bank," this is a bit of a misnomer, as usually somewhere down the line, the financial transaction ends up flowing through a bank, but the idea is that the cash receipt or disbursement begins at a point outside of a traditional bank. The reasons companies use these types of electronic payment services vary widely:

>> A customer paying with a credit card may earn "points" (for travel or cash back)

>> A business paying with a credit card to create separation between its bank and the vendor (and use the financing "float")

>> A large company such as Amazon making sure that every form of customer payment can be accepted to maximize the sales opportunity (to eliminate any reason for the customer to terminate the sale)

>> No actual cash changes hands when a sale is made as all customer payments are processed electronically. This assists with reducing theft risks associated with handling cash.

The point is non-bank forms of electronic payments are here to stay, and you can expect them to continue to increase in use as the world moves rapidly toward a cashless economy.

From a business perspective, it's almost impossible to build payment systems that don't incorporate the use of non-bank forms of payments because this has simply become the norm in today's economy. This doesn't mean that non-bank payments have no risk; plenty of traps and problems may arise when using non-bank forms of electronic payments, including these:

>> Having to absorb merchant fees when accepting customer payments electronically (for example, Visa or PayPal charge the merchant 2.5 percent to process the payment)

>> Controlling consumer personal information (like credit card numbers) that could possibly be hacked and exposed

>> Having to reconcile cash receipts from multiple electronic payment providers against your sales records (to match and properly apply cash receipts)

>> Maintaining agreements with multiple electronic payment providers

REMEMBER

The management and accounting issue is straightforward: The benefit of processing payments electronically must be analyzed and compared with the associated risks and costs. This may seem like a relatively simple cost benefit analysis (on the surface), where the benefits of ease of customer payment are apparent, but the costs need to be thoroughly understood because they relate to not just a stated "processing fee" but also the risks a company takes with managing large amounts of data (and the company's responsibility to protect this data).

Using enhanced accounting controls

One important point I would like to make on the electronic payments front is the need for businesses to develop, implement, and execute enhanced accounting controls, policies, and procedures to proactively manage this new environment. Here, I offer four examples of how companies have developed enhanced controls:

>> **Using real-time reconciliations:** A direct-to-consumer company may generate hundreds of thousands of dollars of sales during a peak holiday season such as Black Friday. When this happens, literally hundreds of individual sales are processed with most payments coming from credit cards, debit cards, PayPal, and other sources. To ensure that all customer sales are matched with customer payments, real-time reconciliations (daily or even more frequently) are performed to ensure that all payments are received and recorded correctly.

>> **Offloading data risks:** Companies may rely on front-end or consumer facing computer platforms such as Shopify to act as a retail storefront on the web.

>> **Monitoring frequency:** In the old days, a bank account could be reviewed and reconciled once a month. Not so today, as bank activity and transactions are constantly monitored for unusual or suspicious activity on a daily, hourly, or even real-time basis. Working closely with your bank and merchant account provider to develop systems to actively monitor financial transactions represents a big win for both parties.

>> **Securing cyber-insurance:** Specific forms of insurance are now widely available for purchase to assist with the financial losses that may arise from data breaches, hacks, and so on. Simply put, a cyber-insurance policy, also referred to as "cyber-risk insurance" or "cyber-liability insurance" coverage, is a financial product that enables businesses to transfer the costs involved with recovery from a cyber-related security breach or similar events. Twenty years ago, this type of insurance was a "nice to have" item. Today, it is a must-have.

CONSIDERING THE FUTURE OF CRYPTOCURRENCIES

I would be remiss if I didn't include a brief discussion on the use of crypto currencies, such as Bitcoin and Ethereum (two of the more popular choices) and associated blockchain technology. A major question to consider is whether cryptocurrencies are even a currency, which I would argue they are not. Given that cryptocurrencies do not represent legal tender of a government or country, have highly volatile price environments, are subject to technology risks (because they basically represent ownership of a series of digits), are not widely accepted as a form of payment, don't have the global economic markets of well-established currencies (such as the U.S. Dollar), and may be subject to significant government regulations, it's difficult, as of the time this book was published, to classify cryptocurrencies as actual currencies on par with the U.S. Dollar, Japanese Yen, Chinese Yuan, and the European Euro. Rather, cryptocurrencies are still functioning at the capacity of a speculative asset class that is rapidly evolving in the new digital-based economy.

Further, the following additional facts should be considered when educating yourself on cryptocurrencies:

- Cryptocurrencies are currently not considered cash, either for financial statement reporting purposes under GAAP or for tax purposes under IRS rules and regulations.

- For GAAP purposes, cryptocurrencies are considered an intangible asset that is recorded at cost with that cost basis written down if the asset is impaired or loses value.

- For IRS purposes, cryptocurrencies are treated like investments in stocks. Cryptocurrencies are carried as an asset on the balance sheet with investment accounts like stocks. When cryptocurrency is acquired, whether by purchase or received in payment for goods or services, it is treated as being purchased at the cost indicated by the value of the currency on the date it is acquired.

In the end, I'm not going to debate the validity and stability of cryptocurrencies, but I would offer this final advice: First, educate yourself thoroughly on the advantages and risks of using cryptocurrencies in your business; second, if you do venture into the cryptocurrency space, tread lightly as volatility will most likely reign for the foreseeable future.

EXAMPLE

Q. You and your team have been assigned the task of researching, evaluating, testing, and identifying a cloud-based accounting system to support the company's expanding business opportunities and rapid growth. What type of professional and personnel resources would you look for to assist with proactively managing this project?

A. I've embedded the most important element right in my question. That is, the company's internal team assigned to support this project should not only have experienced accountants involved, but just as importantly, members of critical business management functions including operations, production, sales and marketing, information technology, and executive management. It is essential that management team members from all critical business operations and functions be involved with this process and actively engaged in making this decision for a number of reasons. First, it is inevitable that non-accountants (such as, a production manager) will actively use the accounting system in one capacity or another. So, the more familiar they are with the system the better. Second, accounting systems don't just produce financial data that appear in financial statements and reports. Vast amounts of data are generally present in the accounting system (for example, sales performance by sales rep) that could be extremely useful to other management functions inside the organization. Again, the more familiar they are with the system the better. Third, cloud-based accounting systems can be relatively complex, from a technical perspective. Hence, you had better have your "tech team" involved to ensure that when the accounting system does hit its first "glitch," your team is ready to respond. I could go on with further examples, but the point I am driving home is that in today's on-demand technology-based world, accounting systems are far more integrated, complicated, and powerful than ever before, and require a team approach to maximize their functionality.

 Identify two benefits and two risks associated with using alternative or non-bank forms of payments.

 Enhanced technological security associated with digital accounting data and payment processing is absolutely essential in today's world. Name three strategies that can be utilized to help manage and control the elevated risks associated with digital accounting data.

Managing the Accounting Function in the On-Demand World

To close this chapter, I cover a variety of items related to managing the accounting function in a world that now is built on accessing large amounts of data or information, efficiency in storing this data or information, speed in accessing the information, and widespread availability to the information. The topics highlighted in the following sections present a basic overview or sampling of the types of changes that are occurring at breakneck speed as the old days of the green eye-shaded bean-counter give way to a tech-enabled financial information provider with access to vital information at the touch of a button.

Source documentation

In the olden days, most source documentation was stored in a "hard format" (such as paper-based storage systems that required large amounts of space). Not so today because the transition to paperless storage systems is now the norm rather than the exception. Companies actively maintain accounting records such as customer sales orders and invoices, shipping or packing slips, purchase orders, vendor/supplier invoices, employee wage records, third-party contracts, and the list goes on and on in a digital format. Basically, anything that was paper based is now being stored in an electronic format such as a PDF, JPEG, PNG, or computer coded.

The good news is that the storage of source documentation is much more efficient, cheaper, and more readily accessible. The bad news is that with so much source documentation available electronically, if proper security and access controls have not been implemented, the risk of vital documents being accessed by unauthorized personnel or outside parties has become much more elevated (see the next section).

Data rooms

Data rooms or internal data centers are virtual locations where basically all digitized documentation resides. Companies such as Dropbox specialize in helping companies organize and safeguard almost any type of digital company data, ranging from simple customer orders or copies of vendor invoices to confidential company formation documentation, third-party agreements, and the like. Businesses have the option to outsource digital documentation storage to a company like Dropbox or manage this process internally by maintaining their own computer systems. Either way, convenience, security and accessibility represent advantages of using data rooms because controls can be built in to give different parties access to different levels of company documentation. For example, a company may want to give its Human Resource Manager access to employee contracts and pay records (in a specific subfolder maintained in the data room) but would not want to provide this person access to critical financing documentation.

WARNING

Well-developed and managed (I cannot emphasize this point enough) data rooms are now the norm, but a word of caution is warranted. Proactive management of data rooms is essential to ensure that only authorized personnel have access to the correct folder or subfolder of source documentation.

Financial reporting

Review and control of input and output is more important now than ever before. With online, cloud-based accounting systems, it can be tempting to simply push a button for a preformatted report, and voilà, just like that, out comes a financial report such as an income statement or balance sheet for review with the management team. I cannot tell you how many times I've seen underqualified or inexperienced parties access the accounting system, produce a financial report, and think they have become an expert because the accounting system is just so easy to use. Worse yet, they then distribute it to a third party without thinking about it twice. (Translation: This is a fatal error.)

REMEMBER

The problem is parties who are not qualified accountants or financial professionals may not understand that critical adjustments and/or financial transactions must be captured in the accounting system to ensure CART (complete, accurate, reliable, and timely) financial reports are ready and available for management review. I cannot emphasize enough that tight controls must be maintained by a business to ensure that critical financial reports and statements are released at the appropriate time, after review by qualified parties, and distributed only to the right parties, supported by a reliable analysis (to assist with understanding the financial results).

Flash reports, dashboards, and KPIs

The real-time economy we live and operate in has resulted in an explosion of what are referred to as flash reports (targeted, high frequency, compressed reports) that generally focus on highlighting a company's KPIs (key performance indicators). Quite often, these are referred to as dashboards, which present critical company information in an easy and effective manner to decipher performance data. For example, a direct-to-consumer company may launch a new social media advertising campaign on Instagram over a three-hour period during a holiday shopping window and wants to have access to sales data from different advertising strategies instantaneously (in other words, a quick flash report).

For our direct-to-consumer company, a critical piece of financial information (a KPI) would be to evaluate the total amount spent on advertising compared to the actual sales generated over that three-hour period. For example, if advertising spends $25,000 over the three-hour period and $60,000 of sales were generated, the financial dashboard would present the total advertising spends of $25,000, the total sales generated of $60,000, and also present what is commonly referred to as a CPA or CAC KPI ratio (such as, cost per acquisition or customer acquisition cost). In our example, the CPA or CAC ratio would be 41.67 percent ($25,000 divided by $60,000). Does this represent a reasonable ratio? Well, that is up for management to decide, but, if this type of flash report and ratio is calculated continually over a period of days or weeks, management would be able to hone in on when the company's advertising spends are the most effective. This real situation happens every day.

REMEMBER

What is important to remember about this type of reporting is that the financial and operational data doesn't always originate from the accounting system but may come from a consumer-facing sales technology platform or other type of company technology management system. Here, the accounting function needs to "extend" beyond the base accounting system to develop and implement controls that ensure the financial information being reported from another source technology platform is consistent with the financial transactions being captured and reported in the accounting system. Again, I cannot tell you how many horror stories have resulted from two different technology systems not being properly monitored and reconciled to ensure consistency and accuracy of financial reporting. These days, financial information is seemingly anywhere and everywhere and easily accessible, which runs the risk of creating an exponential increase in reporting errors and mistakes (if proper controls and security have not been established).

Accounting and financial analysis tools

Countless financial and accounting technology tools, resources, platforms, systems, and the like are available today to assist companies with managing their business. These tools range from the likes of the ever-popular Excel or Google Docs to very specific software platforms that sit on top of accounting systems to help generate periodic financial statements. It would be pointless to attempt to list every financial or accounting technology-based tool available; by the time you prepared the list, a quarter of the systems would be gone, replaced by new solutions.

These tools are very valuable to the accounting and financial groups within a business but must be managed closely for a couple of reasons:

>> First, the business financial information contained in these tools (such as an Excel spread-sheet used to house a company's financial forecasts) tends to be very confidential and needs to be tightly controlled.

>> Second, these tools often are very easy to use, update, change, edit, and so on (by multiple parties), and when changes are made, audit trails (the what and why and how of changes) are often sacrificed.

Disciplined accounting management of these tools is just as important as with the company's primary accounting system used to capture transactional and financial data.

Q. Financial reporting represents the lifeblood of all businesses. Without financial reporting, companies wouldn't know if they are generating a profit or loss, have enough resources to cover liabilities and other obligations, and analyze other critical business performance measurements. Besides producing financial statements, including the income statement, balance sheet, and statement of cash flows, identify three other financial reports that a company may produce in a real time fashion to help assist in managing its business interests?

A. Needless to say, hundreds of examples could be identified, as only identifying three really doesn't even scratch the surface of potential reports, but as with most businesses, the following three non-financial statement reports are almost always relied upon in one form or another, and frequently delivered in the form of a flash report. I would like to highlight two items with each report. First, the frequency of the report (daily, weekly, or 13 weeks) is different in each example. Second, the source of the financial information comes from different technology systems in each case. However, what remains the same in all three cases is that the information reported must be CART and secured (as this data is highly sensitive and confidential).

- Sales Flash Report: A large retailer prepares a daily sales flash report that summarizes sales by product line, location of the sale (by store or on-line), number of sales, average sales per order (AOV), and other critical data. This information then is compared to prior year results and budgeted sales to quickly assess how the company is performing during a critical selling period. This report can be generated from multiple sources, including the accounting system or the sales management software system a company may use (for example, Shopify).

- Short-term Cash Projection: A manufacturer prepares a *13-week* cash flow forecast to assist in understanding anticipated cash inflows, outflows, and available borrowing sources during a "tight" period of the year. Almost all companies use some type of short-term cash flow forecasting tool to ensure that adequate levels of cash are available to support short-term operating needs. This report may be derived from the accounting system (depending on how sophisticated the system is), but most likely will be generated from a software reporting or analysis tool/platform that interfaces with the accounting system to generate this data.

- Sales Bookings & Pipeline Reports: *Weekly*, a technology company prepares a summary report of all potential sales that are in the "pipeline" as well as sales that have been actually "booked." By pipeline, I mean potential sales that have been identified but not formally closed and scheduled for delivery (as the sales rep is still actively attempting to close the sale). By booked I mean pipeline opportunities that have been turned into actual bookings (for example, firm sales orders supported by a signed agreement) but not yet delivered to the customer. Of importance with this report is that the base information reported most likely does not reside in the accounting system but is located in the customer relationship management system (also known as Customer Relationship Management, or CRM, a platform such as Salesforce), a critical technology tool to assist the sales team with managing opportunities.

 True or False? Third-party data rooms offer an efficient means to store vital company information, reports, and data that is safe from prying eyes.

7 Identify four technology software systems or platforms (excluding the primary accounting software system such as QuickBooks or Xero) that can be used to store, access, produce, and/or report important business financial data and information.

Answers to Problems on Accounting in the Digital Age

The following are the answers to the practice questions presented earlier in this chapter.

(1) True or false? Advancements in technology have guaranteed that the accuracy and reliability of accounting information is greater today than it's ever been in the past.

False. The key word here to focus on is the term "guarantee," as technology does not guarantee that the accounting information will be more accurate simply because technology is being used to assist in the production of financial information and accounting data. It is important to remember the concept of DIGO (data in, garbage out), and that if a company's internal controls are poor, no amount of technology is going to cover for a poorly designed, controlled, and managed accounting system.

(2) What statement makes the most sense here? Safeguarding physical or tangible assets such as equipment, inventory, and buildings is more important, of equal importance, or less important than safeguarding intangible assets such as customer data, trade secrets, and critical algorithms?

Of Equal importance is the best response. In today's technology-centric economy, safeguarding both tangible and intangible assets is of equal importance, as security represents an important function of the accounting department.

(3) What does the acronym CART stand for?

This one is easy but extremely important — Complete, Accurate, Reliable, and Timely.

(4) Identify two benefits and two risks associated with using alternative or non-bank forms of payments.

Benefits: Customer preference and earning of points. Business payment flexibility to maximize each sale. Risks: Acceptance and control over confidential personal or business data that could be hacked. Added fees incurred to process payments via these methods.

(5) Enhanced technological security associated with digital accounting data and payment processing is absolutely essential in today's world. Name three strategies that can be utilized to help manage and control the elevated risks associated with digital accounting data.

Needless to say, a long list of possible correct answers could be provided here, but let's focus on three key concepts that most businesses use:

a. First, offload risk to highly qualified and experienced third parties (for example, ADP for payroll processing or Shopify for credit card processing) that are experts in their subject matter, including technology security.

b. Second, increase the frequency of monitoring, analyzing, and reconciling sensitive and high-risk data and assets. The quicker you identify a potential data breach, irregularity, and so on, the lower the ultimate cost should be to your business.

c. Third, tightly control access to and security of sensitive technology-based platforms that harbor large amounts of confidential data. Only the appropriate and qualified parties within an organization should have access to confidential systems and data and even then, active monitoring of access by these parties should be a set policy managed by an independent party.

6　True or False? Third-party data rooms offer an efficient means to store vital company information, reports, and data that is safe from prying eyes.

The first part of the question is TRUE in that third-party data rooms are often viewed as an efficient tool to store vital company information, reports, and data. And further, third-party data rooms do offer advanced security features to help protect company information. However, the second part of the question is FALSE. The reference to "prying eyes" should have been a hint as to what the response will be. A weakness may occur at the user or company end if access to the data room is not controlled properly and/or certain folders or subfolders of critical information become available to unauthorized users. Data room security relies heavily on user access, which is controlled by the end parties. If the end party is inexperienced and provides access to the wrong parties, critical business information may be exposed.

7　Identify four technology software systems or platforms (excluding the primary accounting software system such as QuickBooks or Xero) that can be used to store, access, produce, and/or report important business financial data and information.

Hundreds of examples could be provided here so we'll provide a sampling of different primary software platforms including CRM or customer relationship management systems (such as, Salesforce or HubSpot), financial spreadsheets (such as, Excel or Google Sheets), ERP or enterprise resource planning systems (SAP, Oracle NetSuite, or Sage Business Cloud), and ecommerce-based retail store fronts (Shopify or BigCommerce). The reason I presented this question is twofold. First, almost all of these software platforms will directly interface with the accounting software system in some capacity. And as previously noted, DIGO is a real risk, so it is critical to understand that the data generated from one of these software systems or platforms could "pollute" (for lack of a better term) the accounting system if proper controls, policies, and procedures are not implemented to ensure the exchange of data is accurate. Second, security, control, and management of these systems is just as important as the accounting system.

2

Preparing Financial Statements

Chapter **6**

Understanding Basic Accounting Concepts and Methods

W hat is the purpose of accounting? Check out the following statement, which should be abundantly clear, but you would be amazed at how many businesses fail to keep this simple concept in mind.

To produce accurate financial information, every business must develop, implement, maintain, and manage a properly functioning accounting system, which at its foundation relies on establishing, implementing, and adhering to agreed-upon accounting policies, procedures, and controls applied on a consistent basis and in accordance with GAAP.

Generally Accepted Accounting Principles (GAAP), in the simplest definition, are "a set of rules that encompass the details, complexities, and legalities of business and corporate accounting." These rules are established by various accounting organizations, boards, groups, and so on, with the primary group in the United States being the Financial Accounting Standards Board (FASB), which uses GAAP as the foundation for its comprehensive set of approved accounting methods and practices.

There you have it: When producing financial information, businesses should adhere to GAAP as established by FASB. Seems simple enough, but as you work through this chapter it should become abundantly clear that GAAP is really a series of guidelines businesses can use to provide a certain amount of leeway when actual financial information is produced. Or maybe the best way to think of it is like Captain Barbosa from the *Pirates of the Caribbean* franchise: The code (translation to accounting, GAAP) is more what you'd call "**guidelines**" than actual **rules**. With this said, in this chapter, I expand on your understanding of GAAP by providing a summary of various macro-level accounting concepts that help provide certain guardrails for businesses when producing financial information.

Touching on Basic Accounting Theories and Concepts

One thing that I'm not going to do is get into a detailed discussion on understanding accounting concepts, rules, and principles (from a technical perspective). If you genuinely want to understand accounting in more depth, check out a book I wrote with my father, *Accounting for Dummies* 7th edition, which provides an excellent introduction into the basics of accounting. Further, it would be pointless in the span of one chapter (or for that matter, in one book) to try and explain the concepts that dance around in an accountant's head each day. Even myself, being an accountant, would simply rather be put out of my misery than spending hours upon hours deciphering all the technical concepts and guidelines accountants follow when producing financial statements, reports, and information.

Rather, what I have elected to do is summarize a broader scope of accounting theories and concepts to help you gain a better understanding of how financial information is prepared and what overlying broad governances and yes, politics, come into play when preparing financial information. Here are some key points to keep in mind:

>> **Art vs. science:** Probably the single most important concept to understand with accounting is that it really is more of an art than science. Accounting rules and guidelines are not set in stone or laid out in black-and-white terms. Rather, accounting includes a fair amount of subjectivity when it comes to producing financial information (as you will see later in this chapter as accounting policy examples are provided related to valuing inventory and depreciating fixed assets) and relies just as much on qualitative factors as quantitative analyses.

>> **Internal pressure and politics:** Note that accounting is a profession that is not immune from politics and internal reporting pressures. You can be assured that there have been many lively internal discussions between the executive management team members or "C" suite (chief level positions including the CEO, COO, and so forth), the board of directors, and the finance and accounting groups as to finalizing periodic financial statements and reports to ensure the company "hits the numbers." Please note that I am not saying that companies are committing fraud to achieve certain financial operating results, but rather a more subtle approach may be used to change an estimate here or adjust an analysis there to squeeze a few more dollars out of the financial results.

>> **Accrual vs. cash (or other basis):** Simply put, accrual-based accounting measures a company's performance, position, or results by recognizing economic events regardless of when cash transactions occur. This is the essence of GAAP. For example, in the income statement, revenue is recognized when it is earned (as opposed to collecting cash), and expenses are realized expenses when incurred (as opposed to when cash is disbursed).

Almost every business professional, at one time or another, has heard reference made to financial statements being prepared on accrual versus a cash basis. While cash basis reporting is allowed in certain circumstances (such as, for reporting taxable income to the IRS), it should be noted that no serious business uses the cash basis of reporting for external reporting to capital sources or to make important business and economic decisions. For almost all businesses (and to be taken seriously), GAAP must be implemented. Period!

>> **The matching principle:** This concept is relatively straightforward and best understood by referring to an example from the income statement. Under the matching principle, earned revenues should be matched against appropriate expenses during a given period. For example, if a company recognizes earned revenue of $1 million during a monthly reporting period, any sales commissions that are owed to a sales representative should be expensed in the same period, regardless of when the commissions are paid. Another perfect example relates to Tesla. When Tesla records sales of vehicles, it must also estimate and record an appropriate expense for future warranty claims (as Tesla provides a multi-year warranty for product defects on new auto sales), even though it may be years before the warranty claims are presented and paid by the company.

>> **Conservative by nature:** By being conservative I mean that accounting principles tend to be structured to realize expenses earlier and not recognize revenue/sales until the entire earnings process is complete. Maybe being conservative is not all that fair but maybe it is just smart planning, as the accounting governance organizations realize that companies tend to be more aggressive with presenting results (so building in a conservative bias helps provide some balance). Of course, there are always exceptions to this rule as anyone familiar with the epic failures at Enron will attest.

>> **Policies, procedures, and controls:** The foundation of accuracy is centered in properly functioning accounting policies, procedures, and controls, administered by qualified professionals, adhering to GAAP, and applied on a consistent basis. This practice represents the bedrock of any sound accounting system and incorporates these critical components:

- *Qualified staff:* An experienced, qualified, committed, ethical, and diverse accounting staff is a necessity, which is respected by management and supported by the board of directors. In addition, two traits that are essential (to produce CART financial information and to ensure company assets are safeguarded) are best summarized by the character, Duke, played by Jack Palance in the movie *City Slickers II: The Legend of Curly's Gold* when explaining that "one thing is", Curly responds by raising one finger but references two words: honesty and integrity. For accountants, these two traits are of upmost importance, as there is no room for anything less when preparing critical financial information, reports, and statements for both internal and external use.

- *Segregation of duties:* Accounting and financial functions are intentionally segregated between different staff to protect company assets and produce CART (complete, accurate, reliable, and timely) financial information. Many I am sure have heard the story of the reliable nice old lady who has been the company's bookkeeper for 20 plus years before they realize she has bilked the company out of hundreds and thousands of dollars over the years. What better parties are there at committing and hiding fraud than the top accounting and financial staff, as they know exactly how to hide the dirt and conceal the truth. Therefore, it is always recommended that while it's fine to have the accounting or finance department review, account for, and authorize payments, the movement of cash and final approval of the payments should come from a segregated department.

- *Materiality:* All businesses must evaluate and manage the tradeoff between accounting for every dollar (flowing in and out of a company) compared to the cost of implementing this effort. This represents the heart of the materiality concept, as it is literally impossible for companies like Amazon or McDonalds to ensure 100-percent accuracy with all financial transactions. Companies will establish accounting policies, procedures, and controls to ensure that no material misstatements are present in the financial information produced (but are willing to accept a small tolerance for errors if they are not significant). But remember, different parties have different perspectives on what exactly is "material" so be aware of this concept.

- *Use of estimates:* Basically, every operating business of size, in one fashion or another, will use estimates when preparing financial information. This can range from a large, mature retailer that must record estimated returns and refunds after holiday selling season to a newer company such as Netflix that must estimate how its investments in new content (when it produces a new show) should be amortized or expensed against the periodic subscription fees the company earns from its customers. But similar to the concept of materiality, the use of estimates can be a sign or flag of potential accounting issues or misstatements. As a rule of thumb, the more a company must rely on the use of estimates (to prepare financial statements) or the newer or greener a company is (without having years of data available to properly analyze), the higher a chance an error may occur in the financial information prepared.

- *Disclosing accounting changes:* Speaking of estimates, companies will often update or revise estimates as additional data becomes available. This represents a perfectly normal process (if kept within reason). In addition, companies may also change an accounting policy to improve the accuracy of their financial reporting. Again, this happens from time to time and is not out of the ordinary. What does become a problem is when companies are changing estimates or accounting policies on a suspiciously frequent basis and worse yet, do not properly disclose or communicate these changes (they bury the decision deep in the financial report somewhere). Lack of timely and clear disclosure of accounting changes is definitely a red flag.

Providing Some Examples of Choosing Accounting Methods

You may think that two businesses that are identical in every financial respect and have identical transactions during the year would report identical financial statements. You'd be wrong. The two businesses would have identical financial statements only if they elect to use the same accounting principles and apply those principles in the same way and with the same estimates, and that's very unlikely. For example, similar businesses may choose different methods and different lives (such as, the estimated useful life of an asset) for depreciating similar assets, impacting both the depreciation expense reported on the income statement and the accumulated depreciation reported on the balance sheet.

Accounting is more than just reading the facts or interpreting the financial outcomes of business transactions. Accounting also requires accountants to choose between alternative accounting methods. Similar to the conservative states and liberal states addressed in politics, accounting has

>> **Conservative accounting methods:** These accounting methods delay the recording of revenue and accelerate the recording of expenses. Profit is reported slowly.

>> **Liberal accounting methods:** These accounting methods accelerate the recording of revenue and delay the recording of expenses. Profit is reported quickly.

In rough terms, conservative accounting methods are pessimistic, and liberal methods are optimistic. The choice of accounting methods also affects the values reported for assets, liabilities, and owners' equities in the balance sheet.

The main reason accountants have a bias for following conservative accounting methods is that if the amounts reported turn out to be better than expected, users of the financial statements are less likely to be unhappy and pursue legal action against the accountants than if a more liberal accounting method reports higher income, and it turns out that income is less than was expected. Accountants like to say that you don't want users of the financial statements to have surprises; however, if they are surprised, you prefer the surprises are good surprises (income is better than expected) rather than bad surprises (income is less than expected).

Accounting methods must stay within the boundaries of GAAP. A business can't conjure up accounting methods out of thin air. GAAP isn't a straitjacket; it leaves plenty of wiggle room, but the one fundamental constraint is that a business must stick with its accounting method when it makes a choice. Consistency is the rule; the same accounting methods must be used year after year. (The Internal Revenue Service [IRS] allows businesses to change their accounting methods once in a while, but the justification has to be persuasive.)

Getting Off to a Good Start

A new business with no accounting history has to make its accounting decisions for the first time. If the business sells products, it has to select which inventory valuation and cost of goods sold expense method to use. If it owns fixed assets such as machinery and equipment, it has to select which depreciation method to use. If it makes sales on credit, it has to decide which bad debts expense method to use. These decisions are three of the many accounting decisions a business has to make. For the purposes of this chapter, only three examples of accounting decisions are provided, but trust me when I say that for most large businesses, the list of potential accounting decisions is extensive and easily can exceed 20 or more.

The choices of accounting methods for these three expenses — cost of goods sold, depreciation, and bad debts — can make a sizable difference in the amount of profit or loss recorded for the year. Choosing conservative accounting methods for these three expenses can cause profit for the year to be lower by a relatively large percent compared with using liberal accounting methods for the expenses. The comprehensive problems at the end of the chapter demonstrate this point.

To explain these expense accounting methods, I use a start-up business example. This new business has no accounting history. It must make these expense accounting decisions for the first time. Assume that the business put off making these accounting choices until the end of its first year. Everyone was very busy during the year getting the venture off the ground. Furthermore, waiting until the end of the year gave management and the chief accountant (aka controller) a year to learn more about the operating environment of the business and the kinds of problems the business faces.

One year has passed; it's now the end of the first year of business. One of the things a business does at the end of the year is to prepare a listing of all its accounts, which serves as the main source of information for preparing its financial statements. Figure 6-1 presents the accounts of the company at the end of its first year of business. Note that the total of accounts with debit balances equals the total of accounts with credit balances. (Chapter 3 explains debits and credits.) So, there are no bookkeeping errors (or, at least, none that would cause these totals to be out of balance).

Listing of Accounts of Sample Business at the End of the First Fiscal Year

Description	Debits	Credits
Cash & Equivalents	$559,750	
Trade Accounts Receivable	$645,000	
Allowance for Doubtful Accounts		$0
Inventory	$3,725,000	
Prepaid Expenses	$185,000	
Buildings, Machinery, & Other Fixed Assets	$1,150,000	
Accumulated Depreciation		$0
Trade Accounts Payable		$309,500
Accrued Liabilities		$108,500
Short-term Notes Payable		$350,000
Long-term Notes Payable		$500,000
Owners' Equity - Common Stock		$1,500,000
Retained Earnings		$0
Sales Revenue		$4,585,000
Costs of Goods Sold	$0	
Selling, General, & Administrative Expenses	$1,033,000	
Bad Debt Expense	$0	
Depreciation Expense	$0	
Interest Expense	$55,250	
Totals	$7,353,000	$7,353,000

At this point the chief accountant (aka the controller) sits down with top management to decide which accounting methods the business should use to value inventory and record cost of goods sold expense, depreciation expense, and bad debts expense. The financial statements for the first year cannot be prepared until these accounting choices are made and the three expenses are recorded.

EXAMPLE

Q. Review the company's year-end listing of accounts' balances shown in Figure 6-1.

a. How can you tell from this listing of accounts that the business has not recorded its following three expenses for the year?

- *Bad debts expense:* Caused by uncollectible accounts receivable

- *Cost of goods sold expense:* For the cost of products sold; the revenue from these sales has been recorded in the sales revenue account

- *Depreciation expense:* For the use of fixed assets (property, plant, and equipment) during the year

b. Also, did you notice that there is no income tax expense account? What is the explanation for this omission?

A. a. Taking the expenses in the order listed:

- The ending balances in the bad debts expense account and in the allowance for doubtful account are both zero. Therefore, no bad debts expense has been recorded.

- The balance in the cost of goods sold expense account is zero; also, the balance in the inventory account is very large compared with the balance in the sales revenue account. Therefore, no cost of goods sold expense has been recorded.

- The balance in the accumulated depreciation account is zero, and the balance in the depreciation account is zero. Therefore, no depreciation expense has been recorded.

TIP

b. The reason for no income tax expense is that this business is a pass-through entity for income tax purposes. This means that its annual taxable income or loss is passed through to its individual owners who pick up their respective shares of the taxable income or loss in their individual income tax returns. The business itself doesn't pay income tax. (The main types of businesses that are pass-through income tax entities are partnerships, subchapter S business corporations, and limited liability companies or LLCs.)

1 Does the interest expense in Figure 6-1 look reasonable, or does it need an adjustment at the end of the year?

2 In Figure 6-1, note the Prepaid Expenses asset account at the end of the year. What are three examples of such prepaid costs? Are the methods for allocating these costs to expense fairly objective and noncontroversial?

3 In Figure 6-1, note the Accrued Liabilities account at the end of the year. What are two or three examples of such accrued costs that have been incurred but not yet paid? Are the methods for allocating these costs to expense fairly objective and noncontroversial?

4 In Figure 6-1 the Owners' Equity — Retained Earnings account has a zero balance. Why?

Determining Whether Products Are Unique or Fungible

In deciding on its inventory valuation and cost of goods sold expense method of accounting, the first step a business does is to determine whether the products it sells are fungible or unique. A *unique* product is the only one of its kind; no other product is like it in all respects. For example, given the wide range of options, equipment, colors, and models, every car on the lot of a new auto dealer may be different. Another example of a business that sells unique products is a jeweler that sells high priced rings, necklaces, brooches, and so on. Each piece is different than the others.

Fungible means that products are interchangeable and virtually indistinguishable from one another. The products may have different serial numbers, but customers are indifferent regarding which specific products they receive. Most products you buy in a grocery store are fungible. The iPods that Apple sells are fungible. Apple sells different models of iPods, but within each model category the products are fungible.

When the products it sells are unique, the business uses the *specific identification method* to record cost of goods sold expense. The business keeps a separate record for the cost of each product. The cost of each product is charged to cost of goods sold expense when that particular product is sold.

Generally speaking, unique (non-fungible) products are higher priced than fungible products. Also, unique products are bought one at a time, whereas fungible products are bought in batches. The cost per unit of each successive batch typically fluctuates over time. This poses a dilemma; the business must choose which accounting method to use for recording cost of goods sold expense, which the next section explains.

Contrasting Cost of Goods Sold Expense Methods (for Fungible Products)

REMEMBER

Over the years, the accounting profession hasn't managed to settle on just one method for recording cost of goods sold expense and inventory cost (for fungible products). Different methods have been allowed for many years. A business is entirely at liberty to choose whichever method it wishes from among the generally approved methods, which are as follows:

>> *Average cost method:* The costs of different batches of products are averaged to determine cost of goods sold expense and ending inventory cost.

>> *First-in, first-out (FIFO) method:* The costs of batches are charged to cost of goods sold in the order the batches are acquired, and the cost of ending inventory is from the most recent batch(es) acquired.

>> *Last-in, first-out (LIFO) method:* The costs of batches are charged to cost of goods sold in the reverse order that the batches were acquired, and the cost of ending inventory is from the oldest batch(es) acquired.

The one universal rule is that a business can't mark up its ending inventory (that is, its stockpile of unsold products on hand at the end of the year) to the current replacement cost values of the products. In short, GAAP doesn't allow market value appreciation of inventory to be recorded.

From the listing of accounts in Figure 6-1, you can see that the company's inventory account has a relatively large balance. Product purchases during the year were debited in this account, but no credits have been made for the cost of goods sold during the year. Clearly, the appropriate amount should be removed from the inventory asset account and charged to cost of goods sold expense account.

EXAMPLE

Q. Suppose the business made five purchases during the year. It bought 100,000 units of the one product it sells. Suppose, further, that the cost per unit in all five purchases was the same. In other words, there was no change in the purchase cost per unit during the year. This is not too likely, but this scenario provides a good jumping off point for explaining cost of goods sold expense. During the year, the business sold 80,000 units of product. The revenue from these sales was $4,585,000 (see the sales revenue account in Figure 6-1). What amount of gross profit (margin) did the business earn from sales of products during the year?

A. To determine gross profit, you must first determine the cost of the 80,000 units sold during the year. In this scenario the purchase cost per unit of the products sold by the business remained constant during the year. So, there is only one method to determine cost of goods sold: (80,000 units sold ÷ 100,000 units purchased × $3,725,000 cost of purchases = $2,980,000 cost of goods sold). In other words, 80 percent of the goods purchased and available for sale were sold during the year and, therefore, 80 percent of the total cost of purchases should be charged to cost of goods sold. The following journal entry is made:

	Debit	Credit
Cost of goods sold expense	$2,980,000	
Inventory		$2,980,000

Therefore, the gross margin for the year is

Sales revenue	$4,585,000
Cost of goods sold expense	$2,980,000
Gross margin	$1,605,000

TIP

The cost per unit of products purchased (or manufactured) usually does not stay the same from batch to batch. Usually, the cost per unit fluctuates from batch to batch. This fluctuation creates an accounting problem. Three different methods are used to deal with the fluctuation of cost per unit from batch to batch, which I explain in the following sections.

Figure 6-2 presents the history of products purchased by the business during its first year. The business made five purchases, and the costs per unit (purchase prices) drifted up from purchase to purchase. The business sells only one product, which minimizes the number crunching. (Of course, most businesses sell a variety of products.) I use the information in Figure 6-2 to illustrate the three methods of accounting for cost of goods sold and the cost of inventory.

History of Inventory Acquisitions during the End of the First Fiscal Year			
Description	Quantity of Units	Cost Per Unit	Total Cost
First Purchase	24,000	$35.40	$849,600
Second Purchase	22,500	$35.44	$797,400
Third Purchase	20,000	$37.65	$753,000
Fourth Purchase	10,000	$38.50	$385,000
Fifth Purchase	23,500	$40.00	$940,000
Total Purchases	100,000		$3,725,000

FIGURE 6-2: History of inventory acquisitions during the first year.

Averaging things out

Many accountants argue that when the acquisition cost per unit fluctuates the thing to do is to use the *average cost* of products to determine cost of goods sold expense. The logic of the *average cost method* goes like this: Five batches of products were purchased at different prices, so it's best to lump together all five purchases and determine the *average cost per unit*. From the data in Figure 6-2, the average cost per unit purchased during the year is calculated as follows:

$3,725,000 total cost of purchases ÷ 100,000 units = $37.25 average cost per unit

The cost of goods sold expense for the products sold during the year is calculated as follows:

80,000 units sold during year × $37.25 average cost per unit = $2,980,000 cost of goods sold expense

Alternatively, if you know that the business sold 80,000 of the 100,000 units available during the year, you can calculate cost of goods sold expense the following way:

(80,000 ÷ 100,000) × $3,725,000 total cost of purchases = $2,980,000 cost of goods sold expense

TIP

Unless you've been asleep at the wheel, you should have noticed that the average cost method gives the same answer for cost of goods sold expense as in the example scenario just above in which it is assumed that the purchase cost per unit remained the same during the year. That's the effect of calculating an average. The five different costs per unit figures (see Figure 6-2) are condensed to one average number, as if this had been the cost per unit during the year.

Using the average cost method, the $37.25 average cost per unit is used for the company's 20,000 units of ending inventory (100,000 units acquired less 80,000 units sold):

20,000 units of inventory × $37.25 average cost per unit = $745,000 cost of ending inventory

Summing up, the $3,725,000 total cost of products purchased during the first year of business is divided between $2,980,000 cost of goods sold expense and $745,000 cost of ending inventory.

WARNING The average cost method is not as easy to use in actual practice as this example may suggest. With this method, you face questions such as how often should you determine the average cost per unit? Should you calculate the average just once a year, once each quarter, once each month, or after each purchase? Before computers came along, calculating an average cost per unit was a pain in the posterior.

5 During its first year, a business made seven acquisitions of a product that it sells. Figure 6-3 presents the history of these purchases. Compare the purchases history in Figure 6-3 with the one in Figure 6-2. Does the average cost method make more sense or seem more persuasive in one case over the other?

6 Refer to the purchase history in Figure 6-3. The bookkeeper said he was using the average cost method. He calculated the average by adding the seven cost per unit amounts and dividing by 7 to get an average cost per unit of $24.76 (rounded). He then multiplied this average unit cost by the 158,100 units sold during the year to get a cost of goods sold of $3,914,556. Is this the correct way to apply the average cost method? If not, what is the correct answer for cost of goods sold expense for the year?

History of Inventory Acquisitions during the End of the First Fiscal Year

Description	Quantity of Units	Cost Per Unit	Total Cost
First Purchase	14,200	$25.75	$365,650
Second Purchase	42,500	$23.85	$1,013,625
Third Purchase	16,500	$24.85	$410,025
Fourth Purchase	36,500	$23.05	$841,325
Fifth Purchase	6,100	$26.15	$159,515
Sixth Purchase	52,000	$23.65	$1,229,800
Seventh Purchase	18,200	$26.00	$473,200
Total Purchases	**186,000**		**$4,493,140**

FIGURE 6-3: Acquisition history of products.

Going with the flow: The FIFO method

My uncle worked many years on the receiving and shipping docks of several businesses. If you asked my uncle how to calculate the cost of goods sold, he would point out that the first goods into inventory are the first to be delivered to customers when products are sold. In other words, the sequence follows a *first-in, first-out* order. Businesses don't buy an initial stock of products, put them away in a dark corner, and then take a long time to deliver these products to customers. (Well, wineries may be an exception to this general rule.) The first-in, first-out flow of products delivered to customers means that the business's inventory of products at the end of the year comes from its most recent purchase(s).

The first-in, first-out (FIFO) method of determining cost of goods sold expense follows the flow of products taken out of inventory for delivery to customers. In the example, 80,000 units of product were sold to customers. The calculation of the $2,925,000 total cost assigned to these products by the FIFO method is shown in Figure 6-4. The first 24,000 units sold are assigned a cost of $35.40 per unit, or $849,600; the next 22,500 units sold are assigned a cost of $35.44 per unit, or $797,400; and so on.

FIGURE 6-4: Cost of goods sold expense calculation by the FIFO method.

Costs of Goods Sold Expense
Calculated Using FIFO

Description	Quantity of Units	Cost Per Unit	Total Cost
First Purchase	24,000	$35.40	$849,600
Second Purchase	22,500	$35.44	$797,400
Third Purchase	20,000	$37.65	$753,000
Fourth Purchase	10,000	$38.50	$385,000
Fifth Purchase	3,500	$40.00	$140,000
Total Costs of Goods Sold Expense	80,000		$2,925,000

The entry to record cost of goods sold expense for the year using the FIFO method is

	Debit	Credit
Cost of goods sold expense	$2,925,000	
Inventory		$2,925,000

In internal accounting reports to managers, the accountant presents the cost per unit sold and compares it with the sales price during the year to determine the profit margin per unit. Using the FIFO method, the cost per unit sold is:

$2,925,000 cost of goods sold ÷ 80,000 units sold = $36.5625, or $36.56 rounded cost per unit sold during year

This cost per unit sold doesn't equal any of the five acquisition costs, nor does it equal the average cost per unit purchased during the year, which is $37.25. Business managers are used to dealing with averages, so this discrepancy shouldn't be a problem — although, whenever you're dealing with an average, it's important to know and take into account how the average is determined.

REMEMBER What about ending inventory? By the FIFO method, the cost of ending inventory equals the cost of the most recent acquisition(s) — because the cost of earlier acquisitions is charged to cost of goods sold expense for the year. In the example, $2,925,000 is charged to cost of goods sold expense, which leaves a remainder of $800,000 in the inventory account: ($3,725,000 cost of purchases during the year − $2,925,000 to cost of goods sold = $800,000 cost of inventory). The cost of ending inventory is based on the cost of the last, or fifth, purchase and consists of 20,000 units at $40.00 cost per unit for the total cost of $800,000 (data from Figure 6-2). The total quantity of the last (fifth) purchase was 23,500 units (3,500 units were charged to cost of goods sold expense, and the other 20,000 units remain in ending inventory).

 7 Figure 6-3 presents the inventory acquisition history of a business for its first year. The business sold 158,100 units during the year. By the FIFO method, determine its cost of goods sold expense for the year and its cost of ending inventory.

 8 In the example shown in Figure 6-3, the purchase cost per unit bounces up and down over successive acquisitions, and the quantities purchased each time vary quite a bit. Do these two factors play a role in the choice of a cost of goods sold method?

Going against the flow: The LIFO method

The FIFO method (see the preceding section) has a lot going for it: It follows the actual sequence of products delivered out of inventory to customers, and it's relatively straightforward to apply. But (and this is a very big but), federal income tax law allows businesses to use an opposite method to determine annual taxable income. This method, called *last-in, first-out,* or LIFO, reverses the sequence in which products sold are removed from inventory and charged to cost of goods sold expense.

Since costs of products tends to rise over time, the LIFO method assigns a higher cost to cost of goods sold than does the FIFO method. Note in the examples, the cost of goods sold in Figure 6-4 using FIFO is $2,925,000, while in Figure 6-5 using LIFO the cost of goods sold is $3,017,000.

The higher cost of goods sold under LIFO results in a lower gross profit and lower net income. And since it is unlikely that a business is going to sell the last items purchased and keep the older items in inventory, why would any business choose to use LIFO?

Businesses will state that the logic for using the LIFO method is that products sold must be replaced in order to stay in business and that the closest approximations to replacement costs are the costs of the most recent purchases.

However, the real reason for choosing LIFO is the unique aspect in the tax law for using LIFO for tax purposes. By providing for lower net income, FIFO provides for lower tax liabilities. Congress, not wanting to be criticized for allowing business to report low income for tax while reporting higher income for financial statement purposes, put into the LIFO tax law a requirement that any business using LIFO for tax is required to also use LIFO for financial statement purposes. This is the only place that I am aware of where Congress, through tax legislation or any other legislation, has mandated the accounting principle to be used for financial statement purposes.

The entry to record cost of goods sold expense for the year using the LIFO method is

	Debit	Credit
Cost of goods sold expense	$3,017,000	
Inventory		$3,017,000

Costs of Goods Sold Expense
Calculated Using LIFO

Description	Quantity of Units	Cost Per Unit	Total Cost
First Purchase	4,000	$35.40	$141,600
Second Purchase	22,500	$35.44	$797,400
Third Purchase	20,000	$37.65	$753,000
Fourth Purchase	10,000	$38.50	$385,000
Fifth Purchase	23,500	$40.00	$940,000
Total Costs of Goods Sold Expense	80,000		$3,017,000

FIGURE 6-5: Cost of goods sold expense calculation by the LIFO method.

TIP

What about ending inventory? The cost of ending inventory by the LIFO method depends on whether the business during the year increased the number of products held in inventory. Assume that the business did, in fact, increase its quantity of inventory (it acquired more units than it sold during the year). In this case, the cost of ending inventory equals the cost of its beginning inventory and the cost of the additional units, which is based on the per unit costs from the earliest acquisitions during the year. On the other hand, when a business decreases its inventory during the year, its ending inventory cost is based on the cost(s) per unit in its beginning inventory.

In the example, the cost of ending inventory is $708,000: ($3,725,000 cost of purchases during the year − $3,017,000 to cost of goods sold = $708,000 cost of inventory). In other words, the cost of its ending inventory comes from the oldest purchase and consists of 20,000 units at $35.40 cost per unit for a total cost of $708,000.

WARNING

In the example, the ending balance sheet reports inventory at $708,000 cost value by the LIFO method versus $800,000 cost value by the FIFO method, which is a fairly sizable difference. FIFO gives a more up-to-date inventory cost in the balance sheet. Reporting ending inventory based on the earliest acquisition cost is the Achilles' heel of the LIFO method.

Assume a business has been using LIFO for, say, 40 years. This means that some part of its inventory cost goes back to costs it paid 40 years ago. If the difference between the current cost value of inventory (as measured by FIFO) and the LIFO cost is significant, the business discloses this discrepancy in a footnote to its financial statements.

9 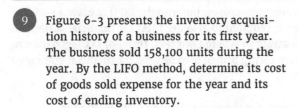 Figure 6-3 presents the inventory acquisition history of a business for its first year. The business sold 158,100 units during the year. By the LIFO method, determine its cost of goods sold expense for the year and its cost of ending inventory.

10 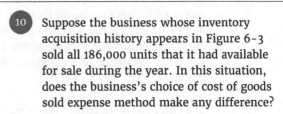 Suppose the business whose inventory acquisition history appears in Figure 6-3 sold all 186,000 units that it had available for sale during the year. In this situation, does the business's choice of cost of goods sold expense method make any difference?

Appreciating Depreciation Methods

REMEMBER

The basic theory of depreciation accounting is unarguable: The amount of capital a business invests in a fixed asset, less its estimated future residual (salvage) value when it will be disposed of, should be allocated in a rational and systematic manner over its estimated useful life to the business.

A fixed asset's cost shouldn't be charged entirely to expense in the year the asset's acquired. Doing so would heavily penalize the year of acquisition and relieve future years from any share of the cost. But the opposite approach is equally bad: The business shouldn't wait until a fixed asset is eventually disposed of to record the expense of using the asset. Doing so would heavily penalize the final year and relieve earlier years from any share of the fixed asset's cost.

Essentially, cost less residual value should be apportioned to every year of the fixed asset's use. (Land has perpetual life, and, therefore, its cost isn't depreciated.) The theory of depreciation is relatively simple, but the devil is in the details. And, I mean details! I should also note that for assets that fall into various categories that have relatively quick obsolescence periods (for example, computers, software, and so on), not only are short depreciation periods utilized to expense the asset, but residual values are often set at zero. The reason for this should be obvious in that most computer and software assets have very short lives (due to technological advancements) and at the end of, let's say, a three- or five-year period, are basically worthless.

REMEMBER

Before I dive into providing a specific example of how depreciation expense is calculated and recorded, it is worth nothing that depreciation expense is to fixed assets (such as tangible or real assets such as equipment, buildings, and computers) as amortization expense is to intangible assets (soft or intangible assets such as the value associated with a patent, the cost incurred to develop software, goodwill associated with a purchase of a company, the purchase of a trademark or tradename, and so on). The same concept applies to both fixed assets and intangible assets over a period of time: The asset being depreciated or amortized is being consumed and losing value. In the case of a patent that has legal protection for 17 years, it is safe to say that the value of the patent at the end of 17 years is worth much less than in year one. Really, the only difference between fixed and intangible assets (other than an actual physical asset being present) is the terminology used — depreciation of fixed or hard assets and amortization of intangible or soft assets. The reason I make mention of this concept here is based in the transition the U.S. economy has undergone over the past 50 years, moving from a production-based economy to a service, data, and technology-based economy (one in which you are far more likely to see intangible assets listed on a company's balance sheet that are subject to amortization expense).

TIP

Frankly, there's not much point in discussing the finer points of depreciation accounting. I could refer you to many books written by accounting scholars on depreciation. But as a practical matter the federal income tax law dictates the depreciation methods and practices used by most businesses. The IRS publication "How to Depreciate Property" (2021 edition, Publication 946) runs 112 pages. You ought to read this pamphlet — if you have the time, stamina, and can endure the pain of reading a document published by the government.

REMEMBER

Let me step on the soapbox for a moment. The depreciation provisions in the income tax law are driven mainly by political and economic incentives, to encourage businesses to upgrade and modernize their investments in long-term operating assets. Although businesses may follow income tax regulations on depreciation, they are not required to use the same methods and lives for financial statement reporting as for tax reporting, like they are required to do so with LIFO inventory. As the result, useful lives for depreciating fixed assets for tax purposes are too short; salvage value is generally ignored; and depreciation is stacked higher in the early years. In other words and excluding technologically sensitive assets such as computers and software, fixed assets generally last longer than their income tax depreciation lives; when disposed of fixed assets often have some salvage value; and, a strong case can be made for allocating an equal amount of depreciation to each year over the useful life of many fixed assets. In short, actual depreciation practices for tax purposes deviates from depreciation theory. And may differ from financial statement reporting, which may closer follow depreciation theory. Okay, I'm off my soapbox now.

EXAMPLE

Figure 6-1 shows the accounts of a business at the end of its first year of operations. No depreciation expense for the year has been recorded yet, but obviously, some amount of depreciation must be recorded. The business purchased all its fixed assets during the first week of the year, and the assets were placed in service immediately, so the business is entitled to record a full year's depreciation on its fixed assets. (Special partial-year rules apply when assets are placed in service at other times during the year.)

The company's buildings, equipment, and other fixed assets account consists of the following components:

Land	$150,000
Building	$468,000
Equipment	$532,000
Total	$1,150,000

REMEMBER

The cost of land is not depreciated. Land stays on the books at original cost as long as the business owns the land. Ownership of land is a right in perpetuity, which does not come to an end. Land does not wear out in the physical sense, and generally holds its economic value over time. Buildings, machines, equipment, computers, and other fixed assets, on the other hand, wear out with use over time and generally reach a point at which they have no economic value.

Assume the business decides to maximize the amount of depreciation recorded in the year, according to the provisions of the income tax law.

EXAMPLE

Q. What depreciation amounts for the year should be recorded on the business's building and machines?

A. Under the federal income tax law, the cost of a building used by a business in its operations is depreciated over 39 years by the straight-line depreciation method of allocation. Therefore, the depreciation on the building for the year equals $12,000 ($468,000 cost ÷ 39 years = $12,000 depreciation per year).

Under the federal income tax law, the machines and equipment used by the business fall into the seven-year useful life class, and they can be (but don't have to be) depreciated by the double-declining balance method of allocation. This is an accelerated depreciation method of allocation that front-loads depreciation, which means that more depreciation is allocated to the early years and less to the later years of the asset's useful life. The applicable percent for the first year is double the straight-line rate. Therefore, 2/7 of the cost of the machines is charged to depreciation in the first year: $532,000 × 2/7 = $152,000 depreciation in the first year.

REMEMBER

In years two, three, and four, the percent is the same but is applied on the *declining balance*, which equals cost less accumulated depreciation at the start of the year. So, for example, in the second year, 2/7 is multiplied by the original cost of the machines minus the first year's depreciation. The business converts to the straight-line depreciation method for the last three years. In these three years, the straight-line depreciation amount is higher on the declining balance than the amount determined by the accelerated rate. By switching to the straight-line depreciation method for the last three years, the original cost of the machines is fully depreciated over the seven-year life of the assets. (Cost wouldn't be fully depreciated if the accelerated rate were used in the last three years.)

11 Determine the annual depreciation amounts on the machines for years two through seven according to the double declining accelerated depreciation method. Also, determine the declining balance of the machines at the end of each year (cost less accumulated depreciation), which is also called the book value of the fixed assets.

12 Instead of using the double-declining depreciation method for its machines, suppose the business used the straight-line depreciation method over seven years. Determine the year-by-year difference in bottom-line profit with the straight-line depreciation method. (Remember that the business doesn't pay income tax because it's a pass-through tax entity.)

Timing Bad Debts Expense

Most businesses extend credit to others, whether that means making sales on credit to other businesses, loaning money to their officers, or loaning money to their vendors and employees. The act of extending credit is backed by some good business reasons, but businesses that do so also take the risk of not being paid. Some debtors may not pay up or pay the full amount owed. Retailers have to live with some amount of shoplifting losses, despite their best efforts to prevent it. In like manner, businesses that extend credit to their customers and make loans have to live with some amount of bad debts expense, despite their best efforts to screen customers and to collect overdue debts. *Bad debts* is the general term for these *uncollectible receivables*.

A business has two options for how it records its bad debts expense:

>> **Specific write-off method:** No entry is made for bad debts expense until specific receivables are actually written off as uncollectible. A receivable is not written off until every conceivable collection effort has been made and the debt has been discharged through bankruptcy proceedings or until the customer (or other debtor) has vanished and can't be traced. One disadvantage of this method is that the receivables asset could be overstated because specific accounts have not as yet been identified as uncollectible that will, in fact, prove to be uncollectible in the future.

>> **Allowance method:** Based on its collection experience with its credit customers (and other debtors) a business records bad debts expense before individual, specific receivables are identified as being uncollectible. The business estimates its bad debts expense, before all the facts are in regarding which particular receivables will have to be written off as uncollectible. This is a more conservative method than the specific write-off method because bad debts expense is recorded sooner. One disadvantage is that the future amount of bad debts (receivables that will eventually be written off) has to be estimated. Another disadvantage is that the income tax law does not permit this method to be used by most businesses.

EXAMPLE

From the data in Figure 6-1, you can see that the business's accounts receivable balance is $645,000 at year-end. The business hasn't loaned money to employees, officers, or vendors. (Non-customer loans are recorded in other accounts, such as loans to officers.) The business didn't write off any customers' receivables during the year; however, at year-end, the amounts owed to the business by a few customers are several months overdue. The business shut off credit to these customers and sent them dunning (please pay now) letters. The customers have assured the business that they will pay but just need more time, so they say.

The business has done everything it can to get the customers to pay up, short of bringing legal action. As far as the business knows, none of these customers have declared bankruptcy, but the business has heard a rumor that one customer has contacted a lawyer about bankruptcy. The total amount overdue from these deadbeat customers is $18,500, and the business is of the opinion that the $18,500 will not be collected.

In addition, some other customers are two or three months overdue in paying their accounts. The business understands that some of these debts may end up being uncollectible, but it's still hopeful that these overdue accounts will be collected in full.

EXAMPLE

Q. Given the preceding background information, how much bad debts expense should the business record at the end of its first year according to

a. the specific write-off method for bad debts expense?

b. the allowance method for bad debts expense (see information in part b. of the answer)?

A. Frankly, coming up with a bad debts expense amount for the year under either bad debts expense accounting method is somewhat arbitrary and relies on the use of making an accounting estimate (refer to this concept discussed earlier in this chapter). Only time will tell exactly how much of the total $645,000 accounts receivable will not be collected.

a. The $18,500 seriously overdue amount of accounts receivable is written off by the specific write-off method for recording bad debts expense. The entry is as follows:

	Debit	Credit
Bad Debts Expense	$18,500	
Accounts Receivable		$18,500

The specific accounts receivable making up this $18,500 have been identified. Considering that the company has identified specific customers and made reasonable efforts to collect the amounts owed to it, the receivables should be written off and charged to bad debts expense. This amount of expense is allowed for federal income tax purposes.

After making this write-off entry, the accounts receivable balance is $626,500 ($645,000 balance before write off – $18,500 write-off = $626,500 adjusted balance of accounts receivable). Some of this total amount of accounts receivable probably will turn out to be uncollectible. But the specific write-off method does not record these future write-offs at this time. The bad debts expense for the first year is $18,500, and the accounts receivable balance reported in its year-end balance sheet is $626,500.

b. Using the allowance method for recording bad debts expense, an additional amount of bad debts expense is recorded for the yet-to-be identified uncollectible receivables. Of course, the accountant has to estimate the amount of future write-offs. (The argument is that some estimate is better than none.) Suppose a conservative estimate of these additional bad debts is $20,000. However, specific customers' accounts haven't been identified for this estimated bad debts amount.

During the year, $18,500 has already been recorded in the bad debts expense account. As the specific receivables were identified as uncollectible during the year, the business had no choice but to write off the receivables and record bad debts expense. Using the allowance method, the accountant makes the following additional entry at the end of the year, which increases the bad debts expense account:

	Debit	Credit
Bad Debts Expense	$20,000	
Allowance for Doubtful Accounts		$20,000

The allowance for doubtful accounts account is the contra account to the accounts receivable asset account. Its balance is deducted from the asset account's balance in the balance sheet. After giving effect to this year-end entry, the company's bad debts expense for the year is $38,500 ($18,500 actually written off during the year + $20,000 estimated uncollectible receivables to be written off in the future). In its year-end balance sheet the business reports accounts receivable at $626,500 and the $20,000 balance in the allowance for doubtful account is deducted from accounts receivable. So, the net amount of accounts receivables in its ending balance sheet is $606,500.

The IRS doesn't allow most businesses to use the allowance for bad debts expense method to determine annual taxable income. (This is a terrible pun, isn't it?) Under the income tax rules, specific accounts receivable must actually be written off in order to deduct bad debts as an expense for determining taxable income. (For more information, you can refer to IRS Publication 535, "Business Expenses" (2021), and pay particular attention to the chapter on business bad debts.)

13 The controller of the business outlined in the example question is from the double-breasted, dull grey suit, old guard school of accounting (and most likely wears a green eye shade). He argues that a customer's account receivable should be written off as uncollectible when it becomes more than 30 days old. The normal credit term offered by the business to customers is 30 days. At the end of its first year, $278,400 of the company's $645,000 accounts receivable is more than 30 days old. What bad debts expense entry would the controller make at the end of the year if he had his way? Do you agree with his approach?

14 The president of the business outlined in the example question attends an industry update seminar at which the speaker says that the average bad debts experience of businesses in this field is about 1 percent of sales. Assume that the business adopts this method. Determine its bad debts expense for the first year and for the balances in its accounts receivable and allowance for doubtful accounts at the end of the year.

The following two questions are comprehensive for this chapter. They draw upon the discussion throughout the chapter and the answers to the example questions in the chapter. In answering these two comprehensive questions you should also refer to the figures in the chapter.

15 Prepare the company's income statement for its first year of business using the conservative accounting methods for cost of goods sold expense, depreciation expense, and bad debts expense.

16 Prepare the company's income statement for its first year of business using the liberal accounting methods for cost of goods sold expense, depreciation expense, and bad debts expense.

Answers to Problems on Choosing Accounting Methods

The following are the answers to the practice questions presented earlier in this chapter.

1 Does the interest expense in Figure 6-1 look reasonable, or does it need an adjustment at the end of the year?

TIP

Asking this kind of question at the end of the year is always a good thing for an accountant to do, to make sure than no account that needs adjustment at year-end is overlooked. In this situation, interest expense is $55,250 (see Figure 6-1). The sum of the business's two notes payable accounts in the year-end listing of accounts is $850,000. From Figure 6-1, you don't know for sure whether these two notes payable were borrowed for the entire year. Assuming that the notes were outstanding the entire year, the following applies:

$55,250 interest expense ÷ $850,000 notes payable = 6.5 percent annual interest rate

If the notes payable were outstanding for less than the full year, then the effective annual interest rate would be higher. Ultimately, the interest expense account probably doesn't need adjusting at the end of the year. The business probably has recorded all interest expense for the year, so it's unlikely that an adjusting entry needs to be recorded at year-end for interest expense.

2 In Figure 6-1, note the prepaid expenses asset account at the end of the year. What are three examples of such prepaid costs? Are the methods for allocating these costs to expense fairly objective and noncontroversial?

Three examples of prepaid expenses are

- *Insurance premiums:* Paid in advance of the insurance coverage. When the premium is paid, the amount is recorded in the prepaid expenses asset account, and then the cost is allocated to each month of insurance coverage.

- *Software subscriptions:* Companies often purchase a license to use software for a period of time, over 3 to 12 months. As such, allocating the expense over the appropriate period that the license covers would be a classic example of a prepaid expense.

- *Property taxes:* Paid at the beginning of the tax year in some states, counties, and cities. The tax paid for the coming year is recorded in the prepaid expenses asset account and then allocated to property tax expense each month or quarter.

TIP

Generally speaking, the allocation of these and other prepaid expenses is objective and non-controversial. At the end of a reporting period, the accountant needs to make sure that any prepaid expenses that have been "used up" have been moved from the prepaid asset account to the expense account. Different accountants use the same allocation methods. However, most businesses don't bother to record relatively minor prepaid costs in the asset account and instead record the costs immediately as expenses. (The materiality concept applies here.) For example, a business may give its delivery truck drivers quarters to feed parking meters as they make deliveries to customers. Theoretically, the amount shouldn't be recorded as an expense until the quarters are actually used, but most companies record the expense as soon as they distribute the quarters.

3 In Figure 6-1, note the accrued expenses payable liability account at the end of the year. What are three examples of such accrued costs? Are the methods for allocating these costs to expense fairly objective and noncontroversial?

Three examples of accrued costs are as follows:

- *Vacation and sick pay:* Businesses should accrue the costs of vacation and sick pay, which is often referred to as PTO or paid time off. These expenses are "earned" by their employees each pay period. (I stress the word "earned" because the actual accumulation of these employee benefits may not be clear-cut and definite. If the business has a collective bargaining contract with its employees, these benefits usually are well-defined.)

- *Warranties and guarantees:* Most products sold by businesses come with a warranty or guarantee. After the point of sale, the business incurs costs to service, repair, or replace a product under the terms of its warranty or guarantee. The business should estimate the future costs of fulfilling these obligations.

- *Property taxes:* The business should determine the amount of the property taxes that are paid at the end of the tax year (in arrears) and accumulate the expense during the year.

The accrual of these and other costs isn't cut and dried and tends to be somewhat controversial. The allocation of accrued costs has many shades of gray — there aren't any "bright" lines to delineate which particular costs should be accrued and which ones don't have to be.

4 In Figure 6-1 the Owners' Equity — Retained Earnings account has a zero balance. Why?

The final entry of the year is the closing entry in which the net profit or loss for the year is entered into the retained earnings account. The closing entry isn't made until all revenues and all expenses for the year are recorded. Because the business has just concluded its first year, its retained earnings account had a zero balance at the start of the year. The closing entry to transfer net profit or loss for the year into the account hasn't been made, so retained earnings still has a zero balance. The items discussed in the Q&A and in questions 1, 2, and 3 need to be resolved and recorded before the final net profit or loss is known and before that profit or loss can be recorded to retained earnings. After the accountant records net profit or loss into retained earnings, the account will have a balance, of course.

5 During its first year, a business made seven acquisitions of a product that it sells. Figure 6-3 presents the history of these purchases. Compare the purchases history in Figure 6-3 with the one in Figure 6-2. Does the average cost method make more sense or seem more persuasive in one case over the other?

This is a hard question to answer, to be frank, because the appropriateness of the average cost method depends on how you look at it. You could argue that you have a little more reason to use the average cost method in the Figure 6-3 scenario because the purchase price bounces up and down, whereas in the Figure 6-2 scenario, the purchase prices are on an upward trend. But, by and large, accountants do not consider whether prices fluctuate up and down or are on a steady up escalator in making the decision to use the average cost method. Accountants like the "leveling out" effect of the average cost method. This is the main reason why they prefer the method.

6 Refer to the purchase history in Figure 6-3. The bookkeeper said he was using the average cost method. He calculated the average of the seven purchase costs per unit and multiplied this average unit cost by the 158,100 units sold during the year to get a cost of goods sold of $3,914,556. His average cost per unit is $24.76 (rounded). Is this the correct way to apply the average cost method? If not, what is the correct answer for cost of goods sold expense for the year?

The bookkeeper made a mistake because the average cost method doesn't use the simple average of purchases prices. The average cost method uses the *weighted* average of acquisition prices, which means that each purchase price is weighted by the quantity bought at that price. In the Figure 6-3 scenario, the $26.15 purchase price carries much less weight because only 6,100 units were bought at this price. The $23.05 purchase price carries more weight because 36,500 units were bought at this price.

The correct average cost per unit is calculated as follows:

($4,493,140 total cost of purchases ÷ 186,000 units purchased) = $24.1567, or $24.16 rounded

Therefore, the correct cost of goods sold expense for the period is $3,819,169. You can calculate this amount by multiplying the exact average cost per unit by the 158,100 units sold, or you can calculate it as follows:

(158,100 units sold ÷ 186,000 units available for sale) × $4,493,140 total cost of goods available for sale = $3,819,169 cost of goods sold expense

7 Figure 6-3 presents the inventory acquisition history of a business for its first year. The business sold 158,100 units during the year. By the FIFO method, determine its cost of goods sold expense for the year and its cost of ending inventory.

The cost of goods sold expense by the FIFO method is determined as follows:

	Costs of Goods Sold Expense Using FIFO		
Description	Quantity of Units	Cost Per Unit	Total Cost
First Purchase	14,200	$25.75	$365,650
Second Purchase	42,500	$23.85	$1,013,625
Third Purchase	16,500	$24.85	$410,025
Fourth Purchase	36,500	$23.05	$841,325
Fifth Purchase	6,100	$26.15	$159,515
Sixth Purchase	42,300	$23.65	$1,000,395
Seventh Purchase	0	$26.00	$0
Total Costs of Goods Sold Expense	158,100		$3,790,535

The cost of ending inventory includes some units from the sixth purchase and all units from the seventh purchase, which is summarized in the following schedule:

Ending Inventory Value Using FIFO			
Description	Quantity of Units	Cost Per Unit	Total Cost
First Purchase	0	$25.75	$0
Second Purchase	0	$23.85	$0
Third Purchase	0	$24.85	$0
Fourth Purchase	0	$23.05	$0
Fifth Purchase	0	$26.15	$0
Sixth Purchase	9,700	$23.65	$229,405
Seventh Purchase	18,200	$26.00	$473,200
Total Costs of Goods Sold Expense	27,900		$702,605

8. In the example shown in Figure 6-3, the purchase cost per unit bounces up and down over successive acquisitions, and the quantities purchased each time vary quite a bit. Do these two factors play a role in the choice of a cost of goods sold method?

Generally speaking, the volatility of acquisition costs per unit isn't a critical factor in choosing a cost of goods sold expense method, nor is the variation in acquisition quantities. The reasons for selecting one method over another don't depend on these two factors.

9. Figure 6-3 presents the inventory acquisition history of a business for its first year. The business sold 158,100 units during the year. By the LIFO method, determine its cost of goods sold expense for the year and its cost of ending inventory.

The cost of goods sold expense as determined by the LIFO is as follows:

Costs of Goods Sold Expense Using LIFO			
Description	Quantity of Units	Cost Per Unit	Total Cost
First Purchase	0	$25.75	$0
Second Purchase	28,800	$23.85	$686,880
Third Purchase	16,500	$24.85	$410,025
Fourth Purchase	36,500	$23.05	$841,325
Fifth Purchase	6,100	$26.15	$159,515
Sixth Purchase	52,000	$23.65	$1,229,800
Seventh Purchase	18,200	$26.00	$473,200
Total Costs of Goods Sold Expense	158,100		$3,800,745

The cost of ending inventory includes all the units from the first purchase and some from the second purchase, which is summarized as follows:

	Ending Inventory Value Using LIFO			
Description		Quantity of Units	Cost Per Unit	Total Cost
First Purchase		14,200	$25.75	$365,650
Second Purchase		13,700	$23.85	$326,745
Third Purchase		0	$24.85	$0
Fourth Purchase		0	$23.05	$0
Fifth Purchase		0	$26.15	$0
Sixth Purchase		0	$23.65	$0
Seventh Purchase		0	$26.00	$0
Total Costs of Goods Sold Expense		27,900		$692,395

(10) Suppose the business whose inventory acquisition history appears in Figure 6-3 sold all 186,000 units that it had available for sale during the year. In this situation, does the business's choice of cost of goods sold expense method make any difference?

No, all three methods (average cost, FIFO, and LIFO) give the same result. The $4,493,140 total purchase cost of the 186,000 units would be charged to cost of goods sold expense.

(11) Determine the annual depreciation amounts on the machines for years two through seven according to the double-declining method. Also, determine the book value (cost less accumulated depreciation) at the end of each year.

The complete depreciation schedule of the machines over their estimated seven years of life is presented as follows:

	Depreciation Expense Using Double Declining Method		
Year	Cost Less Accumulated Depreciation	Annual Depreciation	Fraction or Ratio Applied
1	$532,000	$152,000	2/7
2	$380,000	$108,571	2/7
3	$271,429	$77,551	2/7
4	$193,878	$55,394	2/7
5	$138,484	$46,161	See Note
6	$92,323	$46,161	See Note
7	$46,161	$46,161	See Note
Total		$532,000	

Note: Generally, when the straighline depreciation expense exceeds the DDB depreciation expense the company will move to the straightline method to fully depreciate the asset.

TIP

Note the "Cost less Accumulated Depreciation at Start of Year" column in the schedule. These are the book values of the asset at the start of each year, which are the same as the book value at the end of the previous year. For instance, the $380,000 book value at the start of year 2 is the same as the book value at the end of year 1. And so on. At the end of year 7 the book value is down to zero, because the $532,000 accumulated depreciation equals the original cost of the asset.

12) Instead of using the double-declining depreciation method for its machines, suppose the business used the straight-line depreciation method over seven years. Determine the year-by-year difference in bottom-line profit with the straight-line depreciation method. (Remember that the business doesn't pay income tax because it's a pass-through tax entity.)

	Depreciation Expense Comparison		
	Double Declining Method vs. Straight Line		
Year	Double Declining Method	Straightline Method	Difference
1	$152,000	$76,000	($76,000)
2	$108,571	$76,000	($32,571)
3	$77,551	$76,000	($1,551)
4	$55,394	$76,000	$20,606
5	$46,161	$76,000	$29,839
6	$46,161	$76,000	$29,839
7	$46,161	$76,000	$29,839
Total	$532,000	$532,000	$0

13) The controller of the business outlined in the example question is from the double-breasted, dull grey suit, old guard school of accounting (and most likely wears a green eye shade). He argues that a customer's account receivable should be written off as uncollectible when it becomes more than 30 days old. The normal credit term offered by the business to customers is 30 days. At the end of its first year, $278,400 of the company's $645,000 accounts receivable is more than 30 days old. What bad debts expense entry would the controller make if he had his way at the end of the year? Do you agree with his approach?

If the controller had his way, he would make the following entry:

	Debit	Credit
Bad Debts Expense	$278,400	
Accounts Receivable		$278,400

TIP

I certainly don't agree with writing off such a large amount of accounts receivable. In the real world of business, many customers don't pay on time; indeed, late payment by some customers is expected any time credit is extended. The business would like to receive all payments for its credit sales on time, of course, but it knows that many of its customers probably won't make their payments within 30 days. The chief accountant needs to get real and understand that many customers slip beyond the 30-day credit period but eventually pay for their purchases.

14) The president of the business outlined in the example question attends an industry update seminar at which the speaker says that the average bad debts experience of businesses in this field is about 1 percent of sales. Assume the business adopts this method. Determine its bad

debts expense for the first year and for the balances in its accounts receivable and allowance for doubtful accounts at the end of the year.

The year-end adjusting entry is as follows:

	Debit	Credit
Bad Debts Expense	$45,850	
Allowance for Doubtful Accounts		$45,850

To record bad debts expense equal to 1.0% of total sales for year.

The business also records the write-off specific customers' accounts that have been identified as uncollectible. The write-off entry is as follows:

	Debit	Credit
Allowance for Doubtful Accounts	$18,500	
Accounts Receivable		$18,500

To record write-off of uncollectible accounts.

WARNING

Based on the information provided in the example, using 1 percent of sales to estimate bad debts expense seems too high for this particular business. And, as I mention in the chapter, the IRS doesn't allow the allowance method for income tax purposes.

(15) Prepare the company's income statement for its first year of business using the conservative accounting methods for cost of goods sold expense, depreciation expense, and bad debts expense.

Using LIFO for cost of goods sold expense, accelerated depreciation for machines, and the allowance method for bad debts expense, the income statement of the business for its first year is as follows:

Sample Company Income Statement Using Conservative Accounting Methods	
Income Statement For the Twelve Months Ending	FYE 12/31/2021
Sales Revenue, Net	$4,585,000
Costs of Goods Sold	$3,017,000
Gross Profit	$1,568,000
Selling, General, & Administrative Expenses	$1,033,000
Depreciation Expense (*)	$164,000
Bad Debt Expense	$38,500
Total Operating Expenses	$1,235,500
Operating Income (Loss)	$332,500
Other Expenses (Income):	
Interest Expense	$55,250
Total Other Expenses (Income)	$55,250
Net Profit (Loss) before Income Taxes	$277,250

* - Remember to include the depreciation expense on the building which has a value of $468,000 and is depreciated over a straightline period of 39 years.

16) Prepare the company's income statement for its first year of business using the liberal accounting methods for cost of goods sold expense, depreciation expense, and bad debts expense.

Using FIFO for cost of goods sold expense, straight-line depreciation for machines, and the specific charge-off method for bad debts expense, the income statement of the business for its first year is as follows:

Sample Company Income Statement Using Liberal Accounting Methods	
Income Statement For the Twelve Months Ending	FYE 12/31/2021
Sales Revenue, Net	$4,585,000
Costs of Goods Sold	$2,925,000
Gross Profit	$1,660,000
Selling, General, & Administrative Expenses	$1,033,000
Depreciation Expense (*)	$88,000
Bad Debt Expense	$18,500
Total Operating Expenses	$1,139,500
Operating Income (Loss)	$520,500
Other Expenses (Income):	
Interest Expense	$55,250
Total Other Expenses (Income)	$55,250
Net Profit (Loss) before Income Taxes	$465,250

* - Remember to include the depreciation expense on the building which has a value of $468,000 and is depreciated over a straightline period of 39 years.

TIP For additional insight, compare the net income in your answer using liberal accounting methods to your answer to Question 15, which asks you to use conservative accounting methods. You'll find that net income is $188,000 higher using liberal accounting methods, or 68 percent higher than the profit determined by using conservative accounting methods in Question 15.

IN THIS CHAPTER

» Getting a grip on what profit is and isn't

» Designing the income statement

» Minding your p's and q's with revenue and expenses

» Seeing the effect of profit on assets and liabilities

Chapter **7**

The Effects and Reporting of Profit

L et's start off with a statement that should be a no-brainer. That is, business is profit-motivated. Profit stimulates innovation; it's the reward for taking risks; it's the return on capital invested in business; it's compensation for hard work and long hours; it motivates efficiency; it weeds out products and services no longer in demand; it keeps pressure on companies to maintain their quality of customer service and products. In summary, it is the reason businesses well, are in business.

In short, the profit system delivers the highest standard of living in the world. Despite all this, it's no secret that many in society have a deep-seated distrust toward our profit-motivated, free-enterprise, and open-market system — and not entirely without reason. One only needs to look back over the past 20 plus years and revisit names such as Enron, Madoff, and more recently, Theranos, to understand just how the quest for business profit has led to some of the worst frauds and most spectacular business failures in history.

TIP

The job of accountants is to measure profit performance, not to pass judgment on its morality. Yet, accountants shouldn't behave like the three monkeys who see no evil, speak no evil, and hear no evil. If a business is acting illegally, the last thing it wants to do is record a liability because of the likelihood of losing a major lawsuit or having to pay a huge fine because of its illegal activities. The accounting team, including the controller, the vice president of finance, and the chief financial officer, has to decide whether to be part of the conspiracy to conceal the illegal activities or to leave the business.

This chapter explains the effects of profit or loss on financial condition and how profit and loss performance is reported to external parties in the income statement. The term "income statement" generally means the external income statement reported by a business to its shareowners, lenders, and other third parties with an interest in the business. (In Part 3 of this book, I discuss internal profit reports used by a business's managers; internal management profit reports include much more detailed and confidential information than external income statements.)

Understanding the Nature of Profit

Profit doesn't have just one universal meaning or definition. One concept of profit is to buy low and sell high. This definition applies to investing in stocks and real estate, but it's not a good definition for business profit. Another concept of profit is an increase in the market value of an asset. Accounting for business profit ignores market value increases of operating assets. Except for investment companies, hedge funds, and mutual funds, businesses don't earn profit by holding assets that appreciate in value.

REMEMBER

Most businesses earn profit through an ongoing process of selling products and services for prices that provide revenue higher than the expense of providing the products and services. Business profit is the residual, or the amount remaining after deducting expenses from revenue. To make profit, a business needs to raise capital (generally money) to invest in operating assets that are used in its profit-making activities. These assets aren't held for sale or for market value appreciation but are used, or for lack of a better term, consumed in the profit-making activity. The business's sources of capital expect a return on their capital, and interest is paid on money loaned to the business. The profit remaining after paying interest to lenders and income tax to the government accrues to the benefit of the shareowners of the business.

Of course, a business may pursue profit in many other directions — from trading in pork belly futures to real estate speculation. But this chapter focuses on making profit the old-fashioned way — making sales and controlling expenses. The income statement discussed in this chapter is the standard model for a technology business (software) that sells both products and services.

Keeping standards of reporting in mind

REMEMBER

Externally reported income statements should be bound by authoritative financial reporting standards for measuring and reporting profit. These rules are called generally accepted accounting principles, or GAAP for short. Business profit measurement and reporting shouldn't deviate from these standards in any significant respect. Otherwise, the income statement could be judged as misleading and possibly fraudulent. But a word of caution is warranted here. Larger, publicly traded companies are generally required to obtain audited financial statements (which includes the income statement, the balance sheet, and the statement of cash flows) from an independent third-party CPA firm that provides an opinion supporting that the company has in fact prepared financial statements in accordance with GAAP.

However, for smaller, privately held companies, financial statements (again, which includes the income statement) are often not audited, reviewed, or examined by an external party such as a CPA firm. As such, when financial statements, including the income statement, are prepared by the company, they are generally completed by the internal accounting and company management team, which are hopefully complying with GAAP. But GAAP is constantly changing, and most smaller privately held companies just don't have the resources or experience to prepare GAAP-based financial statements. What is provided to external parties is often best efforts to apply GAAP and prepare reliable financial statements, including the income statement. Please note that this does not mean the financial statements of smaller privately held companies are necessarily fraudulent, but rather the financial statements might not be comparable to larger publicly held companies that are applying a different GAAP standard and that financial statements that are not audited may have a higher risk for errors or mistakes.

Following profit

Profit is a calculated number equal to the difference between total sales revenue and expenses. Sales revenue is on one side of the scale; expenses are on the other side; and profit is the measure of how much the revenue side outweighs the expense side. To locate profit, you must trace the effects of revenue and expenses.

Suppose a business collects cash for all its sales and pays cash for all its expenses during the year. You need look to only one place — its cash account — to find the business's profit. However, a business may make credit sales and not collect cash from all its sales during the year. Furthermore, the typical business doesn't pay all its expenses during the year and may pay some of its expenses after the year-end and other expenses before the start of the year. In summary, sales and expenses affect several assets, including cash and liabilities.

TIP

To follow the trail of profit, keep the following general rules in mind:

>> Sales Revenue = Asset Increase or Liability Decrease

>> Expense = Asset Decrease or Liability Increase

EXAMPLE

Q. During the year, Business A's assets increase $3,000,000, and its liabilities increase $400,000 as the result of its profit-making activities. During the year, Business B's assets increase $2,700,000, and its liabilities increase $100,000 as the result of its profit-making activities. During the year, Business C's assets increase $2,000,000, and its liabilities decrease $600,000 as the result of its profit-making activities. None of these three businesses distributed any part of their annual profit to their shareowners during the year. What is the annual profit of each business?

A. All three businesses earn the same profit for the year: $2,600,000. In Chapter 1, I explain that the accounting equation can be stated as follows:

Assets – Liabilities = Owners' equity

Profit increases the owners' equity of a business, which means that the changes in assets and liabilities have the effect of increasing owners' equity. For each business in this scenario, owners' equity improves $2,600,000, which is the amount of profit for the year.

1 A business reports $346,000 net income (profit) for the year just ended. Determine two valid scenarios for changes in its assets and liabilities resulting from its profit for the year.

2 A business reports $3,800,000 loss for the year just ended. Determine two valid scenarios for changes in its assets and liabilities resulting from its loss for the year.

3 A business reports $5,250,000 net income for the year just ended. In its statement of cash flows for the year (see Chapter 10), the business reports that its cash flow from operating activities (from its profit for the year) is $4,650,000. In other words, its cash balance increased $4,650,000 from its profit-making activities for the year. Determine two valid scenarios for changes in assets other than cash and in liabilities that result from its profit for the year.

4 A business reports $836,000 loss for the year just ended. In its statement of cash flows for the year (see Chapter 10), the business reports that its cash flow from operating activities (from its loss for the year) is a negative $675,000. In other words, its cash balance decreased $675,000 from its profit-making activities for the year. Determine two valid scenarios for changes in assets other than cash and in liabilities resulting from its loss for the year.

Choosing the Income Statement Format

The bottom-line profit (or loss) in an income statement draws the most attention, but the income statement is really about sales revenue and expenses. A business can't make profit without sales and expenses. Therefore, the income statement reports sales revenue and expenses.

An income statement reports three basic items of information, in the following order:

» Sales Revenue

» Expenses

» Profit or Loss

Income statements are reported in two basic formats:

» Multi-step format: This format typically presents four measures of profit — gross margin, operating earnings, earnings before income tax, and net income. One revenue line and four profit lines are presented. One purpose of this format is to disclose gross margin, which is a key determinant in the bottom-line profit performance of businesses that sell products. Any slippage in gross margin as a percent of sales revenue is viewed with alarm.

» Single-step format: In this format, all expenses are added, and their total is deducted from sales revenue. Unlike the multi-step format, there's only one profit line, which is bottom-line net income.

TIP

Figure 7-1 is an illustration of the multi-step format. Reading this income statement is like walking down stairs, one step at a time.

Example of Multi-Step Income Statement

QW Example Tech., Inc.
Income Statements
For the Fiscal Years Ending
12/31/20 & 12/31/21
(all numbers in thousands)

For the Twelve Months Ending	12/31/2020	12/31/2021
Sales Revenue, Net	$53,747	$71,064
Costs of Goods Sold	$23,314	$26,891
Gross Profit	$30,433	$44,173
Selling, General, & Administrative Expenses	$29,286	$36,678
Operating Income (Loss)	$1,147	$7,495
Other Expenses (Income):		
Interest Expense	$400	$350
Net Profit (Loss) before Income Taxes	$747	$7,145
Income Tax Expense (benefit)	$261	$2,501
Net Income (Loss)	$486	$4,644

Confidential - Property of QW Example Tech., Inc.

FIGURE 7-1: Example of multi-step income statement format.

The single-step income statement format for the same business is shown in Figure 7-2. In actual practice, you see countless variations of these two basic income statement formats.

Example of Single-Step Income Statement

QW Example Tech., Inc.
Income Statements
For the Fiscal Years Ending
12/31/20 & 12/31/21
(all numbers in thousands)

For the Twelve Months Ending	12/31/2020	12/31/2020	12/31/2021	12/31/2021
Sales Revenue, Net		$53,747		$71,064
Costs of Goods Sold	$23,314		$26,891	
Selling, General, & Administrative Expenses	$29,286		$36,678	
Interest Expense	$400		$350	
Income Tax Expense (benefit)	$261		$2,501	
Total Expenses		$53,261		$66,420
Net Income (Loss)		$486		$4,644

Confidential - Property of QW Example Tech., Inc.

---

5 The sales revenue and expenses of a business for the year just ended are as follows:

Cost of goods sold expense	$6,358,000
Income tax expense	$458,000
Interest expense	$684,000
Selling and general expenses	$4,375,000
Sales revenue	$13,125,000

Prepare the annual income statement of the business in the multi-step format.

---

6 The sales revenue and expenses of a business for the year just ended are as follows:

Cost of goods sold expense	$598,500
Income tax expense	none
Interest expense	$378,000
Selling and general expenses	$896,500
Sales revenue	$1,698,000

Prepare the annual income statement of the business in the single-step format.

Deciding on Disclosure in the Income Statement

After a business decides on the format for reporting its income statement, (multi-step which I definitely recommend over the less useful single-step; see the preceding section), the next main decision concerns how much information to disclose about its expenses. Public companies are subject to financial disclosure rules issued by the United States Securities and Exchange Commission (SEC) and by the Financial Accounting Standards Board (FASB). A publicly owned business has no choice but to abide by these rules. Otherwise, trading in its stock shares could be suspended by the SEC — the kiss of death for a public company.

WARNING

Income statement disclosure standards for nonpublic businesses (that is, those not subject to the SEC's jurisdiction) are surprisingly vague and permissive. Generally accepted accounting standards (GAAP) say little about how much information should be disclosed about expenses in the income statement. Generally speaking, businesses that sell products report their cost of goods sold expenses, and almost all businesses report their interest and income tax expenses. But, it's much more difficult to generalize about the disclosure of other expenses.

TIP

Figures 7-1 and 7-2 disclose only one conglomerate operating expense: Selling and General Expenses. Some businesses disclose only this expense because they're very stingy about revealing any more detail about their operating expenses. Other businesses report five or ten operating expenses in their income statements, which may include separately reporting marketing and advertising expenses, research and development expenses, and other expenses deemed of significance.

TIP

In deciding how much expense disclosure should be included in income statements, businesses make three main considerations:

>> **Confidentiality:** Many businesses don't want to reveal the compensation of the officers of the business, for example. They argue that this information is private and personal.

>> **Materiality:** Most businesses don't see any point in reporting expense information that's relatively insignificant and would only clutter the income statement. When thinking of materiality, think of information that would affect a decision that a reader of the financial statements is going to make, say whether to lend money to the business or not. If disclosing an expense amount will affect that decision, the disclosure is material and needs to be made.

>> **Practicality:** Businesses limit the income statement contents to what fits on one page. A business can put additional detail about expenses in the footnotes to its financial statements, but many argue that shareowners and lenders have only so much time to read financial statements and putting too much information in their financial reports is counterproductive.

EXAMPLE

Q. Assume that you are one of the major shareowners of the private business whose annual income statement is shown in Figure 7-1. You aren't a manager of the business or on its board of directors, but as an outside investor, you're vitally interested in how the business is doing financially. So, you carefully read the business's financial statements, especially its income statement. You depend on the business making a profit in order to pay dividends from profit to its shareowners. Are you satisfied with the extent of expense disclosure in the income statement? Do you want the income statement to report one or more of the following expenses?

- Compensation of officers and senior level employees

- Salaries, wages, and direct burden (for example, health insurance) of the employees

- Facility operating expenses such as repairs and maintenance, rent, utilities, and so on

- R&D (research and development) (a very important expense in technology companies)

- Marketing, advertising, and promotional expenses

- Depreciation and amortization

- Litigation, legal, and other professional fees

- Royalties and licensing fees

- Employee benefit plans

A. In all likelihood, the business keeps accounts for these expenses because they have to be reported in its annual federal income tax return. So, the information is available and could be reported in the business's income statement. I've definitely seen both sides of the coin as in certain situations, a business hands over the income statement, which lists literally every expense (certainly overkill), while other businesses provide only a couple lines of summarized expenses (generally, not adequate). Ideally, there's a middle ground where businesses provide enough expense detail — to ensure the external party has adequate information on which to complete sound financial analyses and base proper business decisions.

If I were a major outside shareowner in this business, I would request that, either in the income statement itself or in the footnotes to the financial statements, information be reported about four expenses (in addition to costs of goods sold expense): research and development, marketing and advertising, profit-sharing or deferred compensation plans, and employee benefit plans. Why these four? Research and development expense can be manipulated by management to push profit up or down for the year. Marketing and advertising expense is very discretionary, and I'd want to compare that expense to sales revenue to evaluate key ratios and customer acquisition costs. Profit-sharing plans and employee benefit plans can be very large encumbrances on a business and may lead to a bit of the onion (the more you peal back the layers of the onion, the more you find). By this I mean that when companies implement profit-sharing and employee benefit plans, these plans can be very robust and complex and may expose a company to potential unforeseen long-term liabilities if economic or business conditions change. For example, an employee benefit plan may guarantee certain continued health insurance coverage to retired employees. If the market for health insurance coverage changes and the company has to absorb much higher premiums down the road, as a shareholder, I would want to understand this risk every year.

7   A business's income statement doesn't disclose its marketing, advertising, and promotional expenses for the year. Give an argument for not disclosing this expense and give an argument for disclosing this expense.

8   Some years ago, businesses in the cosmetic industry did not report sales revenue and cost of goods sold expense. Their income statements started with the gross profit or margin line, and their gross margins were a very large percent of sales revenue (over 70 percent). The companies argued that if their customers found out that their gross margins were so fat, many would refuse to pay such high prices for lipstick, rouge, and so on. Is this a legitimate reason for a business with high gross profit margins to not report sales revenue and cost of goods sold expense?

Examining How Sales and Expenses Change Assets and Liabilities

In a financial report, the income statement may seem like a tub standing on its own feet, disconnected from the balance sheet and the statement of cash flows. Nothing is farther from the truth. The three financial statements are interdependent and interconnected. For example, if sales revenue or one of the expenses had been just $10 different than the amount reported in the income statement, a $10 difference would appear somewhere in the balance sheet and statement of cash flows.

TIP

As you know, an income statement reports sales revenue, expenses, and profit or loss. But an income statement doesn't report how sales revenue and expenses change the financial condition of the business. For example, in Figure 7-1, $71,064,000 of sales revenue is reported in the annual income statement of a business for the FYE (fiscal year ended) 12/31/21. The business also reports $66,420,000 total expenses for the same year. How did the sales revenue and expenses change its financial condition? The income statement doesn't say.

Business managers rely on their accountants to explain how sales and expenses change the assets and liabilities of their businesses. Business lenders and shareowners also need to understand these effects in order to make sense of financial statements.

EXAMPLE

Suppose you're the chief accountant of the business whose income statement is presented in Figure 7-1. The president asks you to explain the financial effects of sales revenue and expenses reported in its latest annual income statement at the next meeting of its board of directors. To help organize your thoughts for the presentation, you decide to prepare summary sales revenue and expense journal entries for the year. Based on your analysis, you prepare the following summary journal entries for sales revenue and for each of the four expenses reported in the income statement. Remember that for your financial statements to remain in balance, the journal entry has to reflect the accounting equation of Assets – Liabilities = Owners' equity.

Sales Revenue:

Example Journal Entry	Journal Entry Debit FYE 12/31/2021	Journal Entry Credit FYE 12/31/2021
Cash & Equivalents	$69,696	
Accounts Receivable, Net	$2,165	
Other Current Liabilities & Deferred Revenue		$797
Sales Revenue, Net		$71,064

The business makes sales on credit as well as pre-billing customers for certain services (refer to deferred revenue line item). As I note in Chapter 2, deferred revenue is a liability. The business has collected the money for the sale in advance of delivering the product or service. As a result, the business has a liability to either deliver on the product or service or to refund the money collected. When recording a credit sale, the asset account accounts receivable is debited. When the customer pays, accounts receivable is credited. The business collected $69,696,000 from customers. Therefore, its accounts receivable balance increased $2,165,000, but this amount included $797,000 of advance or pre-billings (recorded as deferred revenue), which increased liabilities.

Cost of Goods Sold Expense:

Example Journal Entry	Journal Entry Debit FYE 12/31/2021	Journal Entry Credit FYE 12/31/2021
Costs of Goods Sold	$26,891	
Inventory		$2,328
Accounts Payable		$275
Cash & Equivalents		$24,288

The business purchases $24,563,000 of products and services during the year, and its cost of goods sold was $26,891,000. So, its inventory decreased $2,328,000. It didn't pay for all its $24,563,000 of purchases. Its accounts payable for inventory purchases increased $275,000. Therefore, cash outlay for products and services during the year was $24,288,000.

Selling and General Expenses:

Example Journal Entry	Journal Entry Debit FYE 12/31/2021	Journal Entry Credit FYE 12/31/2021
Selling, General, & Administrative Expenses	$36,678	
Prepaid Expenses	$75	
Cash & Equivalents		$34,851
Accrued Liabilities & Other		$163
Accumulated Depreciation		$1,239
Intangible Assets & Goodwill, Net		$500

Selling and General Expenses is a somewhat complicated entry because operating expenses involve several balance sheet accounts. The business added $75,000 to its prepaid expenses balance during the year. This amount reflects expenses paid for in advance that will be an asset to the business until the expense item is used, at which time it will move from an asset to the income statement as an expense. The business recorded $1,739,000 of depreciation & amortization expense for the year, as you see in the credit to accumulated depreciation and reduction in value of intangible assets. (Depreciation & amortization expense is included in the selling and general expenses amount reported in its income statement.) Not all expenses were paid for by the end of the year; unpaid expenses caused a $163,000 increase in accrued expenses payable. The net result of this is that cash decreased by $34,851,000 during the year.

Interest Expense & Debt Repayment:

Example Journal Entry	Journal Entry Debit FYE 12/31/2021	Journal Entry Credit FYE 12/31/2021
Interest Expense	$350	
Notes Payable & Other Long-Term Debt	$1,000	
Cash & Equivalents		$1,350

The business paid $350,000 interest during the year and repaid $1,00,000 of long-term debt during the year as well, all of which was paid from cash. You may ask why I included the repayment of debt in this entry, activity that does not impact the income statement. Don't worry, there is a method to my madness as you will see at the conclusion of this exercise.

Income Tax Expense:

Example Journal Entry	Journal Entry Debit FYE 12/31/2021	Journal Entry Credit FYE 12/31/2021
Income Tax Expense (benefit)	$2,501	
Cash & Equivalents		$2,501

At the end of last year, the business didn't owe any income tax. During the year, it made $2,501,000 installment payments toward its estimated income tax (as required by law). Based on the final determination of its income tax for the year, the business paid its income tax expense in full. As such, there is no impact on balance sheet accounts other than the reduction in cash of $2,501,000 to reflect the payment of income tax obligations.

Bonus Entry for Activity Not Impacting the Income Statement

Example Journal Entry	Journal Entry Debit FYE 12/31/2021	Journal Entry Credit FYE 12/31/2021
Property, Plant, Equipment, & Machinery	$750	
Dividends Paid	$400	
Cash & Equivalents	$3,850	
Capital Stock - Preferred		$5,000

In this entry, no income statement accounts are impacted as the company a.) purchased $750,000 of long-term capital assets (that will eventually be expensed via depreciation); b.) issued and paid a dividend to the company owners of $400,000; and c.) raised $5,000,000 of new capital via issuing preferred stock. The net impact of these transactions increased cash by $3,850,000.

So why did I include this entry? To provide you with a sneak peak at the topics that will be covered in Chapters 8 through 10 as they relate to tying together how the three primary financial statements interact. If you add up all the transactions impacting cash, including increases of $69,696,000 in the sales revenue entry plus the $3,850,000 in the bonus entry, and then subtract the transaction's decreasing cash of $24,288,000 for costs of goods sold; $34,851,000 for selling, general, and administrative expenses; $1,350,000 for interest expense and repayment of debt; and $2,501,000 for income tax expense, the net total of the increases and decreases amounts to a net increase in cash of $10,556,000. And if you refer to the balance sheet presented in Chapter 8 (Figure 8-1), you should notice that sure enough, the net increase in cash amounts to $10,556,000 (accounting magic of course). As you work through subsequent chapters, the logic of how each of the three primary financial statements work together and are "joined at the hip" (for lack of a better term) will become abundantly clear.

These summary entries aren't actual journal entries recorded by a business; they simply help summarize the effects of sales and expenses on the assets and liabilities of the business, as well as how other transactions that have no impact on the income statement can impact assets and liabilities as well. Also, I should point out that to develop the information for these entries, the accountant has to analyze the balance sheet accounts affected by sales and expenses, which takes time.

EXAMPLE

Q. From the five summary journal entries for sales revenue and expenses for the year, can you determine the cash flow from profit (that is, the net cash increase or decrease from its profit-making activities for the year)?

A. Yes, indeed you can. Each of the summary entries involves a debit (increase) or credit (decrease) to the cash account. The net effect on cash from its sales revenue and expenses for the year is summarized as follows:

Cash Inflows, Collections from Sales	$69,696
Cash Outflows:	
Payments for Products & Other Costs of Goods Sold	($24,288)
Payments for General, Selling, & Admin. Expenses	($34,851)
Payments for Other Expenses	$0
Payments for Interest Expense	($350)
Payments for Income Tax Expense	($2,501)
Net Cash Flow from Operating Activities	$7,706

Note: The $7,706,000 net cash increase is labeled "cash flow from operating activities" in the statement of cash flows. (For more on this financial statement see Chapter 10.)

---

9 Refer to the summary sales revenue entry earlier in this section. Assume that accounts receivable increased $3,165,000 instead of the $2,165,000 increase in that entry. Prepare the summary journal entry for sales revenue.

10 Refer to the summary cost of goods sold expense entry earlier in this section. Assume that inventory decreased $3,500,000 during the year because the business sold more products than it purchased. And assume that accounts payable decreased $250,000 during the year because the business paid more of its purchase liabilities than it bought on credit. Prepare the summary journal entry for cost of goods sold expense.

11 Refer to the summary selling and general expenses entry earlier in this section. Assume that prepaid expenses didn't change during the year. The amounts for depreciation expense and the increases in accounts payable and accrued expenses payable are the same as in the summary journal entry. Selling and general expenses are $36,678,000, the same as in the example. Prepare the summary journal entry for selling and general expenses.

Summing Up the Manifold Effects of Profit

Making sales and incurring expenses cause a multitude of effects on the assets and liabilities of a business. In other words, making profit causes many changes in the financial condition of a business. It would be convenient if a $1 profit caused a $1 cash increase and nothing more, but the effects of making profit are much broader and reach throughout the balance sheet.

TIP

The journal entries in the preceding section summarize the effects of sales and expenses on a business's assets and liabilities. Figure 7-3 shows these changes in T accounts for the assets and liabilities. As you probably know, T accounts aren't the official, formal accounts of a business. Rather, T accounts are like scratch paper that accountants use to analyze and "think out" the effects of transactions. A T account has two columns: Debits are always put in the left column and credits in the right column. The rules for debits and credits are explained in Chapter 3.

In Figure 7-3, I use nine asset and liability accounts to illustrate the recording of sales revenue and expenses for the year. Even a relatively small business keeps 100 or more asset and liability accounts. However, the nine asset and liability accounts in the example are sufficient to illustrate the effects of sales revenue and expenses on the financial condition of a business.

Example T-Accounts

QW Example Tech., Inc.
T-Accounts
For the Fiscal Year Ending
12/31/2021
(all numbers in thousands)

Cash			Accounts Receivable	
Debit	Credit		Debit	Credit
$69,696	$24,288		$2,165	
	$34,851			
	$350			
	$2,501			

Deferred Revenue			Inventory	
Debit	Credit		Debit	Credit
	$797			$2,328

Accounts Payable			Prepaid Expenses	
Debit	Credit		Debit	Credit
	$275		$75	

Accrued Liabilities			Accumulated Depr.	
Debit	Credit		Debit	Credit
	$163			$1,239

Intangible Assets				
Debit	Credit		Debit	Credit
	$500			

Confidential - Property of QW Example Tech., Inc.

FIGURE 7-3: Changes in assets and liabilities caused by sales and expenses.

TIP

In order to help you understand what profit consists of, I collapse the changes in assets and liabilities caused by sales and expenses shown in Figure 7-3 into one comprehensive journal entry that shows the diverse effects of making profit. In this entry, the $ profit for the year is shown as an increase in the retained earnings owners' equity account.

Comprehensive Journal Entry that Summarizes Changes in Assets and Liabilities from Profit-Making Activities During the Year

Example Journal Entry	Journal Entry Debit FYE 12/31/2021	Journal Entry Credit FYE 12/31/2021
Accounts Receivable, Net	$2,165	
Other Current Liabilities & Deferred Revenue		$797
Inventory		$2,328
Accounts Payable		$275
Prepaid Expenses	$75	
Accrued Liabilities & Other		$163
Accumulated Depreciation		$1,239
Intangible Assets & Goodwill, Net		$500
Cash & Equivalents	$7,706	
Retained Earnings		$4,644

EXAMPLE

Q. This comprehensive journal entry for the asset and liability effects of making profit "speaks" to an accountant, who's familiar with journal entries and debits and credits. Translate this journal entry into plain English, giving an explanation that non-accounting business managers, lenders, and investors can understand.

A. A good way of explaining the diverse effects of profit on assets and liabilities is to prepare a summary of the changes in balance sheet accounts affected.

Summary of Asset and Liability Changes from Making Profit

Cash	$7,706,000
Accounts Receivable	$2,165,000
Inventory	($2,328,000)
Prepaid Expenses	$75,000
Fixed Assets (Depreciation)	($1,239,000)
Intangible Assets (Amortization)	($500,000)
Net Increase of Assets	$5,879,000
Accounts Payable	$275,000
Accrued Expenses Payable	163,000
Deferred Revenue	$797,000
Increase of Liabilities	$1,235,000
Net Worth Increase from Profit	$4,644,000

REMEMBER

Profit improves the net worth of a business. Net worth, another name for the owners' equity, equals total assets minus total liabilities. In this example, the business makes a profit, and the effect on the balance sheet is that assets increase more than liabilities, which is the typical profit effect. On the other hand, assets could remain relatively flat, and liabilities could decrease. (Although it isn't very common, profit could consist of a decrease in liabilities more than the decrease in assets.)

12 The effects from sales and expenses for the year just ended for a business (not the sample business) were as follows:

Sales revenue was $15,700,000; the business collected $13,900,000 cash from customers, and accounts receivable increased $1,800,000.

The cost of products sold during the year was $9,800,000, and the business added $500,000 of products to inventory. It didn't pay for all $10,300,000 in purchases. Its accounts payable for inventory purchases increased $250,000.

Selling and general expenses were $4,860,000. The business added $125,000 to its prepaid expenses balance during the year. It recorded a $145,000 depreciation expense for the year. (Depreciation is included in the selling and general expenses amount reported in its income statement.) Not all expenses were paid for by the end of the year; unpaid expenses caused a $150,000 increase in accounts payable and a $225,000 increase in accrued expenses payable.

The business paid $200,000 interest during the year. The amount of unpaid interest at year-end increased $25,000. (Use the general liability account accrued expenses payable.)

The business is organized legally as a limited liability company (LLC) and has elected not to pay income tax. Its taxable income for the year is passed through to its shareowners, who include their respective portions of the business's taxable income in their individual income tax returns.

a. Prepare the annual income statement of the business in single-step form.

b. Prepare a summary journal entry for the sales and for each expense of the business for the year.

c. Prepare a comprehensive entry showing the changes in assets and liabilities from profit for the year.

---

13 The comprehensive entry for this business summarizing the changes in assets and liabilities from its sales and expenses for the year is as follows:

Cash	$280,000
Accounts Receivable	$825,000
Inventory	$375,000
Prepaid Expenses	$25,000
Accounts Payable	$955,000
Accrued Expenses Payable	$475,000
Accumulated Depreciation	$390,000
Owners' Equity — Retained Earnings	$875,000

For the business's board of directors, prepare a schedule of changes in assets and liabilities that summarizes the effects on the business's financial condition from its profit for the year.

Answers to Problems on the Effects and Reporting of Profit

The following are the answers to the practice questions presented earlier in this chapter.

(1) A business reports $346,000 net income (profit) for the year just ended. Determine two valid scenarios for changes in its assets and liabilities resulting from its profit for the year.

The simplest scenario is that assets increase $346,000 and liabilities remain the same (zero change). Another valid scenario is a situation in which assets increase $346,000 more than liabilities increase; for example, assets increase $846,000, and liabilities increase $500,000. An unusual but valid scenario would be that assets remain the same (zero change), and liabilities decrease $346,000. The key point is that if profit is $346,000, then net worth (assets minus liabilities) increases $346,000.

(2) A business reports $3,800,000 loss for the year just ended. Determine two valid scenarios for changes in its assets and liabilities resulting from its loss for the year.

The simplest scenario is that assets decrease $3,800,000, and liabilities remain the same (zero change). Another valid scenario is a situation in which assets decrease $3,800,000 more than liabilities decrease; for example, assets decrease $6,800,000, and liabilities decrease $3,000,000. An unusual but valid scenario would be that assets remain the same (zero change), and liabilities increase $3,800,000. The key point is that if loss is $3,800,000, then net worth (assets minus liabilities) decreases $3,800,000.

(3) A business reports $5,250,000 net income for the year just ended. In its statement of cash flows for the year, the business reports that its cash flow from operating activities (from its profit for the year) is $4,650,000. In other words, its cash balance increased $4,650,000 from its profit-making activities for the year. Determine two valid scenarios for changes in assets other than cash and in liabilities that result from its profit for the year.

$5,250,000 profit less the $4,650,000 cash increase from profit leaves $600,000 to be explained. One asset (cash) increased $4,650,000, so you have to figure out what happened to other assets and to liabilities. One valid scenario is that assets other than cash increased $1,600,000, and liabilities increased $1,000,000. If liabilities remained the same (zero change), then assets other than cash would have increased $600,000. It's possible, though not very likely, that assets other than cash remained the same (zero change), and liabilities decreased $600,000.

(4) A business reports $836,000 loss for the year just ended. In its statement of cash flows for the year, the business reports that its cash flow from operating activities (from its loss for the year) is a negative $675,000. In other words, its cash balance decreased $675,000 from its profit-making activities for the year. Determine two valid scenarios for changes in assets other than cash and in liabilities resulting from its loss for the year.

Not all the loss is accounted for by the cash decrease. The $836,000 loss compared with the $675,000 cash decrease leaves $161,000 to be explained. The simplest scenario is that liabilities remained the same (zero change), and assets other than cash decreased $161,000. The reverse of this scenario is that assets other than cash remained the same (zero change), and liabilities increased $161,000. I wouldn't be surprised if assets other than cash increased, even though the business suffered a loss for the year, in which case liabilities would have increased $161,000 more than assets other than cash.

(5) The sales revenue and expenses of a business for the year just ended are as follows:

Cost of goods sold expense	$6,358,000
Income tax expense	$458,000
Interest expense	$684,000
Selling and general expenses	$4,375,000
Sales revenue	$13,125,000

Prepare the annual income statement of the business in the multi-step format.

The annual income statement in multi-step form is

Sales Revenue	$13,125,000
Cost of Goods Sold Expense	6,358,000
Gross Margin	$6,767,000
Selling and General Expenses	4,375,000
Operating Earnings	$2,392,000
Interest Expense	684,000
Earnings Before Income Tax	$1,708,000
Income Tax Expense	458,000
Net Income	$1,250,000

(6) The sales revenue and expenses of a business for the year just ended are as follows:

Cost of goods sold expense	$598,500
Income tax expense	none
Interest expense	$378,000
Selling and general expenses	$896,500
Sales revenue	$1,698,000

Prepare the annual income statement of the business in the single-step format.

The annual income statement in single-step form is:

Sales Revenue		$1,698,000
Cost of Goods Sold Expense	$598,500	
Selling and General Expenses	896,500	
Interest Expense	378,000	$1,873,000
Net Income (Loss)		($175,000)

(7) A business's income statement doesn't disclose its marketing, advertising, and promotional expenses for the year. Give an argument for not disclosing this expense and give an argument for disclosing this expense.

The main argument for not disclosing advertising expense is that the business may give up a competitive advantage by doing so. The thinking is that it's best if a business's competitors don't know how much it spends on advertising. (Of course, a business may not know how much its competitors spend on advertising, either.) Another argument rests on the general grounds of confidentiality; many private businesses believe that they have rights of privacy about their financial affairs.

One main argument in favor of disclosing an advertising expense is that this particular expense is very discretionary and arbitrary in nature and represents an extremely important expense in today's on-line/ecommerce business world. That is, spending on social media platforms such as Facebook, Google, Instagram, and other social media sites is hugely important to a large number of companies that are targeting specific customers to drive sales. A business could be spending far too much on social media advertising with poor results and little payoff. Conversely, a business could be spending very little on social media advertising conversely, a business may spend very little on social media advertising, yet drive sales levels very high indicating a strong return is being realized on their advertising spends. Many lenders, investors, and analysts would argue that they need to know how much a business spends on this type of advertising so they can compare this expense against sales revenue. Also, how much a business spends on advertising says a lot about its general aggressiveness and strategy. This expense is considered a good indicator of a business's competitive strategy.

(8) Some years ago businesses in the cosmetic industry did not report sales revenue and cost of goods sold expense. Their income statements started with the gross margin line, and their gross margins were a very large percent of sales revenue (more than 70 percent). The companies argued that if their customers found out that their gross margins were so fat, many would refuse to pay such high prices for lipstick, rouge, and so on. Is this a legitimate reason for a business with high gross profit margins to not report sales revenue and cost of goods sold expense?

I remember reading these income statements many years ago and being truly shocked. Today, financial reporting standards for businesses that sell products require that they report sales revenue, cost of goods sold expense, and gross profit (margin) in their income statements. In contrast, many businesses don't sell products, or the products they sell are incidental and secondary to the sale of services, which is the main source of their sales revenue. Airlines and movie theaters are examples of such businesses. Service-oriented businesses generally don't report cost of goods sold expense and, therefore, don't report gross profit. Many report a "cost of sales" expense in their income statements, but this expense usually isn't deducted from sales revenue, and gross profit isn't reported.

(9) Refer to the summary sales revenue entry in the section "Examining How Sales and Expenses Change Assets and Liabilities." Assume that accounts receivable increased $3,165,000 instead of the $2,165,000 increase in that entry. Prepare the summary journal entry for sales revenue.

The summary sales revenue entry for this scenario is as follows:

	Journal Entry Debit FYE 12/31/2021	Journal Entry Credit FYE 12/31/2021
Example Journal Entry		
Cash & Equivalents	$68,696	
Accounts Receivable, Net	$3,165	
Other Current Liabilities & Deferred Revenue		$797
Sales Revenue, Net		$71,064

10 Refer to the summary cost of goods sold expense entry in the section "Examining How Sales and Expenses Change Assets and Liabilities." Assume that inventory decreased $3,500,000 during the year because the business sold more products than it purchased during the year. And assume that accounts payable decreased $250,000 during the year because the business paid more of its purchase liabilities than it bought on credit. Prepare the summary journal entry for cost of goods sold expense.

The summary cost of goods sold expense entry for this scenario is as follows:

Example Journal Entry	Journal Entry Debit FYE 12/31/2021	Journal Entry Credit FYE 12/31/2021
Costs of Goods Sold	$26,891	
Inventory		$3,500
Accounts Payable	$250	
Cash & Equivalents		$23,641

In the summary entry for cost of goods sold expense in the example, cash decreased $24,288,000, whereas in this scenario cash decreased $23,641,000, which is a $647,000 smaller cash outlay for the year. Why? Instead of inventory decreasing by $2,328,000, which required less purchases of goods than the goods that were sold, the business allowed its inventory to fall further by a total of $3,500,000, which meant that its purchases were less than the goods sold and produced a $1,172,000 reduction in cash outlay. In the example, accounts payable increased $275,000, but in this scenario, this liability was decreased $250,000. This difference means additional cash outlay of $525,000. The net cash difference, therefore, is $647,000. The inventory difference reduced cash outlay $1,172,000, and the accounts payable difference increased cash outlay $525,000.

11 Refer to the summary selling and general expenses entry in the section "Examining How Sales and Expenses Change Assets and Liabilities." Assume that prepaid expenses didn't change during the year. The amounts for depreciation expense and the increases in accounts payable and accrued expenses payable are the same as in the summary journal entry. Selling and general expenses are $8,700,000, the same as in the example. Prepare the summary journal entry for selling and general expenses.

The summary selling and general expenses entry for this scenario is as follows:

Example Journal Entry	Journal Entry Debit FYE 12/31/2021	Journal Entry Credit FYE 12/31/2021
Selling, General, & Administrative Expenses	$36,678	
Prepaid Expenses	$0	
Cash & Equivalents		$34,776
Accrued Liabilities & Other		$163
Accumulated Depreciation		$1,239
Intangible Assets & Goodwill, Net		$500

This entry doesn't have any debit or credit to prepaid expenses (an asset account) because its balance didn't change in this scenario. In the example, the business increased its prepaid expenses $75,000, so in this scenario, cash outlay is $75,000 lower because the business didn't increase its prepaid expenses.

(12) The effects from sales and expenses for the year just ended of a business were as follows:

Sales revenue was $15,700,000; the business collected $13,900,000 cash from customers, and accounts receivable increased $1,800,000.

The cost of products sold during the year was $9,800,000, and the business added $500,000 of products to inventory. It didn't pay for $10,300,000 in purchases. Its accounts payable for inventory purchases increased $250,000.

Selling and general expenses were $4,860,000. The business added $125,000 to its prepaid expenses balance during the year. It recorded a $145,000 depreciation expense for the year. (Depreciation is included in the selling and general expenses amount reported in its income statement.) Not all expenses were paid for by the end of the year. Unpaid expenses caused a $150,000 increase in accounts payable and a $225,000 increase in accrued expenses payable.

The business paid $200,000 interest during the year. The amount of unpaid interest at year-end increased $25,000. (Use the general liability account accrued expenses payable.)

The business is organized legally as a limited liability company (LLC) and has elected not to pay income tax. Its taxable income for the year is passed through to its shareowners, who include their respective portions of the business's taxable income in their individual income tax returns.

a. Prepare the annual income statement of the business in single-step form.

The income statement in single-step form is:

Sales Revenue		$15,700,000
Cost of Goods Sold Expense	$9,800,000	
Selling and General Expenses	4,860,000	
Interest Expense	225,000	$14,885,000
Net Income		$815,000

b. Prepare a summary journal entry for the sales and for each expense of the business for the year.

The summary entries are as follows:

Sales Revenue:

Cash	$13,900,000	
Accounts Receivable	$1,800,000	
Sales Revenue		$15,700,000

Cost of Goods Sold Expense:

Cost of Goods Sold Expense	$9,800,000	
Inventory	$500,000	
Cash		$10,050,000
Accounts Payable		$250,000

Selling and General Expenses:

Selling and General Expenses	$4,860,000	
Prepaid Expenses	$125,000	
Cash		$4,465,000
Accounts Payable		$150,000
Accrued Expenses Payable		$225,000
Accumulated Depreciation		$145,000

Interest Expense:

Interest Expense	$225,000	
Cash		$200,000
Accrued Expenses Payable		$25,000

c. Prepare a comprehensive entry showing the changes in assets and liabilities from profit for the year.

The comprehensive entry summarizing the changes in assets and liabilities caused by sales and expenses during the year is as follows:

Accounts Receivable	$1,800,000	
Inventory	$500,000	
Prepaid Expenses	$125,000	
Cash		$815,000
Accounts Payable		$400,000
Accrued Expenses Payable		$250,000
Accumulated Depreciation		$145,000
Owners' Equity — Retained Earnings		$815,000

You may notice that cash decreases in this scenario. In other words, the sales and expenses of the business result in an $815,000 cash decrease even though the business earned $815,000. The fact that the cash decrease and profit are the same amounts is purely coincidental.

(13) The comprehensive entry for this business summarizing the changes in assets and liabilities from its sales and expenses for the year is as follows:

Accounts Receivable	$825,000	
Inventory	$375,000	
Prepaid Expenses	$25,000	
Cash		$280,000
Accounts Payable		$955,000
Accrued Expenses Payable		$475,000
Accumulated Depreciation		$390,000
Owners' Equity — Retained Earnings	$875,000	

Prepare a schedule of changes in assets and liabilities for its board of directors that summarizes the effects on the business's financial condition from its profit for the year.

Summary of Asset and Liability Changes from Making Profit

Cash	($280,000)
Accounts Receivable	$825,000
Inventory	$375,000
Prepaid Expenses	$25,000
Fixed Assets (Depreciation)	($390,000)
Net Increase of Assets	$555,000
Accounts Payable	$955,000
Accrued Expenses Payable	$475,000
Increase of Liabilities	$1,430,000
Net Worth Decrease from Loss	$875,000

TIP

In this scenario, net worth decreased $875,000 because liabilities increased $1,430,000 and assets increased only $555,000. This unfavorable difference is the essence of a loss. Notice that even though the business suffered a loss for the year, its cash balance decreased far less than the amount of loss. The cash decrease is relatively low because the business avoided cash payments due to the relatively large increases in its accounts payable and accrued expenses payable.

Chapter **8**

Reporting Financial Condition in the Balance Sheet

Y ou and a number of your "tech" friends and professional associates have identified a growing technology company that needs a capital infusion to execute its business plan. It's a privately owned corporation that is looking to raise $5 million of capital to execute its business plan and is willing to sell new preferred shares in the company in exchange for a targeted 20 percent ownership (final ownership still to be negotiated). As a starting point, your team asks to see the business's past three years annual financial statements, but before the present owners hand over this information, they ask you to sign a non-disclosure agreement (commonly referred to as an NDA). This agreement (which is really a contract) requires that you must keep confidential all the information in the financial statements. You may not divulge anything you learn from the financial statement. You agree and sign the agreement.

The annual financial statements of a business include five essential elements:

>> Income statements for the years requested

>> Balance sheets at the close of business on the last day of the years requested

>> Statement of cash flows for the years requested

>> Statement of changes in owners' equity for the years requested

>> And, in some cases, footnotes that supplement and are an integral part of the financial statements (for most smaller, private companies, footnotes are not provided)

Financial statements of a publicly held company reporting to the SEC are required to be audited by an independent CPA. The financial statements of a private business may or may not be audited by an independent CPA. An audit opinion adds credibility to the financial statements but doesn't come cheap. Hence, more times than not, a private company's financial statements will not be audited. In fact, you would be amazed at how many privately held businesses that generate under $100 million in annual sales revenue do not have audited financial statements prepared.

I also should note that when investing in a business, a potential investor will perform extensive amounts of due diligence — reasonable steps taken by a party in order to satisfy themselves that the assets and liabilities and the business opportunities are what the seller has represented them to be. Requesting and reviewing financial statements represents a very small portion of the due diligence process as generally speaking, the list of information, data, reports, and so on, requested by an investor when evaluating an investment opportunity is very extensive. For the purposes of this chapter, I'm just going to focus on the financial statements requested in the due diligence process and more specifically, the balance sheet.

So, you begin by studying the annual income statement of the business your team is interested in investing in. All the examples and questions in this chapter are based on the following information for this business, which as a reminder, was provided in Figure 7-1: For FYE 12/31/20, the company reports $53,747,000 in sales revenue and $53,261,000 total expenses for the year, which equals roughly 99 percent of sales revenue. So net income is $486,000 for the year, or roughly 1 percent of sales revenue. In your opinion, its profit performance is extremely low for a company in this line of business and warrants additional review. Subsequent to evaluating the income statement, you now turn your attention to its balance sheet, which is a summary of the business's assets and liabilities and, as such, provides a comprehensive picture of the business's financial condition.

Getting Started on the Balance Sheet

Satisfactory profit performance doesn't guarantee that the financial condition of the business is satisfactory. In fact, the business could have serious financial problems, even though it's earning profit. It may have too little cash and assets that can be converted into cash soon enough to pay its short-term liabilities. It could be operating at the mercy of its creditors. Conversely, the business may be sitting on a hoard of cash. You have to look in the balance sheet to find out what's really going on with the business's financial strength, liquidity, and available sources of capital. I should also note that properly managing and understanding a business's balance sheet is just as important as managing and understanding a business's income statement. Both are of equal importance, even though both present a different financial picture!

The balance sheet is also known as the statement of financial condition, which better indicates its nature and purposes. This financial statement presents a summary of the assets, the liabilities, and equity capital of a business. Liabilities are claims against the assets of the business; they arise from unpaid purchases and expenses and from borrowing money. The readers of a balance sheet compare the liabilities of the business against its assets and judge whether the business will be able to pay its liabilities on time.

REMEMBER

It should go without saying that for most businesses, the total assets of a business should be more than its total liabilities. The excess of assets over liabilities equals the owners' equity of the business. In certain cases, a business may have liabilities that exceed its assets resulting in negative owners' equity, but this tends to be fairly rare and short lived (as the business will be under pressure to resolve this situation by raising equity in some form or another). Liabilities have definite due dates for payment, but owners have no such claims on the business. Owners' equity is in the business for the long haul. By majority vote, the owners can decide to dissolve the business, liquidate all its assets, pay off all liabilities, and return what's left to the owners. But individual owners can't call up the business and ask for some of their equity to be paid out to them. In short, owners' equity is the permanent capital base of the business.

A business corporation and more sophisticated limited liability companies report two primary sources of owners' equity:

>> The total amount of capital its owners invested in the business (potentially in different types of equity, which I will explain later in this chapter)

>> The accumulated amount of profit earned and retained by the business

In contrast, business partnerships, simple limited liability companies, and sole proprietorships typically report just one total amount for owners' equity (all forms of equity are consolidated).

Assets, liabilities, and owners' equity accounts aren't intermingled in the balance sheet. Assets are presented in one grouping, liabilities in another, and owners' equity in a third. Balance sheets typically report five to ten assets, five to ten liabilities, and two, three, or four or more owners' equity accounts. (These are rough averages, I should mention.)

The balance sheet of the business your group is thinking about making an investment in reports the following three basic groups as of 12/31/20: total assets equal $18,160,000, total liabilities equal $10,958,000, and total owners' equity of $7,202,000. Using printing option terminology that appears in almost all programs, the most common format, or layout, of the balance sheet is landscape (horizontal). The following is the company's balance sheet presented in the landscape layout as of 12/31/20:

Balance Sheet Horizontal Format

QW Example Tech., Inc.
Balance Sheet
For the Fiscal Year Ending
12/31/2020
(all numbers in thousands)

Assets	12/31/2020	Liabilities	12/31/2020
Current Assets:		Current Liabilities:	
Cash & Equivalents	$1,142	Accounts Payable	$1,654
Accounts Receivable, Net	$6,718	Accrued Liabilities & Other	$667
Inventory, LCM	$4,061	Current Portion of Debt	$1,000
Prepaid Expenses	$300	Other Current Liabilities & Deferred Revenue	$437
Total Current Assets	$12,221	Total Current Liabilities	$3,758
Long-Term Operating & Other Assets:		Long-term Liabilities:	
Property, Plant, Equipment, & Machinery	$7,920	Notes Payable & Other Long-Term Debt	$7,200
Accumulated Depreciation	($3,081)		
Net Property, Plant, & Equipment	$4,839	Total Liabilities	$10,958
Other Assets:		Stockholders' Equity	
Intangible Assets & Goodwill, Net	$1,000	Capital Stock - Common	$5,000
Other Assets	$100	Capital Stock - Preferred	$0
Total Long-Term Operating & Other Assets	$5,939	Retained Earnings	$2,202
		Total Stockholder's Equity	$7,202
Total Assets	$18,160	Total Liabilities & Stockholders Equity	$18,160

Confidential - Property of QW Example Tech., Inc.

Many businesses use the portrait (vertical) format instead of the landscape (horizontal) format. One advantage of the portrait format is that it allows a business to keep its balance sheet on one page in its financial report, whereas the landscape format may require a business to put its balance sheet on two facing pages in its annual financial report. The following is the company's balance sheet presented in the portrait format:

QW Example Tech., Inc.
Balance Sheet
For the Fiscal Year Ending
12/31/2020
(all numbers in thousands)

Assets	12/31/2020
Current Assets:	
Cash & Equivalents	$1,142
Accounts Receivable, Net	$6,718
Inventory, LCM	$4,061
Prepaid Expenses	$300
Total Current Assets	$12,221
Long-Term Operating & Other Assets:	
Property, Plant, Equipment, & Machinery	$7,920
Accumulated Depreciation	($3,081)
Net Property, Plant, & Equipment	$4,839
Other Assets:	
Intangible Assets & Goodwill, Net	$1,000
Other Assets	$100
Total Long-Term Operating & Other Assets	$5,939
Total Assets	$18,160
Liabilities	
Current Liabilities:	
Accounts Payable	$1,654
Accrued Liabilities & Other	$667
Current Portion of Debt	$1,000
Other Current Liabilities & Deferred Revenue	$437
Total Current Liabilities	$3,758
Long-term Liabilities:	
Notes Payable & Other Long-Term Debt	$7,200
Total Liabilities	$10,958
Stockholders' Equity	
Capital Stock - Common	$5,000
Capital Stock - Preferred	$0
Retained Earnings	$2,202
Total Stockholder's Equity	$7,202
Total Liabilities & Stockholders Equity	$18,160

Confidential - Property of QW Example Tech., Inc.

EXAMPLE

Q. The large majority of businesses use either the horizontal or vertical formats for reporting their balance sheets. However, now and then, you see a third format in which total liabilities are subtracted from total assets to determine owners' equity. What would be the rational for using this type of balance sheet format?

A. There is some benefit in presenting the balance sheet in this format as it makes clear that liabilities have a first, or senior, claim on the assets of the business and that owners get what's left over. After paying liabilities, the owners of a business could end up holding an empty bag.

1   A business has $2,500,000 total assets and $1,000,000 total liabilities. Present three balance sheet formats for the business.

2   A business has $4,800,000 total liabilities and $6,500,000 total owners' equity. Present three balance sheet formats for the business.

3   A business has $3,600,000 total assets and $4,600,000 total liabilities. Present three balance sheet formats for the business.

4   A business has $725,000 total assets and $425,000 total owners' equity. Present three balance sheet formats for the business.

Building a Balance Sheet

A brand-spanking-new business starts with a blank balance sheet. It builds up its balance sheet over time with three basic types of transactions:

>> **Financing activities:** Includes the investment of capital in the business by its owners, the return of some capital to owners (which may happen from time to time), distributions from profit (if the business decides to make such distributions), and securing loans to support investing activities.

>> **Investing activities:** Includes the purchase and construction of long-lived assets used in the operations of the business, the purchase of intangible assets used in manufacturing and making sales, and the disposal of operating assets when they're no longer needed or are replaced.

>> **Operating activities:** Includes the profit-making activities of the business, including sales, expenses, and other income and losses, all of which tend to drive or create balance sheet accounts treated as current assets or current liabilities. For example, if a business makes sales on credit (for example, allowing the customer to pay in 30 days from the date of sale), a trade accounts receivable would result (which represents a current asset in the balance sheet).

In Chapter 7, I explain how sales and expenses change the financial condition of the business. In fact, a good part of its balance sheet is driven by the profit-making transactions of the business. Before a business begins its profit-making activities, it needs to raise capital and invest capital in long-term operating assets. These financing and investing activities are the place to start in building a balance sheet.

EXAMPLE

Q. Several investors come together to start a new business. They raise $1,000,000 and invest this sum in the business. The business issues 10,000 shares of capital stock to them. The business borrows $1,500,000 from a bank on the basis of a long-term interest-bearing note payable. The business purchases various long-term operating assets (fixed assets) for a total cost of $2,000,000. It's now ready to begin hiring employees, manufacturing products, and making sales. Prepare the company's balance sheet after these initial financing and investing activities. Use the landscape (horizontal) format for the balance sheet.

A. The company's balance sheet after its initial financing and investing activities is as follows:

Cash	$500,000	Long-Term Notes Payable	$1,500,000
Fixed Assets	$2,000,000	Owners' Equity	$1,000,000
Total Assets	$2,500,000	Total Liabilities & Owners' Equity	$2,500,000

The business hasn't yet started manufacturing products, making sales, and incurring expenses. Therefore, its balance sheet doesn't yet include certain other assets and liabilities that are generated by operations, the profit-making process.

Q. After its initial financing and investing activities, the business manufactures its first batch of products. The total cost of this production run is $800,000. No sales have been made yet, but the business is poised to send out its sales force to call on customers. Its balance sheet after the first production run is as follows:

Cash	$440,000	Trade Accounts Payable	$225,000
Inventory	$800,000	Short-Term Notes Payable	$500,000
Fixed Assets	$2,000,000	Long-Term Notes Payable	$1,500,000
Accumulated Depreciation	($15,000)	Owners' Equity	$1,000,000
Total Assets	$3,225,000	Total Liabilities & Owners' Equity	$3,225,000

Explain the changes in the company's balance sheet, starting with its balance sheet immediately after its initial financing and investing transactions (see the preceding example question).

A. The changes in its balance sheet caused by manufacturing the first batch of products are summarized in the following journal entry:

Balance Sheet Changes Caused By Manufacturing First Batch of Products

Cash	$60,000
Inventory	$800,000
Accounts Payable	$225,000
Short-term Note Payable	$500,000
Accumulated Depreciation	$15,000

Read this entry as follows. The $800,000 cost of manufacturing the first batch of products was provided by borrowing $500,000, by purchasing $225,000 raw materials on credit, by $15,000 depreciation, and by spending down cash $60,000.

The business realized that it didn't have enough cash to pay for its first production run, so it borrowed an additional $500,000 from its bank on the basis of a short-term note payable. Because it made purchases on credit for the raw materials needed for manufacturing products, accounts payable has a balance of $225,000. The cash balance is $60,000 lower compared with its balance immediately after the initial financing and investing transactions ($500,000 balance before − $440,000 balance after = $60,000 decrease).

To have products available for sale, the business had to first manufacture the products. The cost of manufacturing its first batch of products was $800,000, which is in the inventory asset account. The business recorded depreciation on its fixed assets (property, plant, and equipment) because these resources were used in the manufacturing process. The business recorded $15,000 depreciation, which is included in the cost of products manufactured.

5 Instead of the initial financing and investing transactions presented in the preceding example questions, assume the business issued 100,000 capital stock shares for $1,500,000, borrowed $2,000,000 on a long-term note payable, and invested $2,800,000 in fixed assets. Using the landscape (horizontal) format, prepare its balance sheet after these initial financing and investing transactions.

6 Following its initial financing and investing transactions in Question 5, the business manufactured its first batch of products. The cost of products manufactured was $650,000, depreciation was $20,000, and accounts payable increased $185,000. To provide additional cash, the business borrowed $250,000 and signed a short-term note payable. Using the landscape (horizontal) format, prepare its balance sheet after its first production run. Start with the balance sheet after the initial financing and investing transactions in your answer to Question 5.

7 A new business has just been organized. A group of investors put $5,000,000 in the business, and the business issued 5,000,000 shares of capital stock to them. The business borrowed $2,500,000 from a local bank on the basis of a long-term note payable. (Several of the investors had to guarantee this note, or the bank would not have loaned the money to the business.) The business negotiated the purchase of land and buildings that cost $1,250,000. It also paid $5,250,000 for machinery, production equipment, delivery vehicles, and office equipment and furniture. Using the landscape (horizontal) format, prepare the balance sheet of the business immediately after these initial financing and investing activities.

8 The business introduced in Question 7 manufactured its first batch of products. It has not yet sold any of these products. The balance sheet changes caused by the first production run are summarized in the following journal entry:

Cash	$665,000
Inventory	$2,000,000
Accounts Payable	$550,000
Short-term Note Payable	$750,000
Accumulated Depreciation	$35,000

Using the portrait format, prepare its balance sheet after giving effect to the first production run. Start with your balance sheet answer to Question 7.

Fleshing Out the Balance Sheet

The most recent balance sheet of the business your team is considering investing in is presented in Figure 8-1. Notice that I have presented two balance sheets, one for 12/31/2020 and one for 12/31/21. This was done for comparison purposes to assist you with understanding the changes in the company's balance sheet between the two years. The balance sheet has been building and evolving over the years as the company executed its business plan so the end result are the amounts presented in the balance sheet as of 12/31/2020 (the end of the year on which your team evaluated the company's financial statements).

Two Year Comparative Balance Sheet

QW Example Tech., Inc.
Balance Sheets
For the Fiscal Years Ending
12/31/20 & 12/31/21
(all numbers in thousands)

Assets	12/31/2020	12/31/2021	Change
Current Assets:			
Cash & Equivalents	$1,142	$11,698	$10,556
Accounts Receivable, Net	$6,718	$8,883	$2,165
Inventory, LCM	$4,061	$1,733	($2,328)
Prepaid Expenses	$300	$375	$75
Total Current Assets	$12,221	$22,689	$10,468
Long-Term Operating & Other Assets:			
Property, Plant, Equipment, & Machinery	$7,920	$8,670	$750
Accumulated Depreciation	($3,081)	($4,320)	($1,239)
Net Property, Plant, & Equipment	$4,839	$4,350	($489)
Other Assets:			
Intangible Assets & Goodwill, Net	$1,000	$500	($500)
Other Assets	$100	$100	$0
Total Long-Term Operating & Other Assets	$5,939	$4,950	($989)
Total Assets	$18,160	$27,639	$9,479
Liabilities			
Current Liabilities:			
Accounts Payable	$1,654	$1,929	$275
Accrued Liabilities & Other	$667	$830	$163
Current Portion of Debt	$1,000	$1,000	$0
Other Current Liabilities & Deferred Revenue	$437	$1,234	$797
Total Current Liabilities	$3,758	$4,993	$1,235
Long-term Liabilities:			
Notes Payable & Other Long-Term Debt	$7,200	$6,200	($1,000)
Total Liabilities	$10,958	$11,193	$235
Stockholders' Equity			
Capital Stock - Common	$5,000	$5,000	$0
Capital Stock - Preferred	$0	$5,000	$5,000
Retained Earnings	$2,202	$6,446	$4,244
Total Stockholder's Equity	$7,202	$16,446	$9,244
Total Liabilities & Stockholders Equity	$18,160	$27,639	$9,479

Confidential - Property of QW Example Tech., Inc.

FIGURE 8-1: A two-year comparative balance sheet of the business in question.

What does the balance sheet in Figure 8-1 tell you about the business? In fact, it tells you a lot. You know that the business sells on credit because it reports the accounts receivable asset, and you know that it sells products, the cost of which is reported in the inventory asset. Because it reports prepaid expenses, you know that the business pays some of its expenses in advance, and the report of accrued expenses payable liability indicates that it delays paying some expenses. Also, you can tell that the business buys on credit because it reports the accounts payable liability.

The balance sheet for 12/31/20 reveals that the business borrows money, which is evident in its short-term and long-term notes payable liabilities. It has invested $7,920,000 in long-term operating assets, and over the years, it has depreciated $3,081,000 of the cost of these assets. According to the balance sheet, the owners invested $5,000,000 in the business for which they received common stock. And the business has retained $2,202,000 of its cumulative net income over the years. Did you get all that from reading the balance sheet? If not, read it again!

EXAMPLE

Q. Does the balance sheet shown in Figure 8-1 report the current replacement costs of the business's fixed assets (which are labeled "Property, Plant & Equipment" in the balance sheet)? Also, does the balance sheet indicate which depreciation methods the business uses to depreciate its fixed assets?

A. The short answer to the first question is no, balance sheets don't report current replacement cost values of fixed assets. Indeed, the business probably hasn't taken the time and troubles to estimate these replacement costs because it isn't planning to replace its fixed assets. The answer to the second question is a little more involved. This business, like most businesses, doesn't disclose its depreciation methods in the balance sheet itself, but it discloses depreciation methods in the footnotes to the financial statements. (You have to take my word for it because this example doesn't present the footnotes to the business's financial statements.)

The following questions are based on the balance sheet details outlined earlier in this section.

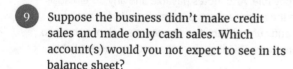

9 Suppose the business didn't make credit sales and made only cash sales. Which account(s) would you not expect to see in its balance sheet?

10 Suppose the business didn't own any of its fixed assets (long-term operating assets). Instead, it entered into rental or lease agreements for all these assets (office space, machinery, equipment, autos, computers, and so on). Which account(s) would you not expect to see in its balance sheet?

11 Suppose the business was very conservative and didn't borrow money. Which account(s) would you not expect to see in its balance sheet?

12 Suppose the business sold only services and not products. Which account(s) would you not expect to see in its balance sheet?

REMEMBER

The balance sheet in Figure 8-1 separates current assets from other assets and separates current liabilities from other liabilities. Financial reporting standards require this classification of assets and liabilities.

>> Current assets are cash and assets that will be converted into cash during one operating cycle, which is the time it takes to manufacture products, to hold the products until they're sold, and to collect the receivables from sales. (Prepaid expenses are also included in current assets because the business uses cash to prepay these costs.) This "from cash back to cash" cycle can be very short, such as a month or so, or it may be relatively long, such as six months or more. Retailers, technology companies, and service organizations tend to have short operating cycles, whereas manufacturers and construction companies have longer operating cycles. As a general rule, current assets are almost always considered to be converted into cash within one year, and current liabilities will be paid or consume cash within one year as well.

>> Current liabilities include those that will be paid within one operating cycle, which mainly are accounts payable and accrued expenses payable. Also, notes payable and any other liabilities that will be paid within one year from the balance sheet date are included in current liabilities. The subtotals of current assets and current liabilities appear in a balance sheet so that the reader can compare these two amounts. Dividing current assets by current liabilities gives the current ratio.

Traditionally, it has been assumed that the current ratio (total current assets divided by total current liabilities) should be at least 2.00 to 1.00, although this minimum has never become a hard-and-fast rule. But if the current ratio dips below 1.00 to 1.00, alarm bells are certain to go off. In fact, many argue that the ratio of cash, cash equivalents (such as short-term marketable investments), and trade accounts receivables divided by current liabilities should be at least 1.00 to 1.00. This is called the quick ratio (total current assets less inventory and prepaid expenses divided by total current liabilities).

EXAMPLE

Q. Referring to the balance sheet in Figure 8-1, how would you assess the short-run solvency of the business as of 12/31/2020? (Solvency refers to the ability of a business to pay its liabilities on time.)

A. The current ratio of the business is 3.25 to 1.00 ($12,221,000 current assets ÷ $3,758,000 current liabilities = 3.25). In other words, for $1.00 of current liabilities, the business has $3.25 of current assets. The question is whether this ratio is high enough to "guarantee" the short-run solvency of the business, or whether there is a serious risk that the business may not be able to pay its short-term (current) liabilities when they come due for payment.

I doubt if the company's bank or shareowners would be upset about its 3.25 to 1.00 current ratio; in fact, they would probably be very happy to see such a strong ratio. The business's quick ratio is also fairly strong at 2.09 to 1.00 ($7,860,000 cash plus trade accounts receivable ÷ $3,758,000 current liabilities = 2.09 to 1.00).

The business's "credit score" (as measured by its current and quick ratios) was solid.

Given the strength of these ratios and the strong credit score, the company's lender (its bank) is likely to decide to renew its short-term loan to the business when it comes due the following month.

The following questions draw on the business whose balance sheet appears in Figure 8-1.

---

 13 Suppose that just before the end of the year, the business paid an additional $400,000 of its accounts payable. Normally, it would not have accelerated payments of accounts payable, but the order to do so came down from "on high," and the payments were made. Why do you think the business may have done this?

 14 Suppose the business held its books open for several days into the next year. It recorded an additional $1,200,000 of payments from customers as if they had been received on December 31 (the last day of its fiscal year) even though the money wasn't actually received and deposited in its bank account until after the end of the year. Why do you think the business may have done this?

This chapter focuses on the balance sheet of a business that sells products and services (see Figure 8-1). I make only a fleeting comment early in the chapter about the annual sales revenue and profit of the business, which, as you know, are reported in its income statement. To recap, its sales revenue for the FYE is $53,747,000, and the business earned $486,000 bottom-line profit for the year. At this point, you can compare the revenue size of the business with its asset size.

The ratio of annual sales revenue to total assets, called the *asset turnover ratio*, varies from industry to industry. Many businesses are *capital intensive*, which means that they need a lot of assets to make sales. For example, companies that sell electricity (such as, utility companies) make huge investments in electric power generating plants. Similarly, airlines make large investments in aircraft, and auto manufacturers invest heavily in production plants and equipment. These types of businesses have relatively low asset turnover ratios. Many other retailers have high asset turnover ratios because they don't need to make large investments in long-lived operating assets.

EXAMPLE

Q. Referring to Figure 8-1, determine whether the size of the business's balance sheet is consistent with the size of its income statement.

A. The business has $18,160,000 total assets (see Figure 8-1), and its annual sales revenue is $53,747,000,000; therefore, its annual sales revenue is 2.96 times total assets (this is its asset turnover ratio). The question asks whether this ratio is consistent with the average asset turnover for industry or not, and in order to answer that, you need to understand that businesses in most industries join trade associations so they can benchmark their financial performance against peers. One of the functions of these trade groups is to collect information from their members and publish norms for the industry. So I look at the trade association information to judge whether the business is significantly above or below the norm for the industry. Generally speaking, an asset turnover ratio of 2.96 to 1.00 is not bad, but again, this will depend on completing "comps" against other businesses operating in the same industry.

Suppose the average asset turnover ratio for businesses in the industry is 5.0 to 1.0. The asset turnover ratio of the business you're considering buying is 2.96 to 1.0; ($53,747,000 annual sales revenue ÷ $18,160,000 total assets = 2.96). What may explain the deviation of the business's asset turnover ratio from the average ratio for the industry?

Does the balance sheet presented in Figure 8-1 give any indication of how old the company is, or how many years it has been in business? Are there any particular accounts or other items in the balance sheet that indicate whether the company is fairly new or has been around for many years?

Clarifying the Values of Assets in Balance Sheets

The evidence is pretty strong that readers of financial reports aren't entirely clear about the dollar amounts reported for assets in a balance sheet. Other than cash — the value of which is clear enough as long as no fraud or shenanigans are present — the amounts reported for assets in a balance sheet aren't at all obvious to non-accountants. Balance sheets don't include reminders or annotations for the valuation basis of each asset. Accountants presume that balance sheet readers understand, or should understand, the asset values that are reported. Accountants are presumptuous, in my opinion.

Of course, accountants should be certain about the valuation of every asset reported in the balance sheet. In preparing a year-end balance sheet, an accountant should do a valuation check on every asset. Recent authoritative pronouncements on financial accounting standards have been moving in this direction. For example, accountants now must check at the end of the accounting year to see whether the value of any asset has been impaired (diminished in economic value to the business), and if so, the book value of the asset should be written down.

REMEMBER

Except for short-term investments in marketable securities that are held for sale, the recorded values of assets aren't written up to recognize appreciation in the replacement or market values of the assets. For example, the current market value of the land and buildings owned by a business may be considerably higher than the cost paid for the real estate many years ago. Or the current replacement value of machinery and equipment owned by a business could be more than the depreciated book value of the assets. These assets are used in the operations of the business and aren't held for sale. Moreover, the assets may not be replaced for many years. Therefore, appreciation in the market and replacement values of these assets aren't recorded. The business makes profit not by holding these assets for sale but rather by using them in the selling of products and services.

The dollar amounts reported for assets in a balance sheet are the amounts that were recorded in the original journal entries made when recording the asset transactions. These journal entries could have been recorded last week, last month, last year, or 20 years ago for some assets. For example,

>> The balance of the asset accounts receivable is from amounts entered in the asset account when credit sales were recorded. These sales are recent, probably within the few months before the end of the year.

>> The balance in the inventory asset account is from the costs of manufacturing or purchasing products. These costs could be from the last two or six months.

>> The costs of fixed assets reported in the property, plant, and equipment asset account in the balance sheet may go back five, ten, or more years — these economic resources are used a long time.

Accountants have devised different ways to record several expenses. The choice of accounting methods affects the balances of several assets, including accounts receivable, inventory, and accumulated depreciation. (I explain these expense accounting methods in Chapter 6.) The reported values of these assets depend on which accounting methods a business adopts to record its expenses. The differences between accounting methods create yet another maddening factor in understanding the dollar amounts reported for assets. No wonder financial report readers are confused about the values reported for assets in balance sheets!

WARNING

Although I don't discuss accounting fraud in this chapter (see Chapter 1), I should point out that, when reading a financial report, you should be alert for any red flags that indicate something may not be right in the financial statements. This vigilance is especially important when you're considering buying or making a major investment in a business. Not to cast aspersions on the present shareowners of the business, but they know you're considering buying the business, and it's conceivable that they may have "suggested" that the chief accountant massage the numbers or even to "cook the books" (that is, the deliberate undertaking of providing misleading financial information) to make the financial statements look as good as possible.

EXAMPLE

Q. Refer to the company's most recent balance sheet in Figure 8-1. The business uses the straight-line depreciation method, by which an equal amount of depreciation is allocated to each year of a fixed asset's estimated useful life. If the business had used accelerated depreciation for its fixed assets instead, the balance in the accumulated depreciation account would be $4,581,000 as of 12/31/2020. How would its balance sheet be different if the business had used accelerated depreciation? (Ignore income tax effects in your answer.)

A. Accumulated depreciation would be $1,500,000 higher, so depreciation expense over the years would be $1,500,000 higher. The higher amounts of depreciation expenses would reduce cumulative net income $1,500,000 (before income tax). Thus, retained earnings would be $1,500,000 lower. The following shows what the balance sheet of the business would be. Note: In the following balance sheet, I've shaded the accounts, subtotals, and totals that differ from amounts reported in Figure 8-1.

Adjusted Balance Sheet

QW Example Tech., Inc.
Balance Sheet
For the Fiscal Year Ending
12/31/2020
(all numbers in thousands)

Assets	12/31/2020
Current Assets:	
Cash & Equivalents	$1,142
Accounts Receivable, Net	$6,718
Inventory, LCM	$4,061
Prepaid Expenses	$300
Total Current Assets	$12,221
Long-Term Operating & Other Assets:	
Property, Plant, Equipment, & Machinery	$7,920
Accumulated Depreciation	($4,581)
Net Property, Plant, & Equipment	$3,339
Other Assets:	
Intangible Assets & Goodwill, Net	$1,000
Other Assets	$100
Total Long-Term Operating & Other Assets	$4,439
Total Assets	$16,660
Liabilities	
Current Liabilities:	
Accounts Payable	$1,654
Accrued Liabilities & Other	$667
Current Portion of Debt	$1,000
Other Current Liabilities & Deferred Revenue	$437
Total Current Liabilities	$3,758
Long-term Liabilities:	
Notes Payable & Other Long-Term Debt	$7,200
Total Liabilities	$10,958
Stockholders' Equity	
Capital Stock - Common	$5,000
Capital Stock - Preferred	$0
Retained Earnings	$702
Total Stockholder's Equity	$5,702
Total Liabilities & Stockholders Equity	$16,660

Confidential - Property of QW Example Tech., Inc.

TIP

Using accelerated depreciation makes the business look different, doesn't it? With that method, total assets are $16,660,000, compared with $18,160,000 total assets by using straight-line depreciation (see Figure 8-1). But of more interest is the change in owners' equity, which decreased from $7,202,000 to $5,702,000 (a 21 percent decrease) and essentially wiped out the retained earnings balance to just $702,000.

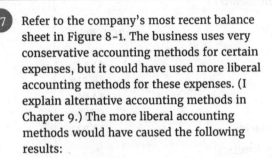

17 Refer to the company's most recent balance sheet in Figure 8-1. The business uses very conservative accounting methods for certain expenses, but it could have used more liberal accounting methods for these expenses. (I explain alternative accounting methods in Chapter 9.) The more liberal accounting methods would have caused the following results:

- Accounts receivable balance would have been $500,000 higher.

- Inventory would have been $250,000 higher.

- Accumulated depreciation would have been $300,000 lower.

Using the landscape/horizontal format, prepare a revised balance sheet for the business giving effect to these differences. (Ignore income tax effects.)

18 Do you see anything suspicious in the balance sheet in Figure 8-1 that may indicate accounting fraud?

Answers to Problems on Reporting Financial Condition in the Balance Sheet

The following are the answers to the practice questions presented earlier in this chapter.

(1) A business has $2,500,000 total assets and $1,000,000 total liabilities. Present three balance sheet formats for the business.

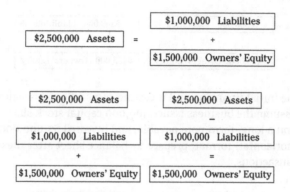

(2) A business has $4,800,000 total liabilities and $6,500,000 total owners' equity. Present three balance sheet formats for the business.

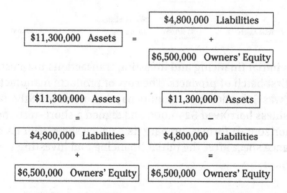

(3) A business has $3,600,000 total assets and $4,600,000 total liabilities. Present three balance sheet formats for the business.

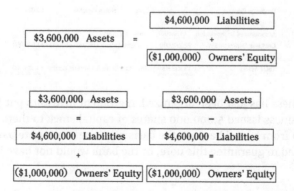

(4) A business has $725,000 total assets and $425,000 total owners' equity. Present three balance sheet formats for the business.

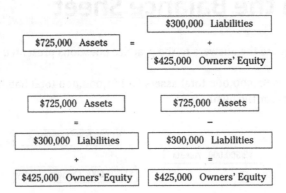

$300,000 Liabilities

$725,000 Assets =

+

$425,000 Owners' Equity

$725,000 Assets $725,000 Assets

=   −

$300,000 Liabilities $300,000 Liabilities

+   =

$425,000 Owners' Equity $425,000 Owners' Equity

(5) Instead of the initial financing and investing transactions presented in the preceding example questions, assume the business issued 100,000 capital stock shares for $1,500,000, borrowed $2,000,000 on a long-term note payable, and invested $2,800,000 in fixed assets. Using the landscape (horizontal) format, prepare its balance sheet after these initial financing and investing transactions.

Assets		Liabilities & Owners' Equity	
Cash	$700,000	Long-term Notes Payable	$2,000,000
Property, Plant, &		Owners Equity:	
Equipment	$2,800,000	Capital Stock (100,000 shares)	$1,500,000
		Total Liabilities &	
Total Assets	$3,500,000	Owners' Equity	$3,500,000

(6) Following its initial financing and investing transactions in Question 5, the business manufactured its first batch of products. The cost of products manufactured was $650,000; depreciation was $20,000; and accounts payable increased $185,000. To provide additional cash, the business borrowed $250,000 and signed a short-term note payable. Using the landscape (horizontal) format, prepare its balance sheet after its first production run. Start with the balance sheet after the initial financing and investing transactions in your answer to Question 5.

Assets		Liabilities & Owners' Equity	
Cash	$505,000	Accounts Payable	$185,000
Inventory	$650,000	Short-term Notes Payable	$250,000
Property, Plant, &		Long-term Notes Payable	$2,000,000
Equipment	$2,800,000		
Accumulated Depreciation	($20,000)	Owners' Equity:	
Cost less Depreciation	$2,780,000	Capital Stock (100,000 shares)	$1,500,000
Total Assets	$3,935,000	Total Liabilities & Owners' Equity	$3,935,000

(7) A new business has just been organized. A group of investors put $5,000,000 in the business and the business issued 5,000,000 shares of capital stock to them. The business borrowed $2,500,000 from a local bank on the basis of a long-term note payable. (Several of the investors had to guarantee this note, or the bank would not have loaned the money to the

business.) The business negotiated the purchase of land and buildings that cost $1,250,000. It also paid $5,250,000 for machinery, production equipment, delivery vehicles, and office equipment and furniture. Using the landscape (horizontal) format, prepare the balance sheet of the business immediately after these initial financing and investing activities.

Assets		Liabilities & Owners' Equity	
Cash	$1,000,000	Long-term Notes Payable	$2,500,000
Property, Plant, &		Owners' Equity:	
Equipment	$6,500,000	Capital Stock (5,000,000 shares)	$5,000,000
		Total Liabilities &	
Total Assets	$7,500,000	Owners' Equity	$7,500,000

8) The business introduced in Question 7 manufactured its first batch of products. It has not yet sold any of these products. The balance sheet changes caused by the first production run are summarized in the following journal entry:

Inventory	$2,000,000	
Cash		$665,000
Accounts Payable		$550,000
Short-term Note Payable		$750,000
Accumulated Depreciation		$35,000

Using the landscape format, prepare its balance sheet after giving effect to the first production run. Start with your balance sheet answer to Question 7.

Assets		Liabilities & Owners' Equity	
Cash	$335,000	Accounts Payable	$550,000
Inventory	$2,000,000	Short-term Notes Payable	$750,000
Property, Plant, &		Long-term Notes Payable	$2,500,000
Equipment	$6,500,000		
Accumulated Depreciation	($35,000)	Owners' Equity:	
Cost less Depreciation	$6,465,000	Capital Stock (5,000,000 shares)	$5,000,000
Total Assets	$8,800,000	Total Liabilities & Owners' Equity	$8,800,000

9) Suppose the business didn't make credit sales and made only cash sales. Which account(s) would you not expect to see in its balance sheet?

The business wouldn't have an accounts receivable asset account because the balance in this asset account comes from credit sales, which the business didn't make. Also, the business shouldn't have a bad debts expense account. This expense comes from uncollectible accounts receivable that are written off; however, a business that sells only for cash has other frustrating expenses, including accepting bad checks from customers, making the wrong change to customers, having to "eat" a fraudulent credit card transaction, and accepting counterfeit currency. These are forms of bad debts that companies have to manage and account for.

10) Suppose the business didn't own any of its fixed assets (long-term operating assets). Instead, it entered into rental or lease agreements for all these assets (office space machinery, equipment, autos, computers, and so on). Which account(s) would you not expect to see in its balance sheet?

In this situation, the business wouldn't have any fixed asset accounts, such as, buildings, machinery, equipment, vehicles, computers, office furniture, and so on. Also the business wouldn't have the accumulated depreciation accounts for fixed asset accounts. Instead of depreciation expense, the business would record rent (or lease) expense.

WARNING

Accountants should examine long-term leases to see whether a lease, in substance, is an installment purchase of the asset. Depending on the terms of the lease and the purchase options at the end of the lease, it may be accounted for as a purchase of the asset. If so, the accountant records the fixed asset and records depreciation over the estimated useful life of the fixed asset.

11. Suppose the business was very conservative and didn't borrow money. Which account(s) would you not expect to see in its balance sheet?

In this unusual situation, the business wouldn't have interest-bearing liability accounts such as notes payable or bonds payable. It wouldn't have an interest expense account, either. The business would have normal operating liability accounts, such as accounts payable and accrued expenses payable, because these operating liabilities don't bear interest.

12. Suppose the business sold only services and not products. Which account(s) would you not expect to see in its balance sheet?

The business wouldn't have an inventory asset account or a cost of goods sold expense account. Also, its accounts payable liability balance would be relatively low compared with a business that sells products. For a company that sells products, a good part of its accounts payable liability balance consists of products purchased on credit (or raw materials used in the manufacturing process that are purchased on credit). In contrast, a business that sells only services doesn't buy products or raw materials on credit.

13. Suppose that just before the end of the year, the business paid an additional $400,000 of its accounts payable. Normally, it would not have accelerated payments of accounts payable, but the order to do so came down from "on high," and the payments were made. Why do you think the business may have done this?

In order to answer this question, you need to look at the business's year-end balance sheet:

Balance Sheet Horizontal Format - Adjusted

QW Example Tech., Inc.
Balance Sheet
For the Fiscal Year Ending
12/31/2020
(all numbers in thousands)

Assets	12/31/2020	Liabilities	12/31/2020
Current Assets:		Current Liabilities:	
Cash & Equivalents	$742	Accounts Payable	$1,254
Accounts Receivable, Net	$6,718	Accrued Liabilities & Other	$667
Inventory, LCM	$4,061	Current Portion of Debt	$1,000
Prepaid Expenses	$300	Other Current Liabilities & Deferred Revenue	$437
Total Current Assets	$11,821	Total Current Liabilities	$3,358
Long-Term Operating & Other Assets:		Long-term Liabilities:	
Property, Plant, Equipment, & Machinery	$7,920	Notes Payable & Other Long-Term Debt	$7,200
Accumulated Depreciation	($3,081)		
Net Property, Plant, & Equipment	$4,839	Total Liabilities	$10,558
Other Assets:		Stockholders' Equity	
Intangible Assets & Goodwill, Net	$1,000	Capital Stock - Common	$5,000
Other Assets	$100	Capital Stock - Preferred	$0
Total Long-Term Operating & Other Assets	$5,939	Retained Earnings	$2,202
		Total Stockholder's Equity	$7,202
Total Assets	$17,760	Total Liabilities & Stockholders Equity	$17,760

Confidential - Property of QW Example Tech., Inc.

WARNING

Pay attention to the current ratio: $11,821,000 current assets ÷ $3,358,000 current liabilities = 3.52 current ratio. By making pay downs on accounts payable very late in the year (perhaps on the very last day of the year), the business improved its current ratio to 3.52 from the 3.25 current ratio in the original scenario (see Figure 8-1). In many cases, a business is under pressure to keep its current ratio as high as possible. What the business in this question did isn't illegal, but the payment should arouse some uneasiness in the accountant. The accountant should make a judgment on the materiality of this action that improves the current ratio from 3.25 to 3.52. Is this a material difference, that is, is it one that could mislead the balance sheet readers? This is a tough question to answer.

The effect on the current ratio isn't material, so nothing would be said about it in the financial statements of the business. If the effect is judged to be material, then the accountant should consider calling it to the attention of the audit committee of the business or another high-level financial officer in the business. The business's financial statements may be audited by an independent CPA firm. The auditors should catch this manipulation of the current ratio, and if they judge it to be material, the CPA firm should bring it to the attention of the audit committee or the board of directors.

14 Suppose the business held its books open for several days into the next year. It recorded an additional $1,200,000 of payments from customers as if they had been received on December 31 (the last day of its fiscal year) even though the money wasn't actually received and deposited in its bank account until after the end of the year. Why do think the business may have done this?

This maneuver is called window dressing; it's done to improve the cash balance reported in the balance sheet and to improve the perceived improvement in liquidity by increasing the cash balance and decreasing trade accounts receivable. In order to answer this question, you need to look at the business's year-end balance sheet:

Balance Sheet Horizontal Format - Adjusted

QW Example Tech., Inc.
Balance Sheet
For the Fiscal Year Ending
12/31/2020
(all numbers in thousands)

Assets	12/31/2020	Liabilities	12/31/2020
Current Assets:		Current Liabilities:	
Cash & Equivalents	$2,342	Accounts Payable	$1,654
Accounts Receivable, Net	$5,518	Accrued Liabilities & Other	$667
Inventory, LCM	$4,061	Current Portion of Debt	$1,000
Prepaid Expenses	$300	Other Current Liabilities & Deferred Revenue	$437
Total Current Assets	$12,221	Total Current Liabilities	$3,758
Long-Term Operating & Other Assets:		Long-term Liabilities:	
Property, Plant, Equipment, & Machinery	$7,920	Notes Payable & Other Long-Term Debt	$7,200
Accumulated Depreciation	($3,081)		
Net Property, Plant, & Equipment	$4,839	Total Liabilities	$10,958
Other Assets:		Stockholders' Equity	
Intangible Assets & Goodwill, Net	$1,000	Capital Stock - Common	$5,000
Other Assets	$100	Capital Stock - Preferred	$0
Total Long-Term Operating & Other Assets	$5,939	Retained Earnings	$2,202
		Total Stockholder's Equity	$7,202
Total Assets	$18,160	Total Liabilities & Stockholders Equity	$18,160

Confidential - Property of QW Example Tech., Inc.

In the original scenario, the quick ratio is 2.09 to 1.00, which is the exact same as the manipulated ratio, as trade receivables is simply being swapped for cash. So why the worry? The answer is simple. The portion of the quick ratio's total assets that is comprised of cash is now $1,200,000 higher than the original calculation and may give the impression that the company has more cash on hand than is actually present. When I was in public accounting years ago, certain audit clients employed window dressing similar to this. I must admit that the CPA auditors tolerated holding the books open for a few days in order to allow the business to report a higher cash balance and give the appearance that trade accounts receivable are lower (reducing questions involving potential bad debts). Current assets and current liabilities don't change, so holding the books open doesn't change the current ratio.

15. Suppose the average asset turnover ratio for businesses in the industry is 5.0 to 1.0. The asset turnover ratio of the business you're considering buying is 2.96 to 1.0; ($53,747,000 annual sales revenue ÷ $18,160,000 total assets = 2.96). What may explain the deviation of the business's asset turnover ratio from the average ratio for the industry?

The business's total assets are too high relative to its annual sales revenue; looking at it another way, its annual sales revenue is too low relative to its total assets. One reason may be that the business has excess capacity, meaning that it may be over-invested in its fixed assets. For example, its building may be too large, or it may have more machines than it needs to manufacture products. Excess capacity is a good place to start, but fixed assets may not be the main reason for a below-normal asset turnover ratio. You should examine all assets to see whether their balances are too big.

The business may have allowed the size of its inventory to get out of control. Perhaps its accounts receivable balance is too high because of lax collection efforts, or it's possible that the business has too much cash relative to its day-to-day operating needs. It could be that the business had a sudden and unexpected dip in sales toward the end of the year. Perhaps it hasn't had time to downsize its assets and adjust to the lower sales level. The business may think that the drop in sales is only temporary and, therefore, it wants to keep its assets at their present levels to support the predicted bounce back in sales next year.

16. Does the balance sheet presented in Figure 8-1 give any indication of how old the company is, or how many years it has been in business? Are there any particular accounts or other items in the balance sheet that indicate whether the company is fairly new or has been around for many years?

One clue regarding the age of the business is the balance in its accumulated depreciation account as a percent of the cost of the fixed assets being depreciated. The higher the percentage, the older the business is likely to be. But this is really just guesswork. Financial statements don't report the age of a business. However, financial reports may include a historical summary of key data (such as annual sales, annual net income, total assets, and so on), which often go back to the first year of business.

17. Refer to the company's most recent balance sheet in Figure 8-1. The business uses very conservative accounting methods for certain expenses, but it could have used more liberal accounting methods for these expenses. (I explain alternative accounting methods in Chapter 9.) The more liberal accounting methods would have caused the following results:

- Accounts receivable balance would have been $500,000 higher.

- Inventory would have been $250,000 higher.

- Accumulated depreciation would have been $300,000 lower.

Using the landscape format, prepare a revised balance sheet for the business giving effect to these differences. (Ignore income tax effects.)

The year-end balance sheet of the business would have been as follows:

Balance Sheet
Horizontal Format - Alternative

QW Example Tech., Inc.
Balance Sheet
For the Fiscal Year Ending
12/31/2020
(all numbers in thousands)

Assets	12/31/2020	Liabilities	12/31/2020
Current Assets:		Current Liabilities:	
Cash & Equivalents	$1,142	Accounts Payable	$1,654
Accounts Receivable, Net	$7,218	Accrued Liabilities & Other	$667
Inventory, LCM	$4,311	Current Portion of Debt	$1,000
Prepaid Expenses	$300	Other Current Liabilities & Deferred Revenue	$437
Total Current Assets	$12,971	Total Current Liabilities	$3,758
Long-Term Operating & Other Assets:		Long-term Liabilities:	
Property, Plant, Equipment, & Machinery	$7,920	Notes Payable & Other Long-Term Debt	$7,200
Accumulated Depreciation	($2,781)		
Net Property, Plant, & Equipment	$5,139	Total Liabilities	$10,958
Other Assets:		Stockholders' Equity	
Intangible Assets & Goodwill, Net	$1,000	Capital Stock - Common	$5,000
Other Assets	$100	Capital Stock - Preferred	$0
Total Long-Term Operating & Other Assets	$6,239	Retained Earnings	$3,252
		Total Stockholder's Equity	$8,252
Total Assets	$19,210	Total Liabilities & Stockholders Equity	$19,210

Confidential - Property of QW Example Tech., Inc.

The expenses of the business over the years would have been $1,050,000 lower; ($500,000 higher sales + $250,000 lower cost of goods sold expense + $300,000 lower depreciation expense = $1,050,000 lower expenses in total). Therefore, cumulative net income would have been $1,050,000 higher (before income tax), and the balance of retained earnings would have been $1,050,000 higher. (Adding the $1,050,000 increase in cumulative net income to the $2,202,000 retained earnings balance in Figure 8-1 equals the $3,252,000 retained earnings balance shown in this answer.)

18) Do you see anything suspicious in the balance sheet in Figure 8-1 that may indicate accounting fraud?

WARNING

I don't see anything suspicious in the balance sheet that may indicate that some accounting hanky-panky is going on, but I will draw your attention to the balance stated in inventory that decreased from $4,061,000 as of 12/31/20 to just $1,733,000 as of 12/31/20. This large decrease, in light of the company making just $486,000 for FYE 12/31/20 (refer to Figure 7-1), could indicate that the company was attempting to shift inventory valuation adjustments (for slow moving or obsolete inventory) into FYE 12/31/20 when profits were much higher. Thus, the company achieved positive net income in both years but might have pushed the envelope a bit by not recognizing that certain inventory was worthless until the next year (to manage or massage profits each year). A good con artist will try to make everything look right. So, who knows for sure? The first rule of an auditor is to be skeptical. I'm an "old auditor" at heart, and I've seen too many fraudulent financial statements in my time. As they say in politics, "Trust, but verify." The problem is that financial report users may not be able to verify the information presented in financial statements. Furthermore, CPA auditors don't necessarily catch accounting fraud in financial statements. Unfortunately, the risk of accounting fraud is always present.

IN THIS CHAPTER

» Rejoining the income statement and balance sheet

» Fitting key pieces into the balance sheet puzzle with operating ratios

» Adding assets to the balance sheet

» Examining debt versus equity on the balance sheet

Chapter **9**

Coupling the Income Statement and Balance Sheet

E very time an accountant records a sale or expense entry using double-entry account-ing, they should see the interconnections between the income statement and balance sheet. (I explain the rules for debits and credits in Chapter 3.) A sale increases an asset or decreases a liability, and an expense decreases an asset or increases a liability. Therefore, one side of every sales and expense entry is in the income statement, and the other side is in the balance sheet. You can't record a sale or an expense without affecting the balance sheet. The income statement and balance sheet are inseparable, but they aren't reported this way!

WARNING

To properly interpret financial statements — the income statement, the balance sheet, and the statement of cash flows — you need to understand the links between the three state-ments, but, unfortunately, the links can be somewhat challenging to see to the untrained eye. Each financial statement appears on a separate page in the annual financial report, and the threads of connection between the financial statements aren't referred to. In reading financial reports, non-accountants especially — and yes, even accountants — usually don't spot these connections.

I explain the income statement in Chapter 7 and the balance sheet in Chapter 8. In this chapter, I stitch these two financial statements together and mark the trails of connections between sales revenue and expenses (in the income statement) and their corresponding assets and liabilities (in the balance sheet). In Chapter 10, I explain the connections between the amounts reported in the statement of cash flows and the other two financial statements.

Rejoining the Income Statement and Balance Sheet

Figure 9-1 shows the lines of connection between income statement accounts and balance sheet accounts. When reading financial statements, in your mind's eye, you should "see" these lines of connection. Because financial reports don't offer a clue about these connections, it may help to actually draw the lines of connection, like you would if you were highlighting lines in a textbook.

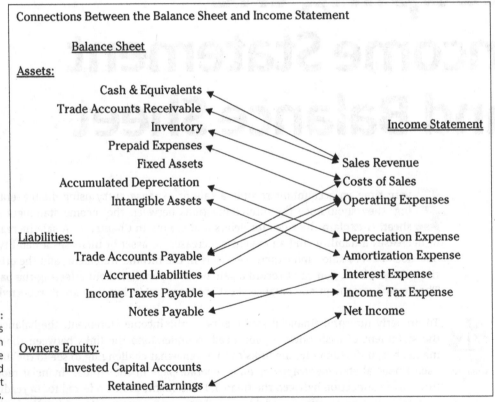

Connections Between the Balance Sheet and Income Statement

Balance Sheet

Assets:
- Cash & Equivalents
- Trade Accounts Receivable
- Inventory
- Prepaid Expenses
- Fixed Assets
- Accumulated Depreciation
- Intangible Assets

Liabilities:
- Trade Accounts Payable
- Accrued Liabilities
- Income Taxes Payable
- Notes Payable

Owners Equity:
- Invested Capital Accounts
- Retained Earnings

Income Statement
- Sales Revenue
- Costs of Sales
- Operating Expenses
- Depreciation Expense
- Amortization Expense
- Interest Expense
- Income Tax Expense
- Net Income

FIGURE 9-1: Connections between income statement and balance sheet accounts.

Here's a quick summary explaining the lines of connection in Figure 9-1, starting from the top and working down to the bottom:

>> Making sales (and incurring expenses for making sales) requires a business to maintain a working cash balance.

>> Making sales on credit generates accounts receivable.

>> Selling products requires the business to carry an inventory (stock) of products.

>> Acquiring products involves purchases on credit that generate accounts payable.

>> Depreciation expense is recorded for the use of fixed assets (long-term operating resources).

>> Depreciation is recorded in the accumulated depreciation contra account (instead decreasing the fixed asset account).

>> Amortization expense is recorded for limited-life intangible assets.

>> Operating expenses is a broad category of costs encompassing selling, administrative, and general expenses:

- Some of these operating costs are prepaid before the expense is recorded, and until the expense is recorded, the cost stays in the prepaid expenses' asset account.

- Some of these operating costs involve purchases on credit that generate accounts payable.

- Some of these operating costs are from recording unpaid expenses in the accrued expenses payable liability.

>> Borrowing money on notes payable causes interest expense.

>> A portion (usually relatively small) of income tax expense for the year is unpaid at year-end, which is recorded in the accrued expenses payable liability.

>> Earning net income increases retained earnings.

EXAMPLE

Q. For the year just ended, a business reports $5,200,000 sales revenue. All its sales are made on credit (to other businesses). Historically, its year-end accounts receivable balance equals about five weeks of annual sales revenue; in other words, an amount equal to five weeks of annual sales revenue is not yet collected at the end of the year. Sales are level throughout the year. What amount of accounts receivable would you expect in the business's year-end balance sheet?

A. Dividing $5,200,000 annual sales revenue by 52 weeks gives $100,000 average sales per week. Based on its past experience, the ending balance of accounts receivables should be about $500,000, which equals five weeks of annual sales revenue.

1 The business in the example question has an annual cost of goods sold expense of $3,120,000. Historically, its ending inventory balance equals about 13 weeks of annual costs of goods sold expense. What amount of inventory would you expect in its year-end balance sheet?

2 The business in the example question has an annual cost of goods sold expense of $3,120,000. Historically, the business's accounts payable for inventory purchases equals about four weeks of annual cost of goods sold. What amount of accounts payable for inventory purchases would you expect in its year-end balance sheet? (Note: The accounts payable balance also includes an amount from purchases of supplies and services on credit; this question concerns only the amount of accounts payable from inventory purchases.)

3 The business in the example question has annual operating expenses in the amount of $1,378,000 (which excludes depreciation, amortization, interest, and income tax expenses). Historically, its year-end balance of accrued expenses payable equals about six weeks of its annual operating expenses. Ignoring accrued interest payable and income tax payable, what amount of accrued expenses payable would you expect in its year-end balance sheet?

4 For the business in the example question, the average amount borrowed on notes payable during the year was $1,500,000. The average annual interest rate on these notes was 6.5 percent. What amount of interest expense would you find in the business's income statement for the year?

Filling in Key Pieces of the Balance Sheet from the Income Statement

Laying the foundation for the balance sheet of a business using its normative *operating ratios* is very instructive. An operating ratio expresses the size of an asset or liability on the basis of sales revenue or an expense in the annual income statement. A *normative* operating ratio refers to how large an asset or liability *should be* relative to sales revenue or its related expense in the annual income statement.

I would like to note that for the remainder of this chapter, I will be using the sample company income statement as a basis to calculate a revised or adjusted balance sheet based on applying normative operating ratios. As such, the balance sheet for the sample company calculated in this chapter will differ from the balance sheet presented in Chapter 8, which is being done for illustrative purposes only. That is, I want to present an alternative balance sheet for the sample company to highlight how the income statement and balance sheet couple together.

EXAMPLE

Suppose the sample business, QW Example Tech, Inc., makes all its sales on credit and offers its customers one month to pay. Very few customers pay early, and some customers are chronic late-payers. To encourage repeat sales, the business tolerates these late-payers, and as a result, its accounts receivable equals five weeks of annual sales revenue. Thus, its normative operating ratio of accounts receivable to annual sales revenue is 5 to 52.

WARNING

The actual ratio of the year-end accounts receivable balance to annual sales revenue is unlikely to be precisely 5 to 52, which equals 9.615 percent of sales revenue. The 5 to 52 operating ratio is the normative ratio between accounts receivable and annual sales revenue; it's based on the sales credit policies of the business and how aggressive the business is in collecting receivables when customers don't pay on time. The 5 to 52 ratio is a benchmark, in other words. Minor deviations are harmless, but significant variances deserve serious management attention and follow-up.

In Chapter 8, I present the balance sheet of our sample company based on the accumulating of actual transactions of the business incurred since its inception. In this section, I start with the normative operating ratios for a business. Based on these critical metrics for the business, I determine the balances for certain of its assets and liabilities. These amounts are what the balances would be if the results of the business's transactions came in right on the money so that every operating ratio ended up being exactly what it should be.

The annual income statement of the sample company is presented in Figure 9-2. From the sales revenue and expenses reported in the income statement, I determine the balances of several assets and liabilities using the normative operating ratios for the business.

Operating ratios can be expressed in terms of weeks of the 52 weeks year (or they can be expressed as percentages of annual sales revenue or annual expense). I use weeks of the year in this example. The normative operating ratios for the business whose income statement is presented in Figure 9-2 are as follows:

>> Cash equals seven weeks of annual sales revenue.

>> Accounts receivable equals five weeks of annual sales revenue.

>> Inventory equals three weeks of annual cost of goods sold.

>> Accounts payable for inventory acquisitions equals one week of annual cost of goods sold.

>> Accounts payable for supplies and services bought on credit equals three weeks of annual selling and general expenses.

>> Accrued expenses payable for operating expenses equals two weeks of annual selling and general expenses.

Income Statement

QW Example Tech., Inc.
Income Statement
For the Fiscal Year Ending
12/31/2021
(all numbers in thousands)

For the Twelve Months Ending	12/31/2021
Sales Revenue, Net	$71,064
Costs of Goods Sold	$26,891
Gross Profit	$44,173
Selling, General, & Administrative Expenses	$36,678
Operating Income (Loss)	$7,495
Other Expenses (Income):	
Interest Expense	$350
Net Profit (Loss) before Income Taxes	$7,145
Income Tax Expense (benefit)	$2,501
Net Income (Loss)	$4,644

Confidential - Property of QW Example Tech., Inc.

FIGURE 9-2: Income statement of sample company for the FYE 12/31/21.

I don't include accrued interest payable and income tax payable in the example for two reasons: First, these year-end liabilities typically are relatively small amounts compared with the major assets and liabilities of a business. Second, the expenses that drive these liabilities aren't operating expenses. The year-end balance of accrued interest payable depends on the terms for paying interest on the business's debt. Income tax expense, as you know, depends on the income tax status of the business and its policies regarding making installment payments toward its annual income tax during the year. In short, it's not possible to apply operating ratios for these two liabilities.

REMEMBER

The ratio of annual depreciation and amortization expense to the original cost of fixed assets or intangible assets (respectively) can't be normalized. Different fixed assets and intangible assets are depreciated and amortized over different estimated useful life spans. For example, some fixed assets are depreciated according to the straight-line method and others according to an accelerated depreciation method. (I explain these depreciation methods in Chapter 6.) The annual depreciation and amortization expense should be a reasonable fraction of the original cost of the fixed assets or intangible assets. It would be unusual, and even suspicious, in fact, if depreciation or amortization expense were more than 30 percent or so of the total original cost of the respective assets.

EXAMPLE

Q. Using the normative operating ratios for the sample company noted previously, whose income statement appears in Figure 9-2, determine the balances for the assets and liabilities driven by its sales revenue and expenses.

A. The asset and liability balances derived from applying the normative operating ratios to the sales revenue and expenses presented in the company's income statement (Figure 9-2) are as follows:

Normative Balance Sheet Amounts (all numbers in thousands)		
Assets		**Computation Notes**
Cash & Equivalents	$9,586	7/52 x $71,064 Net Sales Revenue
Trade Accounts Receivable	$6,833	5/52 x $71,064 Net Sales Revenue
Inventory	$1,551	3/52 x $26,891 Costs of Goods Sold
Liabilities		
Trade Accounts Payable	$2,633	1/52 x $26,891 Costs of Goods Sold + 3/52 x $36,678 SG&A Expenses
Accrued Expenses	$1,411	2/52 x $36,678 SG&A Expenses

TIP

These asset and liability balances are normative, not the actual balances that would be reported in the business's balance sheet. The balances provide a useful benchmark against which the actual balances can be compared. Unusual deviations indicate that something has gotten out of control or that the business has made a fundamental shift in its operating polices and needs to revise its operating ratio yardsticks.

In Figure 9-3, you can see a partial balance sheet that presents only the assets and liabilities determined in the preceding example question. Later in the chapter, I fill in the remainder of the balance sheet, including fixed assets, interest-bearing debt, and owners' equity.

FIGURE 9-3:
Partial balance sheet showing the sample company's asset and liability balances based on normative operating ratios.

Partial Balance Sheet Using Normative Operating Ratios				
QW Example Tech., Inc. Partial Balance Sheet For the Fiscal Year Ending 12/31/2021 (all numbers in thousands)				
Assets	12/31/2021		Liabilities	12/31/2021
Current Assets:			Current Liabilities:	
Cash & Equivalents	$9,566		Accounts Payable	$2,633
Accounts Receivable, Net	$6,833		Accrued Liabilities & Other	$1,411
Inventory	$1,551			

Confidential - Property of QW Example Tech., Inc.

Questions 5 through 9 are based on the sample company's FYE 12/31/21 income statement, but as a result of changing business conditions, the normative operating ratios have changed as well and are now expressed in the following bulleted list as a percent of annual sales revenue and expenses as opposed to weeks in a year:

>> Cash equals 15 percent of annual sales revenue.

>> Accounts receivable equals 12 percent of annual sales revenue.

>> Inventory equals 10 percent of annual cost of goods sold.

>> Accounts payable for inventory acquisitions equals 5 percent of annual cost of goods sold.

>> Accounts payable for supplies and services bought on credit equals 8 percent of annual selling and general expenses.

>> Accrued expenses payable for operating expenses equals 6 percent of annual selling and general expenses.

I should note that in the real world, normative operating ratios are constantly changing as a result of businesses adapting to general market and economic conditions. It is not usual for businesses operating in fast-moving and rapidly changing industries (think technology, retail via the move from brick and mortar to ecommerce, and so on) to have to adjust to new normative ratios. This is just par for the course in today's interconnected global economy.

 5 Determine the balance of cash based on the normative operating ratio for this asset account. (Refer to the preceding list of normative adjusted operating ratios for sample company.)

6 Determine the balance of accounts receivable based on the normative operating ratio for this asset account. (Refer to the preceding list of normative adjusted operating ratios for the sample company.)

7 Determine the balance of inventory based on the normative operating ratio for this asset account. (Refer to the preceding list of normative adjusted operating ratios for the sample company.)

8 Determine the balance of accounts payable based on the normative operating ratios for this liability account. (Refer to the preceding list of normative adjusted operating ratios for sample company.)

9 Determine the balance of accrued expenses payable based on the normative operating ratio for this liability account. (Refer to the preceding list of normative adjusted operating ratios for sample company.)

Putting Fixed Assets in the Picture

Certain assets are obviously missing in the partial balance sheet shown in Figure 9-3: the fixed assets of the business as well as intangible assets. Virtually every business needs these long-lived economic resources to carry on its profit-making activities.

TIP

The cost and accumulated depreciation of a business's fixed assets depends on when the assets were bought (recently or many years ago?), the sort of long-term operating assets the business needs, and whether the business leases or owns these assets. I can't offer you a ratio for the original cost of fixed assets and annual sales revenue because it's very difficult to generalize about the cost of fixed assets relative to annual sales revenue. If I had to hazard a ballpark estimate for this ratio, I would say that annual sales revenue of a business is generally between one to four times the total cost of its fixed assets. But please take this estimation with a grain of salt. The ratio varies widely from industry to industry, and even within the same industry, the ratio can vary from company to company. Generally speaking, retailers have a higher ratio of sales to fixed assets than heavy equipment manufacturers and transportation companies (airlines, truckers, and so on).

In Figure 9-4, you can see an educated guess for the fixed assets' cost, the accumulated depreciation on the fixed assets, and net value of intangible and other assets. The partial balance sheet shown in Figure 9-4 tells an interesting story: The sample company has $22,901,000 total assets, but where did it get that $22,901,000? Its two operating liabilities provided $4,044,000 of the total assets; ($2,633,000 accounts payable + $1,411,000 accrued expenses payable = $4,044,000). So, where did the remaining $18,857,000 come from?

$22,901,000 total assets − $4,044,000 short-term operating liabilities = $18,857,000 needed from sources of business capital

---

Expanded Balance Sheet
Using Normative Operating Ratios

QW Example Tech., Inc.
Expanded Balance Sheet
For the Fiscal Year Ending
12/31/2021
(all numbers in thousands)

Assets	12/31/2021	Liabilities	12/31/2021
Current Assets:		Current Liabilities:	
Cash & Equivalents	$9,566	Accounts Payable	$2,633
Accounts Receivable, Net	$6,833	Accrued Liabilities & Other	$1,411
Inventory	$1,551	Current Portion of Debt	$0
Prepaid Expenses	$0	Other Current Liabilities & Deferred Revenue	$0
Total Current Assets	$17,951	Total Current Liabilities	$4,044
Long-Term Operating & Other Assets:			
Property, Plant, Equipment, & Machinery	$8,670		
Accumulated Depreciation	($4,320)		
Net Property, Plant, & Equipment	$4,350		
Other Assets:			
Intangible Assets & Goodwill, Net	$500		
Other Assets	$100		
Total Long-Term Operating & Other Assets	$4,950		
Total Assets	$22,901	??? - Where From	$18,857

Confidential - Property of QW Example Tech., Inc.

FIGURE 9-4: Sample company's balance sheet that includes all assets and short-term operating liabilities using normative operating ratios.

10. Instead of the amounts shown in Figure 9-4, suppose that the cost of our sample company's fixed assets was $10,170,000 and that accumulated depreciation was $5,120,000. Determine the amount of capital the business would have had to raise in this scenario.

11. Assume that the balances of assets, accounts payable, and accrued expenses payable were the same as shown in Figure 9-4. However, the balance in intangible assets amounted to $1,300,000 and the amount of accumulated depreciation amounted to $5,170,000 Would the sample company need to raise any additional capital?

Completing the Balance Sheet with Debt and Equity

If you owned the sample company, whose balance sheet is depicted in Figure 9-4, how should you have raised the $18,857,000 capital? You can debate this question until the cows come home, because there's no right or best answer. The two basic sources of business capital are interest-bearing debt and equity (more precisely, owners' equity). Where to secure capital is really a business financial management question, not an accounting question per se. As a practical matter, many businesses borrow as much as they can and use owners' equity for the rest of the capital they need.

TIP

Most businesses use debt for part of their capital needs, and this practice makes sense as long as the business doesn't overextend its debt obligations. Because this isn't a book on business finance, a debate concerning debt versus equity isn't in order. Instead, you move on to the complete balance sheet of the business.

Figure 9-5 presents the complete balance sheet for Company X, including its debt and owners' equity accounts. These are the final pieces of the balance sheet puzzle (if you started at the beginning of this chapter, this is what you've been working toward). The business has borrowed $1,000,000 on short-term notes payable (due in one year or less) and $6,200,000 on long-term notes payable (due after one year). Balance sheets may or may not report the annual interest rates on their notes (and bonds) payable in the actual financial statement. If not reported in the balance sheet proper, interest rates and other relevant details of debt contracts are usually disclosed in the footnotes to the financial statements. For example, debt covenants (conditions prescribed by the debt contract) may limit the amount of cash dividends the business can pay to its shareowners.

The original shareowners in the sample company invested $5,000,000 (back in the day), for which they received 1,000,000 capital shares of common stock. Even relatively simple-looking business corporation ownership structures can be more complex than they appear as you can see in the sample company, as it raised another $5,000,000 in 2021 by issuing 500,000 of capital shares of preferred stock. Typically, a footnote is necessary to fully explain the ownership structure of a business corporation including the different types of equity issued, the structure of the equity, any preferences with the equity, and so on. (If you don't believe me, read the shareowners' equity footnotes of any business.) As a general rule, private business corporations don't have to disclose who owns how many of their capital stock shares in their financial statements. In contrast, public business corporations are subject to many disclosure rules regarding the stock ownership, stock options, and other stock-based compensation benefits of their officers and top-level managers.

Complete Balance Sheet
Using Normative Operating Ratios

QW Example Tech., Inc.
Complete Balance Sheet
For the Fiscal Year Ending
12/31/2021
(all numbers in thousands)

Assets	12/31/2021	Liabilities	12/31/2021
Current Assets:		Current Liabilities:	
Cash & Equivalents	$9,566	Accounts Payable	$2,633
Accounts Receivable, Net	$6,833	Accrued Liabilities & Other	$1,411
Inventory	$1,551	Current Portion of Debt	$1,000
Prepaid Expenses	$0	Other Current Liabilities & Deferred Revenue	$0
Total Current Assets	$17,951	Total Current Liabilities	$5,044
Long-Term Operating & Other Assets:		Long-term Liabilities:	
Property, Plant, Equipment, & Machinery	$8,670	Notes Payable & Other Long-Term Debt	$6,200
Accumulated Depreciation	($4,320)		
Net Property, Plant, & Equipment	$4,350	Total Liabilities	$11,244
Other Assets:		Stockholders' Equity	
Intangible Assets & Goodwill, Net	$500	Capital Stock - Common	$5,000
Other Assets	$100	Capital Stock - Preferred	$5,000
Total Long-Term Operating & Other Assets	$4,950	Retained Earnings	$1,657
		Total Stockholder's Equity	$11,657
Total Assets	$22,901	Total Liabilities & Stockholders Equity	$22,901

Confidential - Property of QW Example Tech., Inc.

FIGURE 9-5:
Complete balance sheet of sample company using normative ratios.

Over the years, the business in this scenario retained $1,657,000 of its yearly profits (see retained earnings in Figure 9-5). You can't tell from the balance sheet how much of this cumulative total is from any one year. Nor can you tell from the income statement or the balance sheet how much of its $4,644,000 profit for the year (see Figure 9-2) was distributed as a cash dividend to shareowners during the year just ended. In fact, you may ask yourself how can the business generate a profit of $4,644,000 yet only have retained earnings of $1,657,000? The purpose of the statement of cash flows is to report the cash dividends paid from net income to shareowners during the year (I discuss cash flow statements in Chapter 10). Another possible explanation is that the sample company had cumulative losses prior to the FYE 12/31/21 and has just been able to present a positive retained earnings balance (as a result of the net income generated from the FYE 12/31/21).

Questions 12 and 13 are based on the previously presented balance sheet in Figure 9-5 for our sample company using normative ratios. You're asked to determine certain operating ratios for the business based on the information in its balance sheet.

12　Based on the sample company's income statement and balance sheet, if the company wanted to maintain a total debt to asset ratio of 60 percent, what would the total liabilities of the company amount to?

13　Based on the sample company's income statement and balance sheet, if the company wanted to generate a return on equity (defined as net income divided by total stockholders' equity) of 30 percent, what would the net income amount to?

Answers to Problems on Coupling the Income Statement and Balance Sheet

The following are the answers to the practice questions presented earlier in this chapter.

(1) The business in the example question has an annual cost of goods sold expense of $3,120,000. Historically, its ending inventory balance equals about 13 weeks of annual costs of goods sold expense. What amount of inventory would you expect in its year-end balance sheet?

$3,120,000 ÷ 52 weeks = $60,000 average cost of goods sold per week × 13 weeks operating ratio = $780,000 inventory balance in its year-end balance sheet

(2) The business in the example question has an annual cost of goods sold expense of $3,120,000. Historically, the business's accounts payable for inventory purchases equals about four weeks of annual cost of goods sold. What amount of accounts payable for inventory purchases would you expect in its year-end balance sheet? (Note: The accounts payable balance also includes an amount from purchases of supplies and services on credit; this question concerns only the amount of accounts payable from inventory purchases.)

$3,120,000 ÷ 52 weeks = $60,000 average cost of goods sold per week × 4 weeks operating ratio = $240,000 accounts payable for inventory purchases balance in its year-end balance sheet

(3) The business in the example question has annual operating expenses in the amount of $1,378,000 (which excludes depreciation, amortization, interest, and income tax expenses). Historically, its year-end balance of accrued expenses payable equals about six weeks of its annual operating expenses. Ignoring accrued interest payable and income tax payable, what amount of accrued expenses payable would you expect in its year-end balance sheet?

$1,378,000 ÷ 52 weeks = $26,500 average operating expenses per week × 6 weeks operating ratio = $159,000 accrued expenses payable balance in its year-end balance sheet

(4) For the business in the example question, the average amount borrowed on notes payable during the year was $1,500,000. The average annual interest rate on these notes was 6.5 percent. What amount of interest expense would you find in the business's income statement for the year?

$1,500,000 average notes payable × 6.5 percent interest rate = $97,500 annual interest expense

(5) Determine the balance of cash based on the normative operating ratio for this asset account. (Refer to the preceding list of normative adjusted operating ratios for the sample company.) The correct answer is $10,660,000.

(6) Determine the balance of accounts receivable based on the normative operating ratio for this asset account. (Refer to the preceding list of normative adjusted operating ratios for sample company.)

Use the following:

Normative Adjusted Balance Sheet Amounts (all numbers in thousands)		
Assets		**Computation Notes**
Cash & Equivalents	$10,660	15% x $71,064 Net Sales Revenue
Trade Accounts Receivable	$8,528	12% x $71,064 Net Sales Revenue
Inventory	$2,689	10% x $26,891 Costs of Goods Sold
Liabilities		
Trade Accounts Payable	$4,279	5% x $26,891 Costs of Goods Sold +
		8% x $36,678 SG&A Expenses
Accrued Expenses	$2,201	6% x $36,678 SG&A Expenses

The correct answer is $8,528,000.

(7) Determine the balance of inventory based on the normative operating ratio for this asset account. (Refer to the preceding list of normative adjusted operating ratios for sample company.) Refer to the Normative Adjusted Balance Sheet shown in Answer 6.

The correct answer is $2,689,000.

(8) Determine the balance of accounts payable based on the normative operating ratios for this liability account. (Refer to the preceding list of normative adjusted operating ratios for sample company.)

Refer to the Normative Adjusted Balance Sheet shown in Answer 6.

The correct answer is $4,279,000.

(9) Determine the balance of accrued expenses payable based on the normative operating ratio for this liability account. (Refer to the preceding list of normative adjusted operating ratios for sample company.)

Refer to the Normative Adjusted Balance Sheet shown in Answer 6.

The correct answer is $2,201,000.

(10) Instead of the amounts shown in Figure 9-4, suppose that the cost of the sample company's fixed assets was $10,170,000 and that accumulated depreciation was $5,120,000. Determine the amount of capital the business would have had to raise in this scenario.

Based on the higher amount invested in fixed assets, and taking into account the larger amount of accumulated depreciation, the sample company would have had to raise an additional $700,000 based on the following calculation:

Expanded Balance Sheet for Tech Company (all numbers in thousands)	
Assets	
Adjusted Fixed Asset Gross Balance	$10,170
Adjusted Accumulated Depreciation	($5,120)
Fixed Asset Net Balance	$5,050
Current Fixed Asset Net Balance	$4,350
Additional Capital Required	$700

Correct answer is $700,000.

(11) Assume that the balances of assets, accounts payable, and accrued expenses payable were the same as shown in Figure 9-4. However, the balance in intangible assets amounted to $1,300,000 and the amount of accumulated depreciation amounted to $5,170,000. Would the sample company need to raise any additional capital?

Expanded Balance Sheet for Tech Company (all numbers in thousands)	
Assets	
Current Fixed Asset Gross Balance	$8,670
Adjusted Accumulated Depreciation	($5,120)
Fixed Asset Net Balance	$3,550
Current Fixed Asset Net Balance	$4,350
Additional Capital Required, in this case less (change, a.)	($800)
Adjusted Intangible Asset Balance	$1,300
Current Intangible Asset Balance	$500
Additional Capital Required, in this case more (change, b.)	$800
Total Additional Capital Required (a. plus b.)	$0

The answer is zero as I have intentionally provided an example that highlights that while one asset balance increases (in this case intangible assets), another asset balance decreases through a higher accumulated depreciation figure (in this case, net fixed assets) which when combined offset each other and produce no need for additional capital.

(12) Based on the sample company's income statement and balance sheet, if the company wanted to maintain a total debt to asset ratio of 60 percent, what would the total liabilities of the company amount to?

Normative Sample Company Financial Data (all numbers in thousands)	
Balance Sheet	
Total Assets	$22,901
Target Ratio of Debt to Total Assets	60.00%
Target total Liabilities	$13,740

Correct answer is $13,740,000 of total liabilities. As you can see from the normative balance sheet, total liabilities amount to $11,244,000 so it would appear that the company could take on some additional debt to support its business plan and on-going operations.

(13) Based on the sample company's income statement and balance sheet, if the company wanted to generate a return on equity (defined as net income divided by total stockholders' equity) of 30 percent, what would the net income amount to?

Normative Sample Company Financial Data (all numbers in thousands)	
Return on Equity Calculation	
Total Stockholders' Equity	$11,657
Target Return on Stockholders' Equity	30.00%
Target Net Income	$3,497

Correct answer is $3,497,000, which compares to actual net income of $4,644,000. In this situation, the company's owners, management team, and external creditors are probably pleased with the operating results as actual net income exceeded a targeted net income by more than $1,000,000.

Chapter **10**

Reporting Cash Flows and Changes in Owners' Equity

The financial report of a business consists of three primary financial statements: the *income statement* for the period (such as, for a month, quarter, or fiscal year end), the *balance sheet* at the end of the period (like as of 12/31/21), and the *statement of cash flows* for the period (which is always reported for the same period covered as the income statement). This chapter examines the statement of cash flows, which is often the least understood of the financial statements that are required in business financial reports, but often the most important.

The history of the statement of cash flows is complex; despite repeated calls from the investment community for cash-flow information in financial reports — and after a rather inept experiment with reporting a funds flow statement — in 1987, the accounting profession finally required that a statement of cash flows be included in financial reports. The cash-flow statement has been included in financial reports for more than three decades now, and it's likely to remain a permanent fixture in business financial reporting.

The funny thing about the statement of cash flows is that unlike the balance sheet and the income statement, which represent source based financial statements (as in, specific accounts have been established in the chart of accounts to record financial transactions), the statement of cash flows is basically produced by a) pulling financial balances from the income statement and b) completing simple mathematical calculations by comparing balance sheet accounts between two period ends (that is, addition and subtraction). Simple enough, well, yes, but for some reason this financial statement is even difficult for professional accountants to produce, let alone interpret. So, I'll do my best throughout this chapter to simplify the statement of cash flows to make it less intimidating and easier to understand.

In the simplest form, the statement of cash flow reports a company's sources (such as, how a company generates cash) and uses (such as, how a company consumes cash) of cash, and that seems pretty straightforward. However, many cash-flow statements present tangled cash-flow threads that are very difficult to follow. Accountants are partly to blame for this mess, in my opinion; if I were a paranoid investor, I may think that businesses deliberately make their statements of cash flows difficult to read, which should not be the case, but then again, when you leave a bunch of accountants in a room together with too much time on their hands, this is what you end up with.

WARNING

This chapter carries a disclaimer: The following discussion doesn't adhere to the party line. It's not the standard textbook approach to understanding cash flows. I think it's better. Of course, I might be a wee bit biased.

Figuring Profit from the Balance Sheet

Suppose you're the accountant for a business that suffers a terrible fire that destroys virtually everything, including its accounting records. (In hindsight, the business should have stored back-up accounting records off-premises, but it didn't.) When escaping the burning building, the bookkeeper managed to grab one piece of smoldering paper. The bottom part of the page had already burned away, but the bookkeeper thought that this scrap of paper might be helpful, and he was right. The paper contains the business's balance sheets at the end of its two most recent years, minus the last few lines that burned away.

Figure 10-1 presents the balance sheets of the business at the end of its two most recent years (notice that this is the same balance sheet comparison provided in Chapter 8). The changes between the year-end balances are included, and the balance sheet is presented in the portrait, or vertical format, which accountants sometimes refer to as the *report form*. (The term "report form" is not a very descriptive term, in my opinion.)

Unfortunately, the 2021 income statement was lost in the fire. The president wants to know the net income for the year and asks whether you can determine profit from the information in Figure 10-1. Yes, you can (with a little help) determine profit by comparing the net worth of the business at year-end 2021 against its net worth at the end of 2020.

The net worth of a business equals its total assets minus its total liabilities. Generating net income increases the net worth of the business. The net worth of the business in this example increases $9,244,000 from year-end 2020 to year-end 2021, but this does not mean that the company generated $9,244,000 of net income. You will want to read on to clearly understand other financial transactions that impact a company's net worth.

Two Year Comparative Balance Sheet

QW Example Tech., Inc.
Balance Sheets
For the Fiscal Years Ending
12/31/20 & 12/31/21
(all numbers in thousands)

Assets	12/31/2020	12/31/2021	Change
Current Assets:			
Cash & Equivalents	$1,142	$11,698	$10,556
Accounts Receivable, Net	$6,718	$8,883	$2,165
Inventory, LCM	$4,061	$1,733	($2,328)
Prepaid Expenses	$300	$375	$75
Total Current Assets	$12,221	$22,689	$10,468
Long-Term Operating & Other Assets:			
Property, Plant, Equipment, & Machinery	$7,920	$8,670	$750
Accumulated Depreciation	($3,081)	($4,320)	($1,239)
Net Property, Plant, & Equipment	$4,839	$4,350	($489)
Other Assets:			
Intangible Assets & Goodwill, Net	$1,000	$500	($500)
Other Assets	$100	$100	$0
Total Long-Term Operating & Other Assets	$5,939	$4,950	($989)
Total Assets	$18,160	$27,639	$9,479
Liabilities			
Current Liabilities:			
Accounts Payable	$1,654	$1,929	$275
Accrued Liabilities & Other	$667	$830	$163
Current Portion of Debt	$1,000	$1,000	$0
Other Current Liabilities & Deferred Revenue	$437	$1,234	$797
Total Current Liabilities	$3,758	$4,993	$1,235
Long-term Liabilities:			
Notes Payable & Other Long-Term Debt	$7,200	$6,200	($1,000)
Total Liabilities	$10,958	$11,193	$235
Stockholders' Equity			
Capital Stock - Common	$5,000	$5,000	$0
Capital Stock - Preferred	$0	$5,000	$5,000
Retained Earnings	$2,202	$6,446	$4,244
Total Stockholder's Equity	$7,202	$16,446	$9,244
Total Liabilities & Stockholders Equity	$18,160	$27,639	$9,479

Confidential - Property of QW Example Tech., Inc.

FIGURE 10-1:
Comparative
balance
sheet of the
business.

WARNING

Calculating the net income amount from the change in the balance sheets for this business depends on two other factors, and you need to answer the following questions before you can reach a final answer regarding net income:

>> Did the shareowners invest additional capital in the business? An infusion of new ownership capital in the business increases the net worth of the business. Any amount of net worth increase from owners putting additional capital into the business is deducted from the change in net worth in determining net income for the year.

>> Did the business distribute cash dividends to its shareowners during the year? Cash dividends from profit decrease the net worth of the business. Therefore, the amount of cash dividends is added to the change in net worth in determining net income for the year.

EXAMPLE

Q. The president of the business also serves as the chair of its board of directors. After you have estimated net income for 2021 based on the balance sheet in Figure 10-1, the president tells you that he thinks $400,000 cash dividends were paid to shareowners during 2021. In addition, he reconfirms that the company raised $5,000,000 of new capital in 2021 to support future growth plans. Based on this additional information about cash dividends and the capital raise, what amount of net income did the business earn in 2021?

A. The net worth of the business increased $9,244,000 during the year, as explained earlier in this section. The $400,000 amount of cash dividends to stockholders decreased net worth because $400,000 of owners' equity is taken out of the business. The $400,000 amount of cash dividends is added to the $9,244,000 net worth increase to get $9,644,000 net income for the year. But I'm not done yet, as this figure then needs to be reduced by the amount of new capital raised during the year ($5,000,000), as this increase relates to a cash infusion in the form of an investment and not from internal earnings. So adjusting for this time, the final net income generated by the company amounts to $4,644,000. In other words, even after the $400,000 cash dividends, net worth still increased $4,244,000 (excluding the $5,000,000 of capital raised). Net income had to increase net worth $4,644,000,000 for this to happen.

---

1 After you revise your net income answer (see the example question in this section), the president tells you that he has since talked with other directors of the business and realized that he was wrong about the cash dividends. Now he's fairly certain that $750,000 cash dividends were paid to shareowners during 2021 and that the business issued additional capital stock shares for $5,000,000. Based on this additional information, what amount of net income did the business earn in 2021?

2 A business reports $500,000 net loss for the year just ended. It didn't issue or retire any capital stock shares during the year, and it didn't pay cash dividends because of its loss in the year. Did its net worth decrease $500,000 during the year? Did its cash balance decrease $500,000 during the year because of its loss?

3 Can the net worth of a business go negative? If so, explain briefly how this may happen and if it means that the business would have a negative cash balance.

Reporting the Statement of Changes in Stockholders' Equity

From information about the company's annual profit performance, dividends, and capital invested by or returned to shareowners, the accountant prepares a *statement of changes in stockholders' equity*. This statement is included in the annual financial report of the business. It is called a "statement," but it's really more of a *schedule* of changes in the owners' equity accounts. Because the primary audience of the financial report is the business's shareowners (the stockholders of a business corporation), they're very interested in the changes in their accounts.

TIP

Figure 10-2 presents the basic structure of a statement of changes in stockholders' equity for the business example introduced in Figure 10-1. The statement of changes in stockholders' equity illustrated in Figure 10-2 is actually a fairly straightforward example. A business may have a complicated capital structure, in which case this schedule includes much more detail than shown in Figure 10-2.

TIP

In Figure 10-2, total owners' equity equals $16,446,000 at the end of 2021 ($10,000,000 capital stock including common and preferred + $6,446,000 retained earnings = $16,446,000). You will notice that in 2021, the company had three primary events impact owners' equity including a) undertaking a successful capital raise of $5,000,000, b) generating $4,644,000 of net income, and c) issuing a dividend of $400,000. All these transactions are important for external investors to understand and for most businesses, not all that unusual (as in any given year, businesses tend to undertake financial transactions that impact owners' equity).

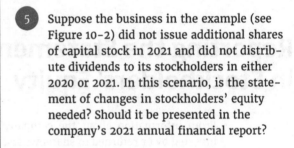

Statement of Change in Stockholders' Equity

QW Example Tech., Inc.
Statement of Changes in Stockholders' Equity
For the Fiscal Year Ending
12/31/2021

Description	Common Stock Shares	Common Stock Amount	Preferred Stock Shares	Preferred Stock Amount	Retained Earnings	Total
Balance, January 1, 2021	1,000,000	$5,000,000	0	$0	$2,202,000	$7,202,000
Sale of Preferred Stock			500,000	$5,000,000		$5,000,000
Net Income					$4,644,000	$4,644,000
Dividends					($400,000)	($400,000)
Other Accumulated Income (Expenses)					$0	$0
Balance, December 31, 2021	1,000,000	$5,000,000	500,000	$5,000,000	$6,446,000	$16,446,000

Fully Diluted Shares:
Common	1,000,000
Preferred	500,000
Stock Option Grants	125,000
Total	1,625,000

Note: The company has issued & outstanding 125,000 employee stock option grants as of 12/31/21.

Confidential - Property of QW Example Tech., Inc.

FIGURE 10-2:
Statement (schedule) of changes in stockholders' equity.

---

4 Please refer to Figure 10-1 that presents the comparative balance sheet of the business and to Figure 10-2 that presents its statement of changes in stockholders' equity. Suppose the business had paid $200,000 cash dividends (instead of $400,000) to stockholders in 2021. In this scenario, which dollar amounts in the business's comparative balance sheet would be different as the result of this one change?

5 Suppose the business in the example (see Figure 10-2) did not issue additional shares of capital stock in 2021 and did not distribute dividends to its stockholders in either 2020 or 2021. In this scenario, is the statement of changes in stockholders' equity needed? Should it be presented in the company's 2021 annual financial report?

Determining Cash Effect from Profit Generating Activities

Someone has to be in charge of managing the cash flows and cash balance of a business. In mid-size and large businesses, the person with this heavy responsibility is probably the treasurer, vice president of finance, or chief financial officer. In smaller businesses, the president may manage cash flows in addition to all his or her other functions. Simply put, if cash isn't managed carefully, the business could run out of cash, and that would be a disaster. (One major consequence is that employees wouldn't be paid on time.) Managing cash flow is a top priority of every business, and this management starts with cash flow from profit.

TIP

Borrowing money and gaining owner investments in the business increase its cash balance. But *cash flow from profit* doesn't refer to these two sources of cash. The term refers to the net cash result from the sales and expenses of the business during the period. Sales and expenses are also called *operating activities* or *profit-making activities*. In the statement of cash flows the increase or decrease of cash during the period from the business's profit-making activities is called *cash flow from operating activities*. This is a rather technical term that is not all that clear in my opinion. For brevity and clarity, I prefer the term *cash flow from profit*, which I use throughout this chapter — except where I have to use the formal term cash flow from operating activities in the statement of cash flows.

EXAMPLE

Q. Continuing the example scenario created earlier in this chapter, the president asks you to determine cash flow from profit (net income) in 2021. In other words, he wants to know how much the business's cash balance increased from making profit in the year. Based on the information in its comparative balance sheet (Figure 10-1) and its statement of changes in stockholders equity (Figure 10-2), determine the business's cash flow from profit for 2021. Did its cash balance increase $4,644,000, the same amount as net income? Or, did cash increase a different amount? Did cash decrease as the result of the company's profit-making activities? (It's possible.)

A. During the year, the business increased its cash in total by $10,556,000. The primary drivers of this increase in cash are as follows:

The business paid down its long-term debt by $1,000,000 during the year. In addition, the business issued additional capital stock shares for $5,000,000 and paid $400,000 cash dividends to shareowners during the year (see Figure 10-2). Therefore, the net cash increase from its financing activities was $3,600,000: ($1,000,000 decrease in debt + $5,000,000 issue of stock shares – $400,000 dividends = $3,600,000 cash increase).

The business spent $750,000 cash for additions and replacements to its property, plant, and equipment (see the increase in this fixed asset account in Figure 10-1). These cash outlays are classified as investing activities.

The combination of the financing and investing activities results in a net cash increase of $2,850,000 ($3,600,000 of financing activity less $750,000 of investments in property, plant, and equipment), yet the total cash increase for the company amounted to $10,556,000. So, why the difference — even if 100% of the net income generated for the year of $4,644,000 was added to the $2,850,000 (just calculated to start this paragraph), this produces an increase of cash of $7,494,000, well below the actual increase of $10,556,000.

This question asks you to determine the business's cash flow from operating activities (cash flow from profit generating activities) for the year. It does not ask you to prepare the formal statement of cash flows for the year (which I explain in the next section). Since the objective is to get cash flow from profit, I favor the method explained in Chapter 1. The four components of cash flow from profit are assembled in the following summary for the business example:

Summary of Cash Flows For the Year

Cash flow from operating activities	????
Cash flow from investing activities	($750,000)
Cash flow from financing activities	$3,600,000
Increase in cash during the year	$10,556,000

Solving for the unknown factor, cash flow from profit generating activities is $7,706,000 for the year. The $7,706,000 cash flow from profit plus the $3,600,000 net cash increase from financing activities provided the business $11,306,000 cash. It used $750,000 for capital expenditures. So, its cash balance increased $10,556,000.

TIP

This analysis method (solving for the unknown factor) is a "backdoor" approach for determining cash flow from profit generating activities. First, you determine the net change in cash caused by the investing and financing activities. Then you compare this amount to the change in cash during the year. The rest of the change in cash during the year must equal the cash flow from profit generating activities. This method is an expedient and practical way to answer the question but is not 100-percent accurate, as the calculated figure should not be assumed to be the actual net profit generated by the company. As I discuss in the next section, changes that occur in net working capital (such as, current asset and current liabilities) also generally impact the change in cash.

If all you need to know is the final amount of cash flow from profit generating activities for the period, the analysis method just demonstrated gives you the correct answer. But I should remind you that the statement of cash flows provides information about several determinants of cash flow from operating activities, as well as the final amount. These determinants of cash flow from profit are explained in the next section.

6 Figure 10-3 presents a business's comparative balance sheet that's missing the information for owners' equity. Assume that the company didn't issue additional capital stock shares during the year and didn't pay cash dividends to its shareowners during the year. Determine its net income for the year 2021.

7 From the information presented in Figure 10-3, determine the company's cash flow from profit (operating activities) for 2021.

Comparative Balance Sheet
without Owners Equity

Sample Company
Balance Sheets
For the Fiscal Years Ending
12/31/20 & 12/31/21

Assets	12/31/2020	12/31/2021	Change
Current Assets:			
Cash & Equivalents	$456,000	$425,000	($31,000)
Accounts Receivable, Net	$386,000	$340,000	($46,000)
Inventory, LCM	$518,000	$576,000	$58,000
Prepaid Expenses	$46,000	$52,000	$6,000
Total Current Assets	$1,406,000	$1,393,000	
Long-Term Operating & Other Assets:			
Property, Plant, Equipment, & Machinery	$897,000	$1,060,000	$163,000
Accumulated Depreciation	($257,000)	($318,000)	($61,000)
Net Property, Plant, & Equipment	$640,000	$742,000	
Total Assets	$2,046,000	$2,135,000	
Liabilities			
Current Liabilities:			
Accounts Payable	$246,000	$230,000	($16,000)
Accrued Liabilities & Other	$204,000	$215,000	$11,000
Current Portion of Debt	$350,000	$300,000	($50,000)
Other Current Liabilities & Deferred Revenue	$0	$0	$0
Total Current Liabilities	$800,000	$745,000	
Long-term Liabilities:			
Notes Payable & Other Long-Term Debt	$400,000	$525,000	$125,000
Total Liabilities	$1,200,000	$1,270,000	

FIGURE 10-3: Comparative balance sheet without owners' equity accounts.

8 A company's net worth decreased $425,000 during the year just ended. It didn't pay cash dividends during the year, and it didn't issue or retire capital stock during the year. Determine its profit or loss for the year.

 9 A company's net worth decreased $585,000 during the year just ended. It didn't pay cash dividends during the year, but it issued additional capital stock shares during the year for $150,000. Determine its profit or loss for the year.

Presenting the Statement of Cash Flows

TIP

A business's accountant prepares the income statement from its sales revenue and expense accounts and prepares the balance sheet from its asset, liability, and owners' equity accounts. However, there are no cash flow accounts from which to prepare the statement of cash flows.

How does an accountant prepare the statement of cash flows without ready-made accounts with cash flow balances? This is an interesting question, well, interesting to accountants I should say. I doubt that non-accountants care a fig about how the accountants do their work in preparing financial statements. Accountants use different techniques for gathering and analyzing the information needed to prepare the statement of cash flows.

Theoretically, an accountant could analyze and classify all the entries in the cash account during the year to collect the information needed to prepare the statement of cash flows. However, going back and looking at the large number of entries in the cash account during the year isn't a very practical method for pulling together the information needed to prepare the statement of cash flows.

Today, businesses use computers in their accounting systems, as you know. It's conceivable that a company could design its data-entry procedures and computer programs such that at the end of the year the computer would spit out exactly the information needed to prepare the statement of cash flows. Evidently this is not done by many businesses. In most businesses this financial statement is assembled the old-fashioned way — the accountant sits down and organizes the information pretty much by hand. The information can be put into a spreadsheet program to do the tedious computations and groupings.

Reporting cash flows

Regardless of how the accountant goes about organizing the information needed to prepare it, the statement of cash flows is fundamentally the same for every business. Figure 10-4 presents the business's statement of cash flows for 2021. The format of this financial statement is in accordance with the official standard governing reporting cash flows. Figure 10-4 presents cash flows for two years, which is common for most public companies (which may even present three years of comparative cash flow statements). Their financial reporting practices are heavily influenced by the requirements of the Securities and Exchange Commission (SEC). (Financial reports of private businesses aren't in the public domain, so it's hard to generalize about their reporting practices in this respect.)

REMEMBER

In the statement of cash flows, transactions are grouped into three types (see Figure 10-4):

>> *Operating activities:* The section reports the determinants of the cash increase or decrease attributable to the profit-making or operating activities of the business during the period, and the final amount of cash flow from operating activities for the period — a positive $7,706,000 in the example.

>> *Investing activities:* This section includes expenditures for long-term operating assets and proceeds from the disposal of these assets (if any), and the net cash increase or decrease from these activities for the period — a negative $750,000 in the example.

>> *Financing activities:* This section includes the cash flows from new borrowings or loans, the payment on company loans or outstanding debt, owners investing capital in the business, any return of capital to them, and cash dividends to owners, and the net cash increase or decrease from these activities for the period — a positive $3,600,000 in the example.

The "bottom line" of the statement is the net cash increase or decrease from the three types of activities reported in the statement — a positive $10,556,000 in the example. As you see in Figure 10-4, this $10,556,000 increase is not the bottom line in the literal sense, because the beginning cash balance is added to the net cash increase during the year to arrive at the ending balance of cash. The $10,556,000 increase in cash during the year is the bottom line in the sense that the three main types of activities caused cash to increase this amount during the year. I would also draw your attention to comparing the net increase in cash for 2021 of $10,556,000 to the paltry change in cash for 2020 of a negative $16,000. This comparison should jump out at you as how can a company generate more than $10 million in cash in one year and basically nothing the previous year. Well, the answer is relatively simple, as between generating net profits of $4.6 million and raising new capital of $5 million, it is easy to understand just how quickly cash can be generated in a business.

Financial statement readers definitely want to know whether the company's cash balance increased or decreased during the year, and they want to know the principal reasons for the increase or decrease. These are the reasons for reporting the statement of cash flows.

Statement of Cash Flows, Indirect Method

QW Example Tech., Inc.
Statement of Cash Flows
For the Fiscal Years Ending
12/31/20 & 12/31/21
(all numbers in thousands)

For the Twelve Months Ending	12/31/2020	12/31/2021
Net Profit (Loss)	$486	$4,644
Operating Activities, Cash provided (used):		
Depreciation & Amortization	$1,631	$1,739
Decrease (increase) in trade receivables	($746)	($2,165)
Decrease (increase) in inventory	$150	$2,328
Decrease (increase) in other current assets	($50)	($75)
Increase (decrease) in trade payables	$111	$275
Increase (decrease) in accrued liabilities	$59	$163
Increase (decrease) in other liabilities	$13	$797
Net Cash Flow from Operating Activities	$1,654	$7,706
Investing Activities, Cash provided (used):		
Capital Expenditures	($720)	($750)
Investments in Other Assets	$0	$0
Net Cash Flow from Investing Activities	($720)	($750)
Financing Activities, Cash provided (used):		
Dividends or Distributions Paid	$0	($400)
Sale (repurchase) of Capital Stock	$0	$5,000
Proceeds from Issuance of Debt	$0	$0
Repayments of Long-term Debt	($1,000)	($1,000)
Other Financing Activities	$50	$0
Net Cash Flow from Financing Activities	($950)	$3,600
Other Cash Flow Adjustments - Asset Impairment	$0	$0
Net Increase (decrease) in Cash & Equivalents	($16)	$10,556
Beginning Cash & Equivalents Balance	$1,158	$1,142
Ending Cash & Equivalents Balance	$1,142	$11,698

Confidential - Property of QW Example Tech., Inc.

FIGURE 10-4:
Statement of
cash flows for
the business.

WARNING

Many investment analysts and financial reporters — who should know better — take an unadvisable shortcut to calculate a number they call cash flow from profit: Depreciation and amortization expense is added to net income to produce cash flow from profit. However, it's misleading to single out depreciation and amortization expense as if it were the only factor that affects cash flow from profit. Depreciation and amortization expense should be put in the broader context of all the asset and liability changes that affect cash flow from profit. This is exactly the purpose of the first section of the statement of cash flows that reports the cash flow from operating activities (see Figure 10-4).

Depreciation and amortization expense is often the largest factor for the difference between cash flow and net income, as it is in the example shown in Figure 10-4. But changes in other assets and liabilities also affect cash flow from profit or operating activities. In some situations, these other changes overwhelm depreciation and amortization expense and are the main reasons for the difference between cash flow and profit. As you can see from Figure 10-4, the large increase in trade accounts receivable and large decrease in inventory also had a significant impact on cash generated from operating activity.

TIP

A business needs to generate sufficient cash flow from profit to pay cash dividends to shareowners. In Figure 10-4, the business generated $7,706,000 cash flow from profit or operating activities for the year, and it paid out $400,000 cash dividends to its stockholders. This comparison is one of many that the reader of the statement of cash flows can make to judge the cash flow policies and decisions of the business. Given that the business needed $750,000 for investments in fixed assets during the year, should it have paid out such a large portion of its cash flow from profit? This is just one of many important issues that creditors and shareowners should ponder in reading a statement of cash flows.

Connecting balance sheet changes with cash flows

As I have said more than once in this book, the three primary financial statements of a business are intertwined and interdependent. The numbers in the statement of cash flows are derived from the changes in the business's balance sheet accounts during the year. Changes in the balance sheet accounts drive the amounts reported in the statement of cash flows.

The lines of connection between changes in the business's balance sheet accounts during the year and the information reported in the statement of cash flows are shown in Figure 10-5. Note that the $4,244,000 net increase in retained earnings is separated between the $4,644,000 net income for the year and the $400,000 cash dividends for the year: ($4,644,000 net income – $400,000 dividends = $4,224,000 net increase in retained earnings).

Balance sheet account changes, such as those shown in Figure 10-5, are the basic building blocks for preparing a statement of cash flows. These changes in assets, liabilities, and owners' equity accounts are the amounts reported in the statement of cash flows (as shown in Figure 10-5), or the changes are used to determine the cash flow amounts (as in the case of the change in retained earnings, which is separated into its net income component and its dividends component).

Note in the cash flow from operating activities section in Figure 10-5 that net income is listed first; then several adjustments are made to net income to determine the amount of cash flow from operating activities. The assets and liabilities included in this section are those that are part and parcel of the profit-making activity of a business. For example, the accounts receivable asset is increased (debited) when sales are made on credit. The inventory asset account is decreased (credited) when recording cost of goods sold expense. The accounts payable account is increased (credited) when recording expenses that haven't been paid. And so on.

Balance Sheet Changes & Connections

QW Example Tech., Inc.
Balance Sheet
For the Fiscal Year Ending
12/31/2021
(all numbers in thousands)

Changes in Period Ending Balances from 2020 to 2021	Change	Cash Flow from Operating Activities	Amount
		Net Profit (Loss)	$4,644
		Depreciation & Amortization	$1,739
Assets		Decrease (increase) in trade receivables	($2,165)
Current Assets:		Decrease (increase) in inventory	$2,328
Cash & Equivalents	$10,556	Decrease (increase) in other current assets	($75)
Accounts Receivable, Net	$2,165	Increase (decrease) in trade payables	$275
Inventory, LCM	($2,328)	Increase (decrease) in accrued liabilities	$163
Prepaid Expenses	$75	Increase (decrease) in other liabilities	$797
Total Current Assets	$10,468	Net Cash Flow from Operating Activities	$7,706
Long-Term Operating & Other Assets:			
Property, Plant, Equipment, & Machinery	$750		
Accumulated Depreciation	($1,239)	Cash Flow from Investing Activities:	
Net Property, Plant, & Equipment	($489)	Capital Expenditures	($750)
Other Assets:			
Intangible Assets & Goodwill, Net	($500)	Cash Flow from Financing Activities:	
Other Assets	$0	Dividends or Distributions Paid	($400)
Total Long-Term Operating & Other Assets	($989)	Sale (repurchase) of Capital Stock	$5,000
Total Assets	$9,479	Repayments of Long-term Debt	($1,000)
Liabilities		Net Change in Cash During Year	$10,556
Current Liabilities:			
Accounts Payable	$275	Beginning Cash Balance	$1,142
Accrued Liabilities & Other	$163		
Current Portion of Debt	$0	Ending Cash Balance	$11,698
Other Current Liabilities & Deferred Revenue	$797		
Total Current Liabilities	$1,235		
Long-term Liabilities:			
Notes Payable & Other Long-Term Debt	($1,000)		
Total Liabilities	$235		
Stockholders' Equity			
Capital Stock - Common	$0		
Capital Stock - Preferred	$5,000		
Retained Earnings	$4,244		
Total Stockholder's Equity	$9,244		
Total Liabilities & Stockholders Equity	$9,479		

Confidential - Property of QW Example Tech., Inc.

FIGURE 10-5:
Connections
between the
balance sheet
changes and
the statement
of cash flows.

The rules for cash flow adjustments to net income are as follows:

TIP

>> An asset increase during the period decreases cash flow from profit activities

>> A liability decrease during the period decreases cash flow from profit activities

>> An asset decrease during the period increases cash flow from profit activities

>> A liability increase during the period increases cash flow from profit activities

Following the third listed rule, the $1,739,000 depreciation and amortization expense for the year is a positive adjustment, or add–back to net income — see Figure 10-4. Recording depreciation and amortization expense reduces the book value of the fixed and intangible assets being depreciated and amortized. Well, to be more precise, recording depreciation and amortization expense increases the balance of the accumulated depreciation contra account that is deducted from the original cost of fixed assets, and amortization expense reduces the net value of the original cost of the intangible asset. Recording depreciation and amortization expense does not involve a cash outlay. The cash outlay occurred when the business bought the assets being depreciated or amortized, which could be years ago.

This format of the cash flow from operating activities section shown in Figure 10-4 is referred to as the indirect method (a rather technical term). The large majority of public businesses use this method to report their cash flow from operating activities. However, the authoritative accounting standard on this matter permits an alternative method for reporting cash flow from operating activities, which is called the direct method (not that this term is any clearer than the other). Very few businesses elect this alternative format, and I do not explain it here. But you should know that a business has this option for reporting cash flow from operating activities.

 The comparative balance sheet for a business (without its owners' equity accounts) is presented in Figure 10-3. (Note that this is a different business example than the main example in the chapter.) The company didn't issue additional capital stock shares during the year and didn't pay cash dividends to its shareowners. Please refer to your answers to Questions 6 and 7. You need to know the net income of the business for the year, and you should use your answer to Question 7 as a check in answering this question. Prepare the company's statement of cash flows for 2021.

11 The beginning and ending balances of certain accounts in a company's balance sheet are as follows:

Partial Balance Sheet for Sample Company			
Description	Beginning Balance	Ending Balance	Change
Accounts Receivable, Net	$500,000	$465,000	($35,000)
Inventory, LCM	$780,000	$860,000	$80,000
Prepaid Expenses	$110,000	$105,000	($5,000)
Accounts Payable	$350,000	$325,000	($25,000)
Accrued Liabilities & Other	$165,000	$175,000	$10,000

The business records $145,000 depreciation expense for the year, and its net income is $258,000 for the year. Determine its cash flow from operating activities for the year. Present your answer in the indirect format for cash flow from operating activities in the statement of cash flows.

12 Referring to the scenario in Question 11, assume that the facts remain the same except that the business doesn't record depreciation expense in the year. Instead, it leases all its fixed assets and pays rent. The rent expense for the year is $145,000. (Note that the rent expense is the same amount as depreciation expense in Question 11.) Determine its cash flow from operating activities for the year. Present your answer for reporting cash flow from operating activities according to the indirect format (as illustrated in Figure 10-4).

Answers for Problems on Reporting Cash Flows and Changes in Owners' Equity

The following are the answers to the practice questions presented earlier in this chapter.

1 After you revise your net income answer (see the example question), the president tells you that he has since talked with other directors of the business and realized that he was wrong about the cash dividends. Now he's fairly certain that $750,000 cash dividends were paid to shareowners during 2021 and that the business issued additional capital stock shares for $5,000,000. Based on this additional information, what amount of net income did the business earn in 2021?

Net income is $4,994,000. This is calculated based on taking the increase in net worth of $9,244,000, subtracting the capital raise of $5,000,000 (which did not change) and then adding $750,000 of dividends.

2 A business reports $500,000 net loss for the year just ended. It didn't issue or retire any capital stock shares during the year, and it didn't pay cash dividends because of its loss in the year. Did its net worth decrease $500,000 during the year? Did its cash balance decrease $500,000 during the year because of its loss?

Yes, net loss decreased net worth (owners' equity) $500,000. There were no other transactions that affected owners' equity during the year (no capital stock issue and no cash dividends).

TIP

To determine whether its cash balance decreased $500,000 because of the business's loss, you need to know the changes in the assets and liabilities of the business that are affected by its sales and expenses. You can't answer this cash flow question without this information. If the business didn't record any depreciation expense in the year, and if the balances of the various assets and liabilities affected by sales and expenses remained absolutely flat during the year, then and only then would the loss decrease cash $500,000 during the year. But this is a highly unlikely scenario for the business.

3 Can the net worth of a business go negative? If so, explain briefly how this may happen and if it means that the business would have a negative cash balance.

Yes, the net worth of a business can go negative. A large enough loss in the year could wipe out all owners' equity and more, or repeated losses year after year could drive owners' equity into the negative column. Remember that a loss decreases the retained earnings balance of a business. The loss for the year or cumulative losses over time can push retained earnings into a large negative balance. The negative balance of retained earnings can become more than the balance in the owners' equity invested capital account. In this case, owners' equity would be negative.

TIP

Regarding the second question, you have to put your finger on what a negative cash balance is. Usually, a negative cash balance refers to an overdrawn bank checking account balance in which the business has written checks for more than exists in its account. In this day and age of electronic payments and banking, banks don't typically allow overdraws to happen and refuse to honor checks after the checking account balance is drawn down to zero. However, a bank may tolerate a temporary negative balance for a good customer, but a business with a negative owners' equity hardly qualifies as a good customer. Generally speaking, the cash balance of a business can't go below zero (or, it can't go negative).

4 Please refer to Figure 10-1, which presents the comparative balance sheet of the business, and to Figure 10-2, which presents its statement of changes in stockholders' equity. Suppose the business had paid $200,000 cash dividends (instead of $400,000) to stockholders in 2021. In this scenario, which dollar amounts in the business's comparative balance sheet would be different as the result of this one change?

Just one relatively small difference, like the one in this problem, causes various changes in the balance sheet. In the following answer, the amounts that are different are shaded so that you can easily identify them.

Alternative Two Year Comparative
Balance Sheets

QW Example Tech., Inc.
Balance Sheets
For the Fiscal Years Ending
12/31/20 & 12/31/21
(all numbers in thousands)

Assets	12/31/2020	12/31/2021	Change
Current Assets:			
Cash & Equivalents	$1,142	$11,898	$10,756
Accounts Receivable, Net	$6,718	$8,883	$2,165
Inventory, LCM	$4,061	$1,733	($2,328)
Prepaid Expenses	$300	$375	$75
Total Current Assets	$12,221	$22,889	$10,668
Long-Term Operating & Other Assets:			
Property, Plant, Equipment, & Machinery	$7,920	$8,670	$750
Accumulated Depreciation	($3,081)	($4,320)	($1,239)
Net Property, Plant, & Equipment	$4,839	$4,350	($489)
Other Assets:			
Intangible Assets & Goodwill, Net	$1,000	$500	($500)
Other Assets	$100	$100	$0
Total Long-Term Operating & Other Assets	$5,939	$4,950	($989)
Total Assets	$18,160	$27,839	$9,679
Liabilities			
Current Liabilities:			
Accounts Payable	$1,654	$1,929	$275
Accrued Liabilities & Other	$667	$830	$163
Current Portion of Debt	$1,000	$1,000	$0
Other Current Liabilities & Deferred Revenue	$437	$1,234	$797
Total Current Liabilities	$3,758	$4,993	$1,235
Long-term Liabilities:			
Notes Payable & Other Long-Term Debt	$7,200	$6,200	($1,000)
Total Liabilities	$10,958	$11,193	$235
Stockholders' Equity			
Capital Stock - Common	$5,000	$5,000	$0
Capital Stock - Preferred	$0	$5,000	$5,000
Retained Earnings	$2,202	$6,646	$4,444
Total Stockholder's Equity	$7,202	$16,646	$9,444
Total Liabilities & Stockholders Equity	$18,160	$27,839	$9,679

Confidential - Property of QW Example Tech., Inc.

You will note that the primary changes are reflected in the retained earnings balance (an increase of $200,000 as a result of the lower dividend amount) and cash (an increase as it is assumed the $200,000 of lower dividends are kept as cash).

(5) Suppose the business in the example (see Figure 10-2) did not issue additional shares of capital stock in 2021 and did not distribute dividends to its stockholders in 2021. In this scenario, is the statement of changes in stockholders' equity needed? Should it be presented in the company's 2021 annual financial report?

You can make a good case that there's no need for presenting the statement of changes in stockholders' equity in the company's annual report because it contains so little information in addition to what's already in the comparative balance sheet. The statement does report that net income is added to the retained earnings balance each year, but most financial statement readers should understand this point. However, for most companies that adhere to best in class accounting policies and procedures, even if limited changes are presented in the stockholders' equity during the year, the statement is generally produced and reported.

WARNING

On the other hand, one could argue that showing no dividends and no issue of capital stock either year sends a message that the company is conserving its cash and presumably has a need for the cash. On balance, therefore, most businesses would go ahead and report a statement of changes in stockholders' equity. If a reader isn't interested enough to read the statement, they can skip it. You never know; some business investors and creditors read every financial statement and every footnote, and these people expect to see the statement of changes in stockholders' equity in the financial report.

(6) Figure 10-3 presents a business's comparative balance sheet that's missing the information for owners' equity. Assume that the company didn't issue additional capital stock shares during the year and didn't pay cash dividends to its shareowners during the year. Determine its net income for the year 2021.

The company's net income for 2021 is determined as follows:

Simple Balance Sheet for Sample Company		
Balance Sheets Years Ending	**12/31/2020**	**12/31/2021**
Total Assets	$2,046,000	$2,135,000
Current Liabilities	($800,000)	($745,000)
Long-Term Debt	($400,000)	($525,000)
Owners' Equity	$846,000	$865,000
Net Profit for 2020		$19,000

The business didn't issue capital stock and didn't pay dividends during the year, so $19,000 is its net income. In other words, the increase in net worth consists entirely of the increase in retained earnings caused by net income for the year.

You may think the net income in this scenario is a rather paltry amount, and you'd be right. Generally, a business expects to earn annual net income equal to 10 to 15 percent or more of its owners' equity. Owners' equity is the investment by the owners in the business, and the owners expect to earn a return on their investment. Based on the $846,000 balance of owners' equity at the start of 2020, a 15 percent return on investment would require about $127,000 net income. The company had better improve its profit performance, or else.

(7) From the information presented in Figure 10-3, determine the company's cash flow from profit-generating activities for 2021.

Using the method of solving for the unknown factor you set up the problem as follows:

Summary of Cash Flows for the Year

Cash flow from operating activities	????
Cash flow from investing activities	($163,000)
Cash flow from financing activities	$75,000
Decrease in cash during the year	($31,000)

Solving for the unknown factor, cash flow from profit generating activities is $57,000 for the year. In Figure 10-3, you can see that the company increased cash $75,000 from its notes payable transactions during the year ($125,000 increase in long-term notes payable – $50,000 pay down on short-term notes payable = $75,000 net increase). The business didn't raise money by issuing capital stock during the year and didn't pay cash dividends during the year. So, the net cash increase from its financing activities is $75,000. It spent $163,000 on property, plant, and equipment (see Figure 10-3). Therefore, cash flow from profit must have increased cash $57,000: ($57,000 cash increase from profit – $163,000 capital expenditures + $75,000 cash from financing activities = $31,000 decrease in cash during year). Did you follow all this? I hope so. Cash flow analysis isn't for sissies, is it?

(8) A company's net worth decreased $425,000 during the year just ended. It didn't pay cash dividends during the year, and it didn't issue or retire capital stock during the year. Determine its profit or loss for the year.

All the decrease in net worth in this scenario must be due to the loss for the year. So, the bottom-line is that the business suffered a $425,000 loss for the year.

Does this loss mean that bankruptcy is just around the corner? A loss doesn't necessarily mean that the business is out of cash and unable to pay its debts on time. The business could have plenty of cash to buy time enough to correct its problems and move into the black. Then again, if this is the tenth straight year of losses, the business may be hanging on by a thread and may have to declare bankruptcy.

(9) A company's net worth decreased $585,000 during the year just ended. It didn't pay cash dividends during the year, but it issued additional capital stock shares during the year for $150,000. Determine its profit or loss for the year.

The company's net worth increased $150,000 from the issue of capital stock. If the business had experienced a break-even year (sales revenue – expenses = 0), its net worth would have increased $150,000. But, its net worth actually decreased $585,000 during the year. Therefore, the company must have reported a $735,000 loss for the year.

(10) The comparative balance sheet for a business (without its owners' equity accounts) is presented in Figure 10-3. (Note that this is a different business example than the main example in the chapter.) The company didn't issue additional capital stock shares during the year and didn't pay

cash dividends to its shareowners. Please refer to your answers to Questions 6 and 7. You need to know the net income of the business for the year, and you should use your answer to Question 7 as a check in answering this question. Prepare the company's statement of cash flows for 2021.

Statement of Cash Flows
for Sample Company

Sample Company
Statement of Cash Flows
For the Fiscal Year Ending
12/31/2021

For the Twelve Months Ending	12/31/2021
Net Profit (Loss)	$19,000
Operating Activities, Cash provided (used):	
Depreciation & Amortization	$61,000
Decrease (increase) in trade receivables	$46,000
Decrease (increase) in inventory	($58,000)
Decrease (increase) in other current assets	($6,000)
Increase (decrease) in trade payables	($16,000)
Increase (decrease) in accrued liabilities	$11,000
Increase (decrease) in other liabilities	$0
Net Cash Flow from Operating Activities	$57,000
Investing Activities, Cash provided (used):	
Capital Expenditures	($163,000)
Financing Activities, Cash provided (used):	
Proceeds from Issuance of Debt	$125,000
Repayments of Long-term Debt	($50,000)
Net Cash Flow from Financing Activities	$75,000
Decrease in Cash During Year	($31,000)
Beginning Cash Balance	$456,000
Ending Cash Balance	$425,000

(11) The beginning and ending balances of certain accounts in a company's balance sheet are as follows:

Partial Balance Sheet
for Sample Company

Description	Beginning Balance	Ending Balance	Change
Accounts Receivable, Net	$500,000	$465,000	($35,000)
Inventory, LCM	$780,000	$860,000	$80,000
Prepaid Expenses	$110,000	$105,000	($5,000)
Accounts Payable	$350,000	$325,000	($25,000)
Accrued Liabilities & Other	$165,000	$175,000	$10,000

The business records $145,000 depreciation expense for the year, and its net income is $258,000 for the year. Determine its cash flow from operating activities for the year. Present your answer in the indirect format for cash flow from operating activities in the statement of cash flows.

```
┌─────────────────────────────────────────────────────────────┐
│              Partial Statement of Cash Flows                  │
│                  for Sample Company                           │
│                                                               │
│                    Sample Company                             │
│             Partial Statement of Cash Flows                   │
│                 For the Fiscal Year Ending                    │
│                      12/31/2021                               │
│                                                               │
│        For the Twelve Months Ending          12/31/2021       │
│  Net Profit (Loss)                            $258,000        │
│  Operating Activities, Cash provided (used):                  │
│    Depreciation & Amortization                $145,000        │
│    Decrease (increase) in trade receivables    $35,000        │
│    Decrease (increase) in inventory          ($80,000)        │
│    Decrease (increase) in other current assets  $5,000        │
│    Increase (decrease) in trade payables      ($25,000)       │
│    Increase (decrease) in accrued liabilities  $10,000        │
│    Increase (decrease) in other liabilities        $0         │
│    Net Cash Flow from Operating Activities    $348,000        │
└─────────────────────────────────────────────────────────────┘
```

12 Referring to the scenario in Question 11, assume that the facts remain the same except that the business doesn't record depreciation expense in the year. Instead, it leases all its fixed assets and pays rent. The rent expense for the year is $145,000. (Note that the rent expense is the same amount as depreciation expense in Question 11.) Determine its cash flow from operating activities for the year. Present your answer for reporting cash flow from operating activities according to the indirect format (as illustrated in Figure 10-4).

```
┌─────────────────────────────────────────────────────────────┐
│              Partial Statement of Cash Flows                  │
│                  for Sample Company                           │
│                                                               │
│                    Sample Company                             │
│             Partial Statement of Cash Flows                   │
│                 For the Fiscal Year Ending                    │
│                      12/31/2021                               │
│                                                               │
│        For the Twelve Months Ending          12/31/2021       │
│  Net Profit (Loss)                            $258,000        │
│  Operating Activities, Cash provided (used):                  │
│    Depreciation & Amortization                     $0         │
│    Decrease (increase) in trade receivables    $35,000        │
│    Decrease (increase) in inventory          ($80,000)        │
│    Decrease (increase) in other current assets  $5,000        │
│    Increase (decrease) in trade payables      ($25,000)       │
│    Increase (decrease) in accrued liabilities  $10,000        │
│    Increase (decrease) in other liabilities        $0         │
│    Net Cash Flow from Operating Activities    $203,000        │
└─────────────────────────────────────────────────────────────┘
```

For added insight, compare this answer with the answer to Question 11. Cash flow from profit in this situation is $145,000 less than in the scenario for Question 11 because the business didn't record depreciation expense. Instead, it paid $145,000 rent expense during the year.

TIP

3

Managerial, Manufacturing, and Capital Accounting

IN THIS PART . . .

Learn the accountant's essential role in helping business managers do their jobs well and assist with driving increased profits.

Take a look at the manufacturing cost accounting fundamentals and concepts. I explain the importance of calculating the burden rate for indirect fixed manufacturing overhead costs that is included in product cost, and how production output (not just sales) affects profit for the period.

Gain an overview of how businesses are capitalized using debt and equity and also discover a range of basic topics that will help you become more familiar with terminology, management issues, and other critical concepts associated with raising capital and managing the sources of capital.

Chapter **11**

Analyzing Profit Behavior

Business managers need a sure analytical grip on the fundamental factors that drive profit. And because profit is an *accounting* measure, chief accountants should help the business's managers understand and analyze profit performance. The trick is not to overload managers with so much detail that they can't see the forest for the trees.

REMEMBER

Now, don't get me wrong. Detail is necessary for *management control*; managers need to keep their eyes on a thousand and one details, any one of which can spin out of control and cause serious damage to profit performance. But too much detail is the enemy of profit analysis for planning and decision-making. Management control requires gobs of detailed information. Management decision-making, in contrast, needs condensed and global information presented in a compact package that the manager can get their head around without getting sidetracked by too many details.

The profit analysis methods that I discuss in this chapter can be done on the back of an envelope. All you need for the number crunching is a basic handheld calculator. More elaborate and detail-rich profit analysis methods need to be done on computers. These sophisticated profit analysis methods have their place, but before they delve into technical profit analysis, managers should be absolutely clear on the fundamental factors that determine profit. The idea is to make sure one knows how to read the dashboard before going under the hood and taking apart the engine.

This chapter tackles three main questions:

>> How did the business make its profit?

>> How can the business improve its profit performance?

>> How would unfavorable changes affect the business's profit performance?

Note: I do not use the same fictious business that was used in Part 2, but rather I provide simpler and more compact fictious business examples to assist you with understanding the concepts more efficiently.

Mapping Profit for Managers

Figure 11-1 lays out an internal profit and loss (P&L) report for the business's managers. The revenue and expense information are for the most recent year of a business that I call Company A. (I introduce two other business examples later in this chapter and call them Company B and Company C, imagine that!) An internal profit report should serve as a profit map that shows managers how to get to their profit destination. The profit report in Figure 11-1 is very condensed; it's stripped down to bare essentials. It includes the five fundamental factors that drive profit performance. These key profit drivers are the following:

>> Sales volume, or the total number of units sold during the period

>> Sales revenue per unit (sales price)

>> Cost of goods sold expense per unit (product cost)

>> Variable operating expenses per unit

>> Fixed operating expenses for the period

The other dollar amounts in the profit report (Figure 11-1) depend on these five profit drivers. For instance, the $24,000,000 sales revenue amount equals the 120,000 units sales volume times the $200 sales revenue per unit (or sales price). And, the $25 fixed operating expenses per unit amount equals the $3,000,000 total fixed operating expenses for the period divided by the 120,000 units sales volume.

TIP

Don't confuse the internal profit report presented in Figure 11-1 with the income statement in the external financial reports a business distributes to its owners and creditors. (I discuss externally reported financial statements in Chapters 7, 8, and 10.) The internal profit report (Figure 11-1) includes sales volume and per unit values, which aren't disclosed in externally reported income statements. Also, the internal profit report separates operating expenses into *variable* and *fixed* categories, which isn't done in externally reported income statements.

Internal P&L Highlighting Profit Drivers Company A		
Income Statement For the Twelve Month Periods Ending	Amount 12/31/2020	Per Unit
Total Unit Sales	120,000	
Sales Revenue, Net	$24,000,000	$200.00
Costs of Goods Sold	($15,600,000)	($130.00)
Gross Profit	$8,400,000	$70.00
Variable Operating Expenses	($3,600,000)	($30.00)
Contribution Margin	$4,800,000	$40.00
Fixed Operating Expenses	($3,000,000)	($25.00)
Operating Profit Before Other Expenses & Taxes	$1,800,000	$15.00

FIGURE 11-1: Internal profit (P&L) report (highlighting profit drivers).

The last line in Figure 11-1 is *operating* profit, which is profit before interest and other expenses, other income, and income tax. Interest and other expenses, other income, and income tax are deducted to reach a business's final, bottom-line net income. Income tax is a very technical topic, which makes it difficult to generalize. Some businesses are pass-through entities and don't pay income tax directly. Some businesses receive special tax breaks, and some businesses operate overseas where income taxes are quite different than in the United States.

WARNING Standard terminology doesn't exist in the area of management profit reporting and analysis. Instead of *gross margin,* you may see *gross profit.* Instead of *operating profit,* you may see *operating earnings* or *earnings before interest and income tax* (EBIT). You may even see other terms than these. Despite the diversity of terminology, in the context of a profit report, the meanings of terms used are usually clear enough.

Before using the five profit factors for analyzing profit performance, a good thing to do is to "walk down the profit ladder" in the internal profit report (Figure 11-1). As you take this "walk," one of the most important factors of analyzing profit behavior is to identify for each rung of the ladder whether that rung represents fixed or variable price and cost behavior. At the top of the ladder is sales, followed by costs of goods sold, variable operating expenses, fixed operating expenses, and finally other business expenses (such as interest expense or income tax expense).

The top rung of the ladder is *sales revenue,* which equals sales price times sales volume. For profit analysis assume that sales is variable, as both the volume of a product sold or service delivered and the price charged to the customer for the product or service may change over time. You can think of sales revenue as profit before any expenses are deducted.

If the business sells products, the first expense deducted against sales revenue is *cost of goods sold,* which equals product cost (cost of goods sold expense per unit) times sales volume. (Chapter 6 explains the different accounting methods for recording this expense.)

Deducting cost of goods sold from sales revenue gives you *gross margin.* Managers keep a close watch on the *gross margin ratio,* which for Company A equals 35 percent ($70 gross margin per unit ÷ $200 sales price = 35% gross margin ratio). Even a relatively small shift in this ratio can have huge impacts on profit.

Virtually all businesses have *variable operating expenses,* which are costs that move in tandem with changes in sales revenue. One example of a variable expense is the commissions paid to salespersons, which typically are a certain percent of sales revenue. Other examples of variable expenses that fluctuate with sales are delivery expenses and bad debts from credit sales. Total variable operating expenses equal variable operating expenses per unit times sales volume. Deducting variable operating expenses from gross margin produces *contribution margin,* or profit before fixed operating expenses are considered.

Businesses commit to a certain level of *fixed operating expenses* for the year. Examples of fixed expenses are property taxes, office rent, employees on fixed salaries, insurance, depreciation, legal and accounting, and so on. In the short run, fixed costs behave like the term implies — they're relatively fixed and constant in amount regardless of whether sales are high or low. Fixed costs aren't sensitive to fluctuations in sales over the short term. Company A's $3,000,000 fixed operating expenses for the period are divided by its 120,000 units sales volume to determine the $25 fixed operating expenses per unit in Figure 11-1. However, as sales volume changes, the operating expense per unit will change. The fixed operating cost in total will not change.

The final step in the walk down the profit ladder is deducting fixed operating expenses from contribution margin. The remainder is the business's *operating profit* for the year. The business earned $1,800,000 operating profit for the year, which is 7.5 percent of its sales revenue for the year. Internal operating profit (P&L) reports often include ratios (percents) for each line item based on sales revenue, so managers can track changes in these important ratios period to period.

Q. Refer to the Company A example presented in Figure 11-1. Purely hypothetically, suppose the business could have sold either 5 percent more sales volume, or it could have sold the same sales volume at a 5 percent higher sales price. Assume other profit factors remain the same. Which change — the 5 percent higher sales volume or the 5 percent higher sales price — would have been better for operating profit?

A. Well, 5 percent additional sales volume means the business would have sold 6,000 more units than in the Figure 11-1 scenario: (120,000 units sales volume in Figure 11-1 × 5% = 6,000 additional units). Each additional unit sold would earn $40 contribution margin per unit (see Figure 11-1). So, total contribution margin would have been $240,000 higher. The business's fixed operating expenses would not have increased with such a relatively small increase in sales volume. Therefore, its operating profit would have been $240,000 higher. Would the sales price increase have been any better? You bet it would!

A 5-percent jump means sales price would have been $10 per unit higher: ($200 sales price in Figure 11-1 × 5% = $10 increase in sales price). This would have increased the contribution margin per unit from $40 (see Figure 11-1) to $50. Therefore, the business's total contribution margin would have been $6,000,000: ($50 contribution per unit × 120,000 units sales volume = $6,000,000 contribution margin). This would be an increase of $1,200,000 over the contribution margin in the Figure 11-1 scenario. There's no reason to think that fixed operating expenses would be any different at the higher sales price, so operating profit would have increased $1,200,000.

In short, the 5 percent gain in sales price would have been much better for operating profit, compared with the 5 percent step up in sales volume.

Analyzing Operating Profit

When handed an internal operating profit report like the one presented in Figure 11-1, a business manager may say "thanks for the information" and leave it at that. An internal profit report like the one in Figure 11-1 is prepared according to the standard accounting approach, which reports *totals* for sales revenue and expenses for the period and which starts with sales revenue and works its way down to bottom line profit (operating profit in the Figure 11-1 example). There's nothing wrong with this sort of report. Indeed, managers would be surprised not to get such profit reports on a regular basis.

However, the layout of the typical accounting internal profit report is cumbersome for analyzing profit behavior. As you know, business managers are busy people. They don't have a lot of time to wade through an accounting profit report to analyze the impact of a change in sales volume, or a change in sales price, or a change in any of the key factors that drive profit. An accounting profit report is not the best format for the efficient analysis of profit behavior.

Busy business managers can analyze the profit performance of their business more efficiently using compact profit models based on the five fundamental profit drivers. There are different analysis methods, each having certain advantages. Managers are best advised to be familiar with three profit analysis methods:

» Contribution margin minus fixed costs method

» Excess over breakeven method

» Minimizing fixed costs per unit method

Analysis method #1: Contribution margin minus fixed costs

The basis of this method is that fixed costs have a first claim on contribution margin, and what's left over is operating profit. This method starts with *contribution margin per unit*, which is the catalyst of profit. To make profit, the business has to have an adequate margin per unit. The second step of this method is to multiply contribution margin per unit by sales volume. Earning a margin on each unit sold doesn't help much if a business doesn't sell many units. (Which reminds me of the old joke, "A business loses a little on each sale, but makes it up on volume.")

Using this method, Company A's profit for the year is analyzed as follows:

Analysis method #1: Contribution margin minus fixed costs (see Figure 11-1 for data)

Analysis Method #1, Contribution Margin Company A	Amount
Contribution Margin per Unit	$40
Times: Annual Sales Volume, In Unit	120,000
Equals: Total Contribution Margin	$4,800,000
Less: Fixed Operating Expenses	($3,000,000)
Equals: Operating Profit (before other)	$1,800,000

Analysis method #2: Excess over breakeven

The thinking behind this method is that a business has to first recover its fixed costs by selling enough units before it starts making profit.

This profit analysis technique pivots on the *breakeven volume* of the business, which you calculate as follows for Company A (see Figure 11-1 for data):

Analysis Method #2, Breakeven Company A	Amount
Annual Fixed Operating Expenses	$3,000,000
Contribution Margin per Unit	$40
Equals: Breakeven Number of Units	75,000

Every additional unit sold over the breakeven volume brings in marginal profit (also referred to as *incremental profit*). The underlying theme of this method is that after you sell enough units to recoup your fixed operating expenses for the year, you're "home free" as it were. (Of course, you can't forget about interest expense and income tax.)

Using this method Company A's profit for the year is analyzed as follows:

Analysis method #2: Excess over breakeven (see Figure 11-1 for data)

Analysis Method #2, Marginal Profit Company A	Amount
Annual Sales Volume in Units	120,000
Less: Breakeven Sales Volume in Units	75,000
Equals: Excess Unit Sales above Breakeven	45,000
Times: Contribution Margin per Unit	$40
Equals: Operating Profit (before other)	$1,800,000

Analysis method #3: Minimizing fixed costs per unit

The thinking behind this method of analyzing profit is that a business has to spread its fixed costs over enough sales volume to drive the average fixed cost per unit below its contribution per unit. In this way, the business makes operating profit.

In this method of profit analysis, you compare the contribution margin per unit with *fixed operating expenses per unit*, which you calculate by dividing annual fixed operating expenses by the number of units sold. For Company A, its average fixed operating expenses per unit are as shown:

Analysis Method #3, Fixed Expenses per Unit Company A	Amount
Annual Fixed Operating Expenses	$3,000,000
Annual Sales Volume in Units	120,000
Equals: Fixed Operating Expenses per Unit	$25

The spread between the contribution margin per unit and the average fixed costs per unit gives the profit per unit, which is scaled up by sales volume as follows:

Analysis method #3: Minimizing fixed costs per unit (see Figure 11-1 for data)

Analysis Method #3, Minimizing Fixed Expenses
Company A

	Amount
Contribution Margin per Unit	$40
Less: Average Fixed Operating Expenses per Unit	($25)
Equals: Average Profit per Unit	$15
Times: Annual Sales Volume in Units	$120,000
Equals: Operating Profit (before other)	$1,800,000

Q. Suppose Company A had sold 125,000 units during the year, instead of the 120,000 units in the Figure 11-1 scenario. Using each of the three analysis methods just explained, determine Company A's operating profit at the 125,000 units sales volume level. Assume other profit factors remain the same.

A. The operating profit of Company A is analyzed for this scenario according to the three methods of profit analysis.

Analysis method #1: Contribution margin minus fixed costs (see Figure 11-1 for data)

Contribution margin per unit	$40
Times annual sales volume, in units	125,000
Equals total contribution margin	$5,000,000
Less fixed operating expenses	$3,000,000
Equals operating profit	$2,000,000

Analysis method #2: Excess over breakeven (see Figure 11-1 for data)

Annual sales volume for year, in units	125,000
Less annual breakeven volume, in units	75,000
Equals excess over breakeven, in units	50,000
Times contribution margin per unit	$40
Equals operating profit	$2,000,000

Analysis method #3: Minimizing fixed costs per unit (see Figure 11-1 for data)

Contribution margin per unit	$40
Less average fixed operating expenses per unit	$24
Equals average profit per unit	$16
Times annual sales volume, in units	125,000
Equals operating profit	$2,000,000

1 One of Company A's marketing managers was overheard to comment, "If we had sold 10 percent more units than we did in the year, our profit would have been 10 percent higher." Do you agree with this comment? (Figure 11-1 presents Company A's operating profit report for the year.)

2 Instead of the scenario shown in Figure 11-1 assume that Company A had a bad year. Its internal operating profit report for this alternative scenario is presented here. Using the three methods explained in this section, analyze why the business suffered a loss for the year.

Internal P&L, Alternative Performance Company A		
Income Statement For the Twelve Month Periods Ending	Amount 12/31/2020	Per Unit
Total Unit Sales	120,000	
Sales Revenue, Net	$21,000,000	$175.00
Costs of Goods Sold	($15,600,000)	($130.00)
Gross Profit	$5,400,000	$45.00
Variable Operating Expenses	($3,150,000)	($26.25)
Contribution Margin	$2,250,000	$18.75
Fixed Operating Expenses	($3,000,000)	($25.00)
Operating Profit Before Other Expenses & Taxes	($750,000)	($6.25)

3 Figure 11-2 presents profit performance information for two businesses for their most recent years. Using the three profit analysis methods explained in this section, analyze the profit performance of Company B. (You may note that both businesses in Figure 11-2 earned exactly the same amount of operating profit as the Company A business example for which I explain three profit analysis methods in this section. This similarity allows you to compare the key differences between businesses that earn the same profit.)

Internal P&L for Two Businesses
Company B & Company C

Income Statement For the Twelve Month Periods Ending	Amount 12/31/2020	Company B Per Unit	Amount 12/31/2020	Company C Per Unit
Total Unit Sales	50,000		1,500,000	
Sales Revenue, Net	$15,000,000	$300.00	$36,000,000	$24.00
Costs of Goods Sold	($7,500,000)	($150.00)	($27,000,000)	($18.00)
Gross Profit	$7,500,000	$150.00	$9,000,000	$6.00
Variable Operating Expenses	($3,750,000)	($75.00)	($4,200,000)	($2.80)
Contribution Margin	$3,750,000	$75.00	$4,800,000	$3.20
Fixed Operating Expenses	($1,950,000)	($39.00)	($3,000,000)	($2.00)
Operating Profit Before Other Expenses & Taxes	$1,800,000	$36.00	$1,800,000	$1.20

FIGURE 11-2: Internal profit (P&L) reports for two business examples.

4 Please refer to Figure 11-2. Using the three profit analysis methods explained in this section, analyze the profit performance of Company C. (You may note that both businesses in Figure 11-2 earned exactly the same amount of operating profit as the Company A business example for which I explain three profit analysis methods in this section. This similarity allows you to compare the key differences between businesses that earn the same profit.)

Analyzing Return on Capital

Evaluating the financial performance of a business includes looking at how its profit stacks up against the capital used by the business. Figure 11-1 presents Company A's profit performance for the year down to the operating profit before interest and income tax. Did the business earn enough operating profit relative to the *capital* it used to make this profit?

Suppose, purely hypothetically, that Company A used $100,000,000 capital to earn its $1,800,000 operating profit. In this situation, the business would have earned a measly 1.8 percent *rate of return* on the capital used to generate the profit:

$1,800,000 operating profit ÷ $100,000,000 capital = 1.8 percent rate of return

By almost any standard, 1.8 percent is a dismal return on capital performance.

TIP

In general terms, the amount of capital a business uses equals its total assets minus its operating liabilities that don't charge interest. The main examples of non–interest bearing operating liabilities are accounts payable from purchases on credit and accrued expenses payable. (I discuss these two liabilities in Chapters 8 and 9.) Operating liabilities typically account for 20 percent or more or a business's total assets. The remainder of its assets (total assets less total operating liabilities) is the amount of capital the business has to raise from two basic sources: borrowing money on the basis of *interest-bearing debt* instruments and raising *equity (ownership) capital* from private or public sources.

Assume the following:

EXAMPLE

Company A's sources of capital include $4,000,000 of debt and $8,000,000 of owners' equity, totaling $12,000,000 of total business capital.

Company A's return on total capital for the year is

$1,800,000 operating margin ÷ $12,000,000 capital = 15.0 percent return on capital

Company A's interest expense for the year on its debt is $240,000. Deducting interest from the $1,800,000 operating profit earned by the business gives $1,560,000 profit before income tax. The rate of return on owners' equity (before income tax) for the business is calculated as follows:

$1,560,000 profit before income tax ÷ $8,000,000 owners' equity = 19.5 percent return on equity

EXAMPLE

Q. Company A earned 15.0 percent return on capital (see the preceding calculation), but its return on equity is 19.5 percent, which is quite a bit higher. How do you explain the difference?

A. The higher rate of return on equity is due to a financial leverage gain for the year.

Debt supplies 1/3 of the company's capital ($4,000,000 ÷ $12,000,000 total capital = 1/3). The business earned 15 percent return on its debt capital ($4,000,000 debt × 15 percent rate of return = $600,000 return on debt capital). Because interest is a contractually fixed amount per period, the business had to pay only $240,000 interest for the use of its debt capital.

REMEMBER

The excess of operating profit earned on debt capital over the amount of interest is called *financial leverage gain*. Company A made $360,000 financial leverage gain for the year ($600,000 operating profit earned on debt capital – $240,000 interest paid on debt = $360,000 financial leverage gain).

The owners supply 2/3 of the total capital of the business, so their share of the $1,800,000 operating profit earned by the business equals $1,200,000 ($1,800,000 operating profit × 2/3 = $1,200,000 share of operating profit). In addition, the owners pick up the $360,000 financial leverage gain. Therefore, the profit before income tax for owners equals $1,560,000 ($1,200,000 owners' share of operating profit + $360,000 financial leverage gain = $1,560,000 profit before income tax). The $1,560,000 profit before income tax yields the 19.5 percent on equity that triggered this question.

WARNING

Financial leverage is a double-edged sword. Suppose, for example, that in the example scenario, Company A earned only $240,000 operating profit for the year. Interest is a contractual obligation that can't be avoided. In this situation, all Company A's operating profit would go to its debt holders, and profit after interest (before income tax) for its owners would be zero. The business would have had a financial leverage loss that wiped out profit for its owners. When a business suffers an operating loss, the burden of interest expense compounds the felony and makes matters just that much worse for shareowners.

 Assume the following:

Company B's sources of capital amounts to $8,000,000 of debt and $4,000,000 of owners' equity for total capital of $12,000,000.

See Figure 11-2 for Company B's operating profit performance for the year. The business paid $480,000 interest for the year. Calculate its financial leverage gain (or loss) for the year.

6   Assume the following:

Company C's sources of capital amounts to $6,000,000 of debt and $6,000,000 of owners' equity for total capital of $12,000,000.

See Figure 11-2 for Company C's profit data for the year. The business paid $360,000 interest for the year. Calculate its financial leverage gain (or loss) for the year.

---

7   Suppose that Company B's fixed operating expenses were $3,030,000 for the year. Otherwise, other profit factors are the same as in Figure 11-2. Using the sources of capital and interest expense presented in Question 5, calculate Company B's financial leverage gain (or loss) for the year.

8   Suppose that Company C's fixed operating expenses were $4,440,000 for the year. Otherwise, other profit factors are the same as in Figure 11-2. Using the sources of capital and interest expense presented in Question 6, calculate Company C's financial leverage gain (or loss) for the year.

Improving Profit Performance

Business managers are always looking for ways to improve profit performance (or they should be). One obvious way to improve profit is to sell more units — to move more units out the door without reducing sales prices. A business may have to increase its market share to sell more volume, which is no easy task as I'm sure you know. Or perhaps the business is in a growing market and doesn't have to increase its market share. In any case, the logical place to begin profit improvement analysis is an increase in sales volume.

Selling more units

Every business would like to have sold more units than they did during the most recent period. Take the publisher of this book for example, Wiley Publishing, Inc. I'm certain that the company would like to have sold more copies of Dummies books than the actual number sold during the past year. All businesses are on the lookout for how to increase sales volume. A fundamental growth strategy is to increase sales volume.

EXAMPLE

Q. According to Figure 11-1, Company A sold 120,000 units during the year. If the business had sold 5 percent more units, would its profit have been 5 percent higher? You might quickly review the answer to the example question in the section "Mapping Profit for Managers," which I extend in the following answer.

A. Before I can answer this question, I need to address an important point: When you start simulating increases in sales volume, you have to make assumptions every step of the way. In this case, the question asks you to simulate a 5 percent (6,000 additional units) increase in sales volume to see what happens in the profit example (shown in Figure 11-1). In order to answer the question, you have to assume

- That the sale price (average sales revenue per unit) stays the same at $200 per unit

- That the product cost per unit remains the same at $130 per unit

- That variable operating expenses hold the same at 15 percent of sales revenue

- That Company A's fixed operating expenses stay the same at $3,000,000 for the year

WARNING

The last assumption is an important one to understand because it means that the business has enough unused, or untapped, capacity to sell an additional 6,000 units of product. In other words, you're assuming that there was some slack in the organization such that it could have sold 6,000 more units without stepping up its fixed costs to support the higher sales volume. For relatively small changes in sales volume, that circumstance is probably true in most situations. But on the other hand, what if the question had asked you to simulate an increase in sales volume of 30, 40, or 50 percent? With a change of this extent, a business probably would have to hire more people, buy more delivery trucks, buy or rent more warehouse space, and so on — with the result that its fixed operating expenses would be higher at the higher sales volume level.

Capacity is a broad concept that refers to the capability of a business to handle sales activity. It encompasses all the resources needed to make sales, including employees, machines, manufacturing and warehouse space, retail space, and so on. Many of the costs of capacity are fixed in nature.

TIP

Keeping in mind the assumptions listed, operating profit would have increased much more than 5 percent if Company A had sold 5 percent more units during the year. The key point is this: Contribution margin would stay the same at $40 per unit because sales price, product cost, and variable operating expenses per unit all remain the same (see Figure 11-1). So, the additional 6,000 units would have generated $240,000 additional contribution margin:

$40 contribution margin per unit × 6,000 units sales volume increase =
$240,000 contribution margin increase

Assuming that fixed operating expenses remain the same at the higher sales volume, operating profit increases $240,000 from a 5 percent increase in sales volume. This is an increase of more than 13 percent:

$240,000 operating profit increase × $1,800,000 operating profit = 13.3 percent
increase in contribution margin

In the end, a sales volume increase of only 5 percent would increase operating profit more than 13 percent! How do you like that?

In the example scenario, the bigger 13.3 percent swing in profit compared with the 5 percent change in sales volume is referred to as operating leverage. At the higher sales volume, the business gets more leverage, or better utilization, from its fixed operating expenses. At a lower sales volume, the percent drop in profit would be more severe than the percent drop in sales volume. In other words, the magnifying effect of operating leverage works both ways.

REMEMBER

 Suppose Company B sold 10 percent more units during the year than it did according to Figure 11-2. Determine Company B's operating profit for this scenario. (Assume fixed operating expenses remain the same at the higher sales volume.)

 Suppose Company B sold 5 percent fewer units during the year than it did according to Figure 11-2. Determine Company B's operating profit for this scenario. (Assume fixed operating expenses remain the same at the lower sales volume.)

11 Suppose Company C sold 5 percent more units during the year than it did according to Figure 11-2. Determine Company C's operating profit for this scenario. (Assume fixed operating expenses remain the same at the higher sales volume.)

12 Suppose Company C sold 10 percent fewer units during the year than it did according to Figure 11-2. Determine Company C's operating profit for this scenario. (Assume fixed operating expenses remain the same at the lower sales volume.)

Improving margin per unit

Another way to improve operating profit is to increase the *contribution margin per unit,* without increasing sales volume. Actually, improving contribution margin per unit is very difficult in the real world of business. To increase contribution margin per unit you have to increase sales price, decrease product cost, decrease variable operating expenses per unit, or some combination of these. None of these profit factors are easy to improve in the real world of business, that's for sure.

EXAMPLE

Q. Suppose Company A (see Figure 11-1) wants to improve its contribution margin per unit as the means to increase its operating profit by $240,000. Assume its 120,000 units sales volume remains the same. Assume, further, that the business targeted its product cost as the most feasible way to improve contribution margin per unit. So, assume that sales price, variable operating expenses per unit, and fixed operating expenses remain the same. How much would product cost have to improve to achieve the $240,000 increase in operating profit?

A. The needed improvement in contribution margin per unit is calculated as follows:

$240,000 desired increase in operating profit ÷ 120,000 units sales volume = $2 improvement needed in contribution margin per unit

TIP

Therefore, the business may start by trying to reduce its product cost (cost of goods sold per unit) by $2, from $130 to $128 per unit. Now, this may not sound like such a difficult task. However, the business may already have cut its product cost to the bone. Trying to squeeze another $2 reduction out of product cost may not be realistic. If the business cannot reduce product cost $2 per unit, it has to look at sales price or variable operating expenses per unit in order to improve contribution margin. Raising sales price $2 per unit, or lowering variable operating expenses $2 per unit may be no easier than reducing product cost $2 per unit.

---

13 Suppose that Company B was able to improve (lower) its product cost per unit $10. Assume that all other profit factors for Company B remain the same as shown in Figure 11-2. Determine its operating profit for this scenario. Also, how does this change affect the company's breakeven sales volume?

 14 Suppose that Company C's product cost increases $0.50 per unit. Assume that all other profit factors for Company C remain the same as shown in Figure 11-2. Determine its operating profit for this scenario. Also, how does this change affect the company's breakeven sales volume?

In the preceding example I focus on lowering product cost as one basic way to improve contribution margin per unit. Another basic strategy for improving contribution margin per unit is to increase sales price. Sales prices are the province of marketing managers. I'd be the first to admit that I am not a marketing expert. Setting sales prices is a complex decision involving consumer psychology and many other factors. Nevertheless, in discussing the general topic of how to improve contribution margin per unit I should say a few words about raising sales price — mainly to show the powerful impact of a higher sales price.

You don't get too far in discussing raising sales price without bumping into a problem concerning variable operating expenses per unit. Most businesses have two types of variable operating expenses. Some vary with *sales volume* (the number of units sold) and some vary with sales revenue (the number of dollars from sales). For example, sales commissions depend on the dollar amount of sales. In contrast, packing and shipping costs depend on the number of units sold and delivered.

EXAMPLE

Q. Suppose that Company B (see Figure 11-2 for its profit data) could increase its sales price $15 per unit and sell the same number of units. Assume Company B's volume-driven variable operating expenses are $15 per unit sold, and its revenue-driven variable operating expenses are 20 percent of sales revenue. How would this $15 sales price increase affect its contribution margin per unit, total contribution margin, and operating profit?

A. If the business raises sales price $15, its volume-driven expenses per unit remain the same, but its revenue-driven expenses increase $3 per unit, which is 20 percent of the $15 sales price increase. So, the net gain in contribution margin per unit is only $12. Therefore,

> $12 net increase in contribution margin per unit × 50,000 units sales volume = $600,000 contribution margin increase

Company B's fixed operating expenses should remain the same (a sales price increase should have no bearing on a business's fixed operating expenses). Therefore, the increase in contribution margin would increase the business's operating profit $600,000.

Another factor to consider when considering raising sales price per unit is the impact on the number of units sold. Assuming that the company can raise the sale price $15 per unit and still sell the same number of units is probably not a realistic assumption. As we all know, when items we buy increase in price, we are likely to buy less of the item, to the extent we have some discretion on the quantity we buy. Think of how the cost of gasoline went from $4 per gallon to $6 or more per gallon in 2022. If we only drive to work and still have to work the same number of days, the gallons of gasoline we purchased did not change. But to the extent we planned on a long, driving vacation, we may decide we can no longer afford to take that vacation and the units (gallons) of gasoline we bought decreased. Estimating the decreased number of units (gallons) we can expect to sell to all of our customers has to be factored into our change in our estimated operating profit.

---

15 Suppose that Company B had to drop its sales price $10 due to competitive pressures. All other profit factors remain the same as shown in Figure 11-2. The company's volume-driven variable expenses are $15 per unit sold, and its revenue-driven variable operating expenses are 20 percent of sales revenue. Determine Company B's operating profit for this scenario. Also, how does this change affect the company's breakeven sales volume?

16 Suppose that Company C increased its sales price $1.50. Sales volume remains the same as shown in Figure 11-2. The company's revenue-driven variable operating expenses are 10 percent of sales revenue, and its volume-driven variable operating expenses are $0.40 per unit sold. Determine Company C's operating profit for this scenario. Also, how does this change affect the company's breakeven sales volume?

Answers to Problems on Analyzing Profit Behavior

The following are the answers to the practice questions presented earlier in this chapter.

(1) One of Company A's marketing managers was overheard to comment, "If we had sold 10 percent more units than we did in the year, our profit would have been 10 percent higher." Do you agree with this comment? (Figure 11-1 presents Company A's operating profit report for the year.)

Increasing sales volume 10 percent would have increased total contribution margin 10 percent, assuming that sales price, product cost, and variable operating expenses remained the same. So far this answer is relatively straightforward. The next step concerns what would happen to the company's total fixed operating expenses at the higher sales volume level.

Fixed operating costs don't increase with an increase in sales volume unless the increase in sales volume is relatively large such that the business would have to expand its capacity to accommodate the higher sales volume. Generally speaking, a business probably can take on a 10 percent sales volume increase without having to increase its capacity, at least in the short run. (Remember, an increase in capacity requires an increase in fixed operating expenses.)

Assuming the company's total fixed operating expenses would have been the same, all of the increase in total contribution margin would "fall down" to operating profit. Operating profit, therefore, would have increased more than 10 percent. The increase in total contribution margin is more than 10 percent of operating profit because operating profit is a smaller amount than the total contribution margin amount.

(2) Instead of the scenario shown in Figure 11-1 assume that Company A had a bad year. The internal operating profit report for this alternative scenario is presented below. Using the three methods explained in this section, analyze why the business suffered a loss for the year.

Refer to profit data for Company A at the end of the question in order to produce this answer.

Analysis method #1: Contribution margin minus fixed costs

Contribution margin per unit	$18.75
Times annual sales volume, in units	120,000
Equals total contribution margin	$2,250,000
Less fixed operating expenses	$3,000,000
Equals operating profit (loss)	($750,000)

Analysis method #2: Shortfall below breakeven

Annual sales volume for year, in units	120,000
Less annual breakeven volume, in units	160,000
Equals shortfall below breakeven, in units	(40,000)
Times contribution margin per unit	$18.75
Equals operating profit (loss)	($750,000)

Analysis method #3: Minimizing fixed costs per unit

Contribution margin per unit	$18.75
Less average fixed operating expenses per unit	$25.00
Equals average profit (loss) per unit	($6.25)
Times annual sales volume, in units	120,000
Equals operating profit (loss)	($750,000)

3 Figure 11-2 presents profit performance information for two businesses for their most recent years. Using the three profit analysis methods explained in this section, analyze the profit performance of Company B. (You may note that both businesses in Figure 11-2 earned exactly the same amount of operating profit as the Company A business example for which I explain three profit analysis methods in this section. This similarity allows you to compare the key differences between businesses that earn the same profit.)

Refer to profit data in Figure 11-2 in order to produce this answer.

Analysis method #1: Contribution margin minus fixed costs

Contribution margin per unit	$75
Times annual sales volume, in units	50,000
Equals total contribution margin	$3,750,000
Less fixed operating expenses	$1,950,000
Equals operating profit	$1,800,000

Analysis method #2: Excess over breakeven

Annual sales volume for year, in units	50,000
Less annual breakeven volume, in units	26,000
Equals excess over breakeven, in units	24,000
Times contribution margin per unit	$75
Equals operating profit	$1,800,000

Analysis Method #3: Minimizing fixed costs per unit

Contribution margin per unit	$75
Less average fixed operating expenses per unit	$39
Equals average profit per unit	$36
Times annual sales volume, in units	50,000
Equals operating profit	$1,800,000

4 Please refer to Figure 11-2. Using the three profit analysis methods explained in this section, analyze the profit performance of Company C. (You may note that both businesses in Figure 11-2 earned exactly the same amount of operating profit as the Company A business example for which I explain three profit analysis methods in this section. This similarity allows you to compare the key differences between businesses that earn the same profit.)

Refer to profit data in Figure 11-2 in order to produce this answer.

Analysis method #1: Contribution margin minus fixed costs

Contribution margin per unit	$3.20
Times annual sales volume, in units	1,500,000
Equals total contribution margin	$4,800,000
Less fixed operating expenses	$3,000,000
Equals operating profit	$1,800,000

Analysis method #2: Excess over breakeven

Annual sales volume for year, in units	1,500,000
Less annual breakeven volume, in units	937,500
Equals excess over breakeven, in units	562,500
Times contribution margin per unit	$3.20
Equals operating profit	$1,800,000

Analysis Method #3: Minimizing fixed costs per unit

Contribution margin per unit	$3.20
Less average fixed operating expenses per unit	$2.00
Equals average profit per unit	$1.20
Times annual sales volume, in units	1,500,000
Equals operating profit	$1,800,000

---

(5) Assume the following:

Company B's sources of capital amounts to $8,000,000 of debt and $4,000,000 of owners' equity for total capital of $12,000,000.

See Figure 11-2 for Company B's operating profit data for the year. The business recorded $480,000 interest for the year. Calculate its financial leverage gain (or loss) for the year.

In this case, debt holders provide two-thirds of the company's total capital ($8 million of the total $12 million capital). Thus, two-thirds of its $1,800,000 operating profit can be attributed to the debt capital used by the business, which equals $1,200,000 (2/3 × $1,800,000 = $1,200,000).

The company paid only $480,000 interest on its debt capital.

> $1,200,000 operating profit attributable to debt capital – $480,000 interest on debt capital = $720,000 financial leverage gain

TIP Here's another way to calculate financial leverage gain: The company earned 15 percent return on capital ($1,800,000 operating profit ÷ $12,000,000 total capital = 15.0 percent return on capital). The company paid a 6 percent interest rate on its debt capital ($480,000 interest ÷ $8,000,000 debt = 6 percent interest rate). There's a favorable 9 percent spread between the two rates. Therefore,

> 9 percent favorable spread between return on capital and interest rate × $8,000,000 debt = $720,000 financial leverage gain.

(6) Assume the following:

Company C's sources of capital amounts to $6,000,000 of debt and $6,000,000 of owners' equity for total capital of $12,000,000.

See Figure 11-2 for Company C's profit data for the year. The business recorded $360,000 interest for the year. Calculate its financial leverage gain (or loss) for the year.

In this case, debt holders provide one-half of the company's total capital ($6 million of the total $12 million capital). Thus, one-half of its $1,800,000 operating profit can be attributed to the debt capital used by the business, which equals $900,000 ($1/2 × $1,800,000 = $900,000).

The company paid only $360,000 interest on its debt capital. So,

$900,000 operating profit attributable to debt capital − $360,000 interest on debt capital = $540,000 financial leverage gain

(7) Suppose that Company B's fixed operating expenses were $3,030,000 for the year. Otherwise, other profit factors are the same as in Figure 11-2. Using the sources of capital and interest expense presented in Question 5, calculate Company B's financial leverage gain (or loss) for the year.

For the year, Company B earned $3,750,000 total contribution margin (see Figure 11-2). If its fixed operating expenses were $3,030,000, its operating profit for the year would be only $720,000. Based on this operating profit, Company B's return on capital would be only 6 percent ($720,000 ÷ $12,000,000 total capital = 6 percent return on capital).

In this case, debt supplies two-thirds of total capital. Therefore, two-thirds of its $720,000 operating profit can be attributed to its debt capital, which is $480,000 ($720,000 operating profit × 2/3 = $480,000). The company paid $480,000 interest in the year. Thus, its financial leverage gain is zero.

TIP

Here's another way to calculate the company's financial leverage gain/loss for the year: The business earned only 6 percent return on capital, and its interest rate on debt is 6 percent ($480,000 interest ÷ $8,000,000 debt = 6 percent). So, there's no spread, or difference, between its 6 percent return on capital and its interest rate. Therefore, there's no financial leverage gain (or loss).

(8) Suppose that Company C's fixed operating expenses were $4,440,000 for the year. Otherwise, other profit factors are the same as in Figure 11-2. Using the sources of capital and interest expense presented in Question 6, calculate Company C's financial leverage gain (or loss) for the year.

For the year, Company C earned $4,800,000 total contribution margin (see Figure 11-2). If its fixed operating expenses were $4,440,000, its operating profit for the year would be only $360,000. Based on this operating profit, the company's return on capital would be a very low 3 percent ($360,000 ÷ $12,000,000 total capital = 3 percent return on capital).

In this case, debt supplies one half of total capital. Therefore, one half of its $360,000 operating profit can be attributed to its debt capital, which is $180,000 ($360,000 operating profit × 1/2 = $180,000). The company paid $360,000 interest in the year. Thus, it has a financial leverage loss equal to $180,000.

TIP

Here's another way to calculate the company's financial leverage loss for the year: The business earned only 3 percent return on capital, and its interest rate on debt is 6 percent ($360,000 interest ÷ $6,000,000 debt = 6.0 percent). So, there's an unfavorable 3 percent spread between return on capital and interest rate. The company's financial leverage loss for the year is $180,000 (3 percent unfavorable spread × $6,000,000 debt = $180,000 financial leverage loss for the year).

9️⃣ Suppose Company B sold 10 percent more units during the year than it did according to Figure 11-2. Determine Company B's operating profit for this scenario. (Assume fixed operating expenses remain the same at the higher sales volume.)

For Company B, selling 10 percent additional units equals 5,000 additional units sold. Given that its contribution margin per unit is $75, the increase in its total contribution margin is

> 5,000 additional units × $75 contribution margin per unit = $375,000 increase in total contribution margin

Because fixed operating expenses don't increase at the higher sales volume level, the gain in total contribution margin increases operating profit $375,000. The 10 percent increase in sales volume increases operating profit 20.8 percent ($375,000 gain in operating profit ÷ $1,800,000 operating profit at the original sales volume level = 20.8 percent increase).

REMEMBER

The percent gain in operating profit is much larger than the percent increase in sales volume. This magnification effect is called operating leverage.

🔟 Suppose Company B sold 5 percent fewer units during the year than it did according to Figure 11-2. Determine Company B's operating profit for this scenario. (Assume fixed operating expenses remain the same at the lower sales volume.)

For Company B, selling 5 percent less units equals 2,500 fewer units sold. Given that its contribution margin per unit is $75, the decrease in its total contribution margin is

> 2,500 fewer units × $75 contribution margin per unit = $187,500 decrease in total contribution margin

Because fixed operating expenses don't decrease at the lower sales volume level, the drop in total contribution margin decreases operating profit $187,500. The 5 percent decrease in sales volume decreases operating profit 10.4 percent ($187,500 fall in operating profit ÷ $1,800,000 operating profit at the original sales volume level = 10.4 percent decrease).

REMEMBER

The percent drop in operating profit is much larger than the percent decrease in sales volume. This magnification effect is called operating leverage.

1️⃣1️⃣ Suppose Company C sold 5 percent more units during the year than it did according to Figure 11-2. Determine Company C's operating profit for this scenario. (Assume fixed operating expenses remain the same at the higher sales volume.)

For Company C, selling 5 percent additional units equals 75,000 additional units sold. Given that its contribution margin per unit is $3.20, the increase in its total contribution margin is

> 75,000 additional units × $3.20 contribution margin per unit = $240,000 increase in total contribution margin

Because fixed operating expenses don't increase at the higher sales volume level, the gain in total contribution margin increases operating profit $240,000. The 5 percent increase in sales volume increases operating profit 13.3 percent ($240,000 gain in operating profit ÷ $1,800,000 operating profit at the original sales volume level = 13.3 percent increase).

(12) Suppose Company C sold 10 percent fewer units during the year than it did according to Figure 11–2. Determine Company C's operating profit for this scenario. (Assume fixed operating expenses remain the same at the lower sales volume.)

For Company C, selling 10 percent less units equals 150,000 fewer units sold. Given that its contribution margin per unit is $3.20, the decrease in its total contribution margin is

> 150,000 fewer units × $3.20 contribution margin per unit = $480,000 decrease in total contribution margin

Because fixed operating expenses don't decrease at the lower sales volume level, the drop in total contribution margin decreases operating profit $480,000. The 10 percent decrease in sales volume decreases operating profit 26.7 percent ($480,000 fall in operating profit ÷ $1,800,000 operating profit at the original sales volume level = 26.7 percent decrease).

(13) Suppose that Company B was able to improve (lower) its product cost per unit $10. Assume that all other profit factors for Company B remain the same as shown in Figure 11–2. Determine its operating profit for this scenario. Also, how does this change affect the company's breakeven sales volume?

The complete schedule of changes in this scenario is as follows:

	Before	After	Change
Sales price	$300.00	$300.00	
Product cost	$150.00	$140.00	($10.00)
Variable operating expenses:			
Volume driven expenses	$15.00	$15.00	
Revenue driven expenses at 20%	$60.00	$60.00	
Contribution margin per unit	$75.00	$85.00	+ $10.00
Times Sales volume, in units	50,000	50,000	
Equals Total contribution margin	$3,750,000	$4,250,000	+ $500,000
Less Fixed Operating expenses	$1,950,000	$1,950,000	
Operating profit	$1,800,000	$2,300,000	+ $500,000

As the schedule shows, operating profit increases $500,000, which is a 27.8 percent increase from a 6.7 percent change in product cost ($10 decrease ÷ $150 = 6.7 percent decrease).

TIP

The company's breakeven decreases because contribution margin per unit is higher than it was before the product cost change:

> $1,950,000 fixed operating expenses ÷ $85 contribution margin per unit = 22,941 units breakeven volume

At the $75 contribution margin per unit, Company B's breakeven volume is 26,000 units sales volume.

(14) Suppose that Company C's product cost increases $0.50 per unit. Assume that all other profit factors for Company C remain the same as shown in Figure 11–2. Determine its operating profit for this scenario. Also, how does this change affect the company's breakeven sales volume?

The impact on contribution margin and operating profit from the seemingly small increase in product cost is shown in the following comparative schedule:

	Before	After	Change
Sales price	$24.00	$24.00	
Less Product cost	$18.00	$18.50	$0.50
Less Variable operating expenses:	$2.80	$2.80	
Equals Contribution margin per unit	$3.20	$2.70	($0.50)
Times Sales volume, in units	1,500,000	1,500,000	
Equals Total contribution margin	$4,800,000	$4,050,000	($750,000)
Less Fixed Operating expenses	$3,000,000	$3,000,000	
Equals Operating profit	$1,800,000	$1,050,000	($750,000)

So, operating profit drops $750,000, from $1,800,000 to only $1,050,000, which is a 41.7 percent decrease! The reason is the relatively large drop in contribution margin per unit, from $3.20 to only $2.70, which is a 15.6 percent decline. The importance of maintaining the contribution margin per unit cannot be overstated.

TIP

If Company C's product cost increases $0.50 per unit, the company's breakeven also increases because contribution margin per unit is lower than it was before the product cost change:

$3,000,000 fixed operating expenses ÷ $2.70 contribution margin per unit = 1,111,111 units breakeven volume

At the $3.20 contribution margin per unit, the breakeven volume is 937,500 units sales volume.

15) Suppose that Company B had to drop its sales price $10 due to competitive pressures. All other profit factors remain the same as shown in Figure 11-2. The company's volume–driven variable expenses are $15 per unit sold, and its revenue–driven variable operating expenses are 20 percent of sales revenue. Determine Company B's operating profit for this scenario. Also, how does this change affect the company's breakeven sales volume?

The circumstances cause the company's operating profit to decrease $400,000, as shown in the following schedule:

	Before	After	Change
Sales price	$300	$290	($10)
Less Product cost	$150	$150	
Less Variable operating expenses:			
Volume driven expenses	$15	$15	
Revenue driven expenses at 20%	$60	$58	($2)
Equals Contribution margin per unit	$75	$67	($8)
Times Sales volume, in units	50,000	50,000	
Equals Total contribution margin	$3,750,000	$3,350,000	($400,000)
Less Fixed Operating expenses	$1,950,000	$1,950,000	
Equals Operating profit	$1,800,000	$1,400,000	($400,000)

TIP

If Company B's sales price drops $10, the company's breakeven increases because contribution margin per unit is lower than it was before the sales price change:

$1,950,000 fixed operating expenses ÷ $67 contribution margin per unit = 29,104 units breakeven volume

At the $75 contribution margin per unit, the breakeven volume is 26,000 units sales volume.

(16) Suppose that Company C increased its sales price $1.50. Sales volume remains the same as shown in Figure 11-2. The company's revenue-driven variable operating expenses are 10 percent of sales revenue, and its volume-driven variable operating expenses are $0.40 per unit sold. Determine Company C's operating profit for this scenario. Also, how does this change affect the company's breakeven sales volume?

The circumstances cause the company's operating profit to increase $2,025,000, as shown in the following schedule:

	Before	After	Change
Sales price	$24.00	$25.50	+ $1.50
Product cost	$18.00	$18.00	
Variable operating expenses:			
Volume driven expenses	$0.40	$0.40	
Revenue driven expenses at 10%	$2.40	$2.55	+ $0.15
Contribution margin per unit	$3.20	$4.55	+ $1.35
Times Sales volume, in units	1,500,000	1,500,000	
Equals Total contribution margin	$4,800,000	$6,825,000	+ $2,025,000
Less Fixed Operating expenses	$3,000,000	$3,000,000	
Operating profit	$1,800,000	$3,825,000	+ $2,025,000

TIP

If Company C's sales price increases $1.50, the company's breakeven decreases because contribution margin per unit is higher than it was before the sales price change:

$3,000,000 fixed operating expenses ÷ $4.55 contribution margin per unit = 659,341 units breakeven volume

At the $3.20 contribution margin per unit, the breakeven volume is 937,500 units sales volume.

Chapter **12**

Tackling Managerial Cost Accounting

I n addition to normal accounting matters, businesses that manufacture products face additional accounting challenges that retailers, service providers, tech companies, and distributors generally do not. That is, unique accounting concepts apply to manufacturers that produce products and those warrant a deeper dive. During the past 30 years, the global trends toward outsourcing manufacturing to cheaper foreign destinations such as China has helped transition the United States into a service and tech-based economy, so you may wonder why an entire chapter has been dedicated to this subject. The answer is simple: The United States still produces a wide range of products, from automobiles to jet engines to agricultural products to you name it, that requires proper accounting policies and procedures be applied to ensure complete, accurate, reliable, and timely financial information is produced.

Throughout this chapter, I use the term *managerial cost accounting*, which is a relatively broad term that encompasses manufacturing cost accounting or quite often referred to as just cost accounting (the primary focus of this chapter). In this day and age, if you have a strong understanding of managerial cost accounting, you will definitely have a leg up on your competition. So, with this said, let's dive into the wonderful world of managerial cost accounting with a specific focus placed on manufacturing companies.

Throughout this chapter, I use the term manufacture in the broadest sense: Automobile makers assemble cars, beer companies brew beer, automobile gasoline companies refine oil, DuPont makes products through chemical synthesis, and so on. Retailers (also called merchandisers) and distributors, on the other hand, buy products in a condition ready for resale to the end consumer. For example, Walmart and Target don't manufacture the products they sell. Other companies manufacture the products that retailers sell — although the manufacturers may put private labels on the goods (which is common practice for grocery stores and other retailers).

This chapter focuses mainly on the accounting procedures used to accumulate the basic types of manufacturing costs and how these pools of costs are used to determine product cost. A manufacturer must know product cost in order to determine its cost of goods sold expense for the period and the cost of its inventory. The chapter explores certain unavoidable problems accountants face in determining product cost. To complete the picture, the chapter also explains how unscrupulous managers can set production output to manipulate profit for the period.

Minding Manufacturing Costs

A manufacturing business, first of all, must separate between its manufacturing costs and non-manufacturing costs. Manufacturing costs are the costs of production that are included in the determination of product cost. Non-manufacturing costs include marketing expenses and the general and administration expenses of the business, which are referred to as period costs. I explain the importance of the distinction between product and period costs later in the section. First, I explain the basic types of manufacturing costs that go into the calculation of product cost.

Manufacturing costs consist of four basic types:

>> *Raw materials:* What a manufacturer buys from other companies to use in the production of its own products. For example, General Motors buys tires from Goodyear (or other tire manufacturers) that become part of GM's cars.

>> *Direct labor:* Compensation of employees who work on the production line.

>> *Variable overhead:* Indirect production costs that increase or decrease as the quantity produced increases or decreases. An example is the cost of electricity that runs a company's production machines: If the business increases or decreases the use of those machines, the electricity cost increases or decreases accordingly.

>> *Fixed overhead:* Indirect production costs that do not increase or decrease as the quantity produced increases or decreases. These fixed costs remain the same over a fairly broad range of production output levels. Fixed manufacturing costs include the following:

   • Salaries for certain production employees who don't work directly on the production line, such as a vice president, safety inspectors, security guards, accountants, and shipping and receiving workers

   • Depreciation of production buildings, equipment, and other manufacturing fixed assets

   • Occupancy costs, such as building insurance, property taxes, and heating and lighting charges

Figure 12-1 presents an internal operating profit report of a manufacturer I call Company X; the report includes information about the company's manufacturing activity and costs for the year. A business may manufacture hundreds or thousands of products, but in the example, Company

X manufactures and sells only one product. The example is realistic yet avoids the clutter of too much detail. Figure 12-1 is a good platform to illustrate the fundamental accounting problems and methods of all manufacturers.

The information in the operating profit report and manufacturing activity summary in Figure 12-1 is confidential and for management eyes only. The company's competitors would love to know this information. For instance, if Company X enjoys a significant product cost advantage over its competitors, it definitely wouldn't want its cost data to get into their hands.

FIGURE 12-1:
Internal
operating
profit
report for
Company X (a
manufacturer).

Operating Profit Report for Year
Company X - a Manufacturer

Operating Profit Report For the Twelve Months Ending	Per Unit	Amount 12/31/2021
Sales Volume in Units		110,000
Sales Revenue	$1,400.00	$154,000,000
Costs of Goods Sold	($760.00)	($83,600,000)
Gross Profit (Margin)	$640.00	$70,400,000
Variable Operating Expenses	($300.00)	($33,000,000)
Contribution Margin	$340.00	$37,400,000
Fixed Operating Expenses		($21,450,000)
Operating Profit Before Other Expenses & Taxes		$15,950,000

Manufacturing Activity For the Twelve Months Ending	Per Unit	Amount 12/31/2021
Annual Production Capacity, in Units		150,000
Annual Output, in Units		120,000
Summary of Costs:		
Raw Material	$215.00	$25,800,000
Direct Labor & Burden	$125.00	$15,000,000
Variable Manufacturing Costs Overhead	$70.00	$8,400,000
Subtotal - Variable Costs	$410.00	$49,200,000
Fixed Manufacturing Costs Overhead	$350.00	$42,000,000
Total Manufacturing Costs, Fixed & Variable	$760.00	$91,200,000

Product costs

Unlike a retailer that purchases products in a condition ready for resale, a manufacturer begins by purchasing the raw materials needed in the production process. Then the manufacturer pays workers to operate the production machines and equipment and to move the products into warehouses after they're produced. All this work is done in a sprawling plant that has many indirect overhead costs. All these different production costs are funneled into product cost.

When manufacturing costs are incurred, they're recorded in an inventory account — in particular, the work-in-process inventory account. I explain the use of this account in the section

"Taking a Short Tour of Manufacturing Entries" later in this chapter. Product costs are later recorded in the cost of goods sold expense when the products are sold.

Pay special attention to the $760.00 product cost and its components in Figure 12-1. In particular, note that the $760.00 is the sum of four separate cost components — raw materials, direct labor, variable manufacturing overhead, and fixed manufacturing overhead. All four of the component costs must be correct to end up with the correct product cost.

TIP

Product costs are said to be capitalized because they're viewed as a capital investment, which is an investment in an asset. Product costs aren't recorded to expense until the products are eventually sold, at which time the appropriate amount of cost is removed from the asset account and recorded in the cost of goods sold expense account.

Period costs

Costs that are charged to expense when they're recorded are known as period costs. Marketing costs (such as advertising, sales personnel, or delivery of products to customers) are period costs. These selling costs are recorded as expenses in the period the costs are incurred. General and administrative costs (such as legal and accounting, compensation of officers, or information and data processing) are also period costs. Period costs do not pass through an inventory account.

Separating period and product costs

The distinction between period and product costs is very important. What if a business deliberately recorded some of its manufacturing costs as period costs instead of as product costs? Suppose that for the year just ended, a business recorded $2,400,000 of its manufacturing costs as marketing expenses. The $2,400,000 should have gone into inventory and stayed there until the products were sold. To the extent the products haven't yet been sold at the end of the year, the business has understated the cost of its ending inventory and overstated its marketing expense for the year. Why would a business do this? To minimize its current year's taxable income, that's why.

Evidently many businesses were in the habit of misclassifying some costs as period costs (immediate expense deduction) instead of product costs. In response the IRS has laid down rules regarding what has to be treated as a manufacturing cost. Nevertheless, many gray areas still exist in which drawing a line between manufacturing and non-manufacturing costs is not entirely clear-cut. In any case, a business should be consistent from period to period regarding how it classifies its manufacturing and non-manufacturing costs.

Wages paid to production line workers are a clear example of a manufacturing cost. Salaries paid to salespeople are a marketing cost and are not part of product cost. Depreciation on production equipment is a manufacturing cost, but depreciation on the warehouse in which products are stored after being manufactured is a period cost. Similarly, moving raw materials and partially completed goods through production process is a manufacturing cost, but transporting the finished products from the warehouse to customers is a period cost. Essentially, product cost stops at the end of the production line — but every cost up to that point is a manufacturing cost.

A manufacturer must design and implement a cost accounting system to determine the cost of every product it manufactures and sells. The business must track the costs of all raw materials that go into the production process and the costs of all production line labor (which may involve hundreds or thousands of operations). Furthermore, the business has to determine and allocate many indirect manufacturing costs to the various products it manufactures. (Although in the example shown in Figure 12-1, the business produces only one product.) Tracking and allocating these costs is a very challenging task, to say the least.

Q. How is the $83,600,000 cost of goods sold expense of Company X determined (see Figure 12-1)?

A. In the example (see Figure 12-1), the business recorded $91,200,000 total manufacturing costs to produce 120,000 units during the year. Therefore, the product cost per unit is $760.00: ($91,200,000 total manufacturing costs ÷ 120,000 units production output = $760.00 product cost per unit). Based on this product cost per unit its cost of goods sold expense for the year is determined as follows:

$760.00 product cost × 110,000 units sales volume = $83,600,000 cost of goods sold expense

TIP

The business uses the LIFO (last-in, first-out) method: All 110,000 units sold are charged out at the $760.00 product cost per unit, which is for the latest batch of units produced. (The example treats the entire year as one production period for determining product cost, whereas in actual practice, product cost is determined monthly or quarterly.) In other words, none of the cost from its beginning inventory is charged to cost of goods sold expense. The cost of beginning inventory most likely is carried on the books at a lower product cost. If the company were to use the FIFO (first-in, first-out) method, some of the units sold during the year would have been charged out based on the product cost in beginning inventory. (I discuss the LIFO and FIFO methods in Chapter 6.)

---

1 The company's total manufacturing costs for the year are $91,200,000 (see Figure 12-1), but only $83,600,000 is charged to cost of goods expense. What happened to the other $7,600,000 ($91,200,000 manufacturing costs for year – $83,600,000 cost of goods sold expense for year = $7,600,000)?

2 As you can see in Figure 12-1, Company X recorded $42,000,000 fixed manufacturing overhead costs in the year. Suppose, instead, that its fixed manufacturing overhead costs were $45,600,000 for the year, which is an increase of $3,600,000. Would the company's operating profit have been $3,600,000 lower? (Assume that variable manufacturing costs per unit and operating expenses remain the same.)

3　Suppose that Company X uses the FIFO method instead of the LIFO method shown in Figure 12-1. The company starts the year with 25,000 units in beginning inventory at a cost of $735 per unit according to the FIFO method. During the year, it manufactures 120,000 units and sells 110,000 units (see Figure 12-1). Determine Company X's cost of goods sold expense for the year and its cost of ending inventory using the FIFO method.

4　Company X produced 120,000 units and sold 110,000 units during the year (see Figure 12-1). Therefore, the company increased its inventory 10,000 units. Does this increase seem reasonable? Or is the company's production output compared with its sales volume out of kilter?

Taking a Short Tour of Manufacturing Entries

When a retailer or wholesaler purchases products, it debits (increases) an inventory account. The cost of the products is held in an inventory account until the products are sold. At that time, the appropriate amount of cost is removed from the inventory account and charged to cost of goods sold expense. The amount of the cost removed from inventory is determined by which cost of goods sold expense method is used, such as FIFO or LIFO. (I discuss inventory valuation and associated cost of goods sold expense methods in Chapter 6.)

In contrast to retailers and wholesalers, a manufacturer has to make more entries to get to its cost of goods sold expense. The following illustrative entries are based on the Company X manufacturing example, whose operating profit report and manufacturing activity summary appear in Figure 12-1.

Company X purchased $27,325,000 of raw materials during the year, which is slightly more than the cost of materials released into the manufacturing process. Therefore, its inventory of raw materials increased during the year. The business has a good credit rating and purchased all its raw materials on credit. Its raw materials purchases during the year are shown in the following entry:

	Debit	Credit
Raw Materials Inventory	$27,325,000	
Accounts Payable		$27,325,000

When raw materials are released from inventory storage into the manufacturing process, the cost is charged to a particular job order or to a particular department. The transfers of raw materials to production during the year are shown in the following entry:

	Debit	Credit
Work-in-Process Inventory	$25,800,000	
Raw Materials Inventory		$25,800,000

REMEMBER The work-in-process inventory account is a special account used by manufacturers to accumulate the costs of products working their way through the production process. These products aren't ready for sale until the production process is completed. At that time, an entry is made to move the product cost out of this temporary holding account into the finished goods inventory account — see the entry that follows (the second to last entry).

The company's direct labor costs consist of all elements of compensation earned by its production line workers. The largest part of the compensation of production line workers is paid in cash, but payroll taxes are withheld, and fringe benefit costs are also recorded in various liability accounts. In the following entries I use accrued payables as the generic title for various liability accounts used to record costs incurred by the business that are paid at a later time. The direct labor costs of the business during the period are shown in the following entry:

	Debit	Credit
Work-in-Process Inventory	$15,000,000	
Cash		$xx,xxx,xxx
Payroll Taxes Payable		$x,xxx,xxx
Accrued Payables		$x,xxx,xxx

The bulk of the company's variable manufacturing overhead costs are paid in cash over the course of the year, but two liability accounts — accounts payable and accrued payables — are involved in recording many of these costs. The business's variable manufacturing overhead costs for the year are shown in the following entry:

	Debit	Credit
Work-in-Process Inventory	$8,400,000	
Cash		$x,xxx,xxx
Accounts Payable		$xxx,xxx
Accrued Payables		$xxx,xxx

Most of the company's indirect fixed manufacturing overhead costs for period are paid in cash during the year, but many involve liability accounts for unpaid manufacturing costs — such as the two shown in the following entry. Also, depreciation is a major fixed overhead cost, so the accumulated depreciation account is credited in recording the depreciation cost component of fixed manufacturing overhead costs. The business's fixed manufacturing overhead costs for the year are shown in the following entry:

	Debit	Credit
Work-in-Process Inventory	$42,000,000	
Cash		$xx,xxx,xxx
Accumulated Depreciation		$x,xxx,xxx
Accounts Payable		$x,xxx,xxx
Accrued Payables		$x,xxx,xxx

When the manufacturing process is completed, products are moved from the production line to the warehouse. The appropriate amount of product cost is removed from the work-in-process inventory account (decreased) and entered in the finished goods inventory account (increased). The transfers of products from the production line to the finished goods warehouse during the year are shown in the following entry, which you will notice is represented in dollars or value and not units. It should be noted that most companies maintain what is call a perpetual inventory system that tracks both values and units or volume of products:

	Debit	Credit
Finished Goods Inventory	$91,200,000	
Work-in-Process Inventory		$91,200,000

Note: In these entries, I assume that there was no work-in-process at the beginning or end of the year. This assumption would be accurate, for instance, if the business shut down its manufacturing activity for a week or two at the end of the year to permit a fumigation of the plant or to give workers a holiday vacation. The entries would be more involved if there was work-in-process inventory at the start and end of the year.

Recording the cost of products sold during the year is shown in the following entry:

	Debit	Credit
Cost of Goods Sold Expense	$83,600,000	
Finished Goods Inventory		$83,600,000

Figure 12-2 presents the internal operating profit reports of two sample manufacturing companies, Company Y and Company Z. Their operating profit reports include information about their manufacturing activity for the year.

Operating Profit Report For the Twelve Months Ending	Company Y Per Unit	Amount 12/31/2021	Company Z Per Unit	Amount 12/31/2021
Sales Volume in Units		500,000		2,000,000
Sales Revenue	$85.00	$42,500,000	$25.00	$50,000,000
Costs of Goods Sold	($56.00)	($28,000,000)	($18.45)	($36,900,000)
Gross Profit (Margin)	$29.00	$14,500,000	$6.55	$13,100,000
Variable Operating Expenses	($12.50)	($6,250,000)	($2.50)	($5,000,000)
Contribution Margin	$16.50	$8,250,000	$4.05	$8,100,000
Fixed Operating Expenses		($5,000,000)		($7,500,000)
Operating Profit Before Other Expenses & Taxes		$3,250,000		$600,000

Operating Profit Report for Year
Company Y & Z - both Manufacturers

Manufacturing Activity For the Twelve Months Ending	Per Unit	Amount 12/31/2021	Per Unit	Amount 12/31/2021
Annual Production Capacity, in Units		800,000		2,500,000
Annual Output, in Units		500,000		2,500,000
Summary of Costs:				
Raw Material	$15.00	$7,500,000	$7.50	$18,750,000
Direct Labor & Burden	$20.00	$10,000,000	$2.75	$6,875,000
Variable Manufacturing Costs Overhead	$5.00	$2,500,000	$5.00	$12,500,000
Subtotal - Variable Costs	$40.00	$20,000,000	$15.25	$38,125,000
Fixed Manufacturing Costs Overhead	$16.00	$8,000,000	$3.20	$8,000,000
Total Manufacturing Costs, Fixed & Variable	$56.00	$28,000,000	$18.45	$46,125,000

FIGURE 12-2: Internal operating profit reports of Company Y and Company Z (two manufacturers).

5 Refer to Figure 12-2 for the operating profit report and manufacturing activity summary of Company Y for the year. Assume that the business had no work-in-process inventory at the start or end of the year. The business purchased $7,800,000 raw materials on credit during the year. Make the basic manufacturing entries for the business by following the series of entries explained in this section.

6 Refer to Figure 12-2 for the operating profit report and manufacturing activity summary of Company Z for the year. Assume that the business had no work-in-process inventory at the start or end of the year. The business purchased $19,500,000 in raw materials on credit during the year. Make the basic manufacturing entries for the business by following the series of entries explained in this section.

7 Assume that Company Y uses the LIFO method to charge out raw materials to production. In this question, assume that supply shortages of raw materials meant that Company Y couldn't purchase all the raw materials it needed for production during the year, and it had to draw down its raw materials inventory. Fortunately, it had an adequate beginning inventory of raw materials to cover the gap in purchases during the year. In this situation, would the cost of raw materials issued to production be different than the $7,500,000 shown in Figure 12-2?

8 Determine what Company Z's operating profit would have been if it had sold 2,100,000 units during the year, which is 100,000 more units than in the example shown in Figure 12-2. Assume that production output had remained the same at 2,500,000 units (the company's production output capacity).

Calculating Product Cost: Basic Methods and Problems

Product cost, $760.00 in the example shown in Figure 12-1, consists of two quite different types of manufacturing costs: variable costs (including raw materials, direct labor, and variable overhead) and fixed overhead costs. Variable manufacturing costs remain the same per unit (except at very low or very high levels of production). Thus, the total of variable manufacturing costs moves up and down with increases and decreases in production output (the number of units produced). In contrast, fixed costs are rigid; these costs remain the same and unchanged over a broad range of production output levels. Many of these fixed costs would have to be paid even if the business had to shut down its manufacturing for several months.

Refer to Figure 12-1 for Company X's manufacturing cost information. Its $760.00 product cost consists of $410.00 total variable costs per unit manufactured and $350.00 fixed manufacturing overhead cost per unit.

If Company X had manufactured ten more units than it did during the year, its total variable manufacturing costs would have been $4,100 higher (10 additional units × $410 per unit = $4,100). The actual number of units produced drives total variable manufacturing costs, so even one more unit would have caused the variable costs to increase $410. But the company's total fixed manufacturing overhead costs would have been the same if it had produced ten more units, or 10,000 more units for that matter. Variable manufacturing costs are bought on a per unit basis, as it were, whereas fixed manufacturing costs are bought in bulk at fixed prices for the whole period.

Total manufacturing costs for the year are calculated as follows:

(Variable manufacturing costs per unit × Number of units produced) + Fixed manufacturing overhead costs = Total manufacturing costs

Connecting fixed manufacturing overhead costs and production capacity

Fixed manufacturing overhead costs present certain problems in determining product cost and operating profit (that is, profit before interest and income tax expenses).

Why in the world would a manufacturer in its right mind commit to fixed manufacturing overhead costs? For example, according to Figure 12-1, Company X has $42,000,000 of these cost commitments hanging over its head for the year whether it produces 15,000 or 150,000 units or any number in between. The answer is that fixed manufacturing costs are needed to provide production capacity — the people and physical resources needed to manufacture products — for the year. When the business has the production plant and people in place for the year, its fixed manufacturing costs aren't easily scaled down. The business is stuck with these costs over the short run.

The fixed manufacturing overhead cost component of product cost is called the burden rate. The burden rate of Company X for the year is computed as follows (see Figure 12-1 for data):

$42,000,000 total fixed manufacturing overhead costs for year ÷ 120,000 units production output for period = $350 burden rate

Now, here's a very important twist on the example: Suppose Company X manufactured only 110,000 units during the period — equal to the quantity sold during the year. Its variable manufacturing costs equal $410.00 per unit. This per unit cost remains the same at the lower production output level. In contrast, the burden rate would be $381.82 per unit at the lower production output level ($42,000,000 total fixed manufacturing overhead costs ÷ 110,000 units production output = $381.82 burden rate). The higher burden rate causes product cost to be $31.82 higher.

Q. What would be the operating profit of Company X if its production output for the year had been 110,000 units (equal to the number of units sold) instead of the 120,000 units production output level assumed in Figure 12-1?

A. Its operating profit at the 110,000 units production output level is $12,450,000, as shown in the following schedule:

Operating Profit Report For the Twelve Months Ending	Per Unit	Amount 12/31/2021
Sales Volume in Units		110,000
Sales Revenue	$1,400.00	$154,000,000
Costs of Goods Sold	($791.82)	($87,100,000)
Gross Profit (Margin)	$608.18	$66,900,000
Variable Operating Expenses	($300.00)	($33,000,000)
Contribution Margin	$308.18	$33,900,000
Fixed Operating Expenses		($21,450,000)
Operating Profit Before Other Expenses & Taxes		$12,450,000

Manufacturing Activity For the Twelve Months Ending	Per Unit	Amount 12/31/2021
Annual Production Capacity, in Units		150,000
Annual Output, in Units		110,000
Summary of Costs:		
Raw Material	$215.00	$23,650,000
Direct Labor & Burden	$125.00	$13,750,000
Variable Manufacturing Costs Overhead	$70.00	$7,700,000
Subtotal - Variable Costs	$410.00	$45,100,000
Fixed Manufacturing Costs Overhead	$381.82	$42,000,000
Total Manufacturing Costs, Fixed & Variable	$791.82	$87,100,000

Operating Profit Report for Year, Alternative Company X - a Manufacturer

A key point of this example is that Company X's product cost is $31.82 higher simply because it produces fewer units. The same total amount of fixed manufacturing overhead costs is spread over fewer units of production output. The higher product cost means that cost of goods sold expense is higher, and therefore, operating profit is lower. At the 120,000 units production output level, operating profit is $15,950,000 (see Figure 12-1). But at the 110,000 units production output level, operating profit dips to $12,450,000, which is a decrease of $3,500,000. This decrease gets the attention of business managers, that's for sure!

9 Company Y was on track to sell 550,000 units in the year, but late in the year, a major customer canceled a large order for 50,000 units. The business reduced its production output to 500,000 units, as you see in Figure 12-2. Determine the operating profit Company Y would have earned if it had manufactured and sold 550,000 units in the year.

10 Assume that Company Z's production output for the year is 2,000,000 units (instead of 2,500,000 units as in Figure 12-2). In other words, assume that the business manufactures the same number of units that it sells in the year. Assume all other manufacturing and operating factors are the same. Determine the company's operating profit for the year.

Boosting profit by boosting production

In the Company X example shown in Figure 12-1, cost of goods sold expense for the year benefits from the fact that the business produced 10,000 more units than it sold during the year. These 10,000 units absorbed $3,500,000 of its total fixed manufacturing overhead costs for the year. The cost of goods sold expense escaped $3,500,000 in fixed manufacturing overhead costs because the company produced 10,000 more units than it sold during the year, thus pushing down the burden rate (see the preceding section for an explanation of burden rate). Until the units are sold, the $3,500,000 stays in the inventory asset account (along with variable manufacturing costs, of course).

The distribution of the company's fixed manufacturing overhead costs for the year is summarized as follows:

Total Fixed Manufacturing Overhead Costs for Year (Divided by 120,000 unit production output gives $350.00 burden rate) $42,000,000

→ $38,500,000   Cost of Goods Sold Expense (110,000 units sold during the year times $350.00 burden rate)

↘ $3,500,000   Finished Goods Inventory (10,000 units increase in inventory times $350.00 burden rate)

Of its $42,000,000 total fixed manufacturing overhead costs for the year, only $38,500,000 ended up in cost of goods sold expense for the year ($350 burden rate × 110,000 units sold = $38,500,000). The other $3,500,000 ended up in the inventory asset account ($350 burden rate × 10,000 units inventory increase = $3,500,000). I'm not suggesting any funny business, but Company X did help its operating profit to the tune of $3,500,000 by producing 10,000 more units than it sold. Suppose that the business had produced only 110,000 units, equal to its sales volume for the year. All its fixed manufacturing overhead costs would have gone into cost of goods sold expense, and operating profit would have been that much lower.

WARNING

It's entirely possible that Company X's 120,000 units production output level is justified as a way to have more units on hand for sales growth next year. But the production output decision can get out of hand. A manufacturer may deliberately pump up production output not to prepare for sales growth next year but to pump up profit this year, and that's massaging the numbers, pure and simple. It falls short of cooking the books, which involves fraudulent accounting practices that are untruthful or fictitious. Nevertheless, pushing up production output for the sole purpose of boosting profit definitely smacks of accounting manipulation.

You need to judge whether an inventory increase is justified. Be aware that an unjustified increase may be evidence of profit manipulation or just good old-fashioned management bungling. The day of reckoning will come when the products are sold and the cost of inventory becomes cost of goods sold expense.

TIP

In Figure 12-1, Company X's production capacity for the year is 150,000 units. It produced only 120,000 units during the year, which is 30,000 units fewer than it could have. In other words, it operated at 80 percent of production capacity (120,000 units output ÷ 150,000 units capacity = 80 percent utilization), which is 20 percent idle capacity. (The average U.S. manufacturing plant normally operates at 80 to 85 percent of its production capacity.) Production capacity, to remind you, is the maximum output that a business could achieve during a period of time given its machinery, equipment, buildings and land, labor force, and other necessary manufacturing factors. Idle capacity is the difference between actual output during the period and production capacity. The term "idle" may be too derogatory. Most manufacturers, as a matter of fact, do not run at full production capacity. So, some idle (unused) production capacity is normal.

Running at 80 percent of production capacity, this business's burden rate for the year is $350 per unit ($42,000,000 total fixed manufacturing overhead costs ÷ 120,000 units output = $350 burden rate). As I explain earlier in this section, the burden rate would be higher if the company produced only 110,000 units during the year. The burden rate, in other words, is sensitive to the number of units produced. This connection can lead to all kinds of mischief.

Suppose that Company X manufactures 150,000 units during the year and increases its inventory 40,000 units, which may be a legitimate move if the business is anticipating a big jump in sales next year. On the other hand, an inventory increase of 40,000 units in a year in which only 110,000 units were sold may be the result of a serious overproduction mistake, and the larger inventory may not be needed next year.

EXAMPLE

Q. In the Figure 12-1 scenario Company X manufactured 120,000 units during the year, which caused its inventory to increase 10,000 units. Suppose, instead, that the company had manufactured 150,000 units during the year, which is its production capacity. Assume sales and other factors were the same in this alternative scenario as shown in Figure 12-1 – only production output is different. What would be its operating profit for the year if it had produced 150,000 units?

A. The following operating profit report and summary of manufacturing activity for Company X shows what would have happened at the 150,000 units production output level. Remember that sales volume doesn't change in this scenario; only production output changes. Comparative data is presented for the 120,000 units production output level in the original scenario (see Figure 12-1).

Operating Profit Report for Year,
Production Boost Company X - a Manufacturer

Operating Profit Report For the Twelve Months Ending	Per Unit	Amount 12/31/2021
Sales Volume in Units		110,000
Sales Revenue	$1,400.00	$154,000,000
Costs of Goods Sold	($690.00)	($75,900,000)
Gross Profit (Margin)	$710.00	$78,100,000
Variable Operating Expenses	($300.00)	($33,000,000)
Contribution Margin	$410.00	$45,100,000
Fixed Operating Expenses		($21,450,000)
Operating Profit Before Other Expenses & Taxes		$23,650,000

Manufacturing Activity For the Twelve Months Ending	Per Unit	Amount 12/31/2021
Annual Production Capacity, in Units		150,000
Annual Output, in Units		150,000
Summary of Costs:		
Raw Material	$215.00	$32,250,000
Direct Labor & Burden	$125.00	$18,750,000
Variable Manufacturing Costs Overhead	$70.00	$10,500,000
Subtotal - Variable Costs	$410.00	$61,500,000
Fixed Manufacturing Costs Overhead	$280.00	$42,000,000
Total Manufacturing Costs, Fixed & Variable	$690.00	$103,500,000

Check out the $23,650,000 operating profit when production output is 150,000 units, compared with the $15,950,000 operating profit when production output is 120,000 units — a $7,700,000 difference even though sales volume, sales prices, and operating expenses all remain the same. Whoa! What's going on here? The simple answer is that the cost of goods sold expense is $7,700,000 less than before. How can cost of goods sold expense be less if the business sells 110,000 units in both scenarios, and variable manufacturing costs are $410.00 per unit in both cases?

The culprit is the burden rate component of product cost. In Figure 12-1, total fixed manufacturing costs are spread over 120,000 units of output, giving a $350 burden rate per unit. In the Operating Profit Report shown here in the Answer portion, total fixed manufacturing costs are spread over 150,000 units output, giving the much lower $280 burden rate, or $70 per unit less. The $70 lower burden rate multiplied by the 110,000 units sold reduces cost of goods sold expense $7,700,000 and increases operating profit the same amount.

WARNING

If the business had produced 150,000 units (its production capacity), its inventory would have increased 40,000 units. This increase is quite large compared to the annual sales of 110,000 for the year just ended. Who was responsible for the decision to go full blast and produce up to production capacity? Do the managers really expect sales to jump up enough next year to justify the much larger inventory level? If their guess is right, they look brilliant. But if the output level was a mistake and sales don't go up next year . . . they have you-know-what to pay, even though profit looks good this year. An experienced business manager knows to be on guard when inventory takes such a big jump.

---

11. Toward the end of the year, the president of Company Y looks at the preliminary numbers for operating profit and doesn't like what he sees. He's "promised" the board of directors that operating profit for the year will come in at $4,850,000. In fact, his bonus depends on hitting that operating profit target. There is still time before the end of the year to crank up production output for the year. Therefore, he orders that production output be stepped up. The president asks you to determine what the production output level for the year would have to be in order to report $4,850,000 operating profit for the year. Of course, you have ethical qualms about doing this, but you need the job. So, you reluctantly decide to do the calculation. Determine the production output level that would yield $4,850,000 operating profit for the year.

12. Refer to your answer to Question 10, in which Company Z produces only 2,000,000 units during the year. In the scenario shown in Figure 12-2, the business manufactures 2,500,000 units, which is its maximum production output for the year. Do you think that Company Z cranked up production output to 2,500,000 units mainly to boost its operating profit for the year?

Calculating Product Cost in Unusual Situations

REMEMBER

The basic calculation model for product cost is

Total manufacturing costs for period ÷ Total units produced during period = Product cost per unit

Total manufacturing costs for the period includes direct manufacturing costs that can be clearly identified with a particular product and indirect manufacturing costs that are allocated to the product.

This product cost calculation method is appropriate in most situations. However, it has to be modified in two extreme situations:

>> When manufacturing costs are grossly excessive or wasteful due to inefficient production operations

>> When production output is significantly less than normal capacity utilization

EXAMPLE

Suppose that Company X had to throw away $1,200,000 of raw materials during the year because they weren't stored properly and ended up being unusable in the production process. The manager in charge of the warehouse received a stiff reprimand.

Q. In Figure 12-1, which shows Company X's operating profit performance and summary of manufacturing activity for the year, it is assumed that there were no wasteful manufacturing costs. In this question, assume, instead, that the business had to throw away $1,200,000 of unusable raw materials. How should the $1,200,000 cost of raw materials that were thrown out be presented in the operating profit report and summary of manufacturing activity?

A. The $1,200,000 cost of raw materials that were wasted and not used in production should not be included in the calculation of product cost. The $1,200,000 cost of wasted raw materials should be treated as a period cost, which means that it's recorded as an expense in the period. The operating profit report and summary of manufacturing activity for the year in this scenario is as follows:

Operating Profit Report for Year,
Unique Scenario Company X - a Manufacturer

Operating Profit Report For the Twelve Months Ending	Per Unit	Amount 12/31/2021
Sales Volume in Units		110,000
Sales Revenue	$1,400.00	$154,000,000
Costs of Goods Sold	($750.00)	($82,500,000)
Gross Profit (Margin)	$650.00	$71,500,000
Variable Operating Expenses	($300.00)	($33,000,000)
Contribution Margin	$350.00	$38,500,000
Fixed Operating Expenses		($21,450,000)
Inventory Write-off Raw Materials		($1,200,000)
Operating Profit Before Other Expenses & Taxes		$15,850,000

Manufacturing Activity For the Twelve Months Ending	Per Unit	Amount 12/31/2021
Annual Production Capacity, in Units		150,000
Annual Output, in Units		120,000
Summary of Costs:		
Raw Material	$205.00	$24,600,000
Direct Labor & Burden	$125.00	$15,000,000
Variable Manufacturing Costs Overhead	$70.00	$8,400,000
Subtotal - Variable Costs	$400.00	$48,000,000
Fixed Manufacturing Costs Overhead	$350.00	$42,000,000
Total Manufacturing Costs, Fixed & Variable	$750.00	$90,000,000

TIP The $1,200,000 wasted raw materials cost is recorded as an expense in the year, as you see in the operating profit report. As a result, the cost of raw materials is reduced the same amount in the manufacturing activity summary for the year with the result that product cost drops to $750 per unit.

13 The president of Company X is puzzled by the operating profit report and summary of manufacturing activity for the year, in which $1,200,000 raw materials cost was wasted and charged to expense in the year. He expected that operating profit would be $1,200,000 lower (as compared to the scenario in Figure 12-1, in which there's no wasted raw materials cost). Operating profit in the wasted raw materials scenario is only $100,000 lower than in Figure 12-1. Explain to the president why operating profit is only $100,000 lower.

14 After Company Y's operating profit report and summary of manufacturing activity for the year has been prepared (see Figure 12-2), you, the chief accountant, learn that $1,000,000 of raw materials were thrown away during the year because the items had spoiled and couldn't be used in the manufacturing process. The company's president knows about this loss and insists that no change be made in the operating profit report and summary of manufacturing activity. Do you go along with the president, or do you argue for changing the operating profit report and summary of manufacturing activity?

As I mention earlier, unused production capacity is called idle capacity. One argument is that the cost of idle capacity should be charged off as a period cost (that is, charged directly to expense in the year and not included in product cost). Generally, the cost of idle capacity is calculated as follows:

Percent of idle capacity × Fixed manufacturing overhead costs = Cost of idle capacity

Refer to Company Y's operating profit report and summary of manufacturing activity for the year (Figure 12-2). Its annual production capacity is 800,000 units, but it produced only 500,000 units during the year. The company's idle capacity is 37.5 percent. In this case, the **EXAMPLE** idle capacity cost is calculated as follows:

37.5 percent idle capacity × $8,000,000 fixed manufacturing overhead costs = $3,000,000 cost of idle capacity

Q. How would Company Y's operating profit report and summary of manufacturing activity be revised if the cost of idle capacity is treated as a period cost in the year?

A. The $3,000,000 cost of idle capacity is taken out of fixed manufacturing overhead costs and moved up to the operating profit report as an expense in the period. The revised operating profit report and summary of manufacturing activity, which you may find somewhat surprising, is as follows:

Operating Profit Report for Year,
Unique Scenario Company Y - a Manufacturer

Operating Profit Report For the Twelve Months Ending	Per Unit	Amount 12/31/2021
Sales Volume in Units		500,000
Sales Revenue	$85.00	$42,500,000
Costs of Goods Sold	($50.00)	($25,000,000)
Gross Profit (Margin)	$35.00	$17,500,000
Variable Operating Expenses	($12.50)	($6,250,000)
Contribution Margin	$22.50	$11,250,000
Fixed Operating Expenses		($5,000,000)
Idle Capacity Expense		($3,000,000)
Operating Profit Before Other Expenses & Taxes		$3,250,000

Manufacturing Activity For the Twelve Months Ending	Per Unit	Amount 12/31/2021
Annual Production Capacity, in Units		800,000
Annual Output, in Units		500,000
Summary of Costs:		
Raw Material	$15.00	$7,500,000
Direct Labor & Burden	$20.00	$10,000,000
Variable Manufacturing Costs Overhead	$5.00	$2,500,000
Subtotal - Variable Costs	$40.00	$20,000,000
Fixed Manufacturing Costs Overhead	$10.00	$5,000,000
Total Manufacturing Costs, Fixed & Variable	$50.00	$25,000,000

ALLOCATING INDIRECT COSTS IS AS SIMPLE AS ABC . . . NOT!

Most manufacturers make many different products. Just think of General Motors or Ford and the number of different car and truck models they assemble. If a separate production plant (building, machinery, equipment, tools, workforce, and so on) were dedicated to making only one product, all manufacturing costs would be direct costs to that one particular product. But in reality, it's the other way around: One production plant is used to make many different products. The result is that many production costs are indirect to the different products manufactured by the business.

Indirect manufacturing costs are allocated among the products produced during the period. Therefore, product cost includes both direct and indirect manufacturing costs. Coming up with a completely satisfactory allocation method is difficult and ends up being somewhat arbitrary — but it must be done in order to determine product cost.

Accountants have developed many methods and schemes for allocating indirect overhead costs, many of which are based on some common denominator of production activity, such as direct labor hours. A different method that has gotten a lot of press is called activity-based costing (ABC).

With the ABC method, you identify each necessary, supporting activity in the production process and collect costs into a separate pool for each identified activity. Then you develop a measure for each activity — for example, the measure for the engineering department may be hours, and the measure for the maintenance department may be square feet. You use the activity measures as cost drivers to allocate cost to products. So, if Product A needs 200 hours of the engineering department's time, and Product B is a simple product that needs only 20 hours of engineering, you allocate ten times as much of the engineering cost to Product A.

The idea is that the engineering department doesn't come cheap; including the cost of their slide rules and pocket protectors as well as their salaries and benefits, the total cost per hour for those engineers could be $150 to $200, or more. The logic of the ABC cost-allocation method is that the engineering cost per hour should be allocated on the basis of the number of hours (the driver) required by each product. In similar fashion, suppose the cost of the maintenance department is $20 per square foot per year. If Product C uses twice as much floor space as Product D, you charge it with twice as much maintenance cost.

The ABC method has received much praise for being better than traditional allocation methods, especially for management decision-making. However, you should keep in mind that it requires rather arbitrary definitions of cost drivers, and having too many different cost drivers, each with its own pool of costs, isn't practical.

Managers should be aware of which cost allocation methods are being used by their companies and should challenge a method if they think that it's misleading and should be replaced with a better (though still somewhat arbitrary) method. I don't mean to put too fine a point on this, but to a large extent, cost allocation boils down to a "my arbitrary method is better than your arbitrary method" argument.

TIP

Note that changing the handling of the cost of idle capacity produces no difference in the company's operating profit for the year. Is this surprising, or what? In this example, the company produces the same number of units it sells during the year. Thus, there's no "inventory effect." One-hundred percent of its manufacturing costs for the year end up in expense regardless of the way in which the idle capacity is handled. In Figure 12-2, the entire $8,000,000 fixed manufacturing overhead costs ends up in cost of goods sold expense. In this example scenario, $3,000,000 of the fixed costs end up in a period expense account (cost of idle capacity), and the other $5,000,000 ends up in cost of goods sold expense.

---

15 Assume that Company Z manufactures 2,100,000 units during the year (instead of the 2,500,000 units production output shown in Figure 12-2). Determine its operating profit for the year. Assume that the cost of idle capacity is treated as a period cost and isn't embedded in product cost.

---

16 Refer to Company X's operating profit report and summary of manufacturing activity presented in Figure 12-1. Note that its annual production capacity is 150,000 units, but the business manufactured only 120,000 units during the year. Therefore, it had 20 percent idle capacity (30,000 units not produced ÷ 150,000 units production capacity = 20 percent idle capacity). However, the cost of idle capacity isn't treated as a separate period cost; all the company's fixed manufacturing overhead costs are included in calculating its product cost.

Suppose that the business treats the cost of idle capacity as a period cost. Prepare a revised operating profit report and summary of manufacturing activity for the business.

Answers to Problems on Manufacturing Cost Accounting

The following are the answers to the practice questions presented earlier in this chapter.

(1) The company's total manufacturing costs for the year are $91,200,000 (see Figure 12-1), but only $83,600,000 is charged to cost of goods expense. What happened to the other $7,600,000 ($91,200,000 manufacturing costs for year − $83,600,000 cost of goods sold expense for year = $7,600,000)?

The business produced 120,000 units, which is 10,000 more units than the 110,000 units it sold during the year. Therefore, 1/12 (10,000 ÷ 120,000) of its total manufacturing costs is allocated to the increase in inventory, and 11/12 is allocated to cost of goods sold during the year:

11/12 × $91,200,000 total manufacturing costs = $83,600,000 allocated to cost of goods sold expense

1/12 × $91,200,000 total manufacturing costs = $7,600,000 allocated to inventory

You can also answer this question by using product cost and number of units sold during the year:

$760 product cost × 110,000 units sold during year = $83,600,000 cost allocated to cost of goods sold expense

$760 product cost × 10,000 units increase in inventory = $7,600,000 cost allocated to inventory

(2) As you can see in Figure 12-1, Company X recorded $42,000,000 fixed manufacturing overhead costs in the year. Suppose, instead, that its fixed manufacturing overhead costs were $45,600,000 for the year, which is an increase of $3,600,000. Would the company's operating profit have been $3,600,000 lower? (Assume that variable manufacturing costs per unit and operating expenses remain the same.)

No, operating profit would not be $3,600,000 lower. The following schedule shows that operating profit would be $3,300,000 lower. The higher fixed manufacturing overhead costs drive up the product cost per unit, from $760 to $790, or $30 per unit. However, the business sold only 110,000 units, so the $30 higher product cost per unit increases cost of goods sold expense only $3,300,000 ($30 increase in product cost × 110,000 units sales volume = $3,300,000). Therefore, operating profit decreases $3,300,000.

Operating Profit Report For Year	Company X	
	Per Unit	Totals
Sales volume, in Units		110,000
Sales Revenue	$1,400.00	$154,000,000
Cost of Goods Sold Expense (see below)	(790.00)	(86,900,000)
Gross Margin	$610.00	$67,100,000
Variable Operating Expenses	(300.00)	(33,000,000)
Contribution Margin	$310.00	$34,100,000
Fixed Operating Expenses		(21,450,000)
Operating Profit		$12,650,000

Manufacturing Activity Summary For Year	Per Unit	Totals
Annual Production Capacity, in Units		150,000
Actual Output, in Units		120,000
Raw Materials	$215.00	$25,800,000
Direct Labor	125.00	15,000,000
Variable Manufacturing Overhead Costs	70.00	8,400,000
Total Variable Manufacturing Costs	$410.00	$49,200,000
Fixed Manufacturing Overhead Costs	380.00	45,600,000
Product Cost and Total Manufacturing Costs	$790.00	$94,800,000

TIP

The operating profit decrease still leaves $300,000 of the total $3,600,000 fixed manufacturing overhead costs increase to explain. The 10,000 units increase in inventory absorbs this additional amount of fixed manufacturing overhead costs; including fixed manufacturing overhead costs in product cost is called absorption costing. Some accountants argue that product cost should include only variable manufacturing costs and not include any fixed manufacturing overhead costs. This practice is called direct costing, or variable costing, and it isn't generally accepted. Generally accepted accounting principles (GAAP) require that fixed manufacturing overhead cost must be included in product cost.

(3) Suppose that Company X uses the FIFO method instead of the LIFO method shown in Figure 12-1. The company starts the year with 25,000 units in beginning inventory at a cost of $735 per unit according to the FIFO method. During the year, it manufactures 120,000 units and sells 110,000 units (see Figure 12-1). Determine Company X's cost of goods sold expense for the year and its cost of ending inventory using the FIFO method.

The business started the year with 25,000 units at $735 per unit for a total cost of $18,375,000, which constitutes one batch of inventory. The business manufactured 120,000 units during the year at $760 per unit for a total cost of $91,200,000, which constitutes the second batch of inventory.

Under FIFO, the cost of goods sold expense is determined as follows:

25,000 units × $735 = $18,375,000
85,000 units × $760 = $64,600,000
110,000 units sold = $82,975,000

Under FIFO, the ending inventory consists of one layer:

35,000 units $\times$ \$760 = \$26,600,000

(4) Company X produced 120,000 units and sold 110,000 units during the year (see Figure 12–1). Therefore, the company increased its inventory 10,000 units. Does this increase seem reasonable? Or is the company's production output compared with its sales volume out of kilter?

It's hard to say for sure whether the increased inventory is reasonable. The key factor is the forecasted sales volume for next year. If the business predicts moderate sales volume growth next year, then increasing inventory 10,000 units seems reasonable. On the other hand, if the sales forecast is flat for next year, why did the business produce more than it sold during the year just ended? The inventory increase could have been a mistake, or taking a more cynical view, perhaps the business deliberately manufactured more units than it sold in order to boost operating profit for the year.

(5) Refer to Figure 12–2 for the operating profit report and manufacturing activity summary of Company Y for the year. Assume that the business had no work-in-process inventory at the start or end of the year. The business purchased \$7,800,000 raw materials on credit during the year. Make the basic manufacturing entries for the business by following the series of entries explained in the section "Taking a Short Tour of Manufacturing Entries."

Note: The following manufacturing entries include short explanations.

	Debit	Credit
Raw Materials Inventory	\$7,800,000	
Accounts Payable		\$7,800,000

Purchase on credit of raw materials needed in the production process.

	Debit	Credit
Work-in-Process Inventory	\$7,500,000	
Raw Materials Inventory		\$7,500,000

Transfer of raw materials to the production process.

	Debit	Credit
Work-in-Process Inventory	\$10,000,000	
Cash		\$x,xxx,xxx
Payroll Taxes Payable		\$x,xxx,xxx
Accrued Payables		\$x,xxx,xxx

To record direct labor costs for period.

	Debit	Credit
Work-in-Process Inventory	\$2,500,000	
Cash		\$x,xxx,xxx
Accounts Payable		\$xxx,xxx
Accrued Payables		\$xxx,xxx

To record indirect variable manufacturing overhead costs for period.

	Debit	Credit
Work-in-Process Inventory	$8,000,000	
Cash		$x,xxx,xxx
Accumulated Depreciation		$x,xxx,xxx
Accounts Payable		$x,xxx,xxx
Accrued Payables		$x,xxx,xxx

To record indirect fixed manufacturing overhead costs for period.

	Debit	Credit
Finished Goods Inventory	$28,000,000	
Work-in-Process Inventory		$28,000,000

To record completion of manufacturing process and to transfer production costs to the finished goods inventory account.

	Debit	Credit
Cost of Goods Sold Expense	$28,000,000	
Finished Goods Inventory		$28,000,000

To record cost of products sold during year.

6. Refer to Figure 12-2 for the operating profit report and manufacturing activity summary of Company Z for the year. Assume that the business had no work-in-process inventory at the start or end of the year. The business purchased $19,500,000 raw materials on credit during the year. Make the basic manufacturing entries for the business by following the series of entries explained in the section "Taking a Short Tour of Manufacturing Entries."

Note: The following manufacturing entries include short explanations.

	Debit	Credit
Raw Materials Inventory	$19,500,000	
Accounts Payable		$19,500,000

Purchase on credit of raw materials needed in the production process.

	Debit	Credit
Work-in-Process Inventory	$18,750,000	
Raw Materials Inventory		$18,750,000

Transfer of raw materials to the production process.

	Debit	Credit
Work-in-Process Inventory	$6,875,000	
Cash		$x,xxx,xxx
Payroll Taxes Payable		$x,xxx,xxx
Accrued Payables		$x,xxx,xxx

To record direct labor costs for period.

	Debit	Credit
Work-in-Process Inventory	$12,500,000	
Cash		$x,xxx,xxx
Accounts Payable		$xxx,xxx
Accrued Payables		$xxx,xxx

To record indirect variable manufacturing overhead costs for period.

	Debit	Credit
Work-in-Process Inventory	$8,000,000	
Cash		$x,xxx,xxx
Accumulated Depreciation		$x,xxx,xxx
Accounts Payable		$x,xxx,xxx
Accrued Payables		$x,xxx,xxx

To record indirect fixed manufacturing overhead costs for period.

	Debit	Credit
Finished Goods Inventory	$46,125,000	
Work-in-Process Inventory		$46,125,000

To record completion of manufacturing process and to transfer production costs to the finished goods inventory account.

	Debit	Credit
Cost of Goods Sold Expense	$36,900,000	
Finished Goods Inventory		$36,900,000

To record cost of products sold during year.

(7) Assume that Company Y uses the LIFO method to charge out raw materials to production. In this question, assume that supply shortages of raw materials meant that Company Y couldn't purchase all the raw materials it needed for production during the year, and it had to draw down its raw materials inventory. Fortunately, it had an adequate beginning inventory of raw materials to cover the gap in purchases during the year. In this situation, would the cost of raw materials issued to production be different than the $7,500,000 shown in Figure 12-2?

TIP

Yes, the cost of raw materials charged to production probably would be lower because the beginning inventory or raw materials probably is on the books at a lower cost per unit compared with current purchase prices. This "aging" of inventory cost is one disadvantage of the LIFO method, which I discuss in Chapter 6. When a business dips into its beginning inventory because it uses more materials than it was able to buy during the period, it has to charge out the raw materials at the costs recorded in its inventory account. These costs may go back several years, and in the meantime, the costs of raw materials have probably escalated to higher prices per unit. If the difference is significant, the chief accountant should warn managers that the raw materials component of product cost is lower than normal because of a LIFO liquidation effect — not because of more efficient production methods or lower raw material purchase prices during the year.

8 Determine what Company Z's operating profit would be if it had sold 2,100,000 units during the year, which is 100,000 more units than in the example shown in Figure 12-2. Assume that production output had remained the same at 2,500,000 units (the company's production output capacity).

The business manufactured 500,000 more units than it sold during the year (see Figure 12-2). Therefore, it certainly had 100,000 additional units available for sale; indeed, it had 500,000 additional units available for sale without having to reach into its beginning quantity of inventory. An additional 100,000 units of sales is only a 5 percent increase (100,000 additional units ÷ 2,000,000 units sales volume = 5 percent.) So, the company's fixed operating expenses probably would not increase at the higher sales volume level.

The company's product cost would be the same at the higher sales level and its fixed operating costs would hold the same. Therefore, its operating profit would increase $405,000:

> $4.05 contribution margin per unit × 100,000 additional units sold = $405,000 operating profit increase

In other words, Company Z's operating profit would increase from $600,000 to $1,005,000, which is an increase of 67.5 percent. But don't get too excited — this large percent increase is due mainly to the low base of only $600,000 operating profit. Nevertheless, the business certainly could have reported a much better operating profit if it had sold just 5 percent more units.

9 Company Y was on track to sell 550,000 units in the year, but late in the year, a major customer canceled a large order for 50,000 units. The business reduced its production output to 500,000 units, as you see in Figure 12-2. Determine the operating profit Company Y would have earned if it had manufactured and sold 550,000 units in the year.

Company Y would have earned $4,875,000 operating profit, as the following schedule shows.

		Company Y
Operating Profit Report For Year	**Per Unit**	**Totals**
Sales volume, in Units		550,000
Sales Revenue	$85.00	$46,750,000
Cost of Goods Sold Expense (see below)	(54.55)	(30,000,000)
Gross Margin	$30.45	$16,750,000
Variable Operating Expenses	(12.50)	(6,875,000)
Contribution Margin	$17.95	$9,875,000
Fixed Operating Expenses		(5,000,000)
Operating Profit		$4,875,000

Manufacturing Activity Summary For Year	**Per Unit**	**Totals**
Annual Production Capacity, in Units		800,000
Actual Output, in Units		550,000
Raw Materials	$15.00	$8,250,000
Direct Labor	20.00	11,000,000
Variable Manufacturing Overhead Costs	5.00	2,750,000
Total Variable Manufacturing Costs	$40.00	$22,000,000
Fixed Manufacturing Overhead Costs	14.55	8,000,000
Product Cost and Total Manufacturing Costs	$54.55	$30,000,000

The canceled order for 50,000 units hit operating profit hard: The company's operating profit fell $1,625,000 as the result, from $4,875,000 (see schedule above) to $3,250,000 (see Figure 12-2, in which only 500,000 units are sold).

REMEMBER

The company has unused production capacity (see Figure 12-2), so producing an additional 50,000 units wouldn't have increased its fixed manufacturing overhead costs. And, its fixed operating costs would not have increased at the higher sales level. The company's variable operating expenses equal $12.50 per unit, and its variable manufacturing costs equal $40.00 per unit. Thus, its total variable costs equal $52.50 per unit. Manufacturing and selling 50,000 additional units causes costs to increase $2,625,000 ($52.50 variable costs per unit × 50,000 units = $2,625,000). Selling an additional 50,000 units increases sales revenue $4,250,000 ($85.00 sales price × 50,000 units = $4,250,000). Therefore,

Incremental sales revenue from additional 50,000 units	=	$4,250,000
Incremental costs from additional 50,000 units	=	($2,625,000)
Incremental operating profit from additional 50,000 units	=	$1,625,000

This calculation is an example of marginal analysis, on analyzing things on the edge. The focus is on the 50,000 units that the company didn't sell (but came close to selling).

(10) Assume that Company Z's production output for the year is 2,000,000 units (instead of 2,500,000 units as in Figure 12-2). In other words, assume that the business manufactures the same number of units that it sells in the year. Assume all other manufacturing and operating factors are the same. Determine the company's operating profit for the year.

In this scenario, the company suffers a $1,000,000 operating loss. See the following schedule:

	Company Z	
Operating Profit Report For Year	**Per Unit**	**Totals**
Sales volume, in Units		2,000,000
Sales Revenue	$25.00	$50,000,000
Cost of Goods Sold Expense (see below)	(19.25)	(38,500,000)
Gross Margin	$5.75	$11,500,000
Variable Operating Expenses	(2.50)	(5,000,000)
Contribution Margin	$3.25	$6,500,000
Fixed Operating Expenses		(7,500,000)
Operating Profit Loss		($1,000,000)

Manufacturing Activity Summary For Year	**Per Unit**	**Totals**
Annual Production Capacity, in Units		2,500,000
Actual Output, in Units		2,000,000
Raw Materials	$7.50	$15,000,000
Direct Labor	2.75	5,500,000
Variable Manufacturing Overhead Costs	5.00	10,000,000
Total Variable Manufacturing Costs	$15.25	$30,500,000
Fixed Manufacturing Overhead Costs	4.00	8,000,000
Product Cost and Total Manufacturing Costs	$19.25	$38,500,000

By producing only 2,000,000 units, the company's burden rate increases to $4.00 per unit from the $3.20 burden rate when it produces 2,500,000 units (see Figure 12-2). This is an increase of $.80 per unit, which decreases Company Z's contribution margin per unit from $4.05 to $3.25 per unit. The company records $.80 less profit on each unit sold, so on its 2,000,000 units sales volume its operating profit drops $1,600,000 — from $600,000 profit (see Figure 12-2) to $1,000,000 loss. It appears that the business boosted production output to 2,500,000 units in order to show a profit for the year. As the result, Company Z's stuck with a surplus inventory that it will have to do something with in the year(s) ahead.

(11) Toward the end of the year, the president of Company Y looks at the preliminary numbers for operating profit and doesn't like what he sees. He's "promised" the board of directors that operating profit for the year will come in at $4,850,000. In fact, his bonus depends on hitting that operating profit target. There is still time before the end of the year to crank up production output for the year. Therefore, he orders that production output be stepped up. The president asks you to determine what the production output level for the year would have to be in order to report $4,850,000 operating profit for the year. Of course, you have ethical qualms about doing this, but you need the job. So, you reluctantly decide to do the calculation. Determine the production output level that would yield $4,850,000 operating profit for the year.

The following schedule shows that if the business manufactures 625,000 units, its operating profit will be $4,850,000:

		Company Y	
Operating Profit Report For Year	**Per Unit**	**Totals**	
Sales volume, in Units		500,000	
Sales Revenue	$85.00	$42,500,000	
Cost of Goods Sold Expense (see below)	($52.80)	(26,400,000)	
Gross Margin	$32.20	$16,100,000	
Variable Operating Expenses	($12.50)	(6,250,000)	
Contribution Margin	$19.70	$9,850,000	
Fixed Operating Expenses		(5,000,000)	
Operating Profit		$4,850,000	

Manufacturing Activity Summary For Year	**Per Unit**	**Totals**
Annual Production Capacity, in Units		800,000
Actual Output, in Units		625,000
Raw Materials	$15.00	$9,375,000
Direct Labor	$20.00	12,500,000
Variable Manufacturing Overhead Costs	$5.00	3,125,000
Total Variable Manufacturing Costs	$40.00	$25,000,000
Fixed Manufacturing Overhead Costs	$12.80	8,000,000
Product Cost and Total Manufacturing Costs	$52.80	$33,000,000

The president wants $1,600,000 more profit than shown in Figure 12-2 ($4,850,000 profit target – $3,250,000 profit at 500,000 units production level = $1,600,000 additional profit). The only profit driver that changes with a higher production level is the burden rate, which has to decline $3.20 per unit in order to achieve the additional profit ($1,600,000 additional profit wanted ÷ 500,000 units sales volume = $3.20 decrease needed in burden rate). The burden rate has to decrease $3.20, from $16.00 (see Figure 12-2) to $12.80. The production output level has to be 625,000 units to get the burden rate down to $12.80 ($8,000,000 fixed manufacturing overhead costs ÷ $12.80 burden rate = 625,000 units).

TIP

Whether it's ethical and above board to jack up production to 625,000 units when sales are only 500,000 units for the year is a serious question. The members of Company Y's board of directors should definitely challenge the president on why such a large inventory increase is needed. I would, that's for sure!

12 Refer to your answer to Question 10, in which Company Z produces only 2,000,000 units during the year. In the scenario shown in Figure 12-2, the business manufactures 2,500,000 units, which is its maximum production output for the year. Do you think that Company Z cranked up production output to 2,500,000 units mainly to boost its operating profit for the year?

WARNING

No one wants to jump to conclusions, but it would appear that boosting operating profit very well may be the reason for Company Z's high production output level. Put another way, the chief executive of the business has to justify the large inventory increase based on legitimate reasons, such as a big jump in sales forecast for next year or a looming strike of employees that will shut down the company's production for several months. Otherwise, the ugly truth is that the business is engaging in some earnings management, also called massaging the numbers. Sophisticated readers of the company's financial statements will notice the large jump in inventory in the balance sheet, and they may press top management for an explanation. Therefore, the attempt at accounting manipulation may not work.

13 The president of Company X is puzzled by the operating profit report and summary of manufacturing activity for the year, in which $1,200,000 raw materials cost was wasted and charged to expense in the year. He expected that operating profit would be $1,200,000 lower (as compared to the scenario in Figure 12-1, in which there's no wasted raw materials cost). Operating profit in the wasted raw materials scenario is only $100,000 lower than in Figure 12-1. Explain to the president why operating profit is only $100,000 lower.

The president is asking about the impact on operating profit. If the $1,200,000 cost of wasted raw materials is included in the calculation of product cost, $1,100,000 of it ends up in cost of goods sold expense because 110,000 of the 120,000 units produced were sold during the year. The other $100,000 is absorbed in the inventory increase. In contrast, if the $1,200,000 is charged to expense directly, none of it escapes into the inventory increase. So, in one scenario, profit is hit with $1,100,000 expense and in the other scenario profit is hit with $1,200,000 expense. The operating profit difference is only $100,000.

14 After Company Y's operating profit report and summary of manufacturing activity for the year has been prepared (see Figure 12-2), you, the chief accountant, learn that $1,000,000 of raw materials were thrown away during the year because the items had spoiled and couldn't be used in the manufacturing process. The company's president knows about this loss and insists that no change be made in the operating profit report and summary of manufacturing activity. Do you go along with the president, or do you argue for changing the operating profit report and summary of manufacturing activity?

If you haven't read my answer to Problem 13, please read it. In that scenario the net error in operating profit is only $100,000 because most of the cost of wasted materials had flowed through to cost of goods sold expense. In this case all of the cost of wasted materials ends up in the cost of goods sold expense, so operating profit is correct. The reason is that all of the manufacturing costs for the year are charged to cost of goods sold because all of the company's output for the year was sold. Note that its entire $28,000,000 manufacturing costs is charged to cost of goods sold expense. (Remember that the company uses the LIFO method.)

TIP

Therefore, the argument in this situation is really about how to classify costs in the internal operating profit report to managers. Would it be better to report a separate cost of wasted raw materials? Yes, I think so. Hopefully, this is a cost the company can avoid from happening again. If the error is not corrected, the managers would be misled into thinking that the true product cost is $16.00, when in fact it is $2.00 lower ($1,000,000 cost of wasted raw materials ÷ 500,000 units production output = $2.00 per unit error).

15   Assume that Company Z manufactures 2,100,000 units during the year (instead of the 2,500,000 units production output shown in Figure 12-2). Determine its operating profit for the year. Assume that the cost of idle capacity is treated as a period cost and isn't embedded in product cost.

The company's operating loss is $680,000, as the following schedule shows.

	Company Z	
Operating Profit Report For Year	**Per Unit**	**Totals**
Sales volume, in Units		2,000,000
Sales Revenue	$25.00	$50,000,000
Cost of Goods Sold Expense (see below)	(18.45)	(36,900,000)
Gross Margin	$6.55	$13,100,000
Variable Operating Expenses	(2.50)	(5,000,000)
Contribution Margin	$4.05	$8,100,000
Fixed Operating Expenses		(7,500,000)
Cost of Idle Capacity		(1,280,000)
Operating Profit		($680,000)
Manufacturing Activity Summary For Year	**Per Unit**	**Totals**
Annual Production Capacity, in Units		2,500,000
Actual Output, in Units		2,100,000
Raw Materials	$7.50	$15,750,000
Direct Labor	2.75	5,775,000
Variable Manufacturing Overhead Costs	5.00	10,500,000
Total Variable Manufacturing Costs	$15.25	$32,025,000
Fixed Manufacturing Overhead Costs (Net of idle capacity cost -- see above)	3.20	6,720,000
Product Cost and Total Manufacturing Costs	$18.45	$38,745,000

The company has 16 percent idle capacity in this scenario (400,000 units not produced ÷ 2,500,000 units capacity = 16 percent idle capacity). So, 16 percent of its $8,000,000 fixed manufacturing overhead costs, or $1,280,000, is removed from the calculation of product cost and treated as a period cost. This action reduces operating profit for the year by this amount, of course.

16   Refer to Company X's operating profit report and summary of manufacturing activity presented in Figure 12-1. Note that its annual production capacity is 150,000 units, but the business manufactured only 120,000 units during the year. Therefore, it had 20 percent idle capacity (30,000 units not produced ÷ 150,000 units production capacity = 20 percent idle capacity). However, in the Figure 12-1 scenario, the cost of idle capacity isn't treated as a separate period cost; all the company's fixed manufacturing overhead costs are included in calculating its product cost.

Suppose that the business treats the cost of idle capacity as a period cost. Prepare a revised operating profit report and summary of manufacturing activity for the business.

Company X's operating profit would be $15,250,000, as the following schedule shows.

Operating Profit Report For Year	Per Unit	Totals
Sales volume, in Units		110,000
Sales Revenue	$1,400.00	$154,000,000
Cost of Goods Sold Expense (see below)	(690.00)	(75,900,000)
Gross Margin	$710.00	$78,100,000
Variable Operating Expenses	(300.00)	(33,000,000)
Contribution Margin	$410.00	$45,100,000
Fixed Operating Expenses		(21,450,000)
Cost of Idle Capacity		(8,400,000)
Operating Profit		$15,250,000

Manufacturing Activity Summary For Year	Per Unit	Totals
Annual Production Capacity, in Units		150,000
Actual Output, in Units		120,000
Raw Materials	$215.00	$25,800,000
Direct Labor	125.00	15,000,000
Variable Manufacturing Overhead Costs	70.00	8,400,000
Total Variable Manufacturing Costs	$410.00	$49,200,000
Fixed Manufacturing Overhead Costs (Net of idle capacity cost -- see above)	280.00	33,600,000
Product Cost and Total Manufacturing Costs	$690.00	$82,800,000

Note that the company's operating profit decreases a relatively small amount, only $700,000, due to treating idle capacity as a period cost instead of a product cost. In Figure 12-1, operating profit is $15,950,000, and in this schedule, it's $15,250,000, or $700,000 less. This $700,000 is "buried" in the ending inventory cost under the method shown in Figure 12-1; in other words, in the scenario shown in Figure 12-1, the cost of idle capacity is included in the $760 product cost. The product cost is $70 higher than the $690 product cost in this schedule (in which idle capacity is pulled out of manufacturing and treated as a period cost). The company sold 110,000 units, and the other 10,000 units of its production output increase its inventory. These 10,000 units absorb $700,000 of the idle capacity cost (10,000 units inventory increase × $70 higher burden rate = $700,000 absorbed by inventory increase).

Chapter **13**

Business Planning and Raising Capital

Before you dive into this chapter, you might be asking yourself two simple questions: What does accounting have to do with the business planning process, and why is this chapter included in the book? Both excellent questions to which I offer a very simple answer – Everything! By this, I mean that accounting often finds itself at the epicenter of the business planning process, and while a business plan can be drafted, it basically is meaningless without including CART financial information, statements, and reports. There's that acronym again, CART, which to refresh your memory stands for complete, accurate, reliable, and timely financial information.

Or looking at it from another perspective, a business plan needs to answer several critical financial and accounting related questions including (but not limited to):

» How much capital (cold hard cash) will I need to execute the business plan?

» What type of capital should be secured, debt and/or equity, and in what amounts?

>> What types of financial returns can be expected by parties that either lend the business money or invest in the business and purchase equity ownership?

>> How long will it take the business to become profitable? *Note:* Rarely will new businesses generate a profit right out of the gate.

>> If the company uses more conservative accounting policies, how will this impact future reported profits?

>> How will the balance sheet most likely evolve in relation to increasing sales revenue, and what types of assets will be needed to support the business plan?

>> Based on the cost structure of the business, what prices should the business set for either the products or services its sells?

Needless to say, the list of financial and accounting related questions is extensive, as the sampling list here offers just a small glimpse of the variety of financial data points that are essential to operating a business successfully. And the party(s) responsible for producing this information, well, it's the accounting and finance group, which represents a critical component of the business planning team. So, before you jump to the conclusion that the accounting function operates more or less in the capacity of a back office administrative task that just adds expenses to operating a business, think again, as successful businesses rely heavily on the accounting and financial function to proactively manage and execute business plans to optimize profits and financial returns. In this chapter, I show just how important accounting is to the entire business planning process.

Starting with the Business Plan

It should go without saying that when either new businesses are formed and launched or an existing business implements a specific strategy (such as, to drive sales growth, improve earnings per share, restructure current operations, and so on), a well-developed, supported, presented, and communicated business plan is an absolute necessity. Business plans provide a road map for company management to implement and execute, as they not only outline the resources that will be required but, more importantly, establish a benchmark on which the company's management team can be evaluated. Further, business plans come in all shapes, sizes, and forms, ranging from an entire company-wide plan (for example, laying out how a company like General Motors will transition from making cars with combustible engines to producing electronically powered vehicles over X years) to something as simple as establishing a revenue goal for a group of sales reps who service a specific geographical region.

Business plans generally include a wide range of information, data, reports, articles, analyses, assessments, and the list goes on and on. The level of detail included in a business plan is usually dependent on the target audience, as what might be presented to an external group of venture capitalists or private equity investors (much more condensed with limitations on disclosing confidential information) would be significantly different than presenting a business plan to a company's board of directors. Also, you may frequently hear the term "The Deck" referenced, which is nothing more than a condensed version of a business plan presented in an easy to understand, logical, and appealing format (such as a PowerPoint or PDF file).

A macro-level, business plan should cover all relevant and critical material, which basically can be broken down into the following five primary buckets:

>> **First, summarize the market environment.** Consider questions such as: What is the current market opportunity or need? What market or industry characteristics and trends are present? What is the size of the market? What competition is present? On the surface, providing market information should be a no-brainer, yet in practice this is one topic that business plans tend to be weak in addressing, as acquiring reliable and credible third-party market information is much easier said than done.

>> **Second, overview what resources will be required.** What physical assets will be needed and when? Will new technology need to be developed? What will the organizational chart (org chart) look like? When will personnel need to be hired? What supply chain consider-ations are present? Again, the potential list of topics is endless, but it should be focused on key operational functions that are critical to the success of the plan.

>> **Third, list the management team.** This is relatively simple and straightforward as there is no way a business plan is going to be executed without a strong, experienced, and commit-ted management team being in place.

>> **Fourth, forecast the potential financial return.** Generally speaking, the financial oppor-tunity or return is highlighted with a forecast or proforma income statement that presents multiple years of business operating results (with three to five years of forecast income statements being common).

>> **Fifth, summarize the amount and type of required financial capital.** A conclusion should be drawn not just as to the amount of capital investment a company needs to make to execute the business plan, but more importantly, what type of capital (debt or equity) will be needed, and even more critical, what will the capital structure be. The financial capital conclusion is often supported by what is referred to as "sources and uses of funds," which outlines total sources of capital and how the capital will be used or deployed.

REMEMBER

Condensing this even further and to keep the concept of the business plan as simple as pos-sible, here is what a business plan really is — it answers these questions: What is the oppor-tunity, what resources will be needed, who is the management team, what is the potential financial return, and how much capital is needed?

The remainder of this chapter is focused on the fourth and fifth points, related to the impor-tance of forecasting and how much and what type of financial capital is needed, as expanding on the first three points would constitute a book of itself. I should also note that the fifth point is where I dive into several basic accounting concepts to provide a more thorough understand-ing of accounting for business capital, both debt and owners' equity.

EXAMPLE

Q. The president of the company is excited about pursuing a new business opportunity outside of the United States and has created an internal task force to develop a business plan to present to the board of directors for consideration. The task force includes senior level managers from multiple functions including sales, marketing, manufactur-ing, information technology, legal, and yes, the accounting department. You've been identified as a key team member and assigned to the task force to support the develop-ment of the business plan at the accounting level. Excited to move forward, identify some basic business information you need to get started.

A. There really isn't a right or wrong answer to this question, as the list of business information requests is most likely going to be extensive. However, the best place to start with a project like this is with the following requests that start at the top of the food chain (such as, starting at the top of the income statement to understand potential sales levels first and then expenses, asset investments, and capital requirements after):

- How big is the potential market for the company's products or services?
- What types of products or services will be sold in this foreign market?
- Have prices been set or does the accounting team need to provide preliminary estimates?
- If products are to be sold, will the products be manufactured in a current company production facility or will a new facility need to be established in the foreign country?
- How many employees will be required to support the new business venture and what type of qualifications will be needed?

I could list 50 or more additional questions and information requests but the point that is being emphasized here is the need to determine a starting point on which to begin to develop a plan and financial projection model. In my experience, the best place to start this process is to understand the market and potential sales levels first, and then let the rest of the financial projections fall out from this data.

The point is that business plans and the conclusion on how much financial capital will be needed are vast, complex, and constantly changing and evolving as market conditions change. Ponder and respond to the following two questions. As a hint, these are not your typical "number crunching" accounting questions, as the goal with these questions is to drive qualitative responses.

 List three sources of information and/or data that a company may use to support the development of a business plan.

 Identify three different business situations or opportunities (other than those previously presented) when a business plan should be developed and implemented by management or the owners.

Realizing the Importance of Business Forecasts

At the opening of this chapter, I introduce you to the importance and concept of business planning, and its role in determining how to capitalize a business. The planning process includes numerous elements ranging from assessing current market conditions to understanding the macroeconomic environment to evaluating personnel resources to preparing budgets, forecasts, and/or projections. One thing that will become clearly evident is that business planning and preparing financial forecasts are closely related and for all intents and purposes, "tied at the hip," as in almost all cases, a business plan will be supported by a well-developed financial forecast.

REMEMBER

For the balance of this chapter, the term *forecasts* is used interchangeably with the terms such as *budgets* or *budgeting*, projections, and proformas (which basically all mean the same thing). I prefer to use the term forecasts, as it is broader in scope and helps drive home a key concept related to building best in class forecast models. But I must caution you that most businesses still reference the term "budgeting," as this has been engrained in the business world for decades. As you can tell, I am not a big fan of this term.

Getting a grip on how forecasting works

I want to make a quick attempt to properly define a forecast. Forecasts *are not* based on the concept of "How much can I spend in my division this year?" Rather, forecasts are more comprehensive in nature and are designed to capture all relevant and critical financial data, including revenue levels, costs of sales, operating expenses, fixed asset expenditures, capital requirements, and the like. All too often, forecasts are associated with expense levels and management, which represent just one element of the entire forecasts.

Further, the forecasting process does not represent a chicken-and-egg riddle. From a financial perspective, the preparation of forecasts represents the end result of the entire planning process. Hence, you must first accumulate the necessary data and information on which to build a forecasting model prior to producing projected financial information (for an entire company or a specific division). There is no point in preparing a forecast that does not capture the real economic structure and viability of an entire entity or operating division.

REMEMBER

I would like to drive home the importance of preparing complete financial information within the financial forecasts. All too often, companies prepare financial forecasts focused on just the income statement and downplay the importance of the balance sheet and statement of cash flows (which may get put on the back burner). Basically, most of the management team wants to dial in on the anticipated profit performance of the company and quickly forget that in order to grow top line sales and produce solid profits, the company must be able to manage its cash flow and support its business with a strong balance sheet. Without these two base pillars, even the best laid growth plans can quickly collapse due to poor financial planning.

The bottom line with forecasting (and the entire planning process) is that without having clearly identified business financial and performance objectives, the business is operating blind. Or, put simply, it would be like flying a plane without having a destination. The need for having clearly identified benchmarks and a road map to reach the benchmarks is essential for every business, regardless of size, shape, or form, as often the most important question of all comes down to this: "How am I doing against the plan?"

Gaining insight into forecasting terms

To get deeper into the forecasting process, it's important to gain an initial understanding of the following concepts and terminology. Please note that the following bullet points offer only a glimpse of the entire forecasting process, as this topic really requires multiple chapters to understand. However, in order to arm you with some basic knowledge, here are some standard concepts and terminology to get you headed in the right direction:

>> **Forecasts are dynamic, not static:** Years ago, businesses tended to manage the forecasting process on an annual or maybe semiannual basis. The standard cycle started toward the end of each current FYE (maybe 30 to 90 days prior) as management would get the annual "budgeting" process fired up to plan for the upcoming year. I have no doubt that this annual forecasting process still occurs and is widely used, but based on the economic realities of today's capitalist markets, the forecasting process must be managed as a living, breathing function that should be constantly updated as frequently as critical business information emerges, evolves, and/or changes. This does not mean that preparing updated forecasts needs to be completed weekly (which would be overkill) but trust me when I say that developing forecasting models that have the flexibility to always be rolled forward to look out 12 to 24 months from the end of any desired reporting period is now standard practice. This is not a nice-to-have, but is now a *must-have*.

>> **The SWOT analysis:** This acronym stands for strengths, weaknesses, opportunities, and threats and is a business management assessment tool designed to assist the company's management team with preparing a qualitative assessment of the business, helping to keep all parties focused on key issues. The SWOT analysis is often incorporated into a company's planning function but can also be extremely helpful with preparing financial forecasts. A SWOT analysis is usually broken down into a matrix of four segments. Two of the segments are geared toward positive attributes — strengths and opportunities — and two are geared toward negative attributes — weaknesses and threats. In addition, the analysis differentiates between internal company source attributes and external, or outside of the company, source attributes.

>> **Top-down forecast:** Top-down forecasting is exactly how it sounds (the top line for a company, which is sales), as it starts with projecting critical sales revenue data, including sales unit volumes (by all significant product lines or SKUs), pricing by product, any potential sales discounts, seasonality in sales, customer contact to sales timing relationships, and similar data. After the top-line sales data is built into the forecast, the balance of the income statement then tends to "fall out" naturally and is projected in various steps starting with costs of goods sold or costs of sales expense (as these expenses tend to vary directly with sales levels), then incorporates direct operating expenses, business overhead expenses, and other expenses or income (such as interest expense, income tax expense, and other expenses). Once the income statement forecast is complete, all critical balance sheet assumptions, are incorporated by utilizing relationships or correlations rather than inputting hard data and information.

>> **Bottom-up forecast:** Using a bottom-up approach is quite different. Although certain key correlations or relationships may be incorporated into the forecast model, this approach tends to be much more detailed and includes a large number of hard or firm data points and assumptions being built into the forecast model. In a top down forecast, sales revenue would be determined by gaining X percent of the total Y dollar market and calculating how many sales reps would be needed. In a bottoms up forecast, sales revenue may be driven by how many sales reps are working or employed, so if ten sales reps are working any given month and, on average, each sales rep should be able to generate $250,000 of sales, total sales for the month would be forecast at $2.5 million.

Quite often, companies use a hybrid of top-down and bottom-up approaches, as almost all financial forecast models use some type of correlation and relationship assumptions as well as incorporate hard data for various overhead or fixed costs. The bottom-up approach tends to be better suited for well-established, predictable business models that have a large amount of historical data and operational stability. The top-down approach tends to be better suited for newer businesses or companies operating in rapidly changing environments where you need to understand important financial results quickly under different or "what-if" operating scenarios.

>> **The "what if":** One concept that is strongly associated with the top-down forecasting approach is the *what-if* analysis. It should be obvious that the purpose of the what-if analysis is just like it sounds — that is, what will the results or impact be if this situation or set of events occurs? For example, if a company has to implement a significant product price reduction to match the competition, a what-if analysis will help it quickly calculate and decipher the potential impact on its operating results and associated cash flows. The reason the what-if analysis is easier to use with a top-down forecast approach is that the goal of this analysis tool is to focus on the macro-level impact (to a business) from a potential material change in key business operating metrics. Thus, by being able to change 6 to 12 key variables or forecast assumptions, a management team can quickly assess the impact on the business (which is one of the key strengths of the top-down forecasting approach). This is not to say that what-if analyses cannot be generated using a bottom-up forecasting approach, but when focusing on macro-level company operating results, starting at the top with sales revenue and watching the waterfall impact on overall operations is a particularly useful and powerful analysis for senior management.

Q. A senior executive approaches you about preparing a forecast for a new opportunity and wants it pronto. The executive also wants you to identify the total amount of capital that will be required to support the opportunity. Can you provide the executive what they want by just preparing a forecast income statement?

A. The answer is no. While preparing a forecast income statement will help identify critical data points such as targeted sales levels, expenses, and potential profitability, the income statement does not identify how much capital will be required. This information is driven from preparing a forecast balance sheet and statement of cash flows, which both should clearly estimate the total amount of capital needed to support the business opportunity.

3. A business prepares three sets of forecast, a high or best case, a medium or expected case, and a low or worst case. What concept best describes this strategy?

4. A blank SWOT analysis is provided for a company that has a new cryptocurrency, which it plans on introducing to the market shortly. Complete the following SWOT analysis by offering one item in each quadrant.

Strength: Weakness:

Opportunity: Threat:

Identifying Types of Available Capital

Time to discuss the options and strategies available to capitalize a business. To keep this simple, capitalizing a business comes down to one of two types — using equity or debt. Up first, I provide an overview of using equity capital to finance a business and the related subject matter (or maybe more appropriately, nuances) that comes along with equity capital. Second, I pivot into a discussion on using debt capital and how and when businesses may pursue securing loans to finance a business. Please note that there is no perfect balance or structure between using equity and debt capital; it is impossible to forecast how markets, interest rates, competition, and so forth change over time and the related impact on a company's capital structure. Rather the idea with presenting this information is to provide a better understanding of the pros and cons of both types of capital and the related impact on accounting.

I should note that, yes, a business can deploy or recycle internal capital that is available from company-generated profits and positive cash flow, but in effect, this is really the same as using equity. Rather than distributing profits via issuing dividends, the company can elect to invest the excess earnings back into or inside the business. Further, larger, and stronger companies can often leverage suppliers (by requesting extended credit terms) or customers (requiring deposits or enticing quicker payments) to "mine" cash or capital from key relationships. However, this just represents using a different type of debt as compared to formally structured and documented lending agreements. A perfect example of this is Tesla, which for years has required customers to provide a deposit or down payment in advance of finalizing the purchase of a car (which may take three to six months).

For the purposes of this chapter, I'm going to focus our discussion on securing capital from external equity and debt sources as when large amounts of capital are required (relatively speaking to the size of the business), companies need to look to external capital sources such as banks, alternative lenders (an extremely broad group), venture capitalists, private equity groups, hedge funds, and, yes, Wall Street.

Utilizing equity to capitalize your business

Raising equity capital amounts to nothing more than selling a portion of the business to an external party that will own X percent of the business moving forward (and have the right to future earnings). For example, if a business has established its fair market value at $20,000,000 (what is often referred to as a "pre-money" valuation) and then sells new equity to secure another $5,000,000 of capital, the total "post-money" valuation of the business would be $25,000,000. Under this scenario, the existing owners of the business would own 80 percent of the company ($20,000,000 divided by $25,000,000) and the new owners or investors would own 20 percent of the company ($5,000,000 divided by $25,000,000).

REMEMBER

The pre-money valuation is not the same figure as the owners' equity figure as presented on the balance sheet. The pre-money valuation is based on an agreed upon fair market value of the company before any investment is received. The owners' equity figure represents the accumulated accounting book value of all historical transactions impacting owners' equity. For our sample company (refer to Figure 13-1), the accumulated value of all historical accounting transactions (before the investment) amounts to $11,446,000 (historical common stock investment of $5,000,000 plus accumulated retained earnings balance of $6,446,000). As you can see, this figure is greater than the estimated pre-money valuation of $10,000,000. Is it fair? Well, that's up to the company and investing party to decide, but the point being made is rarely, if ever, does a company's pre-money valuation equal exactly the balance in owners' equity.

When best to utilize: Equity sources of capital are best utilized when a company is operating in a higher-risk environment (new start-up operations or financing high growth), incurring losses, needs to maintain a proper debt-to-equity balance (to avoid becoming overleveraged), and/or when equity capital markets are very strong (so the company can sell the equity at a maximum price). I will utilize the same sample company introduced in Chapter 7 to highlight how a business raises equity capital.

In the sample company, a decision was made to sell 500,000 shares of preferred equity to an external VC firm for $5,000,000 (refer to Figure 13-1 for the company's balance sheet as of 12/31/21). The 500,000 shares amount to a 33.33 percent (500,000 shares divided by the total common and preferred shares of 1,500,000) ownership stake in the company, based on the issued and outstanding voting shares, assuming all the preferred shares have the same basic rights to earnings as the common shares. Refer to Figure 13-2 for the support of the ownership calculation (known as the cap table). The company elected to raise equity to help strengthen the balance sheet as well as to finance a large and potentially risky investment in an acquisition targeted for the next year.

Balance Sheet Example

QW Example Tech., Inc.
Balance Sheet
For the Fiscal Year Ending
12/31/2021
(all numbers in thousands)

Assets	12/31/2021
Current Assets:	
Cash & Equivalents	$11,698
Accounts Receivable, Net	$8,883
Inventory, LCM	$1,733
Prepaid Expenses	$375
Total Current Assets	$22,689
Long-Term Operating & Other Assets:	
Property, Plant, Equipment, & Machinery	$8,670
Accumulated Depreciation	($4,320)
Net Property, Plant, & Equipment	$4,350
Other Assets:	
Intangible Assets & Goodwill, Net	$500
Other Assets	$100
Total Long-Term Operating & Other Assets	$4,950
Total Assets	$27,639
Liabilities	
Current Liabilities:	
Accounts Payable	$1,929
Accrued Liabilities & Other	$830
Current Portion of Debt	*$1,000*
Other Current Liabilities & Deferred Revenue	$1,234
Total Current Liabilities	$4,993
Long-term Liabilities:	
Notes Payable & Other Long-Term Debt	*$6,200*
Total Liabilities	$11,193
Stockholders' Equity	
Capital Stock - Common	$5,000
Capital Stock - Preferred	*$5,000*
Retained Earnings	$6,446
Total Stockholder's Equity	$16,446
Total Liabilities & Stockholders Equity	$27,639

Confidential - Property of QW Example Tech., Inc.

FIGURE 13-1:
Balance sheet for Sample Company as of 12/31/21.

The *cap table* is really nothing more than a table or spreadsheet that spells out exactly who owns what in terms of the equity issued by a company as presented or listed by what type of equity has been issued. On the surface, reading a cap table should be relatively straightforward, as it should list various parties and their respective ownership percentage in the company's owner equity. However, the devil is absolutely in the detail when understanding cap tables and the potential impact as to what owners truly control the company and have the most advantageous ownership stakes. Figure 13-2 provides an ownership snapshot of our sample company.

Cap. Table Example

QW Example Tech., Inc.
Capitalization Table
as of the Fiscal Year Ending
12/31/2021

Description	Number of Shares	Invested Amount	Voting Issued & O/S % Owned	Fully Diluted % Owned
Preferred Equity:				
H&H Test VC Firm, Fund V	500,000	$5,000,000	33.33%	30.77%
Subtotal - Preferred Equity	500,000	$5,000,000	33.33%	30.77%
Common Equity:				
Founders, Original	800,000	$2,000,000	53.33%	49.23%
Investors, Various Parties	200,000	$3,000,000	13.33%	12.31%
Subtotal - Common Equity	1,000,000	$5,000,000	66.67%	61.54%
Common Equity Options & Warrants:				
Stock options issued & outstanding	75,000	$0	0.00%	4.62%
Warrants issued for common stock purchases	50,000	$0	0.00%	3.08%
Subtotal - Common Equity Options & Warrants	125,000	$0	0.00%	7.69%
Total, All forms of Equity	1,625,000	$10,000,000	100.00%	100.00%

Confidential - Property of QW Example Tech., Inc.

FIGURE 13-2: Cap table for Sample Company as of 12/31/21.

It's important to note the pros and cons of raising equity. The pros of raising equity capital are centered in securing much-needed cash, strengthening the balance sheet, and potentially bringing on a valuable long-term capital and strategic partner (covered later in this chapter), among others. The primary cons are centered in having to sell a portion of the company, diluting the current shareholder's ownership stake (in our example, diluting ownership from 100 percent to 66.67 percent) and possibly relinquishing certain management control over critical business decision-making activity.

EXAMPLE

Q. True or false, the pre-money value of a business is equal to the total amount of owners' equity in the balance sheet.

A. The answer is false, as a company's pre-money valuation is based on the fair market value of the business determined by independent parties operating in an arm's-length manner. In some cases, the pre-money valuation may be significantly higher than the stated amount of owners' equity in the balance sheet and in other cases, substantially lower. Again, business values are set by the "market" and not the cumulative summary of historical accounting financial transactions.

5 Can you determine the ownership percentage for each investor in a company based purely on the amount of money invested or used to purchase stock?

6 Instead of the VC firm investing $5,000,000 for 500,000 shares of preferred stock, update the cap table to reflect that the VC firm invested $8,000,000 and received 800,000 shares of preferred stock. What sticks out or could be concerning to the founders based on the new cap table?

With these basic concepts out of the way, it makes sense to drill down further into the meat and potatoes of the ownership structure of a company. How I present owners' equity is going to move well beyond smaller businesses and be directed toward more complex business capital structures that involve multiple types of equity and even quasi forms of equity disguised as debt. Although all businesses will have retained earnings (as previously discussed) or in the case of multiple years of losses, accumulated deficits (in which cumulative losses are greater than cumulative profits), when companies utilize more complex legal entities such as C corporations or LLCs, they also tend to use a wider range of different types of equity to capitalize their business. In a nutshell, this is what is commonly referred to as the cap table.

I have laid out the topics covered in this section of the chapter from the perspective of the equity owners' rights to claims against the company as opposed to the total amount of equity owned in the company. This may seem somewhat convoluted, but as you read through the material, you will quickly gain an understanding of why it is important to understate rights and preferences in lockstep with total ownership interest. For simplicity, I focus on three main components of a typical cap table:

>> Risk-based debt (such as, convertible notes)

>> Preferred equity

>> Common equity, options, and warrants

Before detailing these topics in more depth, a quick word is warranted on the primary available sources of equity capital (from the market). Raising equity can be achieved by pursuing different sources of capital ranging from tapping what I like to refer to as FF&CBAs (family, friends, and close business associates) who are often unsophisticated when making investment decisions all the way through to taking a company public through an IPO — a complex process targeting sophisticated investors and requiring registration with the U.S. Securities & Exchange Commission (the SEC). The IPO process can be very expensive requiring professional help from attorneys, audit firms, underwriters, and others.

In between these two extremes is a very large middle ground, where capital is usually raised from groups that have a keen expertise in providing the right financial capital at the right time and include VCs (venture capitalists), PEs or PEGs (private equity or private equity groups), HNWIs (high-net-worth individuals, sometimes referred to as angel investors), HFs (hedge funds), and other similar types of capital sources. These groups tend to specialize by industry or company stage, usually have significant amounts of capital to deploy, and employ highly qualified management teams to assess the investment opportunities.

Equity designed as debt (risk-based debt)

Companies that cannot raise capital from traditional debt sources, such as banks or alternative-based lenders, and which do not want to raise equity capital (over fears of diluting the ownership and control of the company) will often use what is commonly referred to as convertible debt (a hybrid form of debt and equity that has characteristics of both). I would like to note that for our sample company presented in Figures 13-1 and 13-2, no convertible debt is present, but I felt it was important to include a brief discussion on this form of capital, as it is widely used in today's business world.

Convertible debt is a form of actual debt (such as, a loan to the company) that is reported on a company's balance sheet as a liability, similar to a note or loan payable. Most convertible debt is structured to be long term, with common repayment terms of two to five years. The reason for the name is that convertible debt, either at the option of the party providing the loan or if a specific event occurs, the debt can be converted into either common or preferred equity of the company. The conversion of the debt may occur for any number of reasons, including the company achieving a milestone such as a predetermined sales revenue level being met, if the company raises a large amount of equity (the triggering event), the company is sold, or if the due date of the convertible debt is reached and the debt cannot be repaid.

A logical question at this point is why would a company want to raise money using convertible debt and, conversely, why would an external party want to invest in convertible debt? I answer both questions as follows:

>> **Issuing convertible debt to raise capital:** Raising capital through issuing convertible debt is often used by companies that need to bridge the business (by providing a capital infusion) to get from point D to point F to help substantiate a higher valuation. If a company is worth $X at point D but can see it being worth three times more at point F (based on achieving key milestones), the company will be able to raise equity capital at a much higher valuation and reduce the risk of ownership dilution. Further, when companies do not qualify for traditional bank or alternative-based loans, they can tap a more junior or subordinated type of debt by raising capital through convertible debt (and if structured correctly by the company, it can avoid providing an actual secured interest in company assets). Other potential benefits of using convertible debt include below market interest rates and favorable repayment terms.

>> **Investing in convertible debt to provide capital:** So why would a convertible debt investment be of interest to third parties? Here is your answer: First up, debt has a higher seniority or claim against company assets than equity. Although convertible debt is often structured in a junior position to bank or alternative lender loans (these lenders have a higher claim to company assets in case of a company liquidation or bankruptcy, so they get paid first, assuming cash is available), they sit higher in the "cap stack." The *cap stack* is nothing more than a financial report or analysis that summarizes the order of which liabilities and equity have priority to company assets in case of a liquidating event such as a bankruptcy. Refer to Figure 13-3 in the next section, as it relates to distributing company assets in the event of an unfortunate or depressed company sale. Second, the convertible debt investors can earn a set return on their investments from the interest rate established (such as 6 percent per annum), even though this may not be paid until the due date.

Third, and maybe most importantly, the convertible debt investors have additional return upside via being able to convert into the company's equity down the road. It is quite common for convertible debt to include a feature that allows the investors to convert into the company's equity at a discount to a future capital raise.

Similar to convertible debt, a company may raise capital through issuing a junior tranche of debt that has set repayment terms and interest rates established. But unlike convertible debt, warrants to purchase equity in the company may be attached instead of allowing the debt to convert. For example, if our sample company needed to sweeten the deal to entice the third-party lender to provide the long-term loan with a balance of $6,200,000 as of 12/31/21, it could offer the lender a warrant to purchase 50,000 common shares at $1 per share at the lender's choice. In fact, and if you refer to Figure 13-2, you will indeed see an outstanding warrant for 50,000 shares. Similar to a discount provided to the investors in the convertible debt, the common stock warrant provides for an "equity kicker" to enhance the overall investment return well above the stated interest rate.

FIGURE 13-3:
Cap stack for Sample Company as of 12/31/21.

Cap. Stack Example			
QW Example Tech., Inc. Estimated Liabilities & Shareholders' Equity For the Fiscal Year Ending 12/31/2021 (all numbers in thousands)			
Summary of Liabilities & Equity	Priority Status	Amount	Notes/Comments
Payroll, Taxes, & Burden Payable	High	$444	Employee obligations are generally at the top of the list.
Income Taxes Payable	High	$87	Governments make sure they get their money.
Loans & Notes Payable, Secured	High	$7,200	Senior debt/secured against company assets.
Trade Payables & Accrued Liabilities	High/Med.	$2,315	Depending on terms with vendors, could be high or med.
Deferred Revenue & Other Current Lia.	Medium	$1,147	Customer advance payments & deposits not secured.
Subtotal Liabilities		$11,193	
Preferred Stock	Med/Low	$5,000	Higher preference than common but lower than debt.
Subtotal Liabilities & Preferred Stock		$16,193	
Common Stock	Low	$5,000	Basically last in priority with rights to company assets.
Common Stock Options & Warrants	Bottom	$0	Value dependent on successful company only.
Subtotal Shareholders' Common Equity		$5,000	
Total Liabilities & Shareholders' Equity		$21,193	
Confidential - Property of QW Example Tech., Inc.			

The nuances, details, and specifics surrounding convertible or junior debt are extensive and complex and well beyond the scope of this book. My goal with overviewing this form of capital was not to make you an expert on this specific subject but rather to socialize the concept of debt/equity hybrid forms of capital and why they are attractive to both the company raising capital and the investors providing capital. In effect, these forms of capital represent a middle-of-the-road strategy to help balance the use of debt and equity in one type of financial capital. As with all forms of financial capital, pros and cons are associated with each form, so the trick is knowing when to use each form and, in all cases, making sure you have proper professional counsel to navigate the capital-raising process.

Preferred equity and real control

Further down the cap table is the wonderful world of preferred equity. Up first is to see where everyone stands in the investor priority list to make sure a clear understanding of the basic order of potential claims that creditors, investors, and owners would have against the company in the event of a company liquidation, dissolution, or bankruptcy. Figure 13-3 provides a simple summary of the cap stack for our sample company.

Our sample company's cap table, presented in Figure 13-2, emphasizes equity ownership (as in, who owns what). The cap stack presented in Figure 13-3 emphasizes the pecking order of creditors', investors', and owners' claims against company assets and provides some comments and thoughts on who would get what in the event of liquidating event. It should be obvious that the cap stack can be a very sobering analysis for equity investors; in this case, if the company had to liquidate and received $15,000,000 for all its assets because of a forced liquidation proceeding, it would have enough to cover the total liabilities with almost enough left over to repay the preferred stock owners (leaving nothing for the common stock owners).

The reason I present the cap stack is to highlight the priority status of the preferred stock owners of being below debt but above common stock owners. This is the first and most critical concept to understand about preferred equity or stock: It almost always has a *preference* to common equity or stock when it comes to not just rights to dividends or earnings (before the common equity) but more importantly, claims against company assets.

The second critical concept to understand about preferred equity is that usually the investors demand a certain amount of management control, either directly or indirectly, with the company's affairs. For large, preferred capital equity raises, it is quite common for investors to demand a seat (or possibly two) on the board of directors. For a company that has five board members prior to the preferred capital raise, the terms of the raise may require that the board of directors increase to seven, of which two will be appointed by the preferred equity investors. There are clear reasons preferred equity investors demand board participation, including the ability for them to monitor their investment more closely, as well as to provide valuable executive management insight they may bring to the table. The point being is that board of director participation represents direct strategic management involvement in the company.

Indirectly, the preferred investors can (and usually do) include several negative control provisions that help protect their investment. Examples of negative control provisions include requiring 100 percent board approval to raise capital through another equity offering (so that better terms cannot be offered to the next investors at the expense of the current preferred investors), limitations on how much and what type of loans or notes payable can be secured (without their approval), and 100 percent board authorization and approval in the event the company sells the majority of its business interests. Examples could go on and on, but by now you should get the picture loud and clear. When capital is raised in the form of preferred equity, the structure of these deals tends to strongly favor the preferred equity investors by providing significant financial preferences (to enhance their return) and management involvement (to protect and control their investments).

There is so much information and knowledge surrounding the subject of preferred equity that an entire book could be written on the terms, conditions, provisions, pros, cons, dos, don'ts, and I should have known betters. See the nearby sidebar "The real market," for a perspective on preferred equity investments, specifically, how the financial community can put a spin on a company and inflate its value.

REMEMBER When you hear about unicorn valuations, this is the value the investors *hope* the company will be worth down the road (not what it is worth now) and, if it is not, well, they can cover their downside by investing in preferred equity with favorable terms. In other words, this is just more financial lingo and terminology to familiarize yourself with to make sure you understand the never-ending flow of garbage oozing from the financial community.

Common equity, options, and warrants

At the end of the cap table, I want to briefly discuss common stock ownership and common stock options or warrants. There is really not a lot to discuss, as the reference to "common" says it all. That is, with common stock, everyone is basically in the same bucket with rights to earnings, voting on company matters, claims against company assets, and similar matters. Larger companies may issue multiple types of common stock with a common feature being that the class A common stock has voting rights and the class B common stock has no voting rights, but this type of equity complexity is generally only found in the largest and most powerful companies (such as, Alphabet, aka Google, Class A and C common stock).

Figure 13-2 presents our sample company's cap table, which now reflects ownership by what type of equity owns what percentage of the company.

The items of importance in the cap table are as follows:

>> Two columns of ownership percentages have been provided, voting and fully diluted. Voting captures only the equity that is issued and outstanding that has voting rights. Since common stock options and warrants are nothing more than having rights to purchase common stock at a later date, they do not have voting rights (thus, the reference to 0 percent ownership in this column). The fully diluted column calculates the ownership percentages of the company if all forms of equity were issued and outstanding and held equal rights.

>> The cap table reconciles to the statement of change in stockholders' equity presented in Figure 10-2 but now presents the information in a different format (to help the investors understand where they rank in the cap table and the ownership percentages in the company).

>> An item of significant importance is the voting ownership percentage of 53.33 percent controlled by the common equity group referenced as "founders." This indicates that the founders of the company still control a majority of the voting shares (just over 50 percent) and, at least through the most recent preferred capital raise, still retain management control of the company (which is especially important for obvious reasons).

>> Completing a little bit of math, you can calculate that the new preferred equity investors purchased their shares at $10.00 each compared to the original founders investing at $2.50 per common share and the other common stock owners at $15.00 per share. In other words, the preferred equity investors are breaking even, the original founders' shares have increased in value, while the other common equities investors are currently holding the bag (with implied losses). Oh, well, not every investment turns out to be a winner (at least based on the current valuation), but the other common equity investors are hopeful that management, by implementing its new business plan, can increase the value of the company so that all investors achieve a positive return on their investments.

>> The final item in the cap table captures the issuance of equity incentive grants in the form of common stock options or warrants. Common stock options and warrants are often issued (with the right to exercise at a set price based on a future event) to key employees, board members, strategic third parties, and others to provide an extra monetary incentive to allow these parties to participate in the increase in a company's value (if all goes well). Almost all large companies utilize these types of incentives to attract top employee talent and keep parties engaged with the business to help build value and achieve a successful exit. If all goes well, everyone makes out, and if it does not, let us just say that more than a few common stock options have turned out to be worthless. Options and warrants may have value to the recipient (eventually), but they only provide an option to purchase, so unless the option is exercised, these types of equity have no rights to earnings and cannot vote. Thus, I place them at the very bottom of the cap table, as this group of (potential) equity owners are truly last in line.

At this point, we've reached the bottom of the food chain as it relates to rights to both earnings and claims against assets. It may seem counterintuitive that the founders and the early other common equity investors along with key insiders (in control of common stock options and warrants), the ones who have poured their blood, sweat, and tears into building the business, stand last in line, but this is the reality of operating a business and building it into something of real value.

Q. As a potential external investor evaluating investing in our sample company, would the cap table, cap stack, or both of these financial reports/analyses be helpful when completing your review and diligence on making a potential investment in the company?

A. Clearly, both the cap table and cap stack would provide invaluable information. The cap table would help you understand ownership control and which parties have voting rights. The cap stack would help you envision just how much risk is present if the company had to liquidate unexpectedly and just how much would need to be received to get your money back. As a side note to all of you potential investors out there, if the cap table and cap stack are not provided by the company during your review or diligence process, either demand it or recreate this financial information, as investment decisions should not be made without understanding this critical financial data.

---

7 Referring to our sample company as presented in Figures 13-1 through 13-3, business issues suddenly arise that force it to sell out for $20,000,000 in early 2021. The acquiring company purchases all assets but assumes no liabilities (so all the liabilities and debt must be paid by our sample company). Based on the facts presented in this chapter, calculate the cap stack and how much the common stockholders would receive under this situation (disregard any value received by the option and warrant holders or dividends owed to the preferred investors).

Leveraging debt to finance business operations

Raising debt capital is nothing more than securing a loan from a financial institution (bank, asset-based lender, risk-based lenders, and so on) that has set repayment terms and performance requirements. The examples I give for a financial institution are a variety of different types of lenders. Historically, most people would tend to associate securing a loan with a bank. Oh, how times have changed as banks represent just one source of loans in a very large and growing ocean of sharks. I use the term sharks, as you would be absolutely amazed at how many different sources of loans are now available in the market, a number of which come with extremely expensive terms (thus, the use of the term "shark").

Referring back to our sample company and Figure 13-1, it previously secured or raised $7,200,000 of debt in the form of both short-term loans totaling $1,000,000 (those loans due and payable under one year) and long-term loans totaling $6,200,000 (those loans due and payable after one year). From the balance sheet you cannot tell how quickly the loans need to be paid off other than $1,000,000 will be due over the next twelve months and $6,200,000 thereafter. Are you able to determine if our sample company has too much or too little debt based on the balance sheet? Well, the answer to this question tends to be very subjective. But from completing a quick review of the balance sheet, you will notice total liabilities of $11,193,000 (including the $7,200,000 of debt) compared to $16,446,000 of total owners' equity for a debt-to-equity ratio of .68 to 1.00 ($11,193,000 divided by $16,446,000). For most companies, a debt-to-equity ratio of less than 1.00 to 1.00 generally indicates solid financial strength and health, as it has a debt load that should be very manageable based on our sample company's financial condition and recent performance.

When best to utilize: Debt sources of capital are best utilized when a company has assets available to pledge as collateral, can document and support internal cash flows adequate to service the debt service debt, and has enough strength in the balance sheet to avoid being overleveraged. For companies that are relatively mature (with stable operations and proven profitability or a defendable path to profitability). As you can see from our sample company in Figure 13-1 and referring back to Figure 7-1 (which reported our sample company generated a net profit of $4,644,000 in 2021), this tech company appears to be on sound footing and has appropriately used debt financing to support ongoing business operations.

Here are the pros and cons of utilizing debt capital. The pros of utilizing debt capital are that it brings in much-needed cash, does not dilute the ownership of the existing investors (an extremely big pro), and helps reduce or limit the potential management influence that may be realized from bringing on new owners. The cons with utilizing debt capital are that the company will generally have to pledge assets as collateral (putting the assets at risk), must adhere to set loan repayment terms (committing future cash flows to repaying the debt), will have to pay interest on the loan, and will most likely have to abide by covenants established by the lender.

I should also note that various forms of capital are available that take on the characteristics of both debt and equity. A perfect example of this is what is commonly referred to as convertible debt (a form of a loan which I discuss in the section "Equity designed as debt (risk-based debt)"). As a refresher, convertible debt has similar characteristics to the debt as previously discussed but often has more flexible terms attached (specific assets do not need to be pledged as collateral) in exchange for having the option of converting into company equity if desired (based on a triggering event). Convertible debt is really just a form of equity capital in disguise, but it does offer significant benefits to both the issuing company and the party providing the loan (which I covered previously in this chapter).

WARNING

Other forms of capital, including technology, human, brand or market awareness, and similar types of nonfinancial capital, are essential to operating a business. Needless to say, these are all critical forms of business capital and are essential to the success of any business but are beyond the scope of discussion for this book, as our goal is to keep you focused on understanding financial capital.

Expanding on our debt capital discussion, it will be worthwhile to review some basic concepts, strategies, and terminologies to better help you understand debt–based capital at a more granular level.

>> **Maturity and security:** To begin, always keep these two words in mind when thinking about debt — maturity and security. Maturity means all debt must be repaid over an agreed-upon period based on the terms and interest rate established. Security refers to what assets are pledged and used as collateral or what type of guarantees are provided to support the loan.

>> **Debt sources (such as, loans):** Literally hundreds of different types of financial institutions are willing to provide loans. In fact, the innovation and evolution of lending sources over the past decade has been nothing short of amazing. But in the end, debt sources still generally fall into one of four primary groupings: traditional banks, risk-based lenders (a very broad group of financing sources, often referred to as shadow banking, that include asset-based lenders, hard money lenders, lenders disguised as companies providing "advances," and the list goes on and on), hybrid debt/equity lenders (such as, convertible debt), and large financial institutions such as insurance companies (that invest in the bonds issued by a public company).

To effectively raise debt capital, companies need to clearly understand where they stand in the lender risk appetite food chain. For stronger operating companies that have solid profits and financial strength, banks should be readily available to provide loans (and should also be the cheapest form of debt). For riskier companies that have shaky profits and are highly leveraged, the risk-based lenders would be more logical to approach given their appetite for these types of loans (which will also be far more expensive than bank). And for the largest publicly traded companies, the public debt or bond markets should be accessible to raise capital (which can offer very inexpensive interest rates in the current environment).

>> **Debt underwriting and costs:** The general rule is that when debt sources underwrite a loan, they first look to a company's ability to generate positive cash flow (to cover debt service payments), look to the value of the collateral second (in case the collateral needs to be liquidated to repay the loan), and finally, will rely on secondary repayment sources that generally fall outside of the company (for example, a personal guarantee — PG — provided by an owner or a parent entity guarantee).

Also, it should be clear that the higher the perceived risk with issuing the loan, the greater the return on the loan needs to be (to the parties providing the loan), which may come from higher interest rates, additional fees, or attaching some type of "equity kicker" (for example, the loan includes an option or warrant to purchase X common shares at a discounted price if desired). However, a word of caution is warranted when raising debt capital, as this ocean is filled with sharks, most of which are full of nasty surprises. You would be absolutely amazed at just how expensive debt can be when secured from the risk-based lenders, so do your homework and read the fine print, as the devil is in the detail.

>> **Debt structure:** The balance sheet provides an important clue related to structuring loans correctly. If you refer to Figure 13-1, you will notice that the balance sheet presents the current portion of debt as a current liability and notes payable and other long-term debt as a long-term liability. This means that as of the FYE 12/31/21, our sample company has $1,000,000 of debt due within the next 12 months and approximately $6,200,000 of long-term debt due past 12 months (in our case, over the next three years).

When securing debt-based capital, it is important to properly match long-term debt with assets that will generate profits and cash flow over a long-term period (for example, five years) such as property, equipment, and intangible assets, as well as to match short-term sources of debt with current assets such as trade accounts receivables or inventory (that are anticipated to turn into cash relatively quickly). The key concept here is to properly match the structure of debt repayment term with the cash generation ability of the asset used as collateral.

>> **Debt covenants:** Almost all loans will include lending covenants that provide guardrails (for lack of a better term) to ensure that a company maintains a certain financial performance to support the repayment of the loan. Lenders will utilize a wide range of other covenants (financial and operational) including maintaining strong current ratios, establishing minimum profitability requirements (that is the company must generate positive earnings), requiring audited financial statements, and restricting the company from securing other loans, just to provide a few examples of other covenants.

The range of covenants is extensive and varies significantly by type of lender, but the key for the borrower is to clearly understand their company's borrowing needs and market conditions to negotiate the covenants in advance (and as part of the loan underwriting process). You should use visibility of your company's financial performance from the forecasting process (covered earlier in this chapter) to identify covenants that may be problematic, allowing you to negotiate more flexible and favorable covenants well in advance.

REMEMBER

One final comment as it relates to covenants. In the current economic environment and capital markets, you might come across the terms cov.-lite or no-cov. loans. These are just as they sound: cov.-lite means that a loan is being provided with noticeably light or low levels of covenants and no-cov. indicates that the loan basically has no covenants. Yes, I agree that it is nothing short of crazy for a lender to issue a loan with basically no covenants, but then again, 2020 and 2021 are about some of the craziest markets I have ever seen.

If there was ever a saying that summed up a discussion on debt capital it's this — "The Devil's in the Detail." Securing a loan for a business is certainly no easy task, as it often takes a significant amount of time, effort, and money. Further, loan documents are often very long, complex, and include terms and conditions that can quickly become problematic for inexperienced borrowers. To this I can only offer the all-important advice of making sure you secure proper legal and financial counsel to protect your interests (as leaving this up solely to the lender can be a fatal mistake).

EXAMPLE

Q. Are loan covenants established and incorporated into a loan agreement just for the benefit of the lender (to protect their interests)?

A. The answer on the surface may appear to be yes, but, in fact, when loan covenants are correctly established, the covenants may provide just as much value and protection to the borrower than the lender as it helps set "guardrails" to operate the business and achievable calculations as to not overly burden the borrower.

8 A simple but very helpful exercise here: Go on-line and type in your search engine "business loans" and see what appears on the first page. More than likely, everyone will see different results, as search engine algorithms take into consideration numerous factors (such as, geographical location). Jot down what you see and what sticks out after completing this search.

9 Review our sample company's financial performance, both the balance sheet and income statement, and offer three potential financial covenants that you feel would be reasonable for a lender to request. To get you headed in the right direction, here is one that would be reasonable: The lender requests, and you agree to maintain a current ratio of at least 1.50 to 1.00. A company's current ratio is calculated by dividing total current assets by total current liabilities. For our sample company as of 12/31/21, the current ratio stands at 4.54 to 1.00 ($22,689,000 of current assets divided by $4,993,000 of current liabilities), which is very healthy and well above the requested level of 1.50 to 1.00. So, with one down, please identify two other financial ratios that would make sense for our sample company.

Noting key points in raising capital

When you raise capital, through debt or equity, and ask other parties to believe in your business, you must remember the golden rule: Whoever has the gold makes the rules! Which brings me to offering these final words of wisdom when it comes to raising and managing capital:

>> **Cash is king.** Businesses must proactively, appropriately, and prudently manage cash resources or, to paraphrase the words of Warden Norton from the movie *Shawshank Redemption* (referring to the escape of Andy Dufresne), "Lord, it's a miracle, he just vanished like a fart in the wind." If not responsibly managed and protected, your cash will vanish like a fart in the wind!

>> **Never run out of cash.** It is somewhat easy to discuss a miss or negative variance in the income statement, especially if you have best-in-class information (to explain the miss). But if you run out of cash and must explain this to an investor/lender, get ready to have a rather unpleasant discussion with your capital sources, as it is going to be painful and most likely involve some very restrictive and unfavorable terms (if they even consider providing more capital).

>> **When capital sources offer extra cash, take it!** Yes, this may translate into more ownership dilution and/or added interest expense, but the ability to build a liquidity cushion for when a business hits the eventual speed bump (which you will), is invaluable. There is nothing worse than having to raise cash when times are tough.

>> **Timing can be everything.** Companies will look to offer equity when the price is high (to limit ownership dilution). This is a quite common tactic with large, hot companies looking to raise extra cash for use down the road as evidenced by Tesla (raising extra capital). You will need to pay close attention to economic and market cycles, which can change quickly.

>> **When cash is tight, know your balance sheet and how to squeeze it.** You could incentivize customers to pay early or make deposits (a strategy used by Tesla) or push your vendors a bit (but not too much). You might also be able to work with key lenders or investors to have a bit of a slush fund to tap when needed. The key is to plan proactively, understand your cash flow statement, and communicate effectively.

>> **Understand that who you take capital from is often more important than the amount, type, and structure of that capital.** Most importantly, having the right financial partners that understand your business and timelines and have vast experience and resources can be invaluable. Securing capital from the right source can really help turn a highly stressful process into a wonderful experience. Secure capital from the wrong source and get ready for hell.

I want to emphasize the importance of understanding and relying on the statement of cash flows and retaining proper levels of liquidity to operate your business in good times or bad. There is nothing worse than having to tap capital markets in a hostile environment, as the terms will most likely be ugly (if you get them at all). Also remember the adage about banks: They will lend when you do not need it, and when you do, they are nowhere to be found.

Answers to Problems on Managing Business Capital

The following are the answers to the practice questions presented earlier in this chapter.

1 List three sources of information and/or data that a company may utilize to support the development of a business plan.

The list of potential information sources is endless, but here are some examples to get you started:

- Industry trade publications.
- Company historical operating results.
- General economic reports (public or private).
- Third-party studies and analyses.
- Your company's internal management team and previous business plans.
- Mine and decipher key customer and vendor information.
- Third-party professionals such as lawyers, accountants, financial advisors, industry experts, lenders, VC or PE groups, and so on.

There really is no right or wrong answer here as the list could go on and on. However, being able to focus on the most pertinent and valuable sources of information to assist with creating a business plan cannot be emphasized enough.

2 Identify three different business situations or opportunities (other than those previously presented) when a business plan should be developed and implemented by management or the owners.

Again, the list of potential operating scenarios is endless, but here are some examples to think about:

- A young couple wants to start a business and are looking at a franchise opportunity in the mobile pet grooming industry.
- A large company is looking to expand and is evaluating buying a competing business to "jump start" its effort.
- A company has hit the end of the line and is evaluating declaring bankruptcy, as it is no longer economically viable. Yes, even when a business fails, it should develop a dissolution plan.
- A business is evaluating expanding into a foreign market and needs to evaluate the potential opportunity.
- A business experienced a catastrophic loss from a natural disaster and needs to relocate to another region of the company to continue operations.

Again, the list could go on and on, as the point with providing these examples is to highlight how many operating scenarios exist that warrant developing a business plan, even if relatively basic.

3. A business prepares three sets of forecast, a high or best case, a medium or expected case, and a low or worst case. What concept best describes this strategy?

This represents a perfect example of a "what if" forecast scenario as the company's management team wants to understand the financial performance under the best and worst case operating scenarios.

4. A blank SWOT analysis is provided for a company that has a new cryptocurrency, which it plans on introducing to the market shortly. Complete the following SWOT analysis by offering one item in each quadrant.

I picked the cryptocurrency industry given how relevant this space is as of the date this book was published. I offer two ideas in each box to help understand the type of expected responses.

Strength:	Weakness:
Best in class company management team and technological resources.	Limited company capital. Need substantial equity raise.
Legally protected algorithms already established.	Company young. No profitability achieved to date with no clear path to profitability present.
Opportunity:	Threat:
TAM (total addressable market) is extremely large on a global scale with limited penetration to date.	Government regulations may be forthcoming that hinder industry.
Adoption by general population gaining traction with widespread use not present.	Significant competition already established with more than 10,000 cryptocurrencies in existence.

5. Can you determine the ownership percentage for each investor in a company based purely on the amount of money invested or used to purchase stock?

No. The reason for this is that there are two critical pieces of information to know including the amount paid for the equity and more importantly, how much equity, or in our sample company's case, how many preferred shares, was received. In our sample company, it is one thing to receive 500,000 preferred shares but if for some reason the investor received 1,000,000 preferred shares (as each share was valued lower), the ownership of the company would change dramatically.

6. Instead of the VC firm investing $5,000,000 for 500,000 shares of preferred stock, update the cap table to reflect that the VC firm invested $8,000,000 and received 800,000 shares of preferred stock. What sticks out or could be concerning to the founders based on the new cap table?

Sample Company Alternative Cap. Table

QW Example Tech., Inc.
Capitalization Table
as of the Fiscal Year Ending
12/31/2021

Description	Number of Shares	Invested Amount	Voting Issued & O/S % Owned	Fully Diluted % Owned
Preferred Equity:				
H&H Test VC Firm, Fund V	800,000	$8,000,000	44.44%	41.56%
Subtotal - Preferred Equity	800,000	$8,000,000	44.44%	41.56%
Common Equity:				
Founders, Original	800,000	$2,000,000	44.44%	41.56%
Investors, Various Parties	200,000	$3,000,000	11.11%	10.39%
Subtotal - Common Equity	1,000,000	$5,000,000	55.56%	51.95%
Common Equity Options & Warrants:				
Stock options issued & outstanding	75,000	$0	0.00%	3.90%
Warrants issued for common stock purchases	50,000	$0	0.00%	2.60%
Subtotal - Common Equity Options & Warrants	125,000	$0	0.00%	6.49%
Total, All forms of Equity	1,925,000	$13,000,000	100.00%	100.00%

Confidential - Property of QW Example Tech., Inc.

You will notice that the ownership percentage for the VC firm has increased to 44.44 percent, the same ownership percentage as the original founders. This represents an important item, as effective management control of the company is not as much in the hands of the VC firm as the original founders.

(7) Referring to our sample company as presented in Figures 13–1 through 13–3, business issues suddenly arise that force it to sell out for $20,000,000 in early 2022. The acquiring company purchases all assets but assumes no liabilities (so all the liabilities and debt must be paid by our sample company). Based on the facts presented in this chapter, calculate the "cap stack" and how much the common stockholders would receive under this situation (disregard any value received by the option and warrant holders or dividends owed to the preferred investors).

Sample Company Liquidation Analysis

QW Example Tech., Inc.
Estimated Liabilities & Shareholders' Equity
For the Fiscal Year Ending
12/31/2021
(all numbers in thousands)

Summary of Liabilities & Equity	Priority Status	Amount	Notes/Comments
Payroll, Taxes, & Burden Payable	High	$444	Employee obligations are generally at the top of the list.
Income Taxes Payable	High	$87	Governments make sure they get their money.
Loans & Notes Payable, Secured	High	$7,200	Senior debt/secured against company assets.
Trade Payables & Accrued Liabilities	High/Med.	$2,315	Depending on terms with vendors, could be high or med.
Deferred Revenue & Other Current Lia.	Medium	$1,147	Customer advance payments & deposits not secured.
Subtotal Liabilities		$11,193	
Preferred Stock w/1.5x liquidation preference	Med/Low	$5,000	Remember the 1.5x liquidation preference.
Subtotal Liabilities & Preferred Stock		$16,193	
Total Amount Received		$20,000	Value received from acquiring company.
Value Available to Common Stockholders	Low	$3,807	Remaining value available for common stockholders.

Confidential - Property of QW Example Tech., Inc.

As you can see, the common investors would receive $3,807,000 compared to their original investment of $5,000,000. Is this fair? Well, as my dad always reminded me, "Nobody said that life is fair." The bottom line here is that the owners of the company probably should have negotiated a better deal with the preferred investors. Oh, well, better luck next time.

8. A simple but very helpful exercise here: Go on-line and type in your search engine "business loans" and see what appears on the first page. More than likely, everyone will see different results as search engine algorithms take into consideration numerous factors (such as, geographical location). Jot down what you see and what sticks out after completing this search.

   Have fun with sorting through the responses received, as this exercise is designed to highlight just how many sources of debt are present in the market. For me, the top search results landed with some relatively big organizations including the SBA (Small Business Administration) and large brand names such as Lending Tree, but no banks. This shows you just how fragmented and large the business lending marketplace is.

9. Review our sample company's financial performance, both the balance sheet and income statement, and offer three potential financial covenants that you feel would be reasonable for a lender to request. To get you headed in the right direction, here is one that would be reasonable. The lender requests and you agree to maintain a current ratio of at least 1.50 to 1.00. A company's current ratio is calculated by dividing total current assets by total current liabilities. For our sample company as of 12/31/21, the current ratio stands at 4.54 to 1.00 ($22,689,000 of current assets divided by $4,993,000 of current liabilities), which is very healthy and well above the requested level of 1.50 to 1.00. So, with one down, please identify two other financial ratios that would make sense for our sample company.

Lender Covenants		
Description	Amount	Covenant
Current Ratio:		
Total Current Assets	$22,689,000	
Total Current Liabilities	$4,993,000	
Current Ratio	4.54	Not to fall below 1.50.
Minimum Net Working Capital:		
Total Current Assets	$22,689,000	
Total Current Liabilities	$4,993,000	
	$17,696,000	Must be greater than the total of the outstanding loan balances plus net profit of $1,000,000.
Net Working Capital		Currently this total is $7,200,000.
Minimum Net Profitability Requirement:		
Required Minimum Net Profitability	$1,000,000	To ensure annual debt payment of $1 million can be met.
Current Year Net Profit	$4,644,000	Current company net profit for FYE 12/31/21.
Clearance or Cushion	$3,644,000	Cushion present.

I offer a couple of simple covenant examples including maintaining a minimum net working capital balance of greater than the outstanding loan balances and a minimum annual net profit requirement of $1,000,000 (to support at least being able to repay $1,000,000 of debt a year). Several other financial covenants could be agreed to by the parties, but the key concept for the borrower to remember when agreeing to financial covenants is the following: Make sure the financial covenants are set with more than enough "head room" so that if a bump in the operating results is realized, the financial covenant is not jeopardized. There's nothing worse (and more expensive) than having to deal with a lender and explain why a covenant was breached.

4

The Part of Tens

For business investors: Find ten things everyone reading a business financial report should know and keep in mind.

For accountants: Take away a ten-point checklist for helping managers in their planning, control, and decision-making.

Chapter **14**

Ten Things You Should Know About Business Financial Statements

F inancial statements, which are one of the main products of the accounting system of a business, serve two broad purposes, one targeted toward internal users of the financial information and one targeted toward external users of the financial information:

» They help managers assess and manage the company's profit performance, cash flows, capital resources, and financial condition of a business.

» They serve as a pipeline of information to business lenders, investors, analysts, and other external parties with a vested interest (for example, taxing authorities). Without this financial information, lenders would balk at loaning money to a business, investors would refuse to invest their hard-earned money in a business, analysts would pass on providing an opinion on the economic viability of the company, and taxing authorities would more than likely have a few concerns.

In short, financial statements are essential in managing a business and in raising the capital a business needs to operate.

Internal financial statements used by managers don't circulate outside the business as they often contain confidential and proprietary information. Internal financial statements are distributed on a need-to-know basis within the business; they contain more-detailed information than the summary-level information presented in external financial statements distributed to lenders and shareowners of a business. But both the internal and external financial statements use the same accounting methods. Businesses keep only one set of books, but they "keep secrets" that aren't disclosed in their external financial reports.

Business managers, business lenders, and business investors should understand certain characteristics and limitations of financial statements. I explain ten of these important points in this chapter.

Rules and Standards Matter

I have seen very few maverick financial statements, although in this day and age of providing non-GAAP financial information (for comparison purposes), companies are once again pushing the limit on disclosing financial results to external parties. Almost all financial statements are (or should be) prepared using generally accepted accounting principles (GAAP) and/or international accounting standards. For most larger and more sophisticated businesses, financial statement readers can assume that American GAAP or the international equivalent have been applied in preparing the financial statements and that there aren't any significant deviations from these rules of the game. If financial statements are prepared on some other basis of accounting, the business should make this fact very clear in its financial report. I should also note smaller, less sophisticated businesses may tend to deviate from preparing financial statements using GAAP. I've seen a wide range of "alternative" (for lack of a better term) accounting methods used including cash basis, tax basis, modified accrual, and even FMV (fair market value). Needless to say, when alternative accounting methods are used, red flags should be raised very quickly.

These accounting rules and standards don't put a business in an accounting straitjacket. A business still has wiggle room in the application of GAAP. For instance, both accelerated and straight-line depreciation expense methods are equally acceptable (see Chapter 6), and a business can adopt either conservative or liberal (aggressive) accounting methods for recording profit, which also affect the values reported for assets and liabilities in its balance sheet. A business has the choice among alternative methods in many areas of accounting.

Exactitude Would Be Nice, but Estimates Are Key

Looking at all the numbers in a financial statement, you may assume that they're accurate down to the last dollar. Not true. The balance in the cash account is exact, but virtually every other number you see in a financial report is based on an estimate. The amounts of expenses, revenue, assets, and liabilities are calculated down to the last dollar, but they're based on estimates, and estimates never turn out to be accurate down to the last dollar.

For example, consider depreciation expense. A business estimates the future useful life of a fixed asset (long-term operating asset) and allocates its cost over this useful life. Another example is accounts receivable — the business estimates how much of the total balance of its accounts receivable will turn out to be bad debts. Yet another example is the accrued liability for product warranty and guarantee costs that will be paid in the future. This amount is only an educated guess (but one that hopefully is based on sound historical data and operating trends).

REMEMBER

Estimates are unavoidable in accounting. Most businesses have enough experience to make pretty good estimates, and they consult experts when they need to. A business can nudge an estimate toward the conservative side or the liberal side. For instance, it can estimate that its future product warranty and guarantee costs will be fairly low or fairly high. Usually, arguments exist on both sides, and the business ends up having to make a somewhat arbitrary estimate.

WARNING

Some estimates are particularly difficult to make, such as the liability for future post-retirement medical and health benefits that a business promises its employees. Another difficult estimate concerns product recalls, estimated warranty claims, or sales returns. Estimating the cost of a major lawsuit in which the decision may go against the business is very difficult. My advice is to be alert in reading financial statements to see if the business is facing any issue that's particularly difficult to estimate. Also, remember that the newer the business is, the higher risk the estimates may not be accurate. For a company such as Ford, it has decades of experience in estimating future warranty claims. For a newer auto manufacturer such as Tesla, it doesn't have 30 years of operating experience so its accounting estimates for future warranty claims may be volatile and subject to subjective opinions.

Financial Statements Fit Together Hand in Glove

The three primary financial statements — the income statement, the balance sheet, and the statement of cash flows — appear on separate pages in a financial report and, therefore, may seem freestanding. In fact, the three financial statements are intertwined and interconnected (see Chapters 9 and 10). Accountants assume that the reader understands these connections, so they don't connect the dots between corresponding accounts in different financial statements. Understanding these tentacles of connection between the statements is extremely important, especially for interpreting the statement of cash flows (see Chapter 10). For example, an increase in accounts receivable during the year that's reported in the balance sheet causes a decrease in cash flow from operating activities.

TIP

For help in understanding financial statements and how all their elements work together, check out the book *How To Read A Financial Report,* 9th Edition (Wiley; written by myself and my dad), which has been in print for more than 40 years. The book clarifies the lines of connection between sales revenue and expenses in the income statement and the assets and liabilities in the balance sheet that are changed by sales revenue and expenses. Profit activities are reported in the income statement, but the results of profit are reported in the balance sheet. I explain why accrual basis profit differs from the cash flow from profit (operating activities) — which is a key point that business managers and investors should understand, but many don't. I use financial statement example templates that can be adapted to fit most businesses. I offer to send readers the Excel spreadsheets for the exhibits in this book. To date, I've received hundreds and hundreds of requests for the spreadsheets. Hands down, the most frequent comment in the emails I receive is that I make clear the lines of connection between accounts in the financial statements.

Accrual Basis Is Used to Record Profit, Assets, and Liabilities

The vast majority of businesses must use the accrual basis of accounting to determine profit or loss and to keep track of their assets and liabilities. Simply put, the accrual basis must be used to reflect economic reality. The following are three examples of the accrual basis at work:

>> A business makes a sale on credit, accepting the customer's promise to pay at a later date and delivering the product. The accountant records the sale by an increase to an asset called accounts receivable.

>> A business buys a building or machine that will be used many years in its operations and pays cash for the asset. The cost of the asset isn't charged to expense right away. Rather, the cost is allocated to expense over the estimated useful life span of the asset.

>> A business records an expense now even though it will not pay for the expense until sometime later. To record the expense, a liability is increased; later, when the expense is paid, the liability is decreased.

Some small businesses don't sell on credit, don't carry inventory, don't invest in fixed assets (long-term operating resources), and pay their bills quickly. They may use the cash basis of accounting instead of the accrual basis. Basically, all they do is keep a checkbook.

Cash Flow Differs from Accrual Basis Profit

WARNING

The accrual basis of accounting (see the preceding section), even though it reflects economic reality, can create a point of confusion: Many people look at the bottom-line profit or loss number in the income statement and jump to the conclusion that it's the amount that cash increased or decreased for the period. Indeed, the expression "a business makes money" suggests that making a profit increases the business's cash account the same amount. But cash flow from profit — the net increase or decrease in cash from the sales and expense activities of a business for a period — almost always differs from the amount of bottom-line profit or loss reported in its income statement.

In one sense, you can blame accounting for speaking with a forked tongue: The income statement reports one number for profit (net income), and the statement of cash flows reports another number for profit (cash flow from operating activities). There's the accrual basis number in the income statement and the cash basis number in the statement of cash flows. Essentially, a financial report has two versions of profit, one presented in the income statement and one in the statement of cash flows. But to emphasize again, the true measurement of profit or loss is reported in the income statement.

TIP

The amount of cash flow from profit (operating activities) in the statement of cash flows tells you what profit would have been on the cash basis of accounting. The statement of cash flows explains why the cash flow from profit is different from the net income for the period. One difference (but certainly not the only one) between cash basis and accrual basis profit accounting is depreciation. On the accrual basis, depreciation expense is deducted from sales revenue to determine profit, which is correct of course. From the cash flow point of view, in contrast, depreciation isn't bad but good. The cash inflow from sales revenue, in part, reimburses the business for using its fixed assets. In other words, depreciation for the year is recovery of the cash invested in fixed assets in prior years. Money is returning to the business.

Profit and Balance Sheet Values Can Be and Often Are Manipulated

I'm sure you've heard about business managers "massaging the numbers" to make profit for the year look better or to make the financial condition of the business look better. (aka "fluffing the pillows.") Managers can and do lay a heavy hand on the accounting process — to pump up sales revenue or to deflate expenses for the year in order to meet pre-established profit goals or to dampen the volatility of reported earnings year to year. There's no end to the tactics for manipulating accounting numbers.

TIP

Rather than presenting a litany of the techniques for massaging the numbers, I offer two observations:

>> Massaging the numbers is expected, and one may even argue that business lenders and investors encourage it — mainly on the grounds that a business is entitled to put its best face forward. Independent CPA auditors go along with a reasonable amount of accounting manipulation.

>> There's a big difference between massaging the numbers and cooking the books. Cooking the books is the playful name for a serious crime, accounting fraud, in which fictitious sales are recorded, expenses aren't recorded, liabilities are hidden, or assets are overstated. Accounting fraud is a felony (if one gets caught and convicted, that is) and is centered in a willful intent to deceive the party receiving the financial information.

Financial Statements May Be Revised
Later to Correct Errors and Fraud

One ominous financial reporting development over the last couple of decades bothers me a great deal (and to which I eluded earlier): An increasing number of businesses revise their financial statements after releasing them to the public. I'm speaking about businesses whose securities are traded in public markets (such as the New York Stock Exchange and NASDAQ). Private businesses don't release their financial reports to the public at large, so their financial reports probably aren't revised and restated as frequently as those of public businesses.

By their very nature, financial statements are tentative and conditional. One of the first things you learn in studying accounting is the going concern assumption. The accountant assumes the business will continue to operate for an indefinite period of time and isn't planning to shut down and liquidate its assets. Financial statements are conditional — the condition being that business will continue to operate in a normal fashion. (If a business is in the middle of bankruptcy proceedings, on the other hand, the accountant has to reckon the chances of the business continuing in operations.)

It's amazing to me that most financial report revisions are made to correct major accounting errors or in the worst case, accounting fraud. How did these errors slip through the system in the first place? Undoubtedly, the Enron scandal from the early 2000s has made people more aware of the possibility of accounting fraud. But even before Enron happened, the pace of financial report revisions had accelerated. All you can do is to take any financial report with a grain of salt and keep in mind that the financial statements may contain serious errors.

Some Asset Values Are Current,
but Others May Be Old

The balance (amount) of an asset in a balance sheet is the result of the entries (increases less decreases) recorded in the account. A balance sheet doesn't disclose whether the ending balance in an asset is from recent entries or from entries made years ago. How recent an ending balance is depends on which asset you're talking about and which accounting method is used for the asset. For example, if a business uses the FIFO (first-in, first-out) method for its cost of goods sold expense, its inventories balance on the balance sheet is from entries recorded recently. In contrast, if the company uses the LIFO (last-in, first-out) method, its inventories balance on the balance sheet is from older entries. How much older? Well, one major equipment manufacturer has been using LIFO for many years and part of its inventories balance goes back more than 50 years.

The balance of property, plant, equipment, machinery, trucks, and the like typically consists of fixed assets that have been on the books for 5, 10, 20, or more years. You should never confuse the original costs in this asset account with the current replacement value of the assets. On the other hand, the accounts receivable balance is current, as is cash, of course.

TIP

The footnotes to the financial statements may include information on the current replacement values of certain assets. For example, if a business uses LIFO and has a large gap between the FIFO and the LIFO balances, the business is required under GAAP to disclose an estimate of the FIFO amount for its balance sheet inventories.

Financial Statements Leave Interpretation to Readers

One guiding rule of financial reporting is to let the financial statements speak for themselves. The financial statements and footnotes report the facts but don't interpret what the facts mean or what the facts portend. The assessment and forecast of a company's financial performance and condition are left for the readers to tackle.

REMEMBER

Having said that, I should quickly point out that the chief executive and other top-level officers of public companies include a good deal of commentary and their interpretations of the company's financial performance in annual financial reports. Indeed, it's useful to carefully read the Management Discussion and Analysis (MD&A) section in a public company's annual financial report. But keep in mind that getting the top officers' take is like asking the captain of a ship how the voyage went when the passengers may have quite a different opinion.

Financial Statements Tell the Story of a Business, Not Its Individual Shareowners

Financial statements tell the story of the business. How well or poorly individual investors in the business have done isn't information you can find in the financial statements. Some shareowners in a business may have had their money invested in the business from day one, whereas other original investors may have sold their shares. The business doesn't record the prices they received for the shares; in other words, dealings and transactions among shareowners aren't recorded or reported by the business. This activity is none of the business's business.

REMEMBER

The owners' equity accounts in a balance sheet report only the original amounts invested by shareowners. What has happened since then in the trading of these ownership shares isn't captured in the financial statements — unless the business itself bought some of the shares from its shareowners. You might find it very interesting to compare the current market price of stock shares you own with the stockholders' equity balances reported in the company's balance sheet. In a rough sort of way, this is like comparing the current market value of your home with the cost you paid many years ago.

Chapter 15

A Ten-Point Checklist for Management Accountants

In a business, accounting has several functions. The responsibilities of the entire accounting team including the CFO, the chief accountant (aka, controller), and the accounting department include the following:

» Complying with the manifold requirements of federal and state income taxes, state and local sales taxes, property taxes, payroll taxes, and countless other forms of taxes, licenses, and fees.

» Designing, operating, and managing a system to capture, record, process, store, and safeguard all relevant documents and information about the financial activities of the business (which is especially important in the new digital age).

» Ensuring the integrity and reliability of the information system and preventing fraud from inside and outside the business (the latter being directed at the business).

» Preparing financial statements that are reported externally to its lenders and shareowners. (If the business is a public company, the accountants are also responsible for preparing filings with the Security and Exchange Commission, or SEC.)

» Preparing financial statements and accounting reports for distribution to the business's managers for their planning, control, and decision-making needs.

Translating all of this into one simple and critical concept to remember, the accounting department must always strive to produce complete, accurate, reliable, and timely (also known as CART) financial information, including financial statements, on which a business can make sound economic decisions and comply with all applicable laws, regulations, and governances.

The last function listed is referred to as *management* or *managerial accounting*. It concerns accounting's role in helping business managers carry out their functions. This chapter offers a ten-point checklist for accountants in fulfilling their functions for managers, somewhat like the checklist for pilots before take-off. Accountants are saddled with the several functions previously mentioned, and under the pressures of time they may end up giving short shrift to their duties to managers — which is understandable. However, the very continuance of the business depends on accountants providing managers information they need to know for making decisions and maintaining control. If managers don't get what they need from their accountants, the business could fail or spin out of control. In this sense, management accounting functions are the most central — if the business fails, the other accounting functions are beside the point.

Designing Internal Accounting Reports

In designing internal accounting reports for managers, the accountant should ask, "Who's entitled to know what?" Generally speaking, the board of directors, the chief executive officer, the president, the chief financial officer, and the chief operating officer are entitled to know anything and everything. (This sweeping comment is subject to exceptions in business organizations that tightly control the flow of financial information.) By virtue of their positions, the financial vice president and chief accountant (aka the controller) have access to all financial information about the business.

Other managers in a business have a limited scope of responsibility and authority. The accountant should report to them the information they need to know to make the decisions they are responsible for making, but no more. For example, the vice-president of production receives a wide range of manufacturing information but doesn't receive sales and marketing information. The accountant should identify a particular manager's specific area of authority and responsibility in deciding the information content of accounting reports to that manager. The reporting of information to individual managers should follow the organizational structure of the business; this practice is called *responsibility accounting*.

From the accounting point of view, the organizational structure of a business consists of *profit centers* and *cost centers*:

>> **A profit center could be a product or service line, or even a specific product model or service offering.** For example, a profit center for Apple Computer is its AirPod line of products; another profit center is its iTunes Music Center (where customers download audio and video files), which is more of a service. Within each broad product line, Apple has sub-profit centers. For example, each type of AirPod is a sub-profit center.

>> **A cost center is an organization unit that doesn't directly generate sales revenue.** For example, the accounting department of a company is a cost center.

The accounting reports that go to the manager of a profit center should be oriented to the profit performance of that organization unit. The accounting reports that go to a manager of a cost center should be oriented to the cost performance of that organization unit.

Helping Managers Understand Their Accounting Reports

Most managers have limited accounting backgrounds; their backgrounds are usually in marketing, engineering, law, human resources, and other fields. Not to sound critical, but most business managers have their desires to learn accounting under control. Furthermore, they're very busy people with little time to spare. Yet accountants often act as if managers fully understand the accounting reports they receive and have all the time in the world to read and digest the detailed information they contain. Accountants are dead-wrong on this point.

One of the main functions of the management accountant is to serve as the translator of accounting jargon and reports to business managers — to take the technical terminology and methods of accounting and put it all into terms that non-accounting managers can clearly understand. Of course, being an author of accounting books for non-accountants, I may be biased, but I believe that management accountants can perform a very valuable service by improving their communication skills with non-accounting managers.

Involving Managers in Choosing Accounting Methods

Some business managers take charge of every aspect of the business, including choosing accounting methods for their businesses. But many business managers are passive and defer to their chief accountants regarding the accounting methods their businesses should use. In my opinion, the hands-off approach is a mistake. Chapter 6 explains three critical accounting issues for which a business has to choose between alternative accounting methods. Ultimately, the chief executive officer of the business is responsible for these decisions, as they are responsible for all fundamental decisions of the business. But such accounting decisions may not be on the radar screen of the chief executive.

REMEMBER In choosing accounting methods, the chief accountant shouldn't allow managers to sit on the sidelines and be spectators. The chief accountant shouldn't select an accounting method without the explicit approval and understanding of top-level managers. In particular, the head accountant should explain the differences in profit and asset and liability values between alternative accounting methods. The business's accounting methods should reflect its philosophy and strategies, so if the business is conservative in its policies and strategies, it should use conservative accounting methods.

Chief accountants can find themselves between a rock and a hard place when top-level managers intervene in the normal accounting process. This interference may be referred to as *massaging the numbers, managing earnings, smoothing earnings,* or good old-fashioned *accounting manipulation.* If the accountant accedes to management pressure, they should make clear to the manager what the consequences will be the following year. Generally speaking, there's a *compensatory effect,* or trade-off, between years; pumping up profit this year, for instance, causes profit deflation next year. Massaging the numbers produces a robbing Peter to pay Paul effect, and the accountant should make this very clear to the manager.

Designing Profit Performance Reports for Managers

The accountant needs to read the mind of the manager in designing the layout and content of reports to the manager. Ideally, the profit report should reflect the manager's profit strategy and tactics. For example, a manager of a profit center focuses on two main things — *margin* and *sales volume.* Therefore, the profit report should emphasize those two key factors. It sounds simple enough, but one impediment exists in designing internal profit reports for managers based on management thinking.

In designing internal profit reports for managers, accountants too often follow the path of least resistance. They use the format and content of the income statement reported outside the business, but this won't do. An external income statement conceals as much information as it reveals. External income statements don't disclose information about margins and sales volumes for each profit center of the business.

The accountant has to break out of their external income statement mentality and think in terms of what managers need to know for analyzing profit performance and making profit decisions. My main advice on this point is straightforward: Listen to how the manager explains their profit strategy, which is called the "business model." Get inside the manager's head. Do your best to understand the mindset of the manager regarding how they see the formula for making profit. Listen carefully to which particular factors the manager thinks are the most important drivers (determinants) of profit. Don't try to remodel the manager's thinking into the accountant's way of thinking. Don't forget that the manager is the boss — even though you might think the manager should go back and learn accounting. In short, don't try to educate the manager on accounting; let the manager educate you on what they need to know in order to make profit.

Designing Cash Flow Reports for Managers

The conventional statement of cash flows is far too technical and intimidating for most managers to make sense of. What managers don't understand, they don't use. In my view, accountants are too bound by their "debits and credits" thinking when it comes to the statement of cash flows. The statement of cash flows is designed to reconcile changes in the balance sheet during the period with the amounts reported in the statement. But should this function also be the purpose of reporting this financial statement to managers? I don't think so.

In mid-size and large businesses, the financial officers of the business manage cash flow. Other managers don't have any direct responsibility over cash flow — although their decisions impact cash flow. Managers of profit and cost centers should have a basic understanding of the cash flow impacts of their decisions. They don't necessarily need cash flow statements, but they need to know how their decisions impact cash flow.

TIP

The cash flow reports to managers of profit and cost centers should focus mainly on the key factors that affect *cash flow from operating activities* (see Chapter 10). These internal management reports should concentrate on changes in accounts receivable, inventory, and operating liabilities (accounts payable and accrued expenses payable). These are the main factors for the difference between cash flow and profit that the managers of profit and cost centers have control over and responsibility for.

Designing Management Control Reports

Management control is usually thought of as keeping a close watch on a thousand and one details, any one of which can spin out of control and cause problems. First and foremost, however, management control means achieving objectives and keeping on course toward the goals of the business. Management control covers a lot of ground — motivating employees, working with suppliers, keeping customers satisfied, and so on. But there's no doubt that managers need control reports that include a lot of detail.

TIP

The trick in management control reports is to separate the wheat from the chaff. Being very busy people, managers can't afford to waste time on relatively insignificant problems. They have to prioritize problems and deal with the issues that have the greatest effect on the business. Therefore, the accountant should design management control reports that differentiate significant problems from less serious problems. In control reports, the accountant should use visual pointers to highlight serious problems. In other words, control reports shouldn't be flat, with all lines of information appearing to be equally important.

Developing Financial Forecast Models for Management Decision-Making Analysis

For decision-making purposes, business managers need a model of operating profit that, theoretically, fits on the back of an envelope. The accounting department is often tasked with the function of designing effective forecast models, some of which are relatively simple and others very complex, to assist business managers with making informed economic decisions. A critical concept to understand when preparing and updating forecasts model is the reference to the "What If" analysis. That is, "if" these critical assumptions change then "what" will be the financial impact or updated output. You would be absolutely amazed at how often companies prepare different forecast models and/or business projections to evaluate how changing business conditions may impact their financial results. A perfect example of a macro level event impacting a business's financial performance would be the COVID-19 pandemic that started in 2020 and is still very much alive as of the date this book was published. The COVID-19 pandemic wreaked havoc on business operations around the globe, resulting in the need to quickly update forecast models and projections to adapt to the new world economic reality.

At a micro level, here's an example of such a compact profit "what if" model, which I adapted from "Analysis method #1: Contribution margin minus fixed costs" in Chapter 11:

(Unit Margin × Sales Volume) − Fixed Expenses = Operating Profit

Suppose the sales price is $100 and variable costs equal $65 per unit. Therefore, unit margin is $35. Assume the business sells 100,000 units, so its total contribution margin for the period is $3,500,000 ($35 unit margin × 100,000 units = $3,500,000 total contribution margin). Last, assume its fixed expenses for the period equal $2,500,000. So, its operating profit is $1,000,000 for the period.

The accountant should develop a condensed profit model, which is limited to the critical factors that tip profit one way or the other. This profit model helps the manager focus on the key variables that drive profit behavior. For example, continuing with the example just mentioned, suppose the manager is contemplating cutting sales price 10 percent to boost sales volume 20 percent. Using the profit model, the manager can quickly do a before and after comparison of the proposed sales price cut:

Before: ($35 unit margin × 100,000 units) − $2,500,000 fixed expenses = $1,000,000 operating profit

After: ($25 unit margin × 120,000 units) − $2,500,000 = $500,000 operating profit

Giving up 10 percent of sales price for a 20 percent gain in sales volume may have intuitive appeal, but this decision would cripple profit. Operating profit would drop from $1,000,000 to only $500,000; the manager would give up $10, or 29 percent of the $35 margin per unit. The sacrifice is too great in exchange for only 20 percent gain in sales volume.

Working Closely with Managers in Planning

One of the most important managerial functions has two parts: forecasting changes that will affect the business (refer to the previous point) and planning the future of the business. This task includes plotting the sales trajectory of the business, the need for additional capital, and shifts in size and makeup of its workforce and other factors. The accountant should be involved in the planning process from the get-go. Otherwise, the accountant is at a disadvantage in preparing budgets and financial projections. The better the accountant understands the planning process, and the closer the accountant works with managers in developing plans, the more useful the financial forecasts and budgets will be. It is absolutely essential for business managers to be actively engaged in the planning process, including working with the accounting team, to develop reliable business plans and financial forecasts on which business economic decisions will be made!

Establishing and Enforcing Internal Controls

Internal controls are the forms and procedures established in a business to deter and detect errors and dishonesty (see Chapter 4). (Internal control certainly isn't the most glamorous accounting function in a business organization.) Even if everyone in the business and everyone the business deals with are as honest as the day is long every day of the year, errors are bound to happen.

Every business should have internal control procedures in place to prevent, or at least to quickly catch, different types of errors. A business is the natural target of all sorts of dishonest schemes and scams by its employees, managers, its customers, its vendors, external technology hackers, and others. To minimize its exposure to losses from embezzlement, pilfering, shoplifting, fraud, and burglary, the accountant should establish and enforce effective internal controls in the business. As the old saying goes, "There's a little bit of larceny in everyone's heart." Internal controls are an example of the principle that an ounce of prevention is worth a pound of cure.

Staying Current in the Digital Age and Global Economy

An entire chapter in this book (see Chapter 5) is on the importance of accounting in the digital age. Quite honestly, there is just no way around this topic as for better or worse (mainly better), the accounting function is now performed in real-time, on-line environment (translation, the cloud) that has resulted in the vast majority of all source documentation being "digitized." For all the benefits associated with technology and the digitization of accounting including improved efficiencies, increased productivity, better and more enhanced reporting, just to name a few, an entirely new set of risks arise as it relates to protecting and managing highly confidential financial information from unwanted prying eyes. It is important to always keep in mind the concept of DIGO (data in, garbage out) as financial information runs the risk of becoming polluted faster than ever if the base accounting data is not managed, recorded, and protected correctly. As a result of this risk, accountants must not only be well versed and educated with the digital accounting environment but more importantly, develop strong working relationships with the company's information technology team (the "tech team") to properly manage accounting technology risks.

Further, accountants are very busy people because they carry out many functions in a business. Like business managers, they don't have a lot of time to spare. One thing that gets no mercy in a crowded schedule is keeping up with changes in accounting and financial reporting standards as well as the global economy. It is absolutely essential that accountants stay informed of the latest changes and global events to ensure they can complete their jobs in a prudent, professional, and credible manner. Accountants simply have to set aside time to read professional journals, peruse websites, maintain and continue with educational updates, attend professional forums and conferences, keep alert regarding developments in accounting and financial reporting, and maybe most importantly, stay in-tune with what's happening around the globe. You may ask why I am emphasizing this last point and the reason is simple. Important to note, most financial accounts, whether reported in the balance sheet or income statement, are based to some degree on the use of accounting estimates. For example, for a large company that generates sales around the world and provides 60-day payment terms to its customers, events can quickly change that may result in the need for the bad debt reserve to be adjusted as an event (such as, a war, natural disaster, health crisis, and so on) could overnight, require the bad debt reserve to be increased from 2 percent of total trade accounts receivables to 8 percent. Yes, in today's hyper-connected global economic, things move extremely quickly so it is essential that the accounting team and function be able to adapt and adjust just as quickly to produce CART financial information and statements.

Index

G

H

I

About the Author

Tage C. Tracy (pronounced "Tog"/Scandinavian descent) has, over the past 25+ years, operated a financial consulting firm focused on offering CFO/executive-level support and planning services to private companies on a fractional basis. These services include providing guidance and support with raising debt and equity capital, completing complex financial analysis, supporting risk management assessments, guiding accounting system designs and structuring, and being an integral part of the strategic business planning management functions. Tage specializes in providing these services to businesses operating at four distinct stages: (1) startups and business launches; (2) rapid growth, ramp, and expansion management; (3) strategic exit and acquisition preparedness and management; and (4) turnarounds, challenged environments, and survival techniques.

Tage is also an active author and has been the lead or coauthor for a number of books, including his most recent title, *Business Financial Information Secrets* (Wiley). Tage has also coauthored (with his late father John A. Tracy) *How to Read a Financial Report*, 9th Edition; *Accounting For Dummies*, 7th Edition, *How to Read a Financial Report, Comprehensive Version*; *Cash Flow For Dummies*; and *Small Business Financial Management Kit For Dummies* (all published by Wiley). Tage received his baccalaureate in accounting in 1985 from the University of Colorado at Boulder with honors. He began his career with Coopers & Lybrand (today PricewaterhouseCoopers) and obtained his CPA certificate in the state of Colorado in 1987 (now inactive). Tage can be reached on his website http://financemakescents.com/ or directly at tagetracy@cox.net.

Dedication

Taking the lead in revising the 2nd Edition of *Accounting Workbook* For Dummies, I would like to dedicate this book to, first and foremost, my dad, John A. Tracy, also known as TOP (The Old Pro), who passed away just prior to me finishing the second edition of this book. It's not often that you see a book dedicated to its original author (as he was responsible for writing the first edition), but in this case, my dad's influence, support, guidance, and dedication to the accounting profession, provided over the past 50+ years, cannot be emphasized enough and warrants, without question, this dedication and my heartfelt thanks. I simply can't tell you how much invaluable guidance my dad provided me over the years on the art of writing books, after he encouraged me to take over the family business a decade or so ago. For me, losing a father, mentor, and friend has been difficult enough but this pales in comparison to the loss millions of people — who he reached through his books over the past 40 years, across the globe — will have to endure as my dad's voice goes silent. While my dad will be sorely missed, his mission, passion, and books ensure he will never be forgotten.

Second, I would like to also remember my mom, who passed away in 2017 and express my thanks for "saving my ass" countless times by editing numerous college papers drafted in decades past (a job thankfully taken over by Wiley's editing department). Her commitment, support, and unconditional love showered on our entire family over the decades, including my dad, my four siblings (and spouses), and me, my parents' 12 grandchildren and five spouses (all recently added), and one great-grandchild that arrived as I started this book has always been the rock we all leaned on when life's road took more than a few unexpected twists and turns.

In an era when economic, business, social, and political trust is in such short supply, I can only look back to the foundation my parents laid for everyone in the extended Tracy family with profound gratitude.

Author's Acknowledgments

I am deeply grateful to everyone at Wiley who helped produce this book. Their professionalism, courtesy, exceptional talent, flexibility, understanding, support, and good humor were very much appreciated and needed when writing this book (especially as I worked through my dad's death towards the end of the book). Editors, Linda Brandon and Kelly Henthorne, were exceptional. It was a pleasure working with them. I send a simple and very big heartfelt "thank you."

This book would not have been possible but for the success of my *Accounting For Dummies* (Wiley, 7th Edition, 2022). I owe Wiley and the several editors on the seven editions of the book an enormous debt of gratitude, which I am most willing to acknowledge. Thanks to all of you! I hope I have done you proud with *Accounting Workbook For Dummies*, 2nd Edition.

Publisher's Acknowledgments

Acquisitions Editor: Lindsay Lefevere
Development Editor: Linda Brandon
Copy Editor: Kelly Henthorne
Technical Editor: Dale Wallis, CPA

Production Editor: Magesh Elangovan
Cover Image: © Andrey_Popov/Shutterstock